Growth Trajectory of Gujarat

Public Policy Intervention

Growth Trajectory of Gujarat

Public Policy Intervention

Editor

Dr. Forum S. Dave

ALLIED PUBLISHERS PVT. LTD.

Noida • Mumbai • Kolkata • Chennai • Bangalore

ALLIED PUBLISHERS PRIVATE LIMITED

D-5, Sector-2, **Noida**–201 301
Ph. Nos.: 0120-4320295/2542557/4352866 • E-mail: delhi.books@alliedpublishers.com

17 Chittaranjan Avenue, **Kolkata**–700072
Ph.: 033-22129618 • E-mail: cal.books@alliedpublishers.com

15 J.N. Heredia Marg, Ballard Estate, **Mumbai**–400001
Ph.: 022-42126969 • E-mail: mumbai.books@alliedpublishers.com

No. 25/10, Commander-in-Chief Road, Ethiraj Lane (Next to Post Office)
Egmore, **Chennai**–600008
Ph.: 044-28223938 • E-mail: chennai.books@alliedpublishers.com

P.B. No. 9932, No. 15, 3rd Floor (Next to Vijaya Bank), 5th Cross, Gandhinagar,
Karnataka, **Bangalore**–560009, Ph.: 080-41530285 / 22386239
E-mail: bngl.books@alliedpublishers.com

Website: www.alliedpublishers.com

ISBN: 978-93-89934-83-0

Published by Sunil Sachdev and printed by Ravi Sachdev at Allied Publishers Pvt. Ltd.,
D-5, Sector-2, Noida–201 301

Preface

Development is the key to measuring the progress of any region. Gujarat is celebrating its 63rd formation year. With only 6 per cent of land masses and 5 per cent of the population, it contributes around 15.5 per cent to India's GDP. However, certain socioeconomic issues are required to be addressed effectively.

Gujarat's rural sex ratio of 949 demonstrates a foundation for gender balance. By focusing on targeted strategies to improve the urban sex ratio of 880, we can build upon existing strengths and create a more equitable future for all. One of the health indicators i.e. infant mortality rate different scenarios in rural and urban areas. It is found that the infant mortality rate in the urban region (17, per thousand) in contrast to the rural region is lower (27 per thousand). This has improved over a period [2011: 27 per thousand (rural) and 48 per thousand (urban)]. It is higher than the national average rate. However, there is always room for improvement, special in infrastructure in rural regions, which requires policy intervention. Education is the key to the development of a state. Sarva Shiksha Abhiyan leads to a positive impact, the dropout remains sticky at around 1 percent (over the period 2016-17 to 2021-22). In secondary education, the dropout rate has steadily reduced from 6.6 % to 3.02 percent. Nevertheless, it is not translating into the formation of human capital. This is reflected in the higher level of educated unemployed in the state (i.e., 2,83,140: the Indian Express). However, this must be seen against the low unemployment rate of 2.3 % (CMIF, 2023). The poverty ratio has decreased over a period of time (31.8% in 2004-05 to 16.6%, 2011), but still, it is higher than smaller non-industrialized states like Himachal Pradesh (8.1%), and Goa (5.1%). %). It is essential to know that the growth engine of Gujarat will slow down if these issues are not addressed and the above trend call for urgent policy measuring.

According to a recent report on Sustainable Development Goals (SDG) by NITI Aayog. Major inadequacies are observed in three indicators, namely the Hunger Index (46), gender equality (49), and the quality of education (52). Despite this, the state is performing well in other indicators such as reduction in poverty (66), health index (86), availability of clean water and sanitation (93), affordable and clean energy (94), industry, innovation, and infrastructure (72) and climate action (67). Given the state's strong performance in the majority of the other measured categories, there is a very good foundation to build upon. Focusing on the areas that are lagging will enable the state to make large gains in overall SDG achievement.

Industrialization and urbanization go hand in hand. For ensuring sustainable urbanization, the formulation of urban policy is essential. The urbanization rate of Gujarat (42%) is higher than the national average (37%). This is well reflected in the contribution of the state in total exports (greater than 30%) as well as the per capita income of the state is higher.

However, the growth story of urbanization is leading to environmental degradation. According to the SDGs (Sustainable Development Goals), a city must provide a healthy life. The river Sabarmati is termed one of the more polluted rivers in the nation due to the continuous dumping of effluents.

The outcome of each sector depends on the structure, formulation, and implementation of its policies. Hence, it is imperative to critically examine the policy performance of various sectors. During the process of implementation, overlapping policies may lead to waste of resources and time and duplication of efforts. Against this backdrop, scrutiny of sectoral policies and their variegated outcome is required. Such analyses can have spatial along with sectoral dimensions example Formation of International Business Units (IBU) in the GIFT City. Additionally, institutional reform accelerates the development process of the state. The Institutional framework has been playing an important role in the sustainable development and growth of various sections in Gujarat. As successful corporatization and splitting up of the state electricity board into various entities i.e., Gujarat Electrical Board- into Gujarat Energy Transmission Corporation Limited (GETCO), GENeration Company (GENCO), and five distribution channels. The importance of Institutional reforms needs to be backed by financial reforms. The necessary steps in simplifying the financial process and rationalizing the tax structure can be helpful to both industries and citizens in general. Also, the augmentation of revenue can play an essential role in economic development. In the Budget 2023–24, incentives have been provided to increase the creditworthiness of municipalities so that they can issue municipal bonds. Similar revenue generation efforts were made by Ahmedabad.

Municipal Corporation (AMC) in the year 1998 by issuing the municipal bond. One of such kind by local government. With the right policy intervention, the state will be on a sustainable trajectory. The book will discuss the challenges and opportunities of Gujarat's growth. It will also scrutinize patterns and sectorial scenarios to attain all-encompassing growth.

Dr. Forum S. Dave

Acknowledgement

Growth Trajectory of Gujarat: Public Policy Intervention explores the state's dynamic progress, tracing its transformation and highlighting key turning points in its development. The research and writing of this book have been an incredibly enriching journey, made possible by the generous support of many individuals and institutions. I am deeply grateful for their guidance, encouragement, and belief in this project, all of which have been truly invaluable.

I sincerely thank the Indian Council of Social Science Research (ICSSR) and the ICSSR-Western Wing for supporting the national seminar on "Growth Trajectory of Gujarat," which laid the groundwork for this book. I am also deeply appreciative of the Sardar Patel Institute of Economic and Social Research (SPIESR), Ahmedabad, for providing the resources and stimulating intellectual environment that nurtured this work. I am particularly indebted to Director Niti Mehta for her invaluable mentorship, insightful feedback, and constant encouragement. I also sincerely thank Dr. Nachiket Gosavi and Dr. Vachaspati for generously sharing their time and expertise. I am grateful to the various departments at SPIESR, especially the Administration and Accounts Department.

I thank all the contributors for sharing their valuable research in the form of the chapters that comprise this book. I also appreciate Allied Publishers' professionalism and commitment to its publication. The publication process was greatly aided by the guidance of Satishbhai, Sarita Ranga, and Pradip Chauhan.

Amiras Pandya, Kajal Giri and Vartik Vyas, provided valuable support during the seminar organization. From seminar inception to publication, my core research team—Ashwinbhai Raval, Pradip Chauhan, Vrinda Dave, and Sumit Goswami—demonstrated unwavering excellence.

I sincerely thank Crazy Lad Animation Studio for their artistic cover design.

I am deeply grateful to my friends and family for their unwavering support and encouragement. Their love and blessings make everything possible.

Lastly, thanks to the Ishwar for guiding me through every step of this journey.

A Journey through Gujarat

Gujarat's sustained influence arises from a compelling convergence of distinct yet interconnected domains: economic strength, cultural richness, historical significance, and global connectivity. This confluence underscores its multifaceted importance as a cornerstone of India's socioeconomic and cultural landscape. Economically, Gujarat's prowess, fueled by diversified industries and strategic trade, positions it as a vital contributor to India's national growth, further enhanced by its strategic coastline, a pivotal gateway for international commerce. Culturally, Gujarat's rich legacy, preserved through vibrant festivals, intricate arts, and architectural marvels, fosters cross-cultural understanding and global appreciation, with its unique culinary traditions attracting international attention. Historically, Gujarat's championing of religious pluralism and its entrepreneurial

spirit have significantly shaped India's social and economic fabric, bolstered by strategic investments in education and infrastructure and evidenced by ancient ports like Dwarka and Lothal, testifying to its role as a hub of international trade. Socially, Gujarat fosters cohesion through festivals and preserves its heritage through museums and archaeological sites, while its diverse landscapes attract global interest, and welfare programs promote equitable growth. Gujarat's historical acts of humanitarianism, such as providing refuge to the Parsi community, and early global trade links, exemplified by connections with Mexico, demonstrate its long-standing international engagement, while narratives like Krishna's gift to Brazil and Maharaja Digvijaysinhji's aid to Polish children underscore its enduring global connections and humanitarian spirit. Ultimately, these combined elements—economic strength, cultural wealth, historical significance, social cohesion, and global connectivity—demonstrate Gujarat's multifaceted importance, with its humanitarian spirit, international relations, and illustrative historical narratives solidifying its position as a cornerstone of India's socioeconomic and cultural landscape.

1. Demographics and Economic Performance: Foundations of Growth

Gujarat's demographic profile served as a crucial foundation for its economic dynamism. According to the 2011 census, the state's population was 6.04 crore, projected to reach 7.15 crore by 2023. This population, despite representing only 4.99% of India's total, contributes a substantial 8.2% to the nation's GDP, highlighting the state's economic efficiency. The state's Gross State Domestic Product (GSDP) was a testament to its robust economic health. In 2022–23, the Real GSDP (at constant 2011–12 prices) was estimated at Rs. 1475629 crore, demonstrating an 8.0% growth. The Per Capita Income at NSDP (at current prices) was Rs. 273558 in 2022–23, marking a significant 15.7% increase. This growth is driven by a balanced sectoral contribution: 20.1% from the primary sector, 44.6% from the secondary sector, and 35.3% from the tertiary sector. The Per Capita Income at NSDP (at current prices) was Rs. 273558 in 2022–23, reflecting a 13.1% rise and indicating improved living standards.

2. Agriculture and Allied Sectors: Diversification and Technological Advancement

Gujarat's agricultural landscape is characterized by its diversity and a shift towards high-value crops. The state's agricultural output saw 104.91% of its average rainfall in 2023. Crop production in 2022–23 included 105.14 lakh tonnes of foodgrains, 100.01 lakh bales of cotton, and 72.57 lakh tonnes of oilseeds.Key agricultural initiatives like the Kisan Parivahan Yojana, Pradhan Mantri Kisan Samman Nidhi Yojana, and Pradhan Mantri Krishi Sinchai Yojana support farmers and enhance productivity. The Minimum Support Price (MSP) policy ensures fair returns, with significant procurement of gram, green gram, and mustard. The state's commitment to technological advancement is evident through subsidies for smartphone purchases and the promotion of drone technology. Horticulture and animal husbandry are crucial sectors, Fruit production reached 82.92 lakh tonnes.Milk production increased to 172.81 lakh tonnes.The fisheries sector produced 8.97 lakh tonnes of fish in 2022–23.

3. Forests, Irrigation, and Disaster Relief: Sustainable Resource Management

Gujarat's forest cover, approximately 11.15% of its geographical area, highlights its commitment to environmental sustainability. Irrigation potential is significant, with projects like the Sujalam Sufalam Yojana and SAUNI Yojana enhancing water availability. The Micro Irrigation Scheme benefits numerous farmers. The state's proactive disaster relief measures, including assistance for Covid-19 and the Biparjoy cyclone, demonstrate its resilience.

4. Industry and Infrastructure: Fostering an Investor-Friendly Environment

Gujarat is a highly industrialized state, known for its investor-friendly environment. The Aatmanirbhar Gujarat Scheme supports MSMEs, with over 1.5 million units receiving Udyam Registration Certificates. The Start-Ups/Innovation Scheme promotes research and development. The Annual Survey of Industries (ASI) shows growth in the number of factories and net value added. Schemes like the Shree Vajpayee Bankable Self Employment Loan Scheme and Manav Kalyan

Yojana support self-employment. Mining operations are conducted for minerals like lignite and bauxite.

Infrastructure development is a priority, with the PM Gati Shakti Gujarat Integrated Master Plan (centre scheme) ensuring coordinated planning. The state's Civil Aviation sector witnessed significant growth in 2022–23, with increased aircraft movements and passenger traffic. Port development, managed by the Gujarat Maritime Board, remains a cornerstone of the economy, handling substantial cargo volumes. Telecommunications infrastructure ensures widespread connectivity.

5. Energy Sector: Transitioning to Renewable Sources

Gujarat's installed energy capacity is expanding, reaching 45314 MW by October 2023. Electricity generation and consumption increased. The Sardar Krushi Jyoti Yojana improves power supply for agriculture. The Solar Rooftop Yojana (Surya-Gujarat) and Pradhan Mantri Kusum Yojana (centre scheme) promote renewable energy. The state's focus on renewable energy aligns with national goals and contributes to environmental sustainability.

6. Financial Sector: Building a Robust Ecosystem

Gujarat's banking sector demonstrates strong growth, with an increasing number of bank branches and rising aggregate deposits and advances. Credit cooperative societies also show growth in working capital, indicating a vibrant financial ecosystem.

7. Safety and Technology: Enhancing Security and Digital Inclusion

The Gujarat State Disaster Management Authority (GSDMA) implements the Emergency Response Support System (ERSS-Dial 112) for rapid disaster response. The "Village Wi-Fi" project and the Digital Seva Setu program enhance digital inclusion. The Gujarat Security Operations Centre (GSOC) protects against cyber threats. The state's IT/ITeS and Electronics policies attract investment and foster innovation.

8. Social Development: Achieving Sustainable Development Goals

Gujarat is committed to achieving Sustainable Development Goals (SDGs), with progress seen in various indicators. The Aspirational Blocks Programme targets development in selected talukas.

9. Education and Health: Investing in Human Capital

Gujarat prioritizes education and health, with initiatives like free textbooks, vocational education, and the Gyan Sahayak initiative in education. The state's health infrastructure includes Community Health Centers, Primary Health Centers, and Sub Health Centers. Initiatives like Janani Suraksha Yojana (JSY) and PMJAY-MA Yojana improve maternal and child health.

10. Women and Child Development, Rural and Urban Development, Social Welfare and Employment, and Public Finance and Planning: Inclusive Growth and Governance

Gujarat implements various schemes for women and child development, rural and urban development, social welfare, and employment. The state's financial management shows growth in receipts and expenditures, with a focus on outcome-based budgeting. The Public Distribution System (PDS) and other social welfare programs ensure food security and address the needs of vulnerable populations.

Gujarat's continued success is underpinned by its strategic location, proactive policies, and commitment to inclusive growth. Its diverse economic base, strong infrastructure, and focus on social development position it as a leading economic powerhouse in India, poised to contribute significantly to national growth and development.

Contents

Environment

Financial Aspects

Student's Corner

Commentary

Section 1

Agriculture

Cost-Benefit Analysis of Hi-Tech Banana Farming in Narmada District

Vijay S. Jariwala[1] **and Palak H. Mehta**[2]

ABSTRACT: Modern agriculture has replaced traditional farming practices to meet the increasing demand for horticultural and agricultural crops. Agriculture has to meet the growing production of horticultural and agricultural crops. India has made fairly good progress in production of fruits and vegetables with a total production of 329.86 million tonnes in 2021–22 from 2857.79 million tonnes in the year 2015–16, against 87.10 million tonnes during 1991–92. Banana is the main fruit in international trade and the most popular one in the world (GoI, 2017). India ranks first in area and production of banana in the world (FAO, 2024). High-tech methods like tissue culture and drip irrigation are crucial for banana cultivation. Tissue Culture plants are healthy, disease free, uniform and authentic for plantation, whereas drip irrigation system precisely controls uniform application of water, nutrients, and other required growth substances directly into the root zone of the plant. The fruits produced by these two technologies are exportable in terms of quality (Rao, 2014). Despite their potential, many farmers believe these advanced technologies benefit large-scale operations more than they benefit small farms. This paper challenges this presumption by using a case study of Narmada District to analyze how small farmers can leverage these methods for increased productivity and profitability.

Keywords: *Tissue Culture, Drip Irrigation, Small Farmers, Cost and Benefits, Banana.*

---

[1] Associate Professor, P.G. Department of Economics, Sardar Patel University, Vallabh Vidyanagar, Anand, Gujarat, India. E-mail: viju_19782004@yahoo.com https://orcid.org/0000-0002-7792-598X

[2] Ph.D. Scholar, Department of Economics, Gujarat Vidyapeeth, Ahmedabad, India.

INTRODUCTION

In developing countries like India, agriculture sector is very important in terms of its size, share in total production, income generation and employment. Therefore, the development of agriculture sector is a major requirement for the prosperity of a country. An important factor in hindering the development of agriculture into India is the fragmentation of land in small parts.

According to Agricultural Census 2010–11, the average size of land holding was 2.08 hectares in 1970–71 which was reduced to 1.84 hectares in 1980–81 and 1.08 hectares in 2015–16. Nearly 85 percent of the 138.348 million farming families hold up to 2 hectares of land. (Mahendra Dev, 2012) Large land holding farmer enables to implement modern agricultural techniques and boost productivity. Small land holdings farmer restricts to use traditional methods of farming and limit productivity. As land holdings are small, more people invariably work on the farms in the rural areas and coupled with the obsolete technology, thus farm income come down.

Bananas and plantains are popular globally not only for their nutritional value but also for their economic importance, especially, to small and marginal farmers in developing countries. These are grown in over 150 countries across the world in an area of 59.4 million ha producing 135.11 million metric tonnes (FAO, 2023). World banana production is concentrated in Africa, Asia, the Caribbean and Latin America because of the climatic conditions. Among the various continents, Asia has the lion's share of 52 percent of the global banana production and India, China, Philippines, and Indonesia are the major producers in the South, South-East Asian regions. India contributes 48 percent of the total production in Asia using 37 percent of total area. India's export share in the global market is only 1% even though the country accounts for 26.45 percent of the world's banana production (35.36 Million Metric Tonnes). In the fiscal year 2022–23, India exported bananas worth USD 176 million, equivalent to 0.36 MMT (Government of India, 2025).

Since banana productivity remains low even today, a large number of farmers use traditional methods for farming. They are reluctant to use modern methods such as tissue culture and drip irrigation. Because they are more expensive than traditional method. These modern practices are not just increasing productivity, but also improving the quality of the fruit. Unlike the rest of the world's major banana growing areas, which are dominated by large-scale commercial farms, the Indian banana industry is based on a large number of small, independent farmers, typically cultivating up to 2 hectares. (FAO, 2018) So, it becomes necessary to study how such practices are beneficial for small farmers.

OBJECTIVES

Hence, the present study is conducted with the following objectives:

1. To assess the resource use efficiency for small and large farmers of banana cultivation.
2. To check whether the modern banana farming system is beneficial for small farmers or not.
3. To find out the possible reasons for the fact that how smaller farmers can gain more profit per hectare by adopting modern methods of banana cultivation.

HYPOTHESIS

H_0 : There is no significant difference between per acre productivity of small and large farmers in Hi-tech farming of banana crop.

H_1 : There is a significant difference between per acre productivity of small and large farmers in Hi-tech farming of banana crop.

METHODOLOGY

The present study has been carried out in Gujarat's Narmada district. Out of five talukas of the district, land and weather in Nandod Taluka are more favourable for banana crop; hence nearly total 78.57 percent area of the district banana cultivation takes place in Nandod Taluka. For this study, 76 small and 74 large banana growers who cultivate bananas using Tissue Culture and Drip Irrigation have been selected from ten villages of Nandod Taluka. Those farmers who have up to 2 hectares of land called small famers and more than 2 hectares of land are called large farmers. Farmers take two crops from a banana planation. The first is the main crop and the second is the ratoon crop. Ratoon cropping simply means the second and subsequent crop grown from the suckers. The cost and income of these two crops have been taken into account. The primary data for the study are collected through personal interview method with the help of pre-tested questionnaire. In the study, one-tenth of the installation cost for the drip irrigation method has been counted, because the lifespan of drip irrigation is at least 10 years as per the farmer's opinion.

Data are analysed using both tabular and functional analysis. Tabular analysis is adopted to study the resource use structure, cost, returns and profits in banana cultivation. Simple statistical tools like averages and percentages are used to interpret the results properly.

Cost of cultivation includes variable and fixed costs. Variable costs include the cost of human labour, seeds, manure, irrigation, fertilizers, etc. Fixed cost comprise depreciation, land revenue, rental value of land and interest on fixed capital.

An attempt is made to examine the effects of variation in major agricultural inputs on crop yield with the help of a log-linear regression model which is estimated for both small and large banana cultivation farmers. The log-linear regression model is used to find out the contribution of each factor to banana productivity by small and large framers. The regression model is explained with a log-linear functional form due to the fact that the agricultural production function is usually assumed to follow a Cobb-Douglas production function that requires a log-linear transformation for estimation of input co-efficient. Thus, the estimable equation is as follows:

$$Y = a.X_1^{b1} . X_2^{b2}, \ldots, X_n^{bn} . e^i \qquad \ldots (1)$$

Where,

Y = dependent variable

X_1 to X_6 = independent variables

a = constant representing intercept of production function

b^i = regression coefficient of respective resource variables

e^i = error term

To fit a production function for both small and large banana growers, six inputs (variables) are considered important factors, by considering the problem of multicollinearity in estimating production function. The equation fitted follows the following formula.

$$Y = ax_1^{b1} X2^{b2} X3^{b3} X4^{b4} X5^{b5} X6^{b6} \quad \ldots (2)$$

The function is transformed into linear form by making the logarithmic transformation of all the variables as follows.

$$\text{Log } Y = \text{Log } a + b_1 \text{ Log } X_1 + b_2 \text{ Log } X_2 + b_3 \text{ Log } X_3 + b_4 \text{ Log } X_4 + b_5 \text{ Log } X_5 + b_6 \text{ Log } X_6 \quad \ldots (3)$$

Where,

Y = per acre production

a = intercept of production function

$b_1, b_2, \ldots b_6$ = regression coefficients

X_1 = area of banana (hectare)

X_2 = number of tissue culture plant

X_3 = number of irrigations

X_4 = cost of chemical fertilizers

X_5 = cost of manures

X_6 = cost of Human Labour

Data satisfied the assumption of homogeneity but did not satisfy the normal distribution assumption. So, Non-parametric Mann-Whitney *U*-test was used to examine hypothesis.

RESULTS AND DISCUSSION

Per hectare cost of production of banana for small and large farmers are presented in the table 1.

In Table 1, it is observed that small farmers are spending more per hectare on both main and ratoon crops than the large farmers. During the main crop, small farmers spend 2.97 percent more per hectare than the large farmer. Whereas during the ratoon crop, they spend 5.80 percent more than the large farmers.

The variable cost for large farmers is more than for small farmers. During the main crop, large farmer's variable cost is 0.40 percent more than small farmers and 0.23 percent more during the ratoon crop.

But the fixed cost is higher for small farmer than for large farmer. During the main crop, small farmer's fixed cost is 15.64 percent more than that of large farmers, while during the ratoon crop fixed cost for small farmers is 16.66 percent more than large farmers.

Table 1: Per Hectare Total Cost of Banana Cultivation for Small and Large Farmer

Sr. No.	Items of Cost	*Small Farmers*				*Large Farmers*			
		Main Crop		*Ratoon Crop*		*Main Crop*		*Ratoon Crop*	
		Value (Rs.)	*% of Total Cost*	*Value (Rs.)*	*% of Total Cost*	*Value (Rs.)*	*% of Total Cost*	*Value (Rs.)*	*% of Total Cost*
1.	Human labour cost	25012	8.68	16905	10.5	24481	8.75	17189	11.3
2.	Tractor cost	8237	2.86	0	0.0	3443	1.23	0	0.0
3.	Tissue culture plant cost	43247	15.00	0	0.0	43244	15.46	0	0.0
4.	Irrigation installationcost	10253	3.56	10253	6.4	9922	3.55	9921	6.5
5.	Electricity cost	13633	4.73	9488	5.9	14755	5.27	10494	7.0
6.	Manure cost	25710	8.92	0	0.0	25378	9.07	0	0.0
7.	Fertilizer cost	30076	10.43	26474	16.5	30312	10.83	25111	16.5
8.	Pesticide cost	713	0.25	620	0.4	544	1.94	355	0.23
9.	Maintenance cost	23289	8.07	0	0	28274	10.04	0	0.0
10.	Harvesting cost	12123	4.20	11946	7.3	12030	4.30	11850	7.8
11.	Interest on working capital	14401	4.99	6367	4.0	14465	5.17	6381	4.2
12.	Other cost	13288	4.61	15264	9.5	14017	5.01	16241	10.7
Total variable cost (1 + 12)		**219982**	**76.36**	**97317**	**60.5**	**220865**	**78.95**	**97543**	**64.3**

Sr. No.	*Items of Cost*	*Small Farmers*				*Large Farmers*			
		Main Crop		*Ratoon Crop*		*Main Crop*		*Ratoon Crop*	
		Value (Rs.)	*% of Total Cost*	*Value (Rs.)*	*% of Total Cost*	*Value (Rs.)*	*% of Total Cost*	*Value (Rs.)*	*% of Total Cost*
13.	Land revenue	36731	12.74	36731	22.9	36700	13.12	36700	24.1
14.	Interest on fixed capital	25292	8.77	25292	15.7	16820	6.01	16820	11.1
15.	Depreciation cost	6058	2.10	1273	0.8	5371	1.92	738	0.5
Total fixed cost (13 + 15)		**68081**	**23.63**	**63296**	**39.4**	**58891**	**21.05**	**54258**	**35.7**
Total cost		**288063**	**100**	**160613**	**100**	**279756**	**100**	**151801**	**100**

Source: Field survey.

Thus, in Hi-tech technology for banana cultivation, the cost per hectare is higher for small farmers than for large farmers.

Table 1: Yield and Returns of Banana Cultivation from Small and Large Farmers

Sr. No.	*Particulars*	*Small Farmer*		*Large Farmer*	
		Main Crop.	*Ratoon Crop.*	*Main Crop.*	*Ratoon Crop.*
1.	Production (Quintal/ha)	756	690	685	592
2.	Price received (Rs./Quintal)	1080	1085	1075	1075
3.	Income (Rs./ha)	816480	748650	736375	636400
4.	Cost (Rs./ha)	288063	160613	279756	151801
5.	Net profit (Rs./ha)	528417	588037	456619	484599

Source: Field survey.

Returns from main crop and ratoon crop for small and large farmers in banana cultivation are shown in Table 2. It can be seen here that during the main crop, the yield per hectare banana cultivation for small farmers is 10.36 percent higher than that of large farmers. Moreover, small farmers can get 5 rupees per quintal more as compared to large farmers. In main crop, small farmers get 15.72 percent more net profit per hectare than large farmers in banana cultivation.

In the ratoon crop, small farmers yield 16.5 percent more per hectare compared to large farmers. They can also get 10 Rs. per quintal more than large farmers. Therefore, small farmers acquire 21.35 percent more net profit per hectare than large farmers.

FUNCTIONAL ANALYSIS

Resources used to find production elasticity for small and large farmers are separately estimated and the results are presented in Table 3.

The co-efficient of multiple determination (R^2) is 0.731 for small farmers indicating that 73.1 per cent of total variation in the production is explained by the six variables for functional analysis. The co-efficient of number of tissue cutler (X_2) and number of irrigation (X_3) are found to be positive and significant at 1 per cent level for small farmers, indicating that quantity of seeds and number of irrigations are the most important variables determining the production for small banana farmers. It indicates that with 1 per cent increase in use of number of tissue cutler plant and number of irrigations in banana cultivation, production would go up by 28 per cent and 16.4 per cent respectively. The co-efficient for cost of labour (X_6) is found positive and significant at 5 per cent level, indicating that labour cost significantly affect on of banana production, with production increasing as labour costs rise. However, the co-efficient for constant is found negative and significant at 1 per cent level, indicating that, apart from these six variables, other factors negatively and significantly affect banana production. The production level will increase with a decline in these constants variables. Furthermore, co-efficient of area (X_1), manures cost (X_4) and chemical cost (X_5) are non-significant at 5 per cent level.

Table 2: Production Elasticity for Small and Large Farmers in Banana Cultivation as Estimated from Cobb-Douglas Production Function

Variables/Method	*Small Farmers*	*Large Farmers*
Adjusted R Square	0.731	0.563
a = (Constant)	–2.579 (.005)**	–13.688 (.120)
X_1 = area under crop (hectare)	–.016 (.099)	–.011 (.513)
X_2 = number of tissue cutler (seed)	.278 (.000)**	1.163 (.338)
X_3 = number of irrigations	1.638 (.000)**	2.449 (.000)**
X_4 = manures cost	–.046 (.202)	–.014 (.314)
X_5 = chemical cost	.035 (.289)	.084 (.143)
X_6 = cost of labour	.059 (.038)*	–.057 (.200)
Returns to scale	1.95	3.61

Note: Figures within the parentheses indicate significant value of corresponding elasticity.

** indicates significant at one per cent level & *indicates significant at five per cent level.

The co-efficient of multiple determination (R^2) is 0.563 for large farmers, indicating that 56.3 per cent of total variation in the production is explained by the six variables used in the functional analysis. The co-efficient for number of irrigations (X_3) is found to be positive and significant at 1 per cent level, indicating that number of irrigations is the most important variable determining banana production for large farmers. A 1 per cent increase in the number of irrigations in banana cultivation would result in a 2.44 per cent increase im production. However, the co-efficients for the constant, area (X_1), tissue cutler (X_2), manure (X_4), chemicals (X_5), and labour (X_6) are non-significant at 5 per cent level.

RETURNS TO SCALE

In Cobb-Douglas production function the returns to scale is obtained by the summation of elasticity co-efficient (Σb_i) of the independent variables.

If $\Sigma b_i > 1$ it is increasing returns to scale

If $\Sigma b_i = 1$ it is constant returns to scale and

If $\Sigma b_i = < 1$ it is decreasing returns to scale.

In the study area, the value of Σb_i is found to be 1.95 for small farmers and 3.61 for large farmers in banana cultivation, indicating increasing returns to scale. Therefore, there is scope to increase production by using maximum production tools for both type of farmers.

Mann-Whitney *U* Test

To test the hypothesis that there is no difference in banana productivity between large and small farmers, the Mann-Whitney U statistic is used. In Tables 4 and 5, it can be observed that there is a significant difference in productivity between small and large farmers. Thus, the null hypothesis is rejected and the alternative hypothesis is accepted, indicating that Hi-tech method of banana cultivation is more profitable for small farmers.

Table 4: Ranks

	Type of Farmer	*N*	*Mean Rank*	*Sum of Ranks*
Hi-tech per acer production	SM (A)	76	111.47	8472.00
	LM (B)	74	38.55	2853.00
	Total	150		

Table 5: Test Statistics[a]

	Hi-tech Par Acer Production
Mann-Whitney U	78.000
Wilcoxon W	2853.000
Z	–10.277
Asymp. Sig. (2-tailed)	.000

a. Grouping Variable: type of farmer.

Possible reasons behind more profit for small farmers in Hi-tech technology banana cultivation.

1. Apart from the modern farming methods, which require more financial support and labour the large land size restricts the large farmers from proper personal observation and necessary care of the crop, resulting in less production per hectare for large farmers than small farmers.
2. Large amount of demand for tissue culture plants arises during the sowing period in the district. Large farmers' demand for tissue culture plants is much more than the small farmers. In such situations many times there arise shortage of tissue culture plants. Therefore, large farmers are forced to plant fewer plants per hectare, resulting in lower production per hectare.
3. In banana cultivation practices like plantation, removal of extra suckers, removing leaves, applying fertilizer, weeding and harvesting require a large amount of manual labour. The district faces shortage of labour during the season. A lot of these works is done by the small farmers on their own or their family members are also engaged in this labour work. So, they do not face such shortage. Whereas the large farmers face labour shortage due to

which such practices are not carried out timely and its effect is seen on production.

CONCLUSIONS

1. The total cost of cultivation per hectare for small farmers is more than that of large farmers. The main reason for this is total fixed cost. The cost per hectare is reduced for the large farmers as the expenses like interest on fixed capital and depreciation cost are distributed over the large land holdings. Due to this even though the variable cost being more than that of small farmers the total cost per hectare turns out to be less than that of small farmers.
2. Small farmers can acquire 10.36 percent and 16.5 percent more production per hectare than the large farmers in both the main and ratoon crops respectively. Thus, modern farming techniques of banana is beneficial to small farmers in addition to the large farmers.
3. The large farmers incurs a loss of Rs. 5 to Rs. 10 per quintal as compared to small farmers in both the main and ratoon crops, which is not a big difference. However, the reason for this difference might be their bargaining capacity in the market. Generally, the one having large quantity is supposed to have more bargaining capacity in the market, but when the quantity is that of a perishable crop like banana the more the quantity the less the capacity to bargain. Thus, for such crops, the farmers tend to forgo Rs. 5 to Rs. 10 to sell their produce as quickly as possible. Such norm is observed more among large farmers.
4. Hi-tech farming technologies benefits both small and large farmers. In the main crop, the net profit obtained by small farmers is Rs. 528,417 per hectare, while large farmers earn Rs. 456,619 per hectare. In ratoon crop the net profit gained by small farmer is Rs. 588037 per hectare and large farmer is Rs. 484599 per hectare. A comparison of the profits obtained during both the crops indicates that the small farmers earn 18.62 percent more profit than the large farmers.

   Hi-tech farming technologies benefit both small and large farmers. In the main crop, the net profit obtained by small farmers is Rs. 528,417 per hectare, while large farmers earn Rs.

456,619 per hectare. In the ratoon crop, the net profit for small farmers is Rs. 588,037 per hectare, whereas large farmers earn Rs. 484,599 per hectare. A comparison of the profits obtained during both crops indicates that small farmers earn 18.62 percent more profit than large farmers.

5. Returns to Scale obtained for both the small and large farmers adopting modern practices of farming indicate that there are many opportunities to increase the banana crop production by increasing the equipment for production.

REFERENCES

[1] FAO (2018, 9 20). Food and Agriculture organization of United Nations. Retrieved from www.fao.org: www.fao.org/fsnforum/.../India%20banana%20case_final.pdf

[2] FAO (2024, 08 27). Food And Agriculture Organization of the United Nations. Retrieved from http://www.fao.org/home/en/: http://www.fao.org/economic/est/est-commodities/bananas/bananafacts/en/#.W4YMUc4zbIU

[3] GoI (2017). Horticultural statistics at a glance 2017. new delhi: Government of India.

[4] Government of India, P.I. (2025, January 19). https://pib.gov.in/. Retrieved from https://pib.gov.in https://pib.gov.in/PressReleaseIframePage.aspx?PRID=2006916#:~:text=India's%20export%20share%20in%20the,million%2C%20equivalent%20to%200.36%20MMT

[5] Mahendra Dev, S. (2012). Small Farmers in India: Challenges and Opportunities. Indira Gandhi Institute of Development Research, Mumbai.

[6] Mustaffa, M.M. and Kumar, V. (2012). Banana production and productivity enhancement through spatial, water and nutrient management. jouranal of horticulture science, 7(1), 1–28.

[7] Rao, K. (2014). Adoption of Tissue Culture in Horticulture: A Study of Banana Growing Farmers from a South Indian State. UK: Cambrige Scholars.

Institutional Barriers to Rural Innovation in Gujarat: An Empirical Assessment

Munish Alagh[1]

ABSTRACT: This study investigates the sustainability of rural institutions in Gujarat by analyzing existing state-level initiatives and their potential to foster medium- and long-term grassroots networks. Initiatives of Governmental Farm and Complementary Private Non-Farm Enterprise in Gujarat are examined. Implementation of Innovative Knowledge and Research requires Enabling Knowledge to be included in the Existing Rural Practices. Particularly we examine whether incremental and strategic support in terms of extension to bring commercial viability in the medium term in Rural Gujarat through certain Farm Initiatives such as Contract farming and Investment in Rural Input Programs and Farm/Non-Farm Enterprise can work? Particularly can policy approaches to economically backward, dryland agriculture succeed in the era of market reforms? Personal Interviews covering a decade; 2011–12 to 2023–24 in village Khandoli in Panchmahals, a dry district in Gujarat is taken to bring to the attention of the Extension Model in Gujarat, possibilities of Change Processes. This includes an assessment of awareness regarding existing projects.

Keywords: *Rural Surpluses, Transaction Costs, Non-Farm Enterprise, Extension Systems, Farmer Input Use, Land Holding Characteristics, Rural Input Investments, Commercial Viability of Farming, Use of Modern Equipment in Farming, Community Retail, District Development.*

[1] Sardar Patel Institute of Economic and Social Research. Ahmedabad, Gujarat, India. E-mail: munish.alagh@gmail.com

INTRODUCTION

Gujarat's Rural Development System has both a Gandhian philosophy (Mehta, N., & Mehta, M.G.; 2013) as well as a Commercially Tuned Perspective. In this article an attempt has been made to delineate the ways in which it is possible that the State sustains Gandhian Economies of Sustainability and yet pursues a dominant position in Commerce in the Country. The Economy has possibilities of Small Farm/Farmer Sustenance notwithstanding Agro-Climatic constraints. Through the State Agricultural Universities Modern Scientific Practices can be absorbed in the State's Agriculture. The Simultaneous achievement of both can be pictured with the ideal of a Village in Gujarat, where in the Village Courtyard a Marginal Farmer is selling Sprouts (Unharvested Green Tur) and a Gandhian Shia Community Retail Super-Market Cooperative Operator is engaged in selling Biryani Masala (Dutta, S. and Alagh, M., 2017).

The State's Socio Economic Review (Government of Gujarat, 2021–22), each year, provides the transformation of Data to Enabling Information for scholars. Yet such Knowledge and Innovation needs to be included in the District Development Plans. Particularly, effective implementation at Village Household Level needs to be examined in terms of the changing circumstances on the ground in Gujarat. We use empirical data collected by the author from field visits (Alagh M., 2014, Dutta S. and Alagh M., 2017) to find whether the Transaction Costs related to the Rural Economy can be reduced.

The article will begin with Development Profile of Rural Gujarat and Possibilities of Transformation, focusing, on how Institutions have functioned and Networks have evolved to support both Agricultural and Non-Farm Growth in the state. There is then a discussion on Rural Development Frameworks with some emphasis on Gujarat. This is followed by a Review of the Literature on Rural Institutions, Transformation and Development. The next Section will be on devising a Problem Statement to Overcome the Climate of Uncertainty. Empirics from Field Visits are used to explore results when Dual goals like Equity and Efficiency are sought to be followed in a Proactive Manner. Also, we will study how a Community Retail Super Market Franchising Enterprise (Dutta S and Alagh, M., 2017) Overcame the odds in Gujarat. Alongside we will Study how

Knowledge Feedback can be internalized in Agriculture in Less Irrigated Areas like Panchmahals (Alagh M., 2014). We expand our Perspective gained from 2011–12 to 2024 with the authors' field visits in Panchmahals exploring awareness of Extension Programs in Practice.

Development Profile of Rural Gujarat and Possibilities of Transformation

In a casual observation, all seems well with Gujarat's agriculture. The main campaigns for Agriculture which have been planned in Gujarat are Krishi Mahotsav Campaign for Input Extension Support, Soil-Card Facility for Soil-Conservation and Improvement, Jyotigram Yojana to Provide Electricity based on Peak Hour Usage by Farmer, Sardar Sarovar Project for the construction of Major and Medium Canal Irrigation, and Management of Groundwater Irrigation under Sardar Patel Sahakari Jal Sanchar Yojana, among other Programs. The Institutional Complements to these Programs include, the Systematic Implementation by Talati and Sarpanch of Ground Level Facilitation of the Systematic Efforts of the Various Departments of the State Sachivalaya at Gandhinagar and District Development Officers. The Village Panchayats are enabled by their own Krushi Sahayaks (Village Representatives of the Taluka Officer) creating Mobility for Economic Activities.

The Village Institutions that are Worthy of Emphasis in the State are: Dairying, Credit Cooperatives, Rural Cooperative Banks, Small Village businesses including retail Stores, Farmer Self-Help Groups and Recent Schemes aimed at Empowering Rural Citizenry with Identification followed by Complementary Incentives such as Liquefied Petroleum Gas Cylinders for Cooking for Rural Households. The State aims for the Transformation of Rural Human Capital and Rural Organizations. These are the alternate mechanisms which lead to: "the policy option of making rural areas the focus of diversified enterprise." (Roy D *et al.*, 2007).

The State's Ground-Level Community Initiatives such as Labour and Land Lease market, Water and Power Use Lending and Well Planned Insurance Mechanisms for Securing Property Rights, are well known.

Affirming Regional Knowledge, specially in Use of Science in Community partnerships through Industrial Training Institutes and State-Agricultural Universities, Model Farms and Government Infrastructure Projects, at a Local level were emphasised in (Sharma H. *et al.*, 2017).

Rural Development: Focus on Gujarat's Frameworks

The Gujarati Farmer is a resilient, commerceminded individual. Bottom Up Institutions are bound to work (Easterly, W. 2007) with participants on the ground who must be supported and made viable. Schultz (1964), has written on the idea that Extension Mechanisms are always successful with traditional farmers, provided the government puts in enough effort. Mellor (2017), built up his thesis on modern technologies for the Commercial Medium Farmer and slowly creating conditions for Rural Transformation. The idea now sees the light of day in the form of Synergy in Rural Ground Level Development, such as Constructed Houses, Village Feeder Roads and access to prosperous Rural Markets.

Gujarat, has in spurts lived up to the Metaphor of a Lighthouse in terms of Rural Development (Shah *et al.*, 2009) to other states. There is a strong system of extension regarding Technology in Seeds, Fertilisers, Pesticides and New Technologies. The Initial success of Monsanto Bt cotton in raising Incomes of Farmers, Sardar Sarovar Narmada Canal in raising the Water table since 2004, and the increase in wheat yields from 2002 to 2007 is a Documented Success Story.

Yet, there is a flip side to the story. Some recent Steps for instance, regarding the success of Water Harvesting and Horticultural Projects by the State Government, are said to be only the tip of the Development Iceberg and further effort is required for more urgent but difficult to achieve Goals with regard to Smaller Farmers. Economic Researchers have documented that Experience from Initiatives such as Contract Farming for Potato (Sharma, V.P., De, S., & Jain, D. 2019). Further, some scholars (Kumar 2010) have opined, that in fact, Water Harvesting for Paddy has been a failure in Saurashtra, since Soil Quality is not Conducive to Absorption of water so the option of Surplus Water from Narmada Canal Distributaries in South Gujarat is a Viable Option.

Water Pumping, Management of Check Dams and Large-Scale Managed Aquifier Recharge have contributed significantly by enhancing the benefits of good Monsoons, particularly by increasing the availability of Groundwater for Supplemental Cultivation (Shah *et al.*, 2009). The Water Table rose in the Sardar Sarovar Basin, and the surplus water from Narmada distributaries has found its way to the fields. Sectors, which have largely contributed to this growth are Milk, Cotton, Fruits and Vegetables, Sugarcane, Groundnut and Wheat.

LITERATURE REVIEW

The focus on entitlements has shifted to Rural Empowerment (Government of India, 2024). The business of Economic Policy became more complex when economists began considering Social and Political Institutions in the Policy. For instance, a famous Institutional Economist (Schmid, 2004) has written about how Organizational Factors or Situational Characteristics need to be emphasized in a theory of Institutional Change.

Besides these, there are other possibile Policy Dilemmas arising from Ground Based Strategies (Easterly, W., 2007). The author while visiting Large Patel farmers in Champaner near Vadodara and Desai farmers in Derol Village near Godhra Town found that on ground facilitation of Farmer Relations—such as leasing in of Small farmer land and efforts by Small Cultivators on the land of large farmers—works only if local labour is available for cultivation (Alagh M., 2014).

There is a rich *literature* dealing with the conundrum of Agricultural development. For instance, Mellor (2017) advocates Modern farming Practices in Rural areas to prevent forced Migration. Instead, he advocated, what modern economists have called a Rural-Urban Continuum (Pahl, 1966): Creating a Pull factor by feeding Rural areas with Roads, Extension Services, Agricultural Mandis, Cottage Industry, Small Retail etc. However, his main stress was on the Agricultural Productivity of Medium Farmers to promote sustainability of Commercial Farming.

Theodore Schultz's (1964), writing on the need for Governments to focus on Extension, arguing that with proper Government support, extension works for Farm Families in any State can be strong. Easterly (2001) wrote on bottom-up development through Local Institutions rather than Top-down Policy from the big Global institutions. In our case, the focus is on creating a Pull from the Opposite direction ie Rural Initiatives encouraging Development of the Village and Indigenous Models of the Rural Transformation.

Trivette (2017), shows how local Food Participants, particularly Farms and Food Retailers, build Trust and Reciprocity with one another to mitigate the challenges imposed by the conventional System. A Food Business Principal can be calculative in his/her decisions to trust an Agent but will be genuinely vulnerable to the betrayal as well. In Gujarat, Farmers prefer selling to Traders as age-old patronage models imply comfort but in the case of well-regulated Agricultural Produce Markets in Unjha and Bavla, Farmers are keen to participate in the Market. This can now be extended to a more widely upscaled online Agricultural Produce Market framework.

PROBLEM STATEMENT

Let us introduce this section with a Case of Managed Uncertainty by a Typical Poor farmer of the State:

Mostly wheat, but in case of marginal and small farmers, Bajra is also the main staple diet of many farm households in the state. Bajra is consumed as a Staple, with Tur dal, rice, pickle, gur (molasses) and sometimes even with some vegetables. If the supply of wheat rises because of the Sardar Sarovar Project, the impact or some other facilitatory mechanism in rural area's growth will also pick up substantially.

Seeing the possibility of two square meals, the farmer completely replaces his basket of Wheat with Bajra rotis—an inferior quality cereal. At the time of an increase in effective income, even relatively more prosperous Farm households will not have more Protein Intensive tur or vegetable, but instead, have wheat or/and rice. Sometimes, they even tend to buy better quality rice like Parmal or even Basmati, with their extra income. Those policymakers who wish to increase nutrition but believe that the income elasticity is small, might be inclined to suggest, alternatives to cash transfers; subsidies or price controls that directly encourage increased consumption of nutritious Milletfoods. Similar policy prescriptions may arise if there is a concern, often stated, that simply giving cash is not desirable because households may spend it on other luxuries (food or nonfood).

Knowledge-Empowered ideas such as use of Nutritious Millets or Enabling of Horticulture will work only if farm surpluses are made sustainable.

EMPIRICAL ANALYSIS OF FARM AND FARMER SUSTAINABILITY IN GUJARAT

In this Context of Surpluses and Cash Flows a study conducted through the Centre for Management of Agriculture in IIM Ahmedabad later brought out as a publication on Marketed Surpluses for Farmers in Gujarat (Alagh, M. 2014). This study shows that out of 359 farmers Medium and Large farms in Gujarat which dominate this study also cultivate the largest proportion of Land holding and have higher Investment per hectare. The Medium Farmer between 2 to 10 hectares being dominant in Gujarat was brought out in the study (ibid, 2014).

Table 1 is a descriptive statistics of land holding pattern for the sample. Large farm households lease in 2.59 hectares of irrigated land per household, as compared to 1.23 hectares per household for all households. This is also understandable considering that irrigated tracts will have a greater demand in the lease market as compared to un-irrigated tracts.

Table 1: Average land Holding Characteristics
(Average Per Household in Hectare)

	Overall	*Owned Land*		*Leased in*	
		Irrigated	*Un-irrigated*	*Irrigated*	*Un-irrigated*
Small	27	1.3	0.14	0	0
Medium	183	4.5	0.64	0.38	0.03
Large	144	15.28	2.2	2.59	0
All Farms	359	8.53	1.22	1.23	0.02

A. Modernizing Tools and Rural Enterprises

For Equity in both a Distributive and Financial Sense Access to Credit and Finance is necessary. In a State beset with the problem of Stakeholders holding conflicting interests, this access is challenging.

Table 2 brings out the idea from the entire sample that:

Table 2

Categories→ Crops ↓	*Average Investment per Farm (Rs.)*			*Average Investment per Hectare (Rs.)*		
Farm Class	*Tractors*	*Threshing Machine*	*Tube Well*	*Tractors*	*Threshing Machine*	*Tube Well*
Marginal	0	0	20000	0	0	28818
Small	0	0	24074	0	0	18487
Medium	62502	7180	81530	12069	1386	15743
Large	183006	10444	160416	9281	529	8135

Use of farm machinery is constrained by profitability considerations. Farmers in these areas reported significant expenditures on tractors, tube wells and threshing machines, indicating prosperity. Farmers across all farm sizes use tubewells but tractor and other large equipment is purchased only by a few and available to the rest on rent according to capacity.

B. Rural Commerce Efficiency: Farmer Viability and Resource Access

We extracted information on farmers cultivating pigeon peas (tur). Subsequently, we subject this data to regression. For understanding factors that behave as enablers for farmers, we have extracted data from the study by Alagh cited above (ibid, 2014). Tur is a Foodgrain, yet a commercially saleable commodity with higher responsiveness compared to other foodgrains because of factors like alternate forms of commodity as dry green tur seed vegetable. The factors related to access to quality input including tools and equipment, even storage are more relevant in this Pulse Crop.

Table 3: Regression Values of Factors Affecting Marketed Surplus of Tur in Gujarat 2011–12

Factors	*Coefficient*	*Std. Error*	*t-Ratio*	*p-Value*	
Access to credit	732.958	317.871	2.3058	0.02568	**
Education in years	127.191	33.7097	3.7731	0.00046	***
No. of tractors	750.269	264.761	2.8338	0.00681	***
No. of cattle	172.139	54.183	3.1770	0.00266	***

Statistics based on the weighted data:

Sum Squared Residual	141.7827	S.E. of Regression	1.755629
R-squared	0.920341	Adjusted R-squared	0.903023

Note: *, ** and ***denote significant at 0.05, 0.01 and 0.001 levels respectively.

The regression tested using the concept of Coefficient of Determination (Rsquared) and Level of Significance by matching the calculated value using software of the predicted line values through the scatter points between marketed surplus *Y* as a result of the facilitatory factors like access to credit, which was explained by the regression and how well it matched the observed scatter. The Significance level was determined by the software using the logic of the sample test statistic fitting a normal population curve parameter, say the sample correctly predicts that the population is commercially responsive to credit, education, mechanised equipment and dairying.

An educated farmer with more cattle and equipped with tractors will be more capable to create surpluses.

C. Modernised Agriculture and Transformative Use of Inputs/ Tools/Equipment

As electricity use gets to be very high for intensive irrigation at certain times of the year the electric supply can sometimes fail and then when the Power Station drops are too frequent one needs to reprice the electricity or even ration it according to demand and use type. Farmers in India still will always use the power generated Tubewells as (Alagh, 2014) shows.

Electric tube wells are the major source of irrigation. In some areas diesel tube wells and bore wells are also used for irrigation. This shows that there is sufficient supply of electricity for irrigation. Our sample shows that investment in tube wells is high. There is a great thirst for water in Gujarat agriculture and this continues with SSP water.

Table 4 (In % of total)

Crops ↓ *Categories* →	*Marginal*	*Small*	*Medium*	*Large*	*All Farms*
Kharif – Paddy					
Canal	0.00	0.00	11.44	2.64	7.40
Electric tube-well	0.00	71.60	88.04	94.07	90.32
Bore well	0.00	0.00	1.56	3.29	2.28
Others	0.00	28.40	4.42	0.00	2.99
Kharif – Other Cereals					
Canal	0.00	2.57	4.59	1.60	3.16
Electric tube-well	15.81	44.24	85.01	95.48	89.13
Bore well	84.19	36.70	5.95	2.65	5.05

It is in this context that in Gujarat the provision of electricity for peak hour farm utilization is relevant.

OVERCOMING CHALLENGES: A GUJARAT COMMUNITY RETAIL FRANCHISE

Accelerating the Transformational process through Non-farm Enterprise.

The Case in point is of a Shia Community (Bohras, Khojas and Momins are examples) Supermarket model. The Entrepreneur in question after making a study of the different retail supermarkets launched his own Franchise Arrangement. He thought of overcoming the limitations of his own Community in Business. But he soon found his franchise owners plagued with the same limitations.

There were some store owners who flouted the norm of the Franchise Arrangement and chose to scale up on their own. In Dholka village where there was a good proportion of Jains and Muslims, the supermarket franchisor succeeded because he openly flouted the supermarket community norm by running a very large supermarket in complete contravention of the slow and incremental progress dictated by the format.

In contrast, Ilol Village in Sabarkantha District towards North Gujarat embodies a hesitation among the Merchant and landowning class of the Muslim franchise Owners to adjust to individual requirements and ground level realities. During my visit to the village while writing my book on a Community Retail Super Market initiative (Dutta S., Alagh, M., 2017) I visited the home of Mohseen and Sarfaraz, two brothers who owned the Super Market next to the Ilol Village's Main Courtyard adjoining the Lake called Ilol Talaav.

The Findings from Interviews led me to conclude the following:

1. Enterprise in these villages was caught in a dichotomy between a commercially active Urban Mercantile class and a Landowning Rural Populace. The Proposition of sale and purchase both needed adjustment to Rural settings.
2. So, for Instance the Landed class owning retail store owners like Sarfaraz in the Village had to be convinced of the Value Proposition of selling Local Denim Brands like Spykar, Newport, Flying machine, Numero Uno etc. The Newport Jeans which sold for Rs. 120 in 2014 in the Wholesale Market at Madhepura near Dariapur in Ahmedabad would be a valueadding transaction to the Franchise owner if he would be able to overcome the initial hesitation of moving away from prestige goods to a sensible customer value proposition.
3. There are ways in which the customer would also need to adjust to the value proposition of foam boxes, dry ice and deep freeze as well as purchase of pulses and edible oil in 1 kilo or 2 kilo packing. Similarly, the bundling of beauty, bath and hair solutions in single packing would need getting used to. At a more basic level rural customers would need to learn to make purchases and more specifically plan their shopping from such stores.

4. As long as the Franchisee maintains earning and incentive compatibility in terms of their unit sales, independent of any external agency and can sustain himself within the existing Community Franchise, local innovation will continue to explain Business Cycle Residuals (Griliches, Z. *et al.*, 1966).

IMPROVING PRACTICAL AWARENESS OF EXTENSION PROGRAMS

While neoclassical markets face limitations in addressing uncertainty (Eyzaguirre H., *et al.*, 2014), our field observations highlight positive trends in Gujarat. Notably, government agricultural initiatives, such as Krushi Rath and Krushi Mela, have demonstrably increased farmer awareness from 2011-12 to 2024 (Alagh, M., 2014, Pattnaik I. *et al.*, 2012).

We see potential for further growth in extension services, particularly in the Panchmahal district, where a significant rural population (80% of 2,390,776, 2011 Census) could benefit. Strengthening Agricultural Produce Market Committees (APMCs) across the state requires collaborative efforts, transcending political differences, to ensure institutional integrity.

Our vision is to build a sustainable agricultural future for all of Gujarat, including its diverse agro-climatic regions, especially the dryland areas. Recognizing the challenges posed by erratic monsoons and varying rainfall (700-800 mm), we aim to address specific needs.

Interviews, such as with farmer Hasmukh Parmar in Khandoli village, Panchmahal, reveal both existing strengths and areas for improvement. While some APMCs, like Unjha and Bavla, demonstrate successful daily operations, others, particularly in less developed districts, face challenges.

We acknowledge the difficulties faced by farmers regarding irrigation, power access, and wildlife damage. Government seed and fertilizer provisions are appreciated, and we see opportunities to build upon these successes by addressing other pressing concerns. We can leverage existing resources, like the SSP water supply, to improve irrigation.

We recognize the need to strengthen farmer cooperatives and self-help groups, fostering collaboration and reducing reliance on external traders. We also observe the need for improved transparency and accountability in APMC operations, ensuring that storage facilities are utilized for the benefit of farmers.

We see the potential for digital tools to empower farmers, but we must address the challenges of digital intermediation to ensure equitable access. By focusing on targeted extension efforts, empowering farmer self-help initiatives, and strengthening market infrastructure, we can create a more resilient and sustainable agricultural sector for all of Gujarat.

CONCLUSION

Despite the presence of the Sardar Sarovar for a water-scarce region, for the market to work efficiently and with long term interests of Rural populace in mind a tripartite initiative between the State Government, Co-operatives, and Farmer Companies needs to be devised. Additionally, Private Rural Initiatives in Education and Information can boost the transformation of Agriculture, by providing Extension Services in far-flung areas. From Field visit interviews it is found that there is a need for long-term redressal of Equity issues. Better links with institutions like Colleges, Agricultural Produce Market yards and good support for Family Health. On the whole, Government initiatives need to be supported by Private Research, Knowledge and Innovation initiatives in the State to go beyond the existing initiatives like Horticulture towards Sustainable Medium/ Large farm productivity Measures and once again reemphasise incremental change. A dynamic change is possible only if the promise of the underlying processes of Research and Innovation in agriculture are well linked with farm activities. In Conclusion, here we can say that farmers have lobbied for legal reforms to agricultural institutions, especially with the introduction of Self-help groups, Model farms, Links with formalized Education and Extension mechanisms like State Agricultural universities, and in a Commercially sensitive state like Gujarat active involvement of Urban Businesses in Contract farming once a certain degree of Rural Sustainability is ensured.

REFERENCES

[1] Acemoglu, D., Johnson, S. and Robinson, J.A. (2005). Institutions as a fundamental cause of long-run growth. *Handbook of economic growth,* 1, 385–472.

[2] Alagh, M. (2014). Assessment of marketed and marketable surplus of major food grains in Gujarat. *Indian Journal of Agricultural Marketing,* 28(2), 60–80.

[3] Dutta, S. and Alagh, M. (2017), A Study of a Community-oriented Social Enterprise in Gujarat, Academic Foundation, New Delhi.

[4] Easterly, W. (2007). "The Ideology of Development", Foreign Policy, 161: 30–35.

[5] Eyzaguirre, H., Ferrarini, T.H. and O'Roark, J.B. (2014). Textbook confessions: Government failure. *Journal of Private Enterprise, 29*(3), 159.

[6] Griliches, Z. and D. Jorgenson "Sources of Measured Productivity Change: Capital Input," *American Economic Review,* May 1966, Vol. 56(2), 50–61.

[7] Government of Gujarat (2022). Socio Economic Review of Gujarat State.

[8] Government of India (2024). Interim Budget.

[9] Kumar, M.D. (2010). Managing water in river basins: Hydrology, economics, and institutions. Oxford University Press.

[10] Mehta, N. and Mehta, M.G. (Eds.). (2013). Gujarat beyond Gandhi: identity, society and conflict. Routledge.

[11] Mellor, J.W. (2017). *Agricultural development and economic transformation: promoting growth with poverty reduction.* Springer.

[12] Pahl, R.E. (1966). The rural-urban continuum. Sociologia ruralis, 6(3), 299–329.

[13] Pattnaik, I., Shah, T., Koppa, G.G. and Shah, A. (2012). *Agricultural extension service through Krishi Mahotsav in Gujarat: a preliminary assessment.* Gujarat Institute of Development Research.

[14] Roy, D. and Thorat, A. (2007). Diversification in Indian Agriculture towards High-Value Crops.

[15] Shah, T., Gulati, A., Shreedhar, G. and Jain, R.C. (2009). Secret of Gujarat's agrarian miracle after 2000. Economic and Political Weekly, 45–55.

[16] Schmid, Allan (2004). Conflict and Cooperation: Institutional and Behavioral Economics, Blackwell.

[17] Schult, T.W. (1964). Changing Relevance of Agricultural Economics, Journal of Farm Economics, Vol. 46, No. 5, *Proceedings Number (Dec.)*, pp. 1004–1014.

[18] Sharma, V.P., De, S. and Jain, D. (2019). Managing agricultural commercialisation for inclusive growth in South Asia. *Gates Open Res*, 3(507), 507.

[19] Sharma, H., Swain, M. and Kalamkar, S.S. (2017). Agro-Economic Research Centre.

[20] Trivette, S.A. (2017). Invoices on scraps of paper: Trust and reciprocity in local food systems. *Agriculture and Human Values*, 34(3), 529–542.

ADDENDA

Knowledge Feedbacks can be Internalized in Local Agriculture

The author returned to Khandoli Village in 2024 February. Four farmers were interviewed and the following observations were made.

Bhav Sinhbhai Parmar (A Conservative Medium farmer); 65 years of age, engaged in farming and dairy, with a family of eight, wife, two sons and their wives and two grandsons. Earning an annual income of 3.5 Lakh Rupees. He owned 2 hectares, about 12 bighas of land out of which half was irrigated. The plot that was irrigated used the borewell to source water from the pipeline linking the village with the Canal System of the Narmada Canal Minors. He grew Rice and Tobacco in Kharif and Wheat and Bajra in Rabi season.

Cropping Pattern 2023–24

Season	*Crop*	*Area (hectares)*	*Production (Qt.)*	*Yield (kg/ha)*	*Sale Price Rs./qtl*	*Source of irrigation*
Kharif	Rice	1.5 ha	2100 kg	15 quintals/ha		borewell
	Others tobacco 5 month continue from end of kharif	1 ha	1000 kg	10 quintals/ha		borewell
Rabi	Wheat	1 ha	2000 kg	20 quintals/ha		borewell
	Bajra	1 ha		10 quintals/ha	1100	borewell

Ownership of Farm Machinery and Livestock

Type of Machinery	*Number*	*Approximate Value (Rs.)*
Tractors and related implements	1	
Threshing machine	Hire	1 hour 900 rupees
Tubewell or Borewell	1	
Buffalo	2	
Desi shankar Cows	4	20 litres @50 Rs fat

Sale Pattern of Selected Crops

Crop	*Total Qty. Sold/Kept for Personal Consumption*	*Place*	*Qty.*	*Price*	*Price*	*Month of Sale*
		Trader from Home		*Varies from 500 Rs/maund to 1500 Rs/maund*		*June*
		Market kalol	1200 kg		450 Rs/ maund	
bajri				1100 rupees per quintal		June July
wheat						April

Mangalbhai Parmar: An uneducated but progressive farmer had for instance build contact with a Hyderabad based company for tissue culture for Saag (wood) Cultivation.

General Information

Name of the Head of Household	*Mangalbhai Moorjibhai Parmar*
Gender of the decision maker	Male
Age (years)	78
Occupation of the Decision-maker 1. Main 2. Subsidiary	Farming
Approximate Family Income from other source Rs./yr.	3.5 lakhs
Education of decision maker (years of schooling)	SSC
Family size (Number of family members) 1. Adult Male 2. Adult Female 3. Children (a) Male iv. labourers @200 rupees per hour for sowing 2,3 days per crop	3 one son working in company 3 1 1 studying

Name of the Head of Household	*Mangalbhai Moorjibhai Parmar*
Social Group	OBC
Village	Khandoli
Taluka/Tehsil	Kalol
District	Panchmahal
State	Gujarat

Operational Holding and Cropping Pattern

A. *Land and Machine Ownership Pattern*

	Irrigated	*Un-irrigated*	*Source of Irrigation*
1. Total owned land	½ hectare = 3 bigha	4 bigha	borewell
2. Machines	owned	hired	
(a) tractor	No	@800 Rs/hour	
3. Leased-out land	No		
4. Total Operational land	½ hectare = 3 bigha	4 bigha	

B. *Cropping Pattern (2023–24)*

Season	*Crop*	*Area (hectares)*		*Production (Qt.)*	*Yield (kg/ha)*	*Sale Price Rs./qtl*
		irri	*unirri*			
Kharif	Rice	½ hectare = 3 bigha		1800	15 quintals/ha	930 kg kept for personal consumption kalol, 430 Rs/maund 930 kg sold
Rabi	Wheat		2 bigha	250 kg	20 quintals/ha	1000 kg kept for personal consumption
	Tobacco		2 bigha	250 kg	10 quintals/ha	

Ownership of Livestock

Type of Machinery	*Number*	*Approximate Value (Rs.)*
Feed	3 sacks 30 kilos	Cost 700 rupees
Buffalo	2	
Working Bullocks	1	
Buffaloes in milk Panchmahal Dairy gives support	1	3 litres 1.5 litres twice a day 52 rupees a litre= Rs 50000

Nareshbhai Himmatsinh Parmar is the sarpanch of the Village a Commercial Progressive Medium Framer who engages in leasing in and out land to needy farmers in the village.

General Information

Name of the Head of Household	*Nareshbhai Himmatbhai Parmar*
Gender of the decision maker	Male
Age (years)	38
Telephone Number	7698273385
Occupation of the Decision-maker Main Subsidiary	 Farming Dairy
Approximate Family Income from other source Rs./yr.	7.2 lakhs
Education of decision maker (years of schooling)	10th Pass
Family size (Number of family members) Adult Male Adult Female	 (a) 1 (b) 2 (Wife and Mother)
Social Group	OBC
Village	Khandoli
Taluka/Tehsil	Kalol
District	Panchmahal
State	Gujarat

Operational Holding and Cropping Pattern

A. *Land Ownership Pattern*

	Irrigated	*Source of Irrigation*
1. Total owned land	½ hectare	Borewell
1.1 Area under cultivation		
2. Leased-in land	3 hectare	
3. Leased-out land	1 hectare	
4. Total Operational land	5 hectares approx	

B. *Cropping Pattern (2023–24)*

Season	*Crop*	*Area (hectares)*	*Production (Qt.)*	*Yield (kg/ha)*	*Sale Price Rs./qtl*	*Source of Irrigation*
Kharif	Rice	2 bigha				
	Others tobacco 5 month continue from end of kharif	6 bigha		35 man	1500 Rs. man	
Rabi	Bajra	3 bigha		50 man		

Ownership of Farm Machinery and Livestock

Type of Machinery	*Number*	*Approximate Value (Rs.)*
Tractors and related implements	Hire 1000 Rs/hour	
Tubewell or Borewell	Canal pipeline	
Cattle		
Buffalo	3	
Buffaloes in milk		4 litres 55 rs a litre every 10 days dairy deposit in bank

Sale Pattern of Selected Crops

Crop	*Total Qty. Sold/Kept for Personal Consumption*	*Place*	*Price*	*Month of Sale*
		Trader from home	1500 Rs/ maund	June
		Apmc kalol		
bajri		Trader	1100 rupees per quintal	June July
wheat	For personal consumption			April

Natural Resources and Agriculture in Gujarat: Recent Trends

Amita Shah[1] and Hasmukh Joshi[2]

ABSTRACT: This paper examines micro-level WDPs in Gujarat, crucial for sustainable resource management in dry regions. While SWC strategies have evolved, long-term sustainability is a challenge. Focusing on implementation, the paper proposes strategies for faster progress and equitable outcomes. Hindered by managerial, financial, and community engagement issues, WDP implementation needs a renewed focus. Analyzing Gujarat's current status, the paper suggests bridging the planning-action gap with a holistic approach, considering ecological, social, and political factors. In line with SDG 15, it highlights the urgent need to address land degradation and promote sustainable agriculture, emphasizing long-term commitment and broader coverage, especially in the context of climate change. It calls for increased government support to ensure equitable water access and balanced agricultural growth.

Keywords: *Watershed Development Programs, Soil Water Conservation, Integrated Watershed Management Programme.*

INTRODUCTION

Soil Water Conservation (SWC) plays a pivotal role in the sustainable management of natural resources, particularly in the context of fostering dry and semi-dryland agriculture in India. The SWC has been an important strategy in this direction. The approach has seen several phases ranging from individual household water conservation to the construction of large-scale dams. Despite these efforts, challenges persist in ensuring the long-term sustainability of watershed development programs (WDPs), especially in the face of climate change uncertainties. This paper focuses on the local-level

[1] Professor, Centre for Development Alternatives, Ahmedabad, India.
E-mail: amitagidr@gmail.com

[2] Research Associate, Centre for Development Alternatives, Ahmedabad, India.

implementation of WDPs in Gujarat, addressing key aspects and suggesting strategies for faster execution and equitable outcomes.

Soil Water Conservation (SWC) has once again emerged as a crucial component of natural resource management, particularly in the context of fostering sustainable agriculture in India. The primary aim of SWC is to enhance the efficient utilization of resources across different levels, often referred to as the 'reach to valley.' However, implementing this objective poses numerous challenges, stemming not only from managerial and financial limitations but also from issues related to community engagement and a focus on medium-term outcomes. To address these challenges, efforts have been undertaken to establish middle-ground SWC initiatives, primarily operating at the meso-level. Despite these efforts, the extent of anticipated outcomes over time remains uncertain. Therefore, it becomes imperative to assess the spread of watersheds, especially at the micro level.

The evolution of the SWC approach has traversed various phases, ranging from water conservation at the individual household level to the construction of large dams spanning multiple districts and states. Nevertheless, there is a unanimous agreement on the significance of capturing water to safeguard the basic livelihoods of those whose primary occupation is farming. As pointed out by Dasgupta (2023), "In no other context does the interplay of the 'macro' and 'micro' receive as much attention; and yet, while farmers, fishermen, woodlanders, and grazers constantly monitor their natural capital assets, the one class of assets conspicuously missing in academic writings and government publications on poverty is the wide range of ecosystems and their services that constitute the biosphere" (p. XXV).

Watershed development for conservation of land and soil-water conservation has a long history and has passed through different phases in India Joy, K.J. and Paranjape, S. (2004). Several steps have been taken to deal with these basic resources. However, the outcomes have remained varied and sporadic. The time has come to get back on the drawing board and look afresh how to bridge the gap, within a set time frame. This is particularly important in the context of climate change, which has brought many unknowns within and across regions.

To what extent Watershed Development Programs (WDPs) have moved and brought sustainable outcomes, with equity, is a moot point. Understanding this requires a fairly closer look at the scale and space. This may help create alternative pathways to achieve optimality in the programmes. Needless to say, the idea is to help policy-making processes and ensure people's long-term involvement. At this point, it may be kept in mind that the selection of micro watersheds has been influenced not only by factors like size and reach of the water source but also by social and political forces. This may have significant implications not only in terms of outcomes and long-term sustainability but also for people's involvement, which is particularly important to ensure food security.

A natural resource, water is spread widely as well as diversely in different parts covering rivers, springs, aquifers, wetlands, etc. Thus, it is a public resource. Therefore, the community has a significant role to play in its equitable distribution and use keeping in view social justice, and long-term ecological sustainability. Consequently, it has always remained an integral part of the water-use guidelines (Planning Commission 2011). Policy discourse thereby is saddled between the required holistic approach (p. 20), and central thrust on groundwater management.

Unfortunately, WDP has yet to adopt an integrated approach, especially at the micro level (Shah and Joshi 2023). The complexity is manifested in terms of a fragmented administrative structure where water at different scales and uses is governed by different policy guidelines and institutional mechanisms, as reflected in different guidelines adopted by major departments such as agriculture, and rural development. While the major focus has been on revitalising rainfed areas on one hand and restoration of hilly ecosystems on the other hand, the programme has passed through several changes over time, as presented in Table 1. Ministry of Rural Development, Government of India, finally provided an overarching guideline for WDPs in 2008 (see, Common Guidelines for Watershed Development Project, Govt. of India 2008, for details).

Moreover, WDP implementation across different administrative areas, their co-ordination, and conversion of organisations remains an unfinished agenda (Reddy 2006). At this point, it is important to remember that the draft National Water Framework Act strongly suggested that WDPs should be federated through an upward sub-basin level for interstate coordination. While this is difficult to achieve at different scales, it would still be useful to highlight some of the major learnings in the recent context and the gaps, especially in terms of coverage within a state.

This requires a fresh discourse on the long-term sustainability of the watershed approach across locations and communities, (being the main users) of SWC. This paper makes an effort to bring out certain key aspects of WDPs at the local level across the districts in Gujarat and provide suggestions for faster execution as well as equitable outcomes in future. This paper attempts to highlight key aspects of WDPs at the local level across the districts of Gujarat and offers suggestions for faster execution and equitable outcomes in the future. This is particularly important, given the complex cobweb of water governance getting entangled through the boundaries of the different Ministries/ Departments in the central and state governments, as noted above. The issues of equity, sustainability, and community participation or decentralized democracy are to be kept at the core of the WDPs (Shah *et al.*, 2011).

Table 1: Changing Focus and Limitations of WDP Guidelines Overtime

Year	*Name*	*Main Focus*	*Learning and Missing Gapes*
1994	Prof. C.H. Hanumanth Rao Committee	Assess the Drought Prone Areas Programme (DPAP) and the Desert Development Programme (DDP) to identify Weaknesses and suggest improvements.	Special focus on DPAP and DDP that need special attention in the context of climate change.
2000	Ministry of Agriculture	The National Watershed Development Project for Rainfed Areas (NWDPRA). The guidelines were intended to be common. Guidelines to make the programme more participatory, sustainable, and equitable	Specific link with the overall growth of the agriculture sector.

Year	*Name*	*Main Focus*	*Learning and Missing Gapes*
2001	Ministry of Rural Development (MoRD)	"Hariyali Guidelines".	Widening the scope by including employment generation through other programmes like MGNREGA and creating better space for non-government organisations across states.
2008	Ministry of Rural Development (MoRD)	Common Guidelines for Watershed Development Projects.	Increasing importance of scientific data analysis from GIS.

ECONOMIC GROWTH IN GUJARAT: A COMPARATIVE PICTURE

Gujarat is the 4th largest economy among all the states of India, contributing 8.3% to the total Gross Domestic Product (GDP). The state is the home of 5% of the country's total population and grew at a CAGR of 11.90% between 2015–16 and 2022–23 (IBEF 2023). It is also a highly urbanised state, covering 42.58% of the population compared to 31% at the India level, as per the Census 2011. It stood second, only after Maharashtra on the State Ranking 2023, on a comprehensive score covering seven pillars (Economic, Fiscal, Social, Infrastructure, Financial Inclusion, Environment and Governance) and 46 indicators to rank the states (CareEdge 2023). The economy of Gujarat is the most industrialised in India, having the largest industrial output of any state in the union. It contributes about 45% to the state SDP and grew at the rate of 12% compound rate of growth between 2016 and 2022 (Government of Gujarat, 2022). It also has the highest exports of any Indian state, accounting for 33% of all Indian exports in 2022–23 (The Times of India 2023).

On the other end agriculture sector suffered from unstable rainfall and a significantly large proportion of dry land across districts, leading to stagnant farm production, between 2011 and 2020. This was further reduced during 2019–20 and 2010–11. The foodgrain productivity in Gujarat was 2236 kg/ha, less than 2325 kg/ha at the national level. Compared to some of the states like Punjab (4519 kg/ha), Haryana (3891) kg/ha) or Andhra Pradesh (3038) kg/ha) and Tamil Nadu (2988) kg/ha), Gujarat's productivity remains a cause of concern (Government of Gujarat, 2022, op. cit.). To some extent, it can be linked to limited and uncertain rainfall on one hand, and large sea coast that has been a major victim of climate change, salinity ingress, saline sea winds, etc., on the other.

Within this broader picture of Gujarat's economic growth, it would be useful to see how WDPs, one of the most important and wide-ranging programmes have moved in the state. Unfortunately, despite significant efforts made mainly by the state, to fill up the gap, what is still missing is a clear map of the treated WDPs at the micro level, i.e., at the state, district, and village level in the state.

Over time, Gujarat has passed through different phases of undertaking SWDPs and remained the second top state with respect to the primary focus on collecting rainwater at villages as well as household levels. However, the issue of using water sustainably and equitably has not been attended to effectively. The time has come to interlink economic growth with the sustainable use of natural resources. We need to understand how far the high economic growth of the state has been linked with the sustainability of natural resources through special programmes such as WDPs needs to be stressed in the ongoing growth processes across states, especially in Gujarat.

It has been recognised that WDPs have moved further in terms of capturing geophysical outcomes at different scales and the specific treatments involved at different phases. The issue of increasing coverage and continuous management of the treated area has largely remained unclear. In this context, identifying the scaler map of the treated land could be seen as an important starting point across different geographies within the state. This is particularly so, as we move forward from districts to villages.

IWMP APPROACH: WIDENING THE SCOPE

Keeping in mind the increasing importance of SWDC Government of India has moved forward by setting up the Integrated Watershed

Management Programme (IWMP) in 2010, covering all the states in India. This involved a wide-ranging approach right from long-term sustainability of various natural resources, to strengthening productivity of agriculture and allied sectors, and also poverty reduction. Gujarat State Watershed Management Agency has been the lead agency for this. Some of the important aspects of the program are: a) creating a map of WDP at different levels within the State, District, and down to the village level; b) categorisation of WDPs by natural resource base, especially through historical data, that include socio-economic aspects; and, c) careful identification of drainage and contours on one hand, and the socio-economic aspect on the other. Ideally, satellite images on this parameter are to be collected and then superimposed in the area which can be used for prioritization.

What is important is that various features of the IWMP are to be followed from the micro to the macro level. This approach, in principle, gives a scientific understanding of how the programme should operate at various scales. Unfortunately, experiences indicate that the WDP in the past few years has weakened, especially in terms of achieving expected outcomes. It seems that the program has not been able to keep up its initial enthusiasm concerning its approach, coverage, impacts, and involvement of various agencies including the state, parastatal and non-governmental organizations.

In the absence of this, it may be difficult to map out and prioritise the next phase of the program, especially within the changing agro-climatic conditions. Given these limitations, in what follows, we present a comparative picture of IWMPs, mapping the coverage across districts in Gujarat between 2009–10 and 2013–14, and subsequently in 2014–15 and 2021–22. These periods are being treated separately because of the lack of comparability owing to the reorganisation of districts in Gujarat, in 2014.

LAND AND WATER IN GUJARAT: A DISTRICT-LEVEL SCENARIO

This section provides an overview of IWMP in Gujarat from 2009–10 to 2013–14. One of the important dimensions is the coverage of the program across different agro-climatic zones. This has special implications, because of the scaler dimension with respect to the coverage of total area per district, which is generally higher in dry land districts. For instance, the total land in Amreli, Rajkot, Surendranagar and Banaskantha districts ranges from 7,29,000 to 11,00,000 hectares in dryland regions. This is besides Kachchh district, which has an area of 45,65,200 hectares. Compared to this, the average land within districts like Anand, Kheda, Navsari, Valsad, and Narmada is fairly low (Appendix 1). Such diversity is also important to keep in mind while looking at the comparative picture.

As noted by Alagh (2018), Gujarat can be broadly divided into eight major agro-climatic zones, covering 26 districts (see Map 1 below).

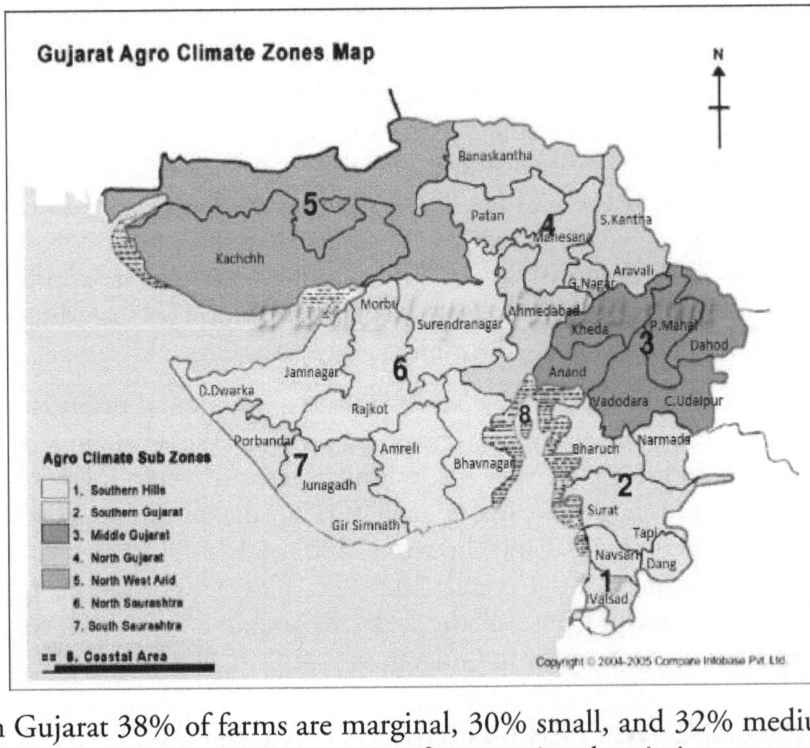

In Gujarat 38% of farms are marginal, 30% small, and 32% medium and large. There is, however, a significant regional variation across the districts. It is, expected that land holdings are higher in dryland regions (e.g., Banas Kantha) as compared to those having assured irrigation (e.g., Kheda). However, the size varies within the agro-climatic zones across districts (Table 2). For instance, the predominant land holding size is smaller in Anand (70%), Kheda (64.35%), Valsad (64.26%), and Navsari (63.83), compared to some of the dry land districts like Surendranagar (14%), Kachchh (13.22%), Jamnagar (18.31%), Banaskantha (28.05%), and so on. In Panchmahal 53% of households have small land holdings which could be due to a large proportion of high land terrain. Therefore, it is important to keep this aspect while selecting WDP across districts. However, at present it is not clear how far this aspect is taken care of.

What is notable is that the proportion of cultivated and net irrigated areas varies significantly across zones. The top 4 districts in terms of cultivated area are Anand (70.3%), Kheda (74.3%), Gandhinagar (76.3) and Mehsana (77.4%). These districts are part of Middle and North Gujarat. What is notable is that these districts also have more than 70% of the net irrigated area, within different agro-climatic zones (Table 2).

Table 2: Diversity in Land Holding Size, along with Cultivated area and Irrigation

Agro-Climatic Zone	*Districts*	*Land Holding Size (%)*			*Agriculture Area*	
		Marginal	*Small*	*Medium + Large*	*% Cultivated Area*	*% Net Irrigated Area*
Southern Hills	Dangs	12.29	15.94	71.77	31.74	7.81
	Navsari	63.83	19.30	16.87	44.40	62.75
	Valsad	64.26	18.54	17.20	53.68	63.80
Southern Gujarat	Bharuch	37.69	28.64	33.67	47.06	34.23
	Narmada	31.97	33.34	34.69	41.17	38.83
	Surat	44.09	28.46	27.45	49.58	67.07
	Tapi	36.16	30.21	33.63	46.44	45.73
Middle Gujarat	Anand	69.97	19.47	10.56	70.26	97.94
	Dahod	35.41	26.33	38.26	61.23	14.93
	Kheda	64.35	21.39	14.27	74.3	81.74
	Panchmahal	52.84	24.1	23.06	54.63	22.93
	Vadodara	48.66	26.61	24.73	67.91	92.68

Agro-Climatic Zone	*Districts*	*Land Holding Size (%)*			*Agriculture Area*	
		Marginal	*Small*	*Medium + Large*	*% Cultivated Area*	*% Net Irrigated Area*
North Gujarat	Ahmedabad	31.94	26.27	41.80	68.14	45.21
	Banaskantha	28.05	30.94	41.01	64.45	61.34
	Gandhinagar	59.05	25.06	15.88	76.3	76.83
	Mahesana	58.23	25.43	16.34	77.44	61.61
	Patan	35.56	27.5	36.94	57.69	61.58
	Sabarkantha	46.54	30.44	23.02	64.01	83.92
North West Gujarat	Kachchh	13.22	29.59	57.19	14.98	37.00
North Saurashtra	Amreli	22.56	37.56	39.88	76.12	46.86
	Bhavnagar	29.44	38.04	32.52	54.23	28.61
	Jamnagar	18.31	40.71	40.98	42.67	88.02
	Rajkot	24.09	42.46	33.45	65.98	61.88
	Surendranagar	14.81	31.52	53.67	69.60	53.64
South Saurashtra	Junagadh	28.52	39.5	31.97	63.82	84.94
	Porbandar	28.39	39.43	32.18	50.39	99.99
All		37.94	30.37	31.69	50.11	56.75

Considering the wide variation in agroclimatic conditions in the state, it is notable that fifteen out of twenty-four districts have more than 60% of their under Irrigation. Of these, Porbandar, Anand, Vadodara, Junagadh, Jamnagar, Sabarkantha and Gandhinagar have more than 75% of the land under irrigation. On the other end, Six Districts (Other than Dangs) have Less than 40% of land under irrigation. What is however important is to consider uncertainty as well as variability of water available for agriculture in different parts of Gujarat. This is particularly important in the context of a significantly large proportion of the irrigated area being dependent on water distributed from other districts. In that case, the issue of equitable distribution of water becomes more concerning (Gujja B. et al. 2006).

IWMP COVERAGES IN GUJARAT: A DISAGGREGATED ANALYSIS

Recognising the wide variation in natural endowments and availability of assured irrigation in different parts of Gujarat, we present a comparative picture of the coverage of IWMPs at the micro level, i.e., at the taluka and village level, to bring out the ground reality. The reason, though limited, is to provide a handy tool to pinpoint the gaps, and to help set up the new phase for IWMP in Gujarat.

Notably, the program has made significant achievements over time. During five years i.e., 2009–10 to 2013–14, for which data are available, the coverage of the Talukas in six districts is as high as 90% and above, even 100%, spread across different parts of Gujarat except in the middle and north Gujarat regions. This is followed by eleven districts covering over 60% to 75% of talukas, mainly in north Gujarat. Against, these the remaining nine districts have low coverage, which includes Banaskantha, ranging between 33% and 57%).

While the coverage of Talukas is quite impressive, the situation is quite different at the village level. For example, though the coverage of IWMP is 100% in a few Talukas, by and large, less than 50% of villages have been covered therein. It is also interesting to note that the districts with high net irrigated areas have low IWMP Projects. For example, Junagadh has almost 100% net irrigated area but has only 12.7% of villages covered under IWMP. Similarly, Vadodara with 92.68% net irrigated area has only 19% villages covered under IWMP. This confirms in negative link between access to irrigation and coverage of IWMPS.

On the other end, districts in dry regions have higher coverage. These include Kachchh, Panchmahal, and to an extent Banaskantha etc. (See Table 3). It is concerning that Dangs being the only hilly district has only 1.4% of villages covered under the Project, and also covers only 7.61% of net irrigated area. There seems to be, overall, an inverse relationship between the net irrigated area in a district and the corresponding coverage of villages under IWMP. This confirms the fact that the districts with high coverage of assured irrigation may not depend much on watershed development projects at least in the medium term. These findings are in line with our inter-state analysis carried out earlier (Shah *et al.* 2023).

Table 3: Coverage of IWMP across Districts, Talukas, and Villages in Gujarat- 2009–10 to 2013–14

Agro-Climatic Zone	*Districts*	*Total No. of Taluka*	*Projects*	*% of Covered Taluka*	*% of Covered Villages*
Southern Hills	Dangs	1	16	100	51.4
	Navsari	5	19	100	46.5
	Valsad	5	16	40	33.8
Southern Gujarat	Bharuch	8	20	37.5	25.8
	Narmada	4	18	75	40.9
	Surat	9	16	44.4	25.1
	Tapi	5	15	100.0	31.1
Middle Gujarat	Anand	8	19	62.5	39.6
	Dahod	7	19	71.4	29.9
	Kheda	10	16	40	21.7
	Panchmahal	11	20	63.6	22.6
	Vadodara	12	23	41.7	19.0
North Gujarat	Ahmedabad	11	19	63.6	17.0
	Banaskantha	12	28	33.3	13.5
	Gandhinagar	4	13	75.0	34.7
	Mahesana	9	16	55.6	25.3
	Patan	7	24	57.1	21.7
	Sabarkantha	13	26	69.2	19.1
North West Gujarat	Kachchh	10	47	90.0	16.3
North Saurashtra	Amreli	11	25	63.6	21.4
	Bhavnagar	11	25	72.7	18.3
	Jamnagar	10	25	60.0	15.7
	Rajkot	14	36	71.4	14.8
	Surendranagar	10	26	90.0	17.3
South Saurashtra	Junagadh	14	23	57.1	12.7
	Porbandar	3	19	100.0	38.8
All (26)		224	569	62.9	22.6

In terms of regional concentration for Talukas and villages, 10 out of 26 districts in Gujarat fall in the category of medium-level concentration both at the taluka level as well as at the village level. On the other end, 13 districts have a low concentration of taluka and villages. To an extent, this suggests the need for strengthening IWMP coverage in these talukas as well as villages (Table 4). What is concerning is that most of the districts within dry and semi-dry regions in Gujarat have fairly low coverage at the village level; such as Dahod, Panchmahal, Banaskantha, Kachchh, and Surendranagar. This calls for detailed analysis to find the reasons behind such a trend and evolve an action plan, especially in the context of changing climatic conditions.

Table 4: Coverage of IWDP

At Taluka Level	*At Village Level*		
	High	*Medium*	*Low*
High	Dangs Navsari	Tapi Porbandar	Kachchh Surendranagar
Medium	Narmada	Anand Dahod Panchmahal Gandhinagar Mehsana	Ahmedabad Patan Sabarkantha Amreli Bhavnagar Jamnagar Rajkot
Low		Valsad Bharuch Surat	Kheda Vadodara Banaskantha Junagadh

We do recognise significant limitations regarding access to relevant data. The information asymmetry suggests the need for better access to information for this sector.

Realising the effectiveness and efficacy of Watershed projects, the Government of Gujarat launched IWMP 6 and IWMP 7 in 2014–15 and 2021–22 respectively to expand its coverage. Table 5 provides information on the expansion at Taluka as well as village levels. By and large, it is expected that the focus of the programme would be relatively more on dry regions, especially in north Saurashtra, covering seven districts. However, no such trend is discernible. While Bhavnagar, Botad and Devbhumi Dwarka have better coverage, districts like Jamnagar, Rajkot and Surendranagar have rather low coverage. On the other hand, a higher proportion of villages are covered in better-endowed districts like Anand (3.83%), Dahod (4.15%), and Gandhinagar (4.12%). Of course, districts like Dangs (4.18%), Gir Somnath and Porbandar, with deficit endowments are relatively better covered. There is still significantly a large gap, that may need immediate attention, especially in the changing climatic conditions.

Table 5: District-wise No. of Projects and Covered No. of Villages in Batch 6 & 7

Agro-climatic Zone	*Districts*	*IWMP-6 (2014-15)*			*IWMP-7 (2021–22)*			*Total IWMP 6 & 7**
		Taluka	*Project*	*No. of Villages*	*Taluka*	*Project*	*No. of Villages*	
Southern Hills (3)	Dangs	1	2	21 (311)	1	1	13	34 (4.18)
	Navsari	1	2	25	1	1	10	35 (2.58)
	Valsad	2	3	31	1	1	9	40 (1.93)
Southern Gujarat (4)	Bharuch	1	1	11	1	1	8	19 (1.19)
	Narmada	1	1	11	2	2	35	46 (5.70)
	Surat	2	2	25	1	1	12	37 (1.62)
	Tapi	2	2	37	1	1	8	45 (1.63)
Middle Gujarat (7)	Anand	1	1	10	1	1	14	24 (3.83)
	Dahod	3	3	25	2	2	29	54 (4.15)
	Kheda	2	2	14	1	1	9	23 (1.43)
	Panchmahal	3	3	27	1	1	5	32 (0.41)
	Mahisagar	1	1	9	1	1	17	26 (2.37)
	Vadodara	1	1	7	1	1	10	17 (0.63)
	Chhotaudaepur	2	2	38	1	1	8	46 (0.89)

Agro-climatic Zone	*Districts*	*IWMP-6 (2014-15)*			*IWMP-7 (2021–22)*			*Total IWMP 6 & 7**
		Taluka	*Project*	*No. of Villages*	*Taluka*	*Project*	*No. of Villages*	
North Gujarat (7)	Ahmedabad	1	2	12	2	2	10	22 (1.82)
	Banaskantha	2	3	12	1	2	5	17 (0.40)
	Gandhinagar	1	1	8	1	1	12	20 (4.12)
	Mahesana	2	2	21	1	1	9	30 (1.46)
	Patan	1	2	6	1	1	9	15 (1.71)
	Sabarkantha	–	–	–	2	2	20	20 (1.43)
	Aravalli	2	2	23	1	1	14	37 (2.07)
North West Gujarat (1)	Kachchh	4	5	13	2	5	22	35 (2.34)
North Saurashtra (7)	Amreli	2	4	24	2	2	10	34 (1.53)
	Bhavnagar	1	1	10	2	2	18	28 (2.21)
	Botad	2	3	15	2	2	8	23 (4.21)
	Jamnagar	1	1	4	2	2	12	16 (1.64)
	Devbhumi Dwarka	1	3	12	2	3	18	30 (7.23)
	Rajkot	3	3	6	2	2	13	19 (1.50)
	Surendranagar	2	2	10	2	2	20	30 (1.03)
South Saurashtra (3)	Junagadh	2	2	19	2	2	8	27 (0.77)
	Gir Somnath	1	1	8	2	2	18	26 (3.71)
	Porbandar	1	1	8	1	1	6	14 (3.19)
All (32)		52	64	502	46	51	419	921 (1.91)

*Figure in parenthesis are percentages of villages covered.

OBSERVATION AND CONCLUSION

Indian agriculture has entered a new phase, where the sustainability of natural resources has become crucial. While there cannot be a disagreement on growth with sustainability, putting that in place within a given time frame seems to be a fairly difficult proposition. The international commitment to Goal 15 of the Sustainable Development Goals reminds us that agricultural growth cannot overlook the sustainability of resource use. There is a strong focus on reversing land degradation and halting biodiversity loss. It calls for a commitment to combat desertification, and restore degraded land and soil by 2030 (United Nations, 2016). In this context, the long-term intervention of the soil-water-conservation programme, in different parts of India, including Gujarat, has become inevitable.

Whereas, SWDPs have been recognized as an important approach, putting that into practice, remains difficult due to various reasons such as financial limitations, lack of organisational capabilities, and long-term involvement of Non-Government Organizations (NGOs)/ Facilitation Agencies (FAs). We argue that the time has come to fill the gap between the approach and the action, for which a map of existing IWMP at the micro (village) level may help as an important starting point.

Despite having increasing coverage in the last few years it is still concerning that the areas once treated are considered as covered forever, and left to individual and/or selected groups or Gram Panchayats involved during the initial phase. This could be quite myopic and may not yield desired result. There is a need to have systematic planning to cover areas that are water deficit, more extensively, especially in view of the fact that the Coverage of IWMP is fairly limited even in dry-semi regions in the state. Government should ensure more judicious, equitable and sustainable access to water, if we desire a balanced regional growth of agriculture, keeping food security in view.

REFERENCES

[1] Alagh, Y.K. (2018). 'Development Perspective of Gujarat', Gujarat Vishvakosh Trust, 21st July.

[2] CareEdge (2023). States' Rankings 2023, https://www.careratings.com/uploads/newsfiles/12012023121156_State_Ranking_-_CareEdge_Report.pdf (accessed on 12 January 2024).

[3] Dasgupta, P. (2023). "Understanding the Role of Nature in Economic Development" In Acharyya Achiransu (ed.), *Environmental Economics in Developing Country: Issues and Challenges,* London. Routledge.

[4] Government of Gujarat (2022). Strategy for Government of Gujarat to Enable India to become a USD 5 Trillion Economy, https://www.gidb.org/Document/2022-5-14_2.pdf (accessed on 12th January 2024).

[5] Government of India (2008). Common Guidelines for Watershed Development Project (2008), Revised Edition – 2011, National Rainfed Area Authority, Planning Commission, Government of India, New Delhi.

[6] Gujarat State Watershed Management Agency (2010). Capacity Building Manual for Integrated Watershed Management Programme.

[7] Gujja, B.; Joy, K.J.; Vispute, Shruti; Paranjape, Suhas and Goud, Vinod (2006). 'Million Revolts' in the Making' in EPW, Vol. 41, Issue No. 07, 18 Feb., 2006.

[8] IBEF (2023). Economic Snapshot, https://www.ibef.org/states/gujarat-infographic (accessed on 12 January 2024).

[9] Joy, K.J. and Paranjape, S. (2004). "Watershed Development Review: Issues and Prospects, Technical Report, *Centre for Interdisciplinary Studies in Environment and Development (CISED),* Bangalore.

[10] Planning Commission (2011). The Draft National Water Framework Act. An input to the Twelfth Plan, Working Group on Water Governance, New Delhi.

[11] Reddy, V.R. and Deshpande, R.S. (2006). 'Sustainable Watershed Management: The GO-NGO Dichotomy' In Book Agricultural Development, Rural Institutions, and Economic Policy, A. Vaidyanathan.

[12] Shah, A., Samuel, A. and Joy, K.J. (2011). Equity in Watershed Development: Imperatives for Property Rights, Resource Allocation, and Institutions: in S.P. Wani, J. Rockstrom and K.L. Saharwat, Eds. Integrated Watershed Management in Rainfed Agriculture, CRC Press, London.

[14] Shah, A. and Hasmukh, Joshi (2023). Sustainable Agriculture and Role of Watershed Development Programs in the Changing Climatic Scenario: Learnings from the Major States in India. CFDA Occasional Paper 1/23.

[15] Shah, Amita, Yagnik, J.R. and Joshi, Hasmukh (2023). "Agro-Ecology and Equity in India: The Status of and Issues in Soil-Water Conservation across the States", *Paper presented in Managing Sustainable Transitions in Agriculture (MST 2023) Conference at IRMA,* Anand Nov. 16–18.

[16] The Times of India (2023). "Third Year in a Row, Gujarat Tops in Exports" https://timesofindia.indiatimes.com/city/rajkot/third-yr-in-row-guj-tops-in-exports/articleshow/100808013.cms (accessed on 12th January 2024)

[17] United Nations (2016). The Sustainable Development Goals Report 2016, New York.

APPENDIX 1

District-wise Land Distribution: 2015–16

Area in '00 ha.

Agro-Climatic Zone	*Districts*	*Geographical Area*	*Net Sown Area*	*Gross Cropped Area*
Southern Hills	Dangs	1776	524	660
	Navsari	2211	1041	1208
	Valsad	3034	1533	1590
Southern Gujarat	Bharuch	6524	3088	3102
	Narmada	2815	1180	1275
	Surat	4418	2486	2790
	Tapi	3249	1591	2061
Middle Gujarat	Anand	2777	1960	3823
	Dahod	3642	2221	3361
	Kheda	3667	2852	4362
	Panchmahal	3281	1681	2038
	Vadodara	4312	2963	3186
North Gujarat	Ahmedabad	7170	4623	6246
	Banaskantha	10770	6370	11725
	Gandhinagar	2163	1480	2102
	Mahesana	4414	2852	4362
	Patan	5771	3446	4982
	Sabarkantha	4233	2745	3607
North West Gujarat	Kachchh	45652	7169	7851
North Saurashtra	Amreli	7295	5272	5817
	Bhavnagar	8334	4682	5265
	Jamnagar	8441	3818	3929
	Rajkot	7750	5264	6021
	Surendranagar	9271	6533	8359
South Saurashtra	Junagadh	5496	3549	4845
	Porbandar	2312	791	1414
All		196024	97656	125797

Source: Directorate of Agriculture, Gujarat State, Gandhinagar.

Section 2
Economic Growth

GSDP Composition and Sector-wise Growth Trends in Gujarat

Ranchhod Gagal[1]

ABSTRACT: The pursuit of a higher standard of living necessitates a balanced focus on both economic growth, the quantitative expansion of output measured by GDP, and economic development, qualitative improvements in living standards and well-being, ensuring economic gains translated into tangible benefits. In today's interconnected world, nations strive for development by optimizing resources and adopting technology, using numerical indicators like GDP and per capita income to track progress and attract investment; Gujarat exemplifies this, contributing disproportionately to India's economy, with robust GSDP growth and rising per capita income reflecting a rapidly expanding economy and improved citizen well-being; analyzing GSDP composition and sectoral growth over the past decade provides insight into the driving forces behind Gujarat's performance, helping to identify areas for future development and evaluating the effectiveness of its economic plans.

Keywords: *GDP, GSDP, Income, Growth, Development.*

INTRODUCTION

An important factor in measuring the economic status of any region is income. Income depends on the economic activities of the entire country or region, the suitability of the economic activity, the activity and efficiency of the available human resources. Gujarat is considered as a developed state of India. Gujarat accounts for 5% of the country's total population but accounts for 8.27% (2021/22) of the national income. Gujarat has a share of 18.14% (2019/20) in the industrial production of the country. Gujarat is a leading state in exports with more than 30 percent share to India's aggregate exports.

[1] Assistant Professor, Department of Economics, Government Arts and Commerce College, Rapar (Dist: Kachchh) Gujarat, India. E-mail: r.college11@gmail.com

In which, the ports are most important contributors. The cargo handled by minor & Intermediate ports in Gujarat have increased significantly from 27.80 lakh tonnes in 1980–81 to 4053.91 lakh tonnes in 2021–22. As per the Quick Estimates, Real GSDP or GSDP at constant (2011–12) prices in 2021–22 has been estimated at Rs. 1382530 crore as against Rs. 1248189 crore in 2020–21, registering a growth of 10.8 percent during the year. Nominal GSDP or GSDP at current prices in 2021–22 have been estimated at Rs. 1957583 crore as against Rs. 1636781 crore in 2020–21, registering a growth of 19.6 percent during the year. The Per Capita Income at Nominal NSDP has been estimated at Rs. 250100 in 2021–22 as against Rs. 212821 in 2020–21, showing an increase of 17.5 percent during the year. The Per Capita Income at Real NSDP (at constant (2011–12) prices) has been estimated at Rs. 174539 in 2021–22 as against Rs. 160321 in 2020–21, registering a growth of 8.9 percent during the year. This paper has tried to find out the GSDP and per capita income trends and GSDP composition and sector wise growth in Gujarat during the last decade.

REVIEW OF LITERATURE

Economic growth measurement and the identification of its determinants has been a subject of long discussion in economic literature ranging from classical model to present economic reforms models. Robinson (1956) gave golden age model of economic growth. She found that rate of capital accumulation and labor force are the main determinants of economic growth and the equality between the two is necessary for equilibrium growth rate. Solow (1956) postulated that growth rate of labour and capital is the crucial determinant of economic growth and capital-labour determines the level of investment and income in the economy. Domar (1957) emphasized upon the role of investment on productivity and growth. Duesenberry (1958) gave optimum growth model recognizing that growth occurs because the actual capital-output ratio lies quite far below the optimum ratio to induce sufficient investment that permits income to grow as fast as of faster than capital accumulation.

OBJECTIVES

1. To know and understanding the trends and growth rate of GSDP.
2. To know and understanding the trends and growth rate of per capita income of State
3. To examine the change in composition of gross state domestic product (GSDP).
4. To examine the change in share of sub-sectors in the aggregate industry and service sectors.
5. To study sector-wise growth trends in Gujarat economy.

RESEARCH METHODOLOGY

This paper is based on secondary data taken from Socio-economic review 2013–14 to 2022–23 of Gujarat, SDP Gujarat State report 2013–14 to 2021–22 of Gujarat Government and performance of development indicators from 2001 to 2022 report of Gujarat.

The composition of GSDP has been studied in terms of percentage share of agriculture & allied activities, industry and service sectors and their sub-sectors viz, mining &quarrying, manufacturing and electricity, gas and water supply for industry sector and construction, trade, hotel, transport and communication, financing, insurance, real estate & business and community, and social and personal services for service sector.

The collected data is processed to analyze the pattern of GSDP and per capita income, sector-wise changes in GSDP. Suitable tables are used to illustrate the facts and analysis.

GROSS STATE DOMESTIC PRODUCT (GSDP)

The states being the subset of the Nation are presented of the economic performance of nation in a disaggregated manner. GSDP means Gross Domestic Product (GDP) at State level, which is aggregated measure of the economic output of a state. Each state in India has its own GSDP, which is calculated by the directorate of economics and statistics. The GSDP of each state used to determine its contribution to the overall economy of India and to compare the economic performance of different states. GSDP is the most important single economic indicator used to measure the growth and to study the structural changes taking place in the economy of State.

Trends of GSDP at current and constant (2011–12) prices (2011–12 to 2022–23)

Year	*Gross Domestic Product at Market Prices*			
	Current Prices (In Cr.)	*Growth Rate*	*Constant Prices (In Cr.)*	*Growth Rate*
2011–12	615606	–	615606	–
2012–13	724495	17.7	682650	10.9
2013–14	807623	11.5	734284	7.6
2014–15	921773	14.1	811428	10.5
2015–16	1029010	11.6	894465	10.2
2016–17	1167156	13.4	981342	9.7
2017–18	1329095	13.9	1086570	10.7
2018–19	1492156	12.3	1183020	8.9
2019–20	1617143	8.4	1265277	7.0
2020–21(R)	1636781	1.2	1248189	–1.4
2021–22 (Q)	1957583	19.6	1382530	10.8

Source: State Domestic Product, Gujarat State 2011–12 to 2021–22 base year 2011–12 report, Directorate of economics and statistics, Government of Gujarat, Gandhinagar, R – Revised estimates, Q – Quick estimates.

Real gross state domestic product (GSDP) or GSDP at market constant (2011–12) prices in 2021–22(Q) has been estimated at Rs. 13,82,530 crore as against Rs. 12,48,189 crore in 2020–21(R) registering a growth of 10.8 percent during the year. Nominal GSDP of GSDP at market current prices in 2021–22(Q) has been estimated at Rs. 19,57,583 crore as against Rs. 16,36,781 crore in 2020–21(R), indicating a growth of 19.6 percent during the year.

Above tables presented trends of GSDP of Gujarat at current prices and constant prices 2011–12 to 2021–22. It is evident from the table that Gujarat economy is clearly on growing as the gross domestic product at market prices at current prices has constantly increased from 6,15,606 caror in 2011–12 to 1,61,7143 crore in 2019–20, average decadal growth rate has been more than 12% annually. GSDP at constant prices has been increased from 6,15,606 crore in 2011–12 to 12,65,277 crore in 2019–20, here average annually growth rate more than 8% reported during same period.

Real gross state domestic product (GSDP) or GSDP at market constant (2011–12) prices in 2021–22(Q) has been estimated at Rs. 13,82,530 crore as against Rs. 12,48,189 crore in 2020–21(R) registering a growth of 10.8 percent during the year. Nominal GSDP of GSDP at market current prices in 2021–22(Q) has been estimated at Rs. 19,57,583 crore as against Rs. 16,36,781 crore in 2020–21(R), indicating a growth of 19.6 percent during the year.

Per Capita Income

Per capita income refers to the average amount of money earned by person in a particular area or country over a specified period, typically one year. It is calculated by dividing the income in the area or country by the total number of people living there. Per capita income is often used as an indicator of a country's economic development and standard of living.

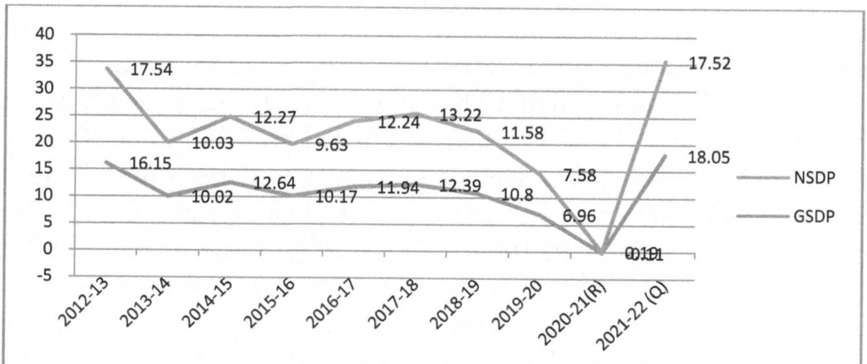

Figure 1: Growth Rate of Per Capita Income

Trends of Per Capita Income GSDP and NSDP at current prices (2011–12 to 2022–23)

Year	*Per Capita Income GSDP and NSDP at Market Prices at Current Prices*			
	Per Capita Income GSDP (In Rs.)	*Growth Rate*	*Per Capita Income NSDP (In Rs.)*	*Growth Rate*
2011–12	101075	–	87481	–
2012–13	117398	16.15	102826	17.54
2013–14	129158	10.02	113139	10.03
2014–15	145484	12.64	127017	12.27
2015–16	160284	10.17	139254	9.63
2016–17	179427	11.94	156295	12.24
2017–18	201650	12.39	176961	13.22
2018–19	223430	10.80	197457	11.58
2019–20	238978	6.96	212428	7.58
2020–21(R)	238716	–0.11	212821	0.19
2021–22 (Q)	281804	18.05	250100	17.52

Source: State Domestic Product, Gujarat State 2011–12 to 2021–22 base year 2011–12 report, Directorate of economics and statistics, Government of Gujarat, Gandhinagar. R – Revised estimates, Q – Quick estimates

Above tables presented trends of per capita income GSDP and NSDP at current prices of Gujarat. Per capita income GSDP has been constantly increased from Rs. 101075 in 2011–12 to Rs. 238978 in 2019–20; it was more than 10% annual growth rate in many years. Per capita income NSDP has increased from Rs. 87481 in 2011–12 to Rs. 212428 in 2019–20. Average growth rate of per capita income 11% annually reported. The per capita income at current prices has been estimated at Rs. 2,50,100 in 2021–22(Q) as against Rs. 2,12,821 in 2020–21(R), showing an increase of 17.5 percent during the year. The per capita income at constant (2011–12) prices has been estimated at Rs. 1,74,539 in 2021–22(Q) as against Rs. 1,60,321 in 2020–21(R), registering a growth by 8.9 percent during the year.

State Gross Domestic Product Composition

GSDP composition implies the contribution of different sectors in the gross state domestic product of the State. Viz, Primary (agriculture and allied activities), secondary (Industry sector and tertiary (service sector) during 2011–12 to 2021–22 period is shown below table.

Sector-wise Composition of GSDP in Percent (2011–12 to 2021–22) at current price

Year	*Agriculture and Allied Activities*	*Industry Sector*	*Service Sector*
2011–12	22.8	40.5	36.7
2012–13	19.0	43.5	37.5
2013–14	20.9	41.9	37.2
2014–15	19.4	44.3	36.3
2015–16	19.8	44.7	35.6
2016–17	21.1	43.7	35.2
2017–18	21.1	43.9	35.0
2018–19	19.0	45.3	35.7
2019–20	19.5	45.0	35.5
2020–21(R)	20.1	44.2	35.7
2021–22 (Q)	19.6	45.3	35.1

Source: State Domestic Product, Gujarat State 2011–12 to 2021–22 base year 2011–12 report, Directorate of economics and statistics, Government of Gujarat, Gandhinagar. R - Revised estimates, Q - Quick estimates

It is evident from the above table that Gujarat economy is clearly on path of developed as the contribution of primary sector in GSDP has constantly slowly declined, secondary sectors share has been growing and tertiary sectors has been constantly stable or minor declined in the last ten years. During the last decadal, there has been a drastic change in the GSDP composition as primary sector contribution has declined from 22.8% in 2011–12 to 19.6% in 2021–22(Q). The share of secondary sector in the GSDP constantly increased from 40.5% in 2011–12 to 45.3% in 2021–22 as per quick estimates. The share of tertiary sector in the GSDP has minor declined from 36.7% in 2011–12 to 35.1% in 2021–22 but it is stabled and not major changed from 2015–16.

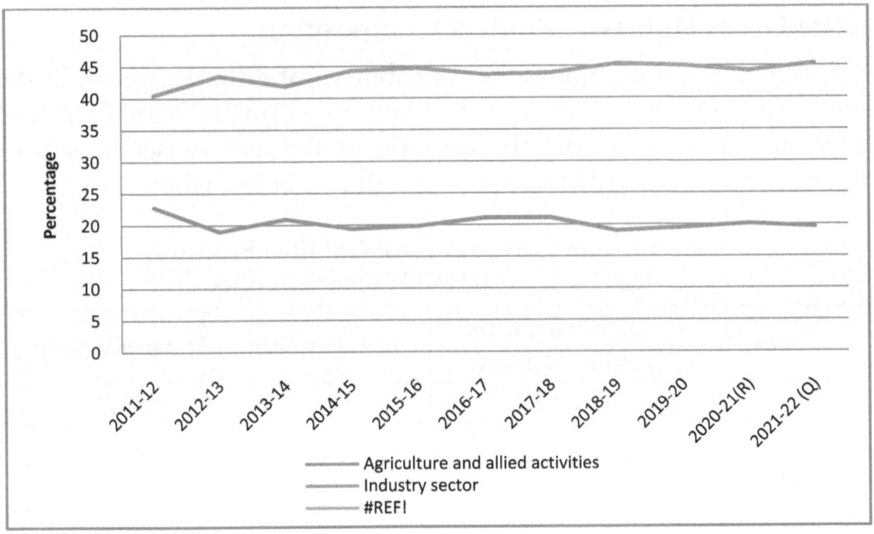

Figure 2: Share of Percent by Sector in GSDP

Contribution of Primary Sub-sectors in Aggregate Primary sector in State & GSDP (In percent)

Year	*Crops*		*Livestock*		*Forestry and Logging*		*Fishing and Aquaculture*		*Mining and Quarrying*	
	SP	*SPGSDP*	*SP*	*SPGSDP*	*SP*	*SPGSDP*	*SP*	*SPGSDP*	*SP*	*SPGSDP*
2011–12	63.17	12.92	14.70	3.01	4.86	0.99	2.57	0.53	14.70	3.01
2012–13	55.32	9.34	16.44	2.78	6.30	1.06	3.01	0.51	18.93	3.20
2013–14	63.43	11.83	15.37	2.87	4.75	0.89	3.00	0.56	13.45	2.51
2014–15	60.34	10.48	16.84	2.93	4.75	0.82	3.99	0.69	14.08	2.45
2015–16	51.96	9.13	17.22	3.02	6.53	1.15	3.84	0.68	20.44	3.59
2016–17	50.01	9.40	15.86	2.98	11.63	2.19	3.51	0.66	18.98	3.57
2017–18	50.89	9.47	16.07	2.99	9.83	1.83	4.12	0.77	19.08	3.55
2018–19	44.75	7.49	18.34	3.07	9.54	1.60	4.52	0.76	22.85	3.82
2019–20	52.60	9.14	17.52	3.04	7.89	1.37	4.37	0.76	17.62	3.06
2020–21(R)	55.83	9.79	18.98	3.33	8.10	1.42	3.42	0.60	13.67	2.40
2021–22 (Q)	52.93	8.93	18.04	3.04	7.36	1.24	3.92	0.66	17.75	2.99

Source: Calculated from State Domestic Product, Gujarat State 2021–22 base year 2011–12 report, Directorate of economics and statistics, Government of Gujarat, Gandhinagar.

R - Revised estimates, Q - Quick estimates, SP- Share of Percent in Primary sector, SPGSDP- Share of percent in GSDP.

The contribution of primary sub sectors in aggregate primary sector and Gujarat GSDP are shown in above table. The share of crops production in aggregate primary sector and GSDP has declined during the period 2011–12 to 2018–19. Its share of percent in aggregate primary sector has declined from 63.17% in 2011–12 to 44.75% in 2018–19 and same trend in GSDP. Livestock and its related activities are constantly growing in agriculture sector. Its share of percent in aggregate primary sector has increased from 14.70% in 2011–12 to 18.04% in 2021–22(Q) and 3.04 percent share in GSDP. The share of percent of forestry and logging in aggregate primary sector has increased from 4.86% in 2011–12 to 7.36% in 2021–22(Q). Fishing and aquaculture and mining and quarrying have slowly increasing in both aggregate primary sector and GSDP.

Contribution of Secondary Sub-sectors in Aggregate Secondary sector in State & GSDP (In percent)

Year	*Manufacturing*		*Electricity, Gas, Water Supply and Other Utility Services*		*Construction*	
	SS	*SPGSDP*	*SS*	*SPGSDP*	*SS*	*SPGSDP*
2011–12	70.19	25.47	9.80	3.56	20.00	7.26
2012–13	73.70	28.56	9.54	3.70	16.75	6.49
2013–14	72.74	27.24	9.56	3.58	17.70	6.63
2014–15	76.38	30.24	8.33	3.30	15.28	6.05
2015–16	78.57	31.21	7.96	3.16	13.47	5.35
2016–17	79.87	31.08	7.18	2.79	12.95	5.04
2017–18	80.33	31.14	6.97	2.70	12.70	4.92
2018–19	80.86	32.25	6.61	2.64	12.53	5.00
2019–20	80.15	32.10	7.65	3.06	12.20	4.89
2020–21(R)	80.18	31.02	7.97	3.08	11.85	4.58
2021–22(Q)	80.90	31.62	7.07	2.76	12.03	4.70

Source: Calculated from State Domestic Product, Gujarat State 2021–22 base year 2011–12 report, Directorate of economics and statistics, Government of Gujarat, Gandhinagar.

R - Revised estimates, Q - Quick estimates, SS - Share of Percent in Secondary sector, SPGSDP - Share of percent in GSDP.

Contribution of Tertiary Sub-sectors in Aggregate Tertiary Sector in State & GSDP (In percent)

Year	*Trade, Hotel and Restaurants*		*Transport, Storage, Communication & Services Related to Broadcasting*		*Financial Services, Real Estate, Ownership of Dwelling & Professional Services*		*Public Administrative*		*Other Services*	
	ST	*SPGSDP*	*ST*	*SPGSDP*	*ST*	*SPGSDP*	*ST*	*SPGSDP*	*ST*	*SPGSDP*
2011–12	32.80	10.80	16.05	5.28	31.70	10.44	9.46	3.11	9.98	3.29
2012–13	34.94	11.67	15.35	5.13	30.70	10.26	9.03	3.02	9.99	3.34
2013–14	33.55	11.13	14.98	4.97	32.39	10.75	8.85	2.94	10.22	3.39
2014–15	33.50	10.87	14.67	4.76	32.01	10.39	9.46	3.07	10.36	3.36
2015–16	32.64	10.33	15.22	4.82	32.18	10.19	9.27	2.94	10.69	3.38
2016–17	33.18	10.39	15.10	4.73	31.57	9.89	9.38	2.94	10.77	3.37
2017–18	34.03	10.51	13.92	4.30	31.56	9.74	9.75	3.01	10.74	3.32
2018–19	34.52	10.84	13.26	4.16	31.19	9.79	10.08	3.17	10.95	3.44
2019–20	34.60	10.94	12.20	3.86	32.13	10.16	9.58	3.03	11.49	3.63
2020–21(R)	31.88	9.96	12.67	3.96	34.53	10.79	9.86	3.08	11.07	3.46
2021–22 (Q)	33.17	10.06	15.78	4.78	31.72	9.62	8.91	2.70	10.42	3.16

Source: Calculated from State Domestic Product, Gujarat State 2021–22 base year 2011–12 report, Directorate of economics and statistics, Government of Gujarat, Gandhinagar.

R - Revised estimates, Q - Quick estimates, ST - Share of Percent in Tertiary sector, SPGSDP - Share of percent in GSDP.

The share of crop production in the agriculture sector is declining and is a relative decline, as total crop production has steadily increased, with the total value of crop production in Gujarat increasing from 79,510 crores in 2011–12 to 1,74,765 crores in 2021. However, one of the main reasons behind the decline in crop production is climate change. Another reason is that farmers do not get remunerative prices at the time of production. Every crop needs a suitable environment. Some unit studies in Kutch district have found that rainfall has increased in the district in the last decade and this has affected the production of low irrigated crops. While the overall rainfall has decreased in north-central Gujarat and this has affected the production of rice. Wheat production was affected in Kutch district last year due to December being warmer than other years.

Secondary sector plays an important role in the economic development of any State/country. Above table shows the contribution of secondary sub-sectors in aggregate secondary sector and Gujarat GSDP. The share of manufacturing in aggregate secondary sectors has increased from 70.19% in 2011–12 to nearly 81% in 2021–22 and its share in GSDP has increased from 25.47% in 2011–12 to 31.62% in 2021–22. The share of electricity, gas, water supply and other utility services has declined during the period of 2011–12 to 2021–22 in both aggregate secondary sector and GSDP. Examining the above table, it is seen that the share of construction sector in the aggregate secondary sector has decreased alarmingly. It's declined from 20% in 2011–12 to 12% in 2021–22. Share of construction sector in GSDP is 4.7% in 2021–22, it was 7.26% in 10 year before.

The share of percent of Service sector in India's GDP has continuing increased but this trend is opposite in Gujarat economy. Above table shows the percentage contribution of tertiary-sub sectors in tertiary sector and GSDP. Many sub-sectors like, Trade, hotel & restaurant, Transport, storage, communication & services related to broadcasting and public administrative has normal declined from 2012–13 to 2021–22 in entire tertiary sector and GSDP. However, share of financial services, real estate and ownership of dwelling & professional services has declined from 10.44% in 2011–12 to 9.62% in 2021–22. Share of other services has increased from 9.98% in 2011–12 to 10.42% in 2021–22 in Tertiary sector but its share has declined in GSDP.

CONCLUSION

Gujarat is considered as a developed and industrialized state of India. Gujarat's gross domestic product at current prices has more than doubled in the last ten years, recording double-digit growth in every year except the two recession years of 2019–20 and 2020–21. While at constant prices total production has increased three times in ten years. This trend is also visible in the per capita income of Gujarat. At current prices, the total per capita income of Gujarat was Rs. 101,075 in 2011–12 and has become Rs. 281,804 in 2021–22 according to quick estimates. Net per capita income of Gujarat is also estimated to increase by 17.52% in this year compared to last year.

Since 1951, there has been a share of sector-wise change in the India's GDP in such a way that the share of percent of industrial sector has been increasing at a slower rate, while the share of percent of the agricultural sector has been steadily declining and may be it has been transformed into the service sector, currently the largest sector is service sector in GDP as per share of percent. The sector-wise percentage share in Gujarat GSDP is different from the situation to India. The industry sector (45.3%) accounts for the largest share percent in the GSDP, followed by the service sector (35%). The share of industry sector has increased from 40.5% in 2011–12 in a revised estimate of around 45.3% in 2021–22. There has been a modest decline in the share of the service sector over this period, while the share of the agriculture sector has declined from 22.8% to 19.6% during this period. In short, examining the overall study, it is found that there has been no major change in the sector-wise structure of GSDP in the last ten years.

The main reason for the decline in the agriculture sector in GSDP is the decline in the share of percent of crop production, as all other agriculture sub-sectors, such as livestock, forestry and logging, fishing and aquaculture and mining and quarrying has increased both in aggregate agriculture sector and GSDP. Share of percent of manufacturing is the main reason for the increase and growth of industrial sector in the GSDP. The share of percent of other secondary sub-sectors like, electricity, gas, water supply and other utility services and construction has remarkable declined in the aggregate secondary sector and GSDP. The share of percent of service sub-sectors in the aggregate tertiary sector and GSDP has seen little changes over ten years.

The share of percent of service sector in Gujarat has decreased as compared to industrial sectors but, it does not mean that the output of service sector has declined. The production of service sector was 2,02,633 crore in 2011–12, it has reached 5,93,396 crore in the year 2021–22. That is, from 2011–12 to 2021–22, there has been an increase of 193%. However, the service sector's share in GSDP has declined as the industrial sector has grown by 242% during this period. In the year 2021–22, compared to the previous year, the services sector grew by 16%, while the industrial sector grew by 21%. The main reason behind the decline in the service sector is that, Gujarat is an industrial state. In terms of the rate of investment in the industrial sector, Gujarat is among the leading states in India.

As per Deccan herald report, Gujarat's success in attracting investments has been attributed to the state's adequately developed infrastructure and its effective workforce, thereby making it a chosen hub for investment. The fact that the state also houses several Special Economic Zones (SEZs) that offer incentives to investors is also a contributing factor. The year 2022–23 has seen five states accounting for more than half of the total bank-assisted investment proposals, as per a report in The Indian Express. The overall investment plans went up by 79 per cent with Uttar Pradesh and Gujarat far ahead of other states in the country. A study by the Reserve Bank of India (RBI) found that the five states accounted for 57.2 per cent of the total investment proposals in the year (or Rs. 2,01,700 crore in total project cost), higher than 43.2 per cent share during 2021–22. Declining public expenditure on education and health in Gujarat also affects the growth of the service sector.

REFERENCES

[1] Domar, E. (1957). Essays in the Theory of economic growth, Oxford University press.

[2] Duesenberry, J. (1958). Business cycles and economic growth, New York: McGrawHill.

[3] Handbook of statistics on India economy, RBI, 2019–20.
[4] Harrod, Ray F. (1948). Toward a dynamic planning, Asia Publishing house, 33.
[5] Nurkse, R. (1963). Problems of capital formation in underdeveloped countries. New York: Oxford University press.
[6] Mangal, S.K. and Agarwal, D.R. (2013). GDP Composition and sector wise growth trends in India: Evidences from post reform period, Dias technology review, Vol. 9, No. 2.
[7] Performance of development indicators from: 2001 to 2022 report, Directorate of economics and statistics, Government of Gujarat, Gandhinagar.
[8] Robinson, J. (1956). The accumulation of capital, London: Macmillan, 2nd edition, 1965, 3rd edition, 1969.
[9] Socio-economic review (2022–23). Gujarat State, Directorate of economics and statistics, Government of Gujarat, Gandhinagar.
[10] Solow, R. (1956). A contribution to the theory of economic growth, quarterly journal of economics, 70, 65–94.
[11] State Domestic Product, Gujarat State 2011–12 to 2021–22 base year 2011–12 report, Directorate of economics and statistics, Government of Gujarat, Gandhinagar.
[12] www.deccanherald.com
[13] www.indianexpress.com

An Analysis of Sectoral Growth and its Contribution to Economic Development in Gujarat

Pinky Desai[1] and Aditee Sharma[2]

ABSTRACT: The article examines growth experience in various sectors of the state and analyses the medium- and long-term growth potential of the economy. Sector-wise performance of Gujarat's economy is analysed with a focus on key engines of growth and the effective role of these growth engines in macroeconomic acceleration of Gujarat Economy. During the nineties, Gujarat improved its economic performance remarkably in almost all secondary and tertiary sectors. While Gujarat has very strong performance in the manufacturing, electricity, construction, transport & communication, and services sector, its major weaknesses is in the primary sector. The article attempts to identify principal drivers of the economy in the state and their contribution to economic growth. The sectors are overall economic growth in terms of GSDP, Agricultural growth including top crops and livestock production, major port of Gujarat, health care facilities etc. Concluding section highlights policy recommendations for sustained economic growth including land reform, investment in education and infrastructure, ports, more FDI, transparency and efficiency in administration, attaining social cohesion, macroeconomic management etc.

Keywords: *Economic, Growth, Performance, Indicator, Sectors.*

[1] [1]Head, Department of Economics, St. Xavier's College, Ahmedabad, India.
[2] PhD Scholar, Gujarat University, Teaching & Research Associate, Gujarat National Law University, Gandhinagar, India. E-mail: asharma@gnlu.ac.in

INTRODUCTION

Economic growth is the most widely acknowledged metric for measuring a country's or state's economic health. Economic growth is a quantitative term that refers to a growth in national product with associated income, as well as an increase in various economic performance indices, such as increased industrial and agricultural production, employment levels, and a decrease in the number of poor people living below a specific poverty line. Meanwhile, economic development is a larger term covering good social improvements and economic progress. It is a qualitative increase in human quality of life and well-being achieved by increasing per capita income.

Structural changes are seen as a critical aspect of economic growth. It has been suggested that economic development is inextricably linked to structural changes: "Structural change facilitates economic growth and economic growth encourages structural change." As a result, economic growth is required for structural changes to occur. Economic structural changes relate to a movement in an economy's economic structure from reliance on agriculture to a more modern, urbanized, and industrially diverse manufacturing and services sector. It is also marked by changes in sectoral employment, with employment rising fast in non-farm sectors and labour being drawn out of agriculture at a rate determined by the labour intensity of industry and services. Rapid increases in agricultural productivity allow for lower worker input per unit of output. In the agricultural industry, there comes a moment when the labour share falls faster than the production.

Gujarat is one of India's most progressive states, with a key role in the country's economy. The state government has framed policies in almost all key sectors such as industry, power, ports, roads, agriculture and minerals. Having estimated GSDP at Rs. 2261 lakhs crore in FY2023. One of the most industrially developed state. Contributes about quarter of India's goods exports. Also, state has developed 46 ports, 17 domestic airports and 3 international airports and 2200 kms gas grids supply gas to industrial areas. Economic changes that began in the mid-1980s and were implemented in the early 1990s have reignited interest in examining sectoral performance and its implications for general economic development, employment, and income distribution. An effort has been made to assess the overall growth performance of various industries in Gujarat using this framework. Key policies by the Gujarat Government to accelerate faster growth rate is Gujarat New Industrial policy 2020, Garments Apparel Policy 2017, Solar Power Policy 2015, Electric Vehicles Policy and Jal Jeevan Policy covering almost all the important sectors of the economy. No doubt, looking at growth trends in different sectors will help you figure out which areas need to improve the most.

Prime minister's 2014 election campaign was largely based on what he called 'the Gujarat model'. Arvind Panagariya, former vice-chairman of the NITI Aayog that has replaced India's Planning Commission, once described Gujarat's success in achieving high rates of economic growth under Modi as 'miraculous. Gujarat has only 5% of India's population, but has remained the strong arm of nation's industrial and trade performance, accounting for about a seventh of India's industrial output and around a fifth of its industrial investment. It is expected that with successful implementation of Narmada Project, Gujarat would be ready for a second green revolution and this revolution would involve value additions in the form of agro-based and food processing industries. The Planning Commission has projected Gujarat as one of the fastest growing states in the tenth plan. In the post-reforms period, Gujarat, in particular, has witnessed high growth in sectors like, chemicals and petrochemicals, engineering, agro and food processing. Demographic trends in Gujarat, especially a slowing population growth rate and a rising share of the population of working age, contribute to an increase in per capita income.

Against this context, the present study attempts to analyse growth experience in various sectors of the state and assess the medium- and long-term growth potential of the economy. Sector-wise performance of Gujarat economy is analysed with a focus on key engines of growth and the effective role of these growth engines in macroeconomic acceleration of Gujarat Economy. Gujarat's economy has undergone structural changes in terms of sectoral composition over the years. The GSDP and NSDP's varying shares of the agricultural, industrial, and services sectors are the best illustrations of this pattern. Gujarat's economy shifted from being predominantly agro-based in the 1960s to being dominated by the services sector in the 1990s. This change in composition has led to significant changes in the production and demand links across different sectors, which have had significant ramifications for Gujarat's economic growth and development. The study attempts to identify principal drivers of the economy in the state and their contribution to economic growth. The sectors are- Energy, Oil & Gas, Agro &food processing, Textiles, Diamonds, Petrochemicals, Engineering, SEZ, Medical Tourism, Biotechnology and IT. Concluding section highlights policy recommendations for sustained economic growth including land reform, investment in education and infrastructure, ports, more FDI, transparency and efficiency in administration, attaining social cohesion, macro-economic management etc.

LITERATURE REVIEW

Reviews of International Theories of Economic Growth

Advanced countries such as the USA and the UK have experienced structural transformation in their economies. These countries have passed through a series of stages in the course of development.

S. Kuznets (1966) found that high countries saw relative industrial expansion until the middle of the twentieth century. He outlined the structural changes that occur as a result of economic progress, highlighting "the shift away from agriculture to non-agricultural pursuits and, then, away from industry to services". Three forces, according to Simon Kuznets, are causing structural changes in the economy. They are:

1. High rate of per capita income growth which brings changes in the elasticities of demand for finished goods, thereby bringing a change in the structure of domestic demand.
2. Development of transport and communications and foreign relations of a country would affect the comparative advantage in the world market.
3. Technological changes bring an impact on the process of production, regardless of changes in the structure of foreign demand.

Thus, modem economic growth is characterized by rapid shifts in the industrial structure of the product and consequently by rapid shifts in shares of labour attached to various sectors in the economy. Trends in the sectoral origin of aggregate output includes a weakening in the share of agriculture and related industries, in the share of manufacturing and public utilities, a shift within manufacturing from less to more durable products and to a limited extent from consumer to produce goods.

Prof. A.G.B. Fisher and Prof. J. Faurosite have also suggested that the swing from primary to secondary and then tertiary is an unavoidable reflection of economic advancement. Apart from the fact that tertiary items have a larger income elasticity of demand than secondary products, Prof. Faurosite has shown that when the industrial sector gets saturated, workers are relocated to the tertiary sector, where goods and services are in great demand.

Lewis Analyses the process of economic development in a dual economy self-possessed of a capitalist sector and a socialist sector. The former the capitalist sector is defined as the segment of the economy with a large amount of replicable capital for profit making reasons when employee wages are lower. The subtract sector does not produce reproducible assets. At this point output per head is much power than in the capitalist sector.

Samuelson remarks that in a mixed economy, the wholesome capitalistic and socialistic economic concepts are reconciled. This kind of compromise has resulted in continuous development in both the public and private sectors at the same time. The authors went on to say that straight capitalism has been turning into a mixed economy with both private and state initiatives and regulations, almost subconsciously.

"Economic development will not occur unless the environment is conducive to it, "UN experts said," underlining the significance of non-economic players in the growth process. People in a nation must want development, and their social, economic, legal, and political circumstances must support it.

Reviews Related to the Economy of Gujarat

Dholakia R.H. (2002), in his paper on "Economic reforms and development strategy in Gujarat", examines the development strategy followed by the Gujarat state government during the nineties. It has followed the strategy focused on industrialization and urbanization with an open-door policy ever since its inception in 1960. Economic reform measures at the Centre with an explicit emphasis on trade and industry considerably benefited Gujarat, making its economic performance outstanding. The state government only facilitated the growth of private enterprise since its strategy was already consistent with the changes in the policy reforms at the Centre. Since the mid-nineties, however, when the reform process at the Centre slowed down, the state government in Gujarat started taking the major initiative to liberalise and reform its policies further. In this process, the focus of the development strategy seems to have shifted away from organized manufacturing to the unorganized sectors and given protection to the SMEs.

Mr Iyengar Sudarshan (2000) found in his article on the level and pattern of economic development in Gujarat that the examination of Gujarat's growth experience did not reveal any special consequences of economic reforms on the regional economy and its vulnerable sectors. The development trend of Gujarat implies that these are inherent in the structure of the economy. Despite the fact that the percentage of commercial crops in the gross cultivated area has been continuously high since the late 1960s, the mean value of indices for the primary sector is quite low. Agricultural productivity is not stable, in large part due to a lack of irrigation. The investment in huge irrigation projects seems to have taken a long time to mature. Since the 1980s, growth in the secondary sector, which is dominated by the manufacturing sector, has slowed. In comparison to the preceding decades, the growth rate from 1980 to 1994 was lower.

Indira Hirway's (2004) study showed significant regional variations in levels of development and stated that the pattern of development in Gujarat is skewed in favour of developed areas and comparatively better-off portions of the population. She also noted in her other work (2000) that during the post-reform period, Gujarat's economic growth was associated with a highly diversified economic structure and that government measures had contributed to that diversification. She does, however, say that the approach does not seem to be sustainable since it has altered the state's agricultural industry relationship.

Shah Amita (1986) argued in a review paper on rural industrialization in Gujarat that, despite their importance, consumer connections have remained relatively stable due to modest but regionally unequal agricultural expansion and whatever demand is sparked, it is generally absorbed by the industrial sector in cities rather than rural communities.

Dholakiya Archana (2000) attempted to investigate the challenges that arose in the state's budget consolidation throughout the reform process. She has called attention to the reasons for Gujarat's budgetary problems. She believes that in order to accelerate development while maintaining fiscal discipline, Gujarat must increase non-tax income to cover its fiscal obligations. In her research, she examines Gujarat's non-tax income and subsidies in order to identify areas for improvement. In contrast to the current stage of reforms in Gujarat, the state is more involved in areas where it should withdraw, as seen by large economic subsidies, and less active in areas where intervention is required, as evidenced by low social sector subsidies.

Bagchi Amiya, Das P. and Chattopadhyay S.K. (2005) have critically explored the Gujarat model of growths by studying the trends in the growth rates from 1970–2000 using State Income, Employment and Annual Survey of Industries data. The study calculates growth rate trends using OLS and linear, semi-log, and quadratic equations. The paper's findings are that (i) the primary and agricultural sectors' growth has been stagnant and declining, (ii) the secondary and tertiary sectors in the state of Gujarat have shown statistically significant, and high rates of growth, mainly due to the manufacturing sector, trade, transportation, banking, real estate, and so on, (iii) the economic growth sustained by secondary and tertiary sectors has had no positive impact on the primary sector, and (iv) the ratio of the dome to dome has According to the research, which reveals rising inter-sectoral inequality, the rural sector is being sidelined from the development process.

OBJECTIVES OF STUDY

1. To identify features of economic growth of Gujarat.
2. To check potentiality of Gujarat for its sustainable development.

METHODOLOGY

This study is purely based on secondary data. Data have been used from government publications like report by NITI AAYOG, UNDP report, socio-economic reviews etc. newspaper articles like published in Times of India, Indian Express and articles published in journals like EPW have been considered to prepare this paper. Analysis encompasses period from 2011–2021. The acquired data must be presented, evaluated, and categorised methodically to develop meaningful conclusions. To figure out what happened, the data were put into an excel spreadsheet and looked at using simple and logical statistical methods, like averages, growth rates, percentages, and ratios.

> *"In search of sustainability and applicability of economy of Gujarat......"*

Sustainable development requires growth that reaches to the lowest echelon of the society. Another condition is natural environment protection for development process to be continued. To be more precise, an economy's growth potential depends on two factors, they are social environment and natural environment. Society's ability to identify and convert resources into prosperity is the main ingredient of development recipe. For this paper some representative indicators of social and natural environment have been taken. Human Development Index is considered here to see the social strength and sustainability of Gujarat. For natural environment sustainability, forest cover of total geographical area of Gujarat has been considered. Some other supportive data like population below poverty line, per capita income, sex ratio are studied. To know economic and social history of Gujarat, this paper has gone through some milestone like decisions of Gujarati people, which reflect their attitude and aptitude, as, ultimately growth and development depend on people's propensity to develop (W. W. Rostow).

OVERVIEW OF GUJARAT

Geography: Gujarat is a state of Republic of India, situated in the western part of the country. The state is covered by Pakistan at the North and North-western part, Rajasthan in the North-east, by Madhya Pradesh in the East and by Maharashtra and Union territories of Diu, Daman and Dadra and Nagar Haveli in the South. South western and Western parts of Gujarat are covered by the Arabian Ocean.

Political History: Gujarat has been ruled by the Gujjars, Mughals, Marathas and British respectively. Some states like the Baroda state had direct relationship with British Governor General, and therefore retained local self-rule.

After independence, the Mahagujarat movement took place and resulted in separation on 1st May, 1960. This separation from the Maharashtra state was based on Gujarati's spiking population for administrative ease.

Demography: Population and decadal growth rate with their density/ km^2 is shown in table 1 below.

Table 1

Census Year	*Population (million)*	*Population Decadal Growth Rate (%)*	*Density/km²*
1961	20.63	26.88	105
1971	26.70	29.39	136
1981	34.09	27.67	174
1991	41.31	21.19	211
2001	50.67	22.66	258
2011	60.38	19.28	308

Source: Handbook of Indian economy by RBI.

GUJARAT'S ROLE IN INDIA'S ECONOMY

Since the reforms begins in 1992–93, Gujarat has been the frontline state of the Indian economy. Its performance in terms of economic growth has always been better than all-India. Nearly 5% of the population of the country lives in the Gujarat, covering the 6% of total land area of the country. Its performance in terms of economic growth has always been better than all-India. The state has the high degree of an entrepreneurial culture, a state government that promotes private initiative and people's participation in development process. It is also enriched with several natural advantages. Gujarat has a diversified structure of economy with a large and expanding industrial sector, highly commercialized agriculture and allied activities.

Economic growth has, in general, three connotations when referred to in professional or political circles. They are volume, efficiency and welfare. Examination of Growth experience in various sectors over the last decade so as to identify the growth potential of the state economy. The States being the subset of the Nation, are presenters of the economic performance of Nation in a disaggregated manner. GSDP is similar to Gross Domestic Product (GDP) at state level, which is aggregated measure of the economic output of a country. Gujarat contributes about 8.6% to India's total GDP having estimated GSDP at 15.5% for the financial year 2022–23. Gujarat ranked 1st in Export Preparedness Index 2021 with the highest exports worth US$ 131 billion (April 2022–January 2023). In 2020–21, the secondary sector contributed 42.9% to the state's GSDP (at current prices), followed by tertiary (37.3%) and primary (19.8%) sectors. While India's share of various sectors in GDP is estimated as 53.89% of service sector followed by 24.29% of secondary sector and 21.29% of agriculture sector. Per capita income of India stands at Rs. 172000 while Gujarat has the Per capita income of Rs. 250100 for the year 2022–23. Gujarat ranks fourth among states in terms of FDI received, with an 83% increase in FDI over the previous year.

Gujarat at National Level

Good Governance Index 2023 (Economic Governance)	Gujarat is ranked first.
Logistics Performance Index 2022	Gujarat tops
Export Preparedness Index 2023	Gujarat ranked fourth with a score of 73.22

Foreign Direct Investment	The state has attracted FDI of $4.71 billion during the year 2022–23, named under top 5 states receiving highest FDI in India
State Food Safety Index 2022–23	Gujarat is the best State in the Country in terms of food safety with 72 points.
First Power Surplus State	Gujarat is the first power surplus state in the country. In a recent ranking conducted in 2020, out of 19 DISCOMs across India, DISCOMs of Gujarat have ranked as the top 4 on key operational and financial performance indicator
Smart City Projects	In 2023, 2 cities from Gujarat featured in the top 10 smart city projects of India by Government of India. The cities included Ahmedabad (5st), Surat (3rd).
National Ease of Doing Business (EoDB) Rankings	Gujarat has consistently ranked among top 5 leading Indian states and Top Achievers.

DRIVERS OF STATE'S ECONOMY

Gujarat is one of the key drivers of India's economic development. The state has demonstrated leadership in many sectors including manufacturing, infrastructure, environment, tourism, healthcare, pharmaceuticals, textiles, innovation and R&D, defence and aerospace, argo & food processing, among others, that reflect the diversity and vibrancy of the state's industrial landscape. Gujarat is one of the most industrially developed states of India, a manufacturing hub with fourth largest economy. Gujarat is tipped as the Growth Engine of India. A state with the largest investor's base and people with natural and inherent entrepreneurial skills is an attractive option to *set up a business* here in India.

Economic and Agricultural Growth of the State

Economic growth is indicator that shows the growth path of the state, trend of the economic growth can be inclusive of many factors. In short, it is a report card of the state showing the performance over the year. Gujarat is agricultural rich state, which makes it important to show the agricultural trends also. As seen in the line chart above, given the Economic growth rate as per GSDP and Agricultural growth rate at constant price. It can be interpreted that in year 2012–13 economic growth rate was 10.9% while agricultural growth rate was at –16.02 i.e., having negative growth rate. But agriculture showed a tremendous growth just in next year 2013–14 at 30.57% but having ups and downs over the 10 years underlying the various factors that has affected agriculture sector. On the other hand, economic growth has also shown the ups and down trends over the years. Having the highest GSDP in 2012–13 at 10.9% and lowest in the year 2020–21 at –1.4 i.e., negative growth rate this is due to worldwide pandemic situation. But the state has shown the fastest recovery from the drastic situation and has the second highest economic growth rate over 10 years of study period at 10.8%.

Agricultural and Live Stock Production of Gujarat having the Significant Value in the Country

India, being a country with diverse climatic conditions, offers a favourable environment for the cultivation of various crops. One such significant cash crop is cotton, with Gujarat leading as the highest cotton-producing state in the country. As of July 31, farmers in Gujarat – the largest cotton producer of India – have completed sowing cotton in 26,64,565 hectares (ha), data released by the state Directorate of Agriculture shows. While this is the highest sowing area since 2015–16 when farmers had sown cotton in 27.21 lh, this is also the third highest sowing area for cotton over the last decade in Gujarat. The state of Gujarat is the largest producer of the most amount of groundnut in India.

Gujarat also is responsible to provide groundnut to export. This state is followed by some other states including Rajasthan, Tamil Nadu, Andhra Pradesh, Karnataka, Maharashtra, Madhya Pradesh, West Bengal, and Maharashtra. The western state of Gujarat, which is also one of the leading agricultural states in India, is the location of India's largest groundnut-producing facility, making it one of the most important agricultural states in the country. The majority of Gujarat's land is used for growing groundnuts during the Kharif season. This crop is responsible for more than 40 percent of India's entire output and is grown throughout the majority of Gujarat.

Gujarat has retained its first position in the country in terms of the value of oilseed and fibre output, according to a recent report prepared by the Union Ministry of Statistics and programme implementation (MoSPI). The state recorded the highest production in 2013–14 at 74.35 lakhs tonnes and 70.72 lakhs tonnes in 2021–22, reaffirming its leadership in this sector.

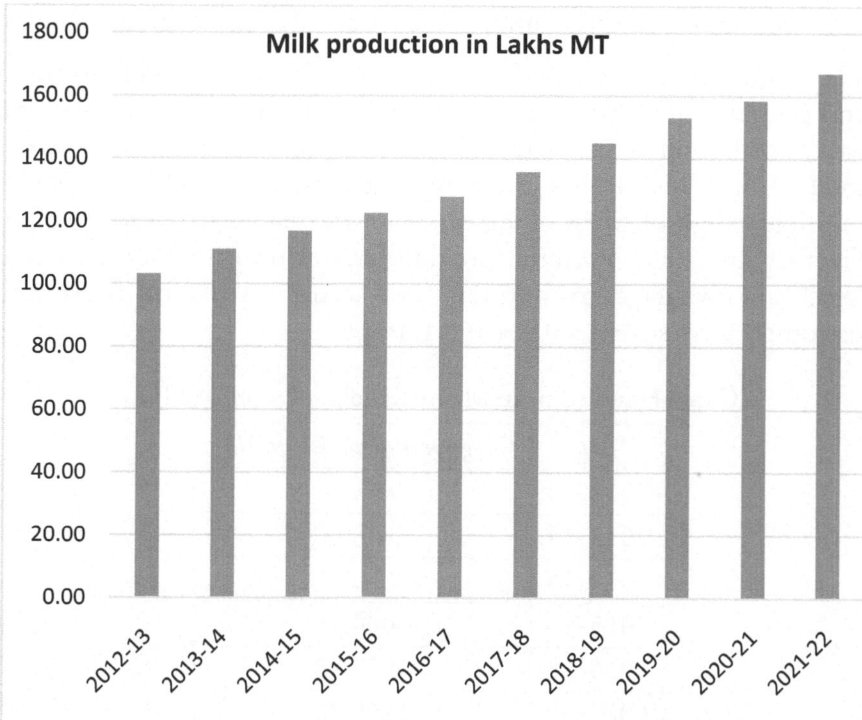

Source: DES Gujarat.

Gujarat has earned the title of milk capital of the country for the strides it has made in the organised dairy sector. A report compiled by Union Ministry of statistics and programme implementation which compares the value of milk output of state over the past decades

(2012–2022) says that milk output of Gujarat rose by 54.8% in the last decade. Gujarat also shares of organised dairy sector and that of dairy co-operatives in the country.

Ports-Cargo Handled

Gujarat is strategically located with India's longest coastline of 1600 km and is the nearest maritime outlet to Middle East, Africa and Europe. The state has the highest number of operational ports and commercial cargo ports. The state ranks first in cargo throughput amongst all Indian ports. The state has 42 ports which include 1 major port and 41 non-major ports which are geographically dispersed across south Gujarat, Saurashtra and Kutch region.

The State acts as a natural gateway to the rich land-locked northern and central hinterland. It has a vast and fertile hinterland comprising west, north, and central India that constitutes a large amount of the total India trade. It has the longest coastline in India and has a multiple range of ports along with a wide range of cargo. Gulf of Cambay and Gulf of Kutch provide natural navigational safety and logistical advantage to northern and central parts of India and proximity to west Asia, Africa and Europe.

Cargo Handled from Major Kandla – Deendayal Port

Year	*Cargo handled (Lakh MT)*
2012–13	936.19
2013–14	870.05
2014–15	924.97
2015–16	1000.51
2016–17	1054.42
2017–18	1100.99
2018–19	1154.01
2019–20	1226.07
2020–21	1175.66
2021–22	1271.00

Source: DES Gujarat.

Kandla – Deendayal, one of the largest major port in India. Given the data from 2012–13 to 2021–22 it can be found that the export has continuously increasing from this port.

Health Indicators of Gujarat

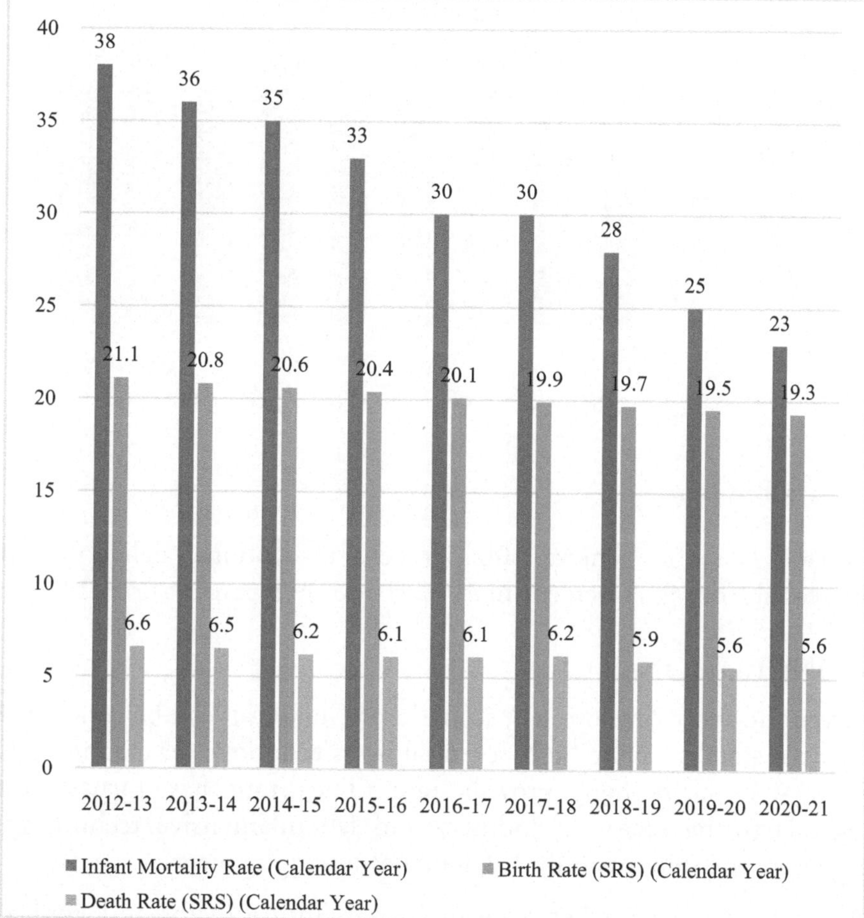

Source: DES Gujarat.

- **Infant Mortality Rate:** The Infant Mortality Rate in Gujarat has reduced sharply by half from 38 in 2012 to 23 in 2021.
- **Birth Rate (SRS):** The birth rate of the state has almost maintaining on the constant rate having 21.1 per 1000 live births in 2021–13 to 19.3 per 1000 live births in 2020–21.

- **Death Rate (SRS):** Death rate is also maintained an almost constant rate as a result of improved health care facilities in the state. Having 6.6 per 1000 live births in 2012–13 to 5.6 per live births in 2020–21.

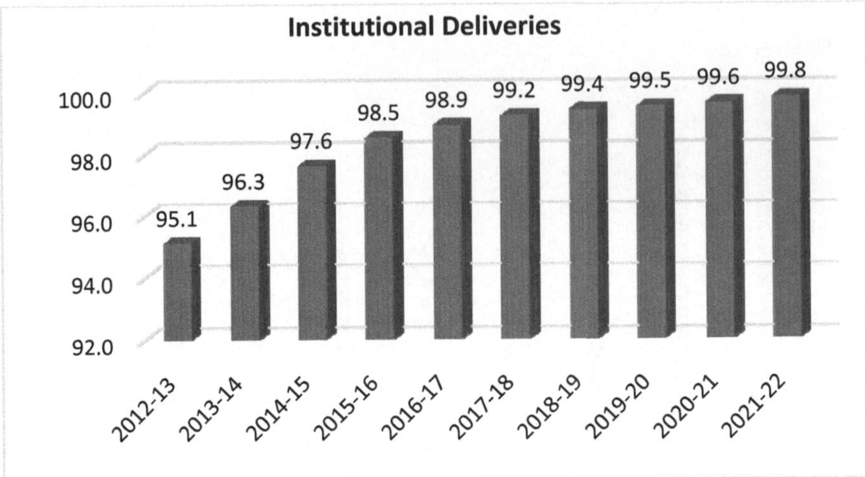

Source: DES Gujarat.

Gujarat is set to achieve 100 per cent institutional delivery as it increased from 95.1 percent in 2012–13 to 99.8 percent in 2020–21.

CONCLUSION

Given the short development scenario of Gujarat, it can be concluded that the state is having high potential in its economic development. It is a state with high growth rate. The state has focused on manufacturing sector of industry and labour-intensive technology, therefore the state has only 1.2% rate of unemployment.

Also, the state has taken care of its agriculture sector and applied innovative ideas through its agriculture universities and recent soil testing process. People of Gujarat, whether they are civilians or political authorities, have used natural environment and have converted them for commercial benefits like development of ports and production of renewable energy by windmills and so on. Although, the state has very high per capita income, compared with other Indian states, the state has very big number of people below poverty line. This shows income inequality, which needs to be corrected out.

The people of Gujarat and the government of Gujarat both have played major role in utilizing their skills. Not only people, nor the government only is responsible for status of a developed state. People have induced and reacted to government policies. Also, for future development or in other words for sustainable development, people and government both have to be serious. With a growth of around 10% p.a. in real terms and a high IRR in excess of 20%, there seems to be tremendous potential for FDI in Gujarat. We should also learn from Andhra Pradesh in matters relating to labour laws and from Maharashtra in matters relating to land laws. Gujarat already has significant thrust on exports. We need to build further and focus more sharply in those modern areas of agri-business, bio-technology and pharma sectors where the market potential world over is tremendous and where Gujarat has a latent or potential comparative advantage. Guaranteeing quality of soft infrastructure valuing high skilled professionals and entrepreneurs, and providing basic amenities to the masses is the key to achieve future looking targets.

REFERENCES

[1] Bagchi Amiya, P. Das and Chattopadhyay, S.K. (2004). "Growth and structural change in economy of Gujarat, 1970–2000", *Economic and Political Weekly,* Vol. XI, No. 28, p. 3029–3047.

[2] Dholakiya, Archana (2000). "Fiscal Imbalance in Gujarat (28), Non tax revenues and Subsides" in Economic and Political weekly Aug. 26 – Sept. 2, 2000, Page No. 3217–3227.

[3] Dholakiya Ravindra, H. (2000). "Liberalization" of Gujarat Review of Recent Experience in Economic and Political Weekly (Aug. 26 – Sept.and development strategy in Gujarat"

[4] Fisher, AGB (1964). "Economic Progress and Social Security", Macmillan, London

[5] Hirway, Indira (2004). "Human Development Report, Gujarat 2004", Mahatma Gandhi Labour Institute Ahmedabad.

[6] Hirway, Indira (2004). "Human Development Report, Gujarat 2004", Mahatma Gandhi Labour Institute Ahmedabad.

[7] Iyengar, Sudarshan (2000). "Level and Pattern of Economy growth in Gujarat – 1980–1994", Occasional Paper Series, Gujarat Institute of Development Research, January-2000

[8] Krishna, K.L. (2004). "Patterns and Determinants of Economic Growth in Indian States", Working Paper No. 144, September, 2004, Indian Council for Research on International Economic Relations, New Delhi.

[9] Kuznets, S. (1966). "Modem Economic Growth - Rate, Structure and Spread", Yale University Press, New Haven

[10] Shah, Amita (1986). "Rural Industrialization in Gujarat", *Indian Journal of Rural Science*, Vol. 18, No. 1.

[11] Shetty, S.L. (2003). "Growth of SDP and Structural Changes in State Economies Interstate Comparisons", Economic and Political Weekly December 6, 2003, PP. 5189–5200

[12] http://164.100.161.63/central-statistics-office-cso-1

[13] https://gujecostat.gujarat.gov.in/publications/index/2

[14] https://m.rbi.org.in/scripts/AnnualPublications.aspx?head=Handbook+of+ Statistics+on+Indian+States

[15] https://www.census2011.co.in/census/state/gujarat.html

[16] https://www.niti.gov.in/working-papers-policy-papers-and-research papers

Online Food Delivery in Gujarat: A Study of Consumer Experiences

Nishi Mehta[1] **and Hastimal Sagara**[2]

ABSTRACT: It's critical to understand whether demand for online meal delivery services varies by region. Applications for online meal delivery are probably influenced by factors including gender, age, and education. It is necessary to look into customer preferences for applications, payment methods and their satisfaction levels. The paper provides valuable insights into the growth trajectory of the online food delivery industry in Gujarat and its implications for both consumers and businesses. It aims at exploring factors driving adoption of online food delivery services, consumer experiences, and understand the implications for the industry stakeholders. The discussion and arguments in this paper are primarily based on interpretation of the data collected through an extensive field survey of consumers of the online food delivery in the state of Gujarat. This research contributes to understanding consumer behaviour in the context of online food delivery services in India, offering insights for businesses aiming at enhancing customer satisfaction.

Keywords: *Cash on Delivery, Online Food Delivery, E-commerce, Payment Methods, Food Technology, Consumer Experiences.*

INTRODUCTION

With the introduction of new digital technologies, particularly the spread of smartphones, India's online food delivery industry seen an unprecedented growth over the past ten years. The fundamental behaviour and shopping pattern towards online food delivery application has significantly changed in India, and has increased

---

[1] Faculty of Commerce, Centre of Excellence, Gujarat University, India.
E-mail: nishimehta081996@gmail.com

[2] Assistant Professor, GLS University, India.
E-mail: hastimal.sagara@glsuniversity.ac.in

particularly after COVID-19. Ordering food online has become more than just a convenience; millions of people choose it for time, cost and situation perspectives. This industry has bridged the gap between customers and their favourite eateries, providing a wide range of cuisines at their fingertips. Food delivery apps enable restaurant companies to fulfil the expectations and needs of rapidly growing customers and better serve them by offering a personalised experience. Applications like Zomato, Swiggy, Food Panda and Uber Eats are major players in online food delivery in the Indian market.

Today, many businesses are setting up online stores due to the availability of technology and acceptance of the people. Other factors that play an important role in development of online business are cheap smartphones, lower cost of internet, free mobile applications, etc. Major advantage of online food ordering is it reduces the load on both the ends i.e., customer and seller. Customers can take as much time as they want to explore the menu without any pressure of ordering hastily.

The online food delivery (OFD) service has emerged as a popular trend in ecommerce space, and serves as a tool to reach a larger number of consumers in a cost-effective manner (Ray *et al.*, 2019). Interestingly, food delivery services have existed in India since the 1890s with services such as the Mumbai dabbawallas (Baindur and Macário, 2013). However, the growth of the various OFDs in India came about in the 2010s with the emergence of Food panda, Swiggy and Domino's.

REVIEW OF LITERATURE

The last ten years, particularly after the global pandemic, have seen an expansion in India's online meal delivery market, which has completely changed how customers access and use food services. Even as the food-delivery ecosystem continues to expand, its economic structure is still evolving and policy initiatives are still at the nascent stage. Bain & Company and Swiggy (2024) in its study titled 'How India Eats' found that the food services market in India, is currently valued at Rs 5.5 lakh crore and the online food delivery penetration in India has gone up from 8% to 12% between 2019 and 2023, representing a 2.8 times growth in online food delivery compared to overall food services. Online food delivery is not universal both geographically as well as demographically. About 70% of food services consumption as of 2023 is concentrated in the top 50 cities and among upper-middle and high-income segments, which are expected to remain demand hotspots in the medium term (Bain & Company and Swiggy, 2024).

Zomato and Swiggy initiated their business from a very small scale, within very few years with their excellent marketing strategies, promotion on social media through hashtags proper funding raised from various investors, including Bessemer Venture Partners, Norwest Venture, Accel Partners, SAIF Partners, Harmony Venture Partners and RB Investments (Gupta, 2019).

The online food delivery service, for various reasons, is preferred by the young. Around 55 per cent of millennials prefer the convenience of meal kits, which can be ingredient-based kits or ready-made meals, over traditional dining experiences for their ease of use and time-saving attributes (Ahuja, *et al.*, 2021). Pal, *et al.* (2021) in their study on university students in India using online food delivery applications found that satisfaction is the greatest predictor of loyalty, followed by food quality and among the mobile app attributes information design has the highest impact on both satisfaction and loyalty, followed by navigational and visual design respectively. Dwi, *et al.* (2019) in their study on Indonesia confirmed a direct effect of food quality on online loyalty, but not e-service quality and disclosed a partial mediation role of customer satisfaction and perceived value on the relationship between both food quality and e-service quality on online loyalty toward OFD services.

There are a number of factors that affect consumer behaviour related to online food delivery. Giri and Yajurvedi (2022) in their study listed down factors affecting consumer behaviour as price and hygiene of the food, food quality, service quality, offers & discounts, taste, speed of delivery, attitude of delivery person, packaging, convenience, menu, advertisement, delivery tracking, payment options and number of restaurants in their descending order. Pal, *et al.* (2021) observed that service quality of food application is most important for consumer satisfaction as well as consumer loyalty, delivery time and food quality also have positive influence on consumer satisfaction and loyalty. Katoch and Sidhu (2021) concluded that core factor influencing online food delivery is quality of food with greater variety and affordable pricing, and the role of technological leverage in determining users' satisfaction is less important in India. Annaraud and Berezina (2020) investigated customer intentions to use OFD services through the evaluation of satisfaction, food quality, and OFD service quality and observed that food quality, control, customer service, and service fulfilment affect customer satisfaction in online food delivery services.

Online food delivery consumers are mostly motivated when they receive any rewards & cashbacks followed by loyalty points or benefits (Saxena, 2019). Bagla and Khan (2017) found food variety and pricing offers in form of cash backs are considered to be the major factors that drive consumers online purchase intention. Most of the consumers use online food delivery application as they want to avail discounts through the application, maybe for getting better discount the consumers in this study use Paytm as the most preferred mode of payment (Beliya *et al.*, 2019). Gupta and Duggal (2021) observed that consumers' usage and selection behaviour related to online food delivery applications are not only influenced by the perceived risk and benefit factors but are also responsible for their overall attitudinal and behavioural variations and found that a decrease in risk perception or an increase in benefit perception of consumers will positively influence their overall attitude towards the use of OFDAs.

Chorneukar (2014) observed that consumers were not comfortable with making online payment rather they prefer to pay through cash-on-delivery (COD) and recommended to improve their quality of service and to maintain the quality of food delivered to consumers. Zomato, Swiggy and Pakwan food paradise (local online food delivery application) are the online food delivery applications accepted by most of the population and majority of consumers are not willing to pay through digital payment rather they would prefer pay cash at the time of delivery of food (Aditya *et al.*, 2022). Gera and Jain (2020) observed that eye catchy images and successive marketing strategies attracted most of the consumers, more than 50% of the consumers were satisfied with the services provided by the food delivery applications.

Wen *et al.* (2011) in their study found that there is no direct relationship between trust of the consumer and their online repurchase intention, therefore E-commerce websites are advised to incorporate proper descriptions of the product on their website. Further they found that almost half of the respondents (students) spent more than 15 minutes per week on commerce websites, and 44.4% of respondents spent nearly $200 per week on online shopping. More than 85% of Internet users all over the world have made at least one online purchase, and between 2006 and 2008.

RESEARCH OBJECTIVES

1. To study the pre-purchase intentions of consumers using online food delivery applications.
2. To study the post-purchase usefulness of food ordered from online food delivery applications.
3. To map the mode of payment by consumers using online food delivery applications.

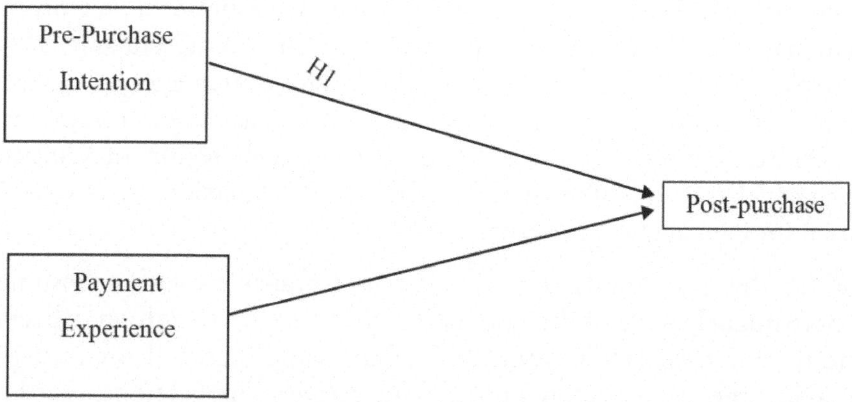

Figure 1: Model Used in the Paper

Source: Designed by the authors based on review of literature of Ramesh *et al.* (2021), Yusra (2020), Vincent Cheow *et al.* (2017) and Seong and Kyung (2020).

HYPOTHESES

1. H0: There is no positive relation between pre-purchase intention and post-purchase usefulness.

   H1: There is a positive relation between pre-purchase intention and post-purchase usefulness.

2. H0: There is no positive relation between payment experience and post-purchase usefulness

   H1: There is a positive relation between payment experience and post-purchase usefulness.

RESEARCH METHODOLOGY

This study attempted to map the purchase intentions, post-purchase usefulness and payment experiences of consumers towards online food delivery application industry. The discussion and arguments in this paper are based on both primary and secondary data. The secondary data have been sourced from reliable and authentic data sources. And, the primary data were collected through a pre-determined and structured questionnaire targeting a sample size of 558 determined through reliability tests. The geographical scope of data collection was the state of Gujarat – dividing it into five subregions namely South Gujarat, North Gujarat, Central Gujarat, Saurashtra region of Gujarat and Kutch region of Gujarat. From South Gujarat 24%, North Gujarat 8%, Central Gujarat 44%, Saurashtra region of Gujarat 22% and Kutch region of Gujarat 2% has been taken into consideration based on the population of each region of Gujarat. Statistical methods like t-test, ANOVA test, regression analysis were used for data analysis purpose.

When the usual mode of payment is not available for the consumer approximately 46% of the responding preferred to use cash on delivery, nearly 6% used credit card, 24% of the sample used debit card for making the payment on online food delivery applications. Further around 23% of the respondents use online banking while 37% of the participants use UPI transactions and lastly around 50% use wallet as their alternate mode of payment when the usual mode of payment is not available. Almost half of the participants use wallet payment as their alternate mode of payment this may be because wallet payment is the easiest mode of payment after cash on delivery for old age people who are not very friendly with technology and even parents prefer not to give credit card debit card or banking details to the children instead, they would choose to give funds or money in wallet.

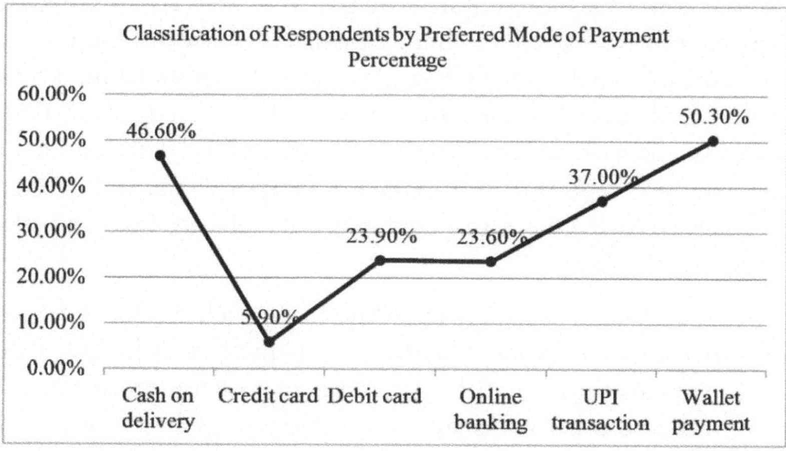

Figure 2: Classification of Respondents by Preferred Mode of Payment
Source: Calculated by the authors from the data collected through a field survey.

There are many local as well as branded applications which deliver food online consumers prefer to order from the application which is mostly used in the market and even trustworthy application as many times one has to enter the banking details or card details in the application for making the payment, show the consumer prefer to use the safest online food delivery application available in the market.

Table 1: Classification of Respondents by Most Used Application

Applications	*Number of Respondents*	*Percentage*
Zomato	434	93.30
Swiggy	332	71.40
Food panda	66	14.20
Uber eats	98	21.10
Eat sure	78	16.80
Restaurants application	239	51.40

Source: Calculated by the author from the data collected through a field survey.

Nearly 93% of the participants use Zomato application, Swiggy is used by 71% of the respondents, approximately 51% use restaurants application (Table 1). Further Food Panda is used by 14% of the participants, around 21% use Uber Eats application and lastly 16% of respondents use Eat Sure application for food delivery in Gujarat. As per the data, it is clearly seen that Zomato (93% uses) is the most used application followed by Swiggy and restaurants application. This may be because of the advertisement strategy, customer service, delivery time etc. of the Zomato and Swiggy application. Even restaurants own application is accepted in the market by respondents. It can even be noted that Food Panda, Uber Eats and Eat Sure are least accepted in the market of Gujarat.

When the consumer is ordering online food, each different consumer has his own different taste. This particular question is included in the study as we can find out the consumers of Gujarat are interested in which kind of food. In this survey question respondents was given a choice to fill more than one option as we can find out which kind of food do the respondents usually order.

Table 2: Classification of Respondents by Type of Food Ordering

Type of Food	*Number of Respondents*	*Percentage*
Fast food	320	57.30
Punjabi	299	53.60
Chinese	253	45.30
Gujarati	248	44.40
South Indian	252	45.20
Italian	239	42.80
Snacks	233	41.80
Non-veg food	123	22.00

Source: Calculated by the authors from the data collected through a field survey.

Approximately 57% of the respondents' fast food by ordering through online for delivery applications, 53% of the respondents preferred to order Punjabi food, 45% preferred Chinese food, 44% preferred Gujarati food, 45% preferred South Indian food, 43% preferred Italian food, 43% prefer snacks and lastly 21% of the population of Gujarat before to order non-veg food through online delivery application (Table 2). From the above graph and table, it can be noted that majority of the respondents of Gujarat to order fast food followed by Punjabi food through online delivery application. Even though Gujarat being a vegetarian state 21% of the sample population order and consumes non veg food through online food delivery applications.

Union of two different variables, mode of payment consumers use and various regions of Gujarat are taken into account. Mode of payment and different regions of Gujarat are given importance to find out if people in different regions use different pattern for payment or they follow the same pattern for making payment when ordered food through online food delivery application. The change in pattern of payment is mostly as per the mindset of the consumers of the particular region or area.

Table 3: Mode of Payment across Region

Cross Tabulation Mode of Payment across Region

Which mode of payment you usually use?		*Region*					*Total*
		North	*South*	*Central*	*Saurashtra*	*Kutch*	
Cash on delivery	Count	11	47	101	37	3	199
	%	23.9%	35.3%	41.2%	30.3%	25.0%	35.7%
Credit card	Count	4	17	27	20	2	70
	%	8.7%	12.8%	11.0%	16.4%	16.7%	12.5%
Debit card	Count	15	32	29	19	3	98
	%	32.6%	24.1%	11.8%	15.6%	25.0%	17.6%
Online banking	Count	10	28	21	23	3	85
	%	21.7%	21.1%	8.6%	18.9%	25.0%	15.2%
UPI transaction	Count	5	7	49	12	1	74
	%	10.9%	5.3%	20.0%	9.8%	8.3%	13.3%
Wallet payment	Count	1	2	18	11	0	32
	%	2.2%	1.5%	7.3%	9.0%	0.0%	5.7%
Total	Count	46	133	245	122	12	558
	%	100.0%	100.0%	100.0%	100.0%	100.0%	100.0%

Source: Calculated by authors from the data collected through a field survey.

In all the regions of Gujarat say North region, South region, central region, Saurashtra region and Kutch region cash on delivery is the most used mode of payment (Table 3). Respondents of Saurashtra region use the maximum credit card for making payments compared to all the regions of Gujarat, while use of debit card is 32.6% in North region of Gujarat which is highest of all regions. In the Kutch region of Gujarat online banking is widely accepted at 25%, why online banking is least accepted at 8.6% in Central Gujarat. UPI transactions are mostly accepted in Central Gujarat at 20% while it is least accepted in South Gujarat for the talking about wallet payment 9% of the participants from Saurashtra region uses it.

Most favourite mode of payment of all the five regions of Gujarat is cash on delivery this maybe because even today after the development of technology people feel safe while giving cash at the time of receiving the parcel as there is no or very less chances of fraudulent activities. After cash on delivery consumers prefer to use either debit card or credit card this maybe because online banking, UPI transactions and wallet payment are comparatively new in the market so yet people are not comfortable or may be do not feel a sense of security to use on each and every platform.

H0: Frequency of mode of payment and region are independent.

H1: Frequency of mode of payment and region are not independent.

Table 4: Mode of Payment across Regions

Chi-Square Tests			
	Value	*df*	*Asymp. Sig. (2-sided)*
Pearson Chi-Square	60.959[a]	20	0.000
Likelihood Ratio	64.096	20	0.000
Linear-by-Linear Association	0.671	1	0.413
Number of Valid Cases	558		

Source: Calculated by author from the data collected through a field survey.

From the results of the chi square table presented above it can be seen from the table that H0 is rejected (60.959, $p < 0.005$) thus it can be concluded that the frequency of mode of payment is not independent of region. Taking into consideration research model given earlier in the paper, the hypotheses for the thesis have been finalized. Some tests like regression analysis test and ANOVA test have been applied to find out the relationship between each hypothesis (Table 5).

Table 5: Results of Hypotheses

Hypothesis	*Regression Weights*	*Beta Coefficient*	*R2*	*F*	*t-Value*	*p-Value*	*Results*
1	PPU•PPI	0.301	0.159	104.892	10.242	0.000	Support
2	PPU•PE	0.517	0.233	168.984	12.999	0.000	Support

Source: Calculated by authors from the data collected through a field survey.

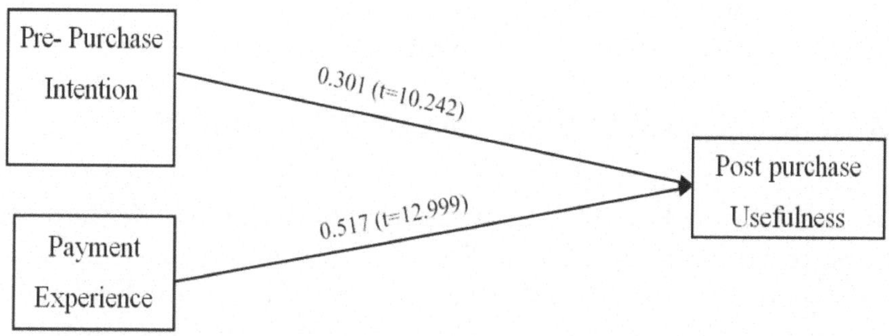

Figure 3: Model of Objectives Showing Research Hypotheses
Source: Calculated by authors from the data collected through a field survey.

(a) Relation between post-purchase usefulness and pre-purchase intention

H0: There is no positive relation between post-purchase usefulness and pre-purchase intention.

H1: There is positive relation between post-purchase usefulness and pre-purchase intention.

In this hypothesis post-purchase usefulness is dependent on pre-purchase intention. As it can be noted 30.1% change in pre-purchase intention can be accounted by post-purchase usefulness. Post-purchase usefulness and pre-purchase intention have positive relationship with each other. Thus, the null hypothesis is rejected, and the alternative hypothesis is not rejected.

(b) Relation between post-purchase usefulness and payment experience

H0: There is no positive relation between post-purchase usefulness and payment experience.

H1: There is positive relation between post-purchase usefulness and payment experience.

In this hypothesis post-purchase usefulness is dependent on payment experience. As it can be noted in table 51.7% change in payment experience can be accounted by post-purchase usefulness. Post-purchase usefulness and payment experience have positive and strong relationship with each other. Thus, the null hypothesis is rejected, and the alternative hypothesis is not rejected.

MAJOR OBSERVATIONS AND CONCLUSION

In Gujarat state, around 57% of the respondents preferred to order fast food through online food delivery applications. Zomato was found to be the most used application (93% respondents) in all the five regions of Gujarat. Wallet payment for their online food orders was used the most by the respondents in all the regions of Gujarat. In their research on online food ordering and delivery services, Kumari and Yadav (2022) found that faster delivery was the most important factor, and discounts and special offers were the second most important factors. The post-purchase usefulness was found dependent on pre-purchase intention and have positive significant relationship. However, Cheow *et al.* (2017) with almost same variables i.e. prior online purchase experience and post-usage usefulness found a negative relationship. Moreover, the post-purchase usefulness is dependent on payment experience of the consumer and both these variables have strong and positive relationship with each other.

REFERENCES

[1] Ahuja, K., Chandra. V., Lord, V. and Peens, C. (2021). "Ordering in: The rapid evolution of food delivery", *Mckinsey & company.*

[2] Baindur, D. and Macário, R. (2013). "Mumbai lunch box delivery system: A transferable benchmark in urban logistics?" *Research in Transportation Economics,* 38(1): 110–121.

[3] Bagla, R. and Khan, J. (2017). "Customers' Expectations and Satisfaction with Online Food Ordering Portals", *Prabandhan Indian Journal of Management,* 10(11).

[4] Beliya, A., Kujur, R., Verma, M., Nagwanshi, V., Sahu, S., Uikey, N. and Bhat, A. (2019). "Satisfaction of Consumers by Using Online Food Services", *International Journal of Humanities and Social Sciences,* 8(4): 35-44.

[5] Cheow, V., Yeo, S., Goh, S.K. and Rezaei, S. (2017). "Consumer experiences, attitude and behavioral intention toward online food delivery (OFD) services", *Journal of Retailing and Consumer Services,* 35: 150–162.

[6] Chorneukar, M.J. (2014). "To Study the Customer Perceptions of Electronic Food", St. Joseph's Evening College, Marketing.

[7] Duggal, S. and Gupta, V. (2020). How the consumer's attitude and behavioural intentions are influenced: A case of online food delivery applications in India. *International Journal of Culture Tourism and Hospitality Research,* 15(1): 77–93.

[8] Gera, B. and Jain, R. (2020). "Post Purchase Behaviour of the Consumers towards Digital Food Ordering and Delivery Service" *International Journal for Research in Applied Science & Engineering Technology (IJRASET),* 8(3): 150–156.

[9] Gupta, M. (2019). "A Study on Impact of Online Food delivery app on Restaurant Business special reference to zomato and swiggy", *International Journal of Research and Analytical Reviews,* 6(1): 890–893.

[10] Katerina, B. and katerina, A. (2020). "Predicting satisfaction and intentions to use online food delivery: What really makes a difference?", *Journal of Food Service Business Research,* 23(4).

[11] Katoch, R. and Sidhu, A. (2021). "Online Food Delivery Industry in India: A Case of Consumer", *Advances in Mathematics: Scientific Journal,* 10: 507–516.

[12] Pal, D., Funilkul, S., Eamsinvattana, W. and Siyal, S. (2021). "Using online food delivery applications during the COVID-19 lockdown period: What drives University Students' satisfaction and loyalty?", *Journal of Foodservice Business Research,* 25(3): 1–45.

[13] Ramesh, R., Prabhu, S.V., Sasikumar, B., Kiruthika Devi, B.S., Prasath, P., Praveena, S. and Kamala, R. (2021). "An empirical study of online food delivery services from applications perspective", *Materials Today: Proceedings,* 80(3): 1–5.

[14] Ray, A., Dhir, A., Bala, P. and Kaur, P. (2019). "Why do people use food delivery apps (FDA)? A uses and gratification theory perspective", *Journal of Retailing and Consumer Services,* 51: 221–230.

[15] Saxena, A. (2019). "An Analysis of Online Food Ordering Applications in India: Zomato and Swiggy", *International Journal of Research in Engineering, IT and Social Sciences,* 9(Special Issue): 13–21.

[16] Seong, S. and Kyung, B. (2020). "The Effect of Food Delivery Application on Customer Loyalty in resttaurant", *Journal of Distribution Science,* 18(4), 5–12.

[17] Suhartanto, D., Ali, M.H., Tan, K.H. and Sjahroeddin, F. (2018). "Loyalty toward online food delivery service: the role of e-service quality and food quality", *Journal of Foodservice Business Research,* 22(2): 1–17.

[18] Swiggy and B. & Company (2024). "*Food services market to reach Rs 10L crore, online food delivery to grow 18% by 2030: Study",* Bengaluru: The New Indian Express.

[19] Vandakudari, A., Tapashetti, R. and Hunnur, R. (2022). "A Study on Consumer Perception & satisfaction towards online Food delivery Applications", *Journal of Emerging Technologies and Innovative Research,* 9(9): b451–b470.

[10] Wen, C., Prybutok, V.R. and Xu, C. (2011). "An integrated model for customer online repurchase intention. *Journal of Computer Information Systems",* 52(1): 14–23.

[11] Yadav, A.K. and Kumari, P. (2022). "Revolutionising Online Food Ordering & Delivery Services, A Comparative Study in Gorakhpur City", *International Journal of Creative Research Thoughts,* 10(7): 972–980.

[12] Yajurvedi, A.G. and N. (2022). "Factors Affecting Consumer Behaviour Towards Online Food Delivery Services Providers in Delhi-NCR", *Journal of Arts, Humanities and Social Sciences,* 5(11): 39–47.

[13] Yusra, A.A. (2020). "The Influence of Online Food Delivery Service Quality on Customer Satisfaction and Customer Loyalty: The Role of Personal Innovativeness", *Journal of Environmental Treatment Techniques,* 8(1): 6–12.

SECTION 3

EDUCATION AND HEALTH

Gujarat's Growth and Human Capital: A Virtuous Cycle?

Mona Khare[1], Sandhya Dubey[2] and Sonam Arora[3]

ABSTRACT: This paper examines the relationship between economic growth and human capital in Gujarat, India, questioning whether its high growth is "virtuous." While economic growth is often linked to human development through education and employment, market imperfections and inequalities can hinder this relationship, creating vicious or lopsided growth cycles. Gujarat, despite strong economic growth, lags in social progress and human development indicators, raising concerns about the sustainability of its growth model. The paper analyzes Gujarat's performance compared to other Indian states, exploring whether its growth is inclusive and equitable. It concludes that Gujarat's growth model, while economically successful, currently falls into a pattern of high economic growth but low social progress, highlighting the need for increased investment in education, particularly higher education, and stronger linkages across all levels of education to ensure long-term sustainable and equitable development.

***Keywords:** Human Capital, Virtuous Cycle, Growth Miracle, GSDP.*

---

[1] Director, UGC-Malaviya Mission Teacher Training Centre, Head, Department of Educational Finance, NIEPA, New Delhi, India.
E-mail: monakhare@niepa.ac.in

[2] Consultant, Department of Educational Finance, NIEPA, New Delhi, India.
E-mail: sandhya@niepa.ac.in

[3] PhD Scholar, Department of Educational Finance, NIEPA, New Delhi, India.
E-mail: sonamarora.nuepa@gmail.com

INTRODUCTION

The circular relationship between economic growth, employment, and education is profusely discussed both theoretically and empirically in the existing literature. While Nurkse (1953) presents a traditional model of the vicious circle of poverty that describes how low income leads to low productivity due to insufficient savings and limited capital formation, Meier and Baldwin (1957) attribute this circular nature to market imperfections and the quality of human resources. They argue that these market imperfections hinder the optimal allocation and utilization of natural resources, resulting in underdevelopment and economic stagnation. Emphasizing the importance of human resource characteristics, they further explain that lack of skills and knowledge contributes to keeping natural resources unutilized or misused—thus perpetuating backwardness: "underdeveloped resources becoming both a consequence and cause of backwardness," setting off a mutually exacerbating cycle. The proposal finds further support in the Human Capital theory of recent years, which presents substantial evidence of increased investment in education for developing human capital and its role in economic development and growth (Shultz, Becker, Hanushek and Kimko 2000; Krueger and Lindahl 2000; Hanushek and Woessmann 2007; Kingdon and Soderbom 2007a, 2007b; Khare, 2019; Chadha 2004, Mathur 1990). Education is the most important form of investment in human capital (Weil, 2004). Mincer (1974) examined human capital as worth of a country, "just as accumulation of personal human capital produces individual economic (Income) growth, so do the corresponding social or national aggregates. In fact, the new trend of linking "education to work" arising from emerging labour market needs, along with evidence of higher salaries and better quality jobs with a growing "skills hierarchy" from primary to tertiary levels (Khare, 2019), further reinforces the previously mentioned arguments. Obtaining quality education as the basis for improving people's lives and achieving sustainable development has become a widely acknowledged model for equitable growth. In this context, Meier and Baldwin's explanation of vicious circle and market imperfections appears to be more closely aligned with the contemporary concept of sustainable development.

The current market is rife with various imperfections, including the newly emerging human capital and complex labour markets. These imperfections encompass educational disparities on the supply side and unequal employment opportunities on the demand side. The interplay of these inequalities contributes to economic disparities, potentially perpetuating a cycle of unequal growth. Moreover, there exists a reciprocal relationship between economic growth and human development, where nations can either enter an upward spiral of development or become trapped in a poverty cycle, as shown in literature (Ranis 2004; Ranis *et al.*, 2000; Mayer-Foulkes 2003). The third scenario might involve unbalanced economic growth, with either relatively strong growth and weak human development or vice versa. Research indicates that most countries with uneven economic growth struggle to maintain their momentum and eventually fall into a cycle of low economic growth and low human development. These experiences demonstrate that human development is essential for long-term sustainable growth. Additionally, the distribution of growth, increased investment, higher productivity, and improved employment are equally important in turning successes in human development into lasting economic prosperity - creating a sustained upward spiral of positive economic expansion.

Gujarat, a prosperous state in India has been known for its unique model of economic growth popularly known as the "Gujarat Model". Gujarat aspires to become a USD 1 trillion economy by 2030 and is positioned to contribute significantly to India's journey towards achieving a USD 5 trillion economy. While the state has witnessed remarkable economic growth and an increase in formal employment opportunities, there remains another aspect that needs to be examined in the light of Human capital theory and endogenous growth models, which emphasise investments in education for achieving equitable economic growth and sustainable development.

The paper seeks to investigate the relative status of Gujarat in terms of a virtuous, vicious, or lopsided circle of economic growth. It aims to identify if Gujarat is on the path towards inclusive development or may be is at risk of being trapped in a model that perpetuates unequal and unsustainable growth. The main questions addressed include why Gujarat despite with high-growth is not experiencing lower inequalities, improved higher education status, improvement in health status and better performance in social indicators over time.

To establish the relationship between the economic growth and the social progress, four scenarios are possible as shown in Figure 1. The concept of different circles of sustainable economic growth in the context of the four quadrants has been adopted (Khare M., 2019). The framework is used to examine Gujarat's experience. Whether it follows a positive cycle of consistent relationship between economic growth of human and social development (Figure 2). A high rate of growth results in higher per capita incomes and lower unemployment rates, subsequently leading to improved employment quality and better education status, which contributes to reduced inequalities and sustained fair growth that mutually reinforces each other.

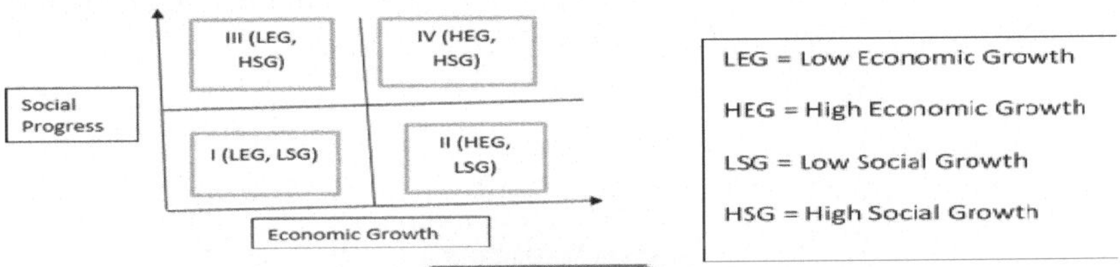

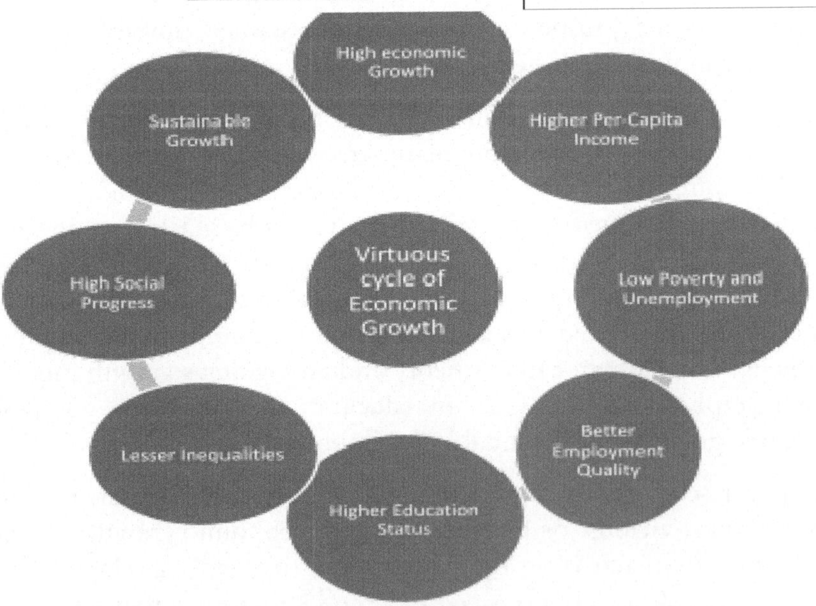

Figure 2: Virtuous Cycle of Sustainable Economic Growth.
Source: Adopted and modified from (Khare M., 2019).

The paper is structured into five parts. First part describes the conceptual framework used in the analysis. Second part aims to investigate the growth pattern of Gujarat Model vis-a-vis All India average and other key Indian states. Third part concentrates on the inter-state scenario regarding social progress and its relationship with economic growth. Fourth part seeks to explore the employment and educational quality indexes and its relationship with economic growth and social progress to understand the nature and the sustainability of Gujarat's growth against the framework of virtuous, vicious or lopsided growth. Fifth part finally focuses on drawing crucial policy implications for the state.

THE GUJARAT MODEL VIS-À-VIS OTHER MAJOR STATES

Since 1960, when Gujarat became an independent state, its growth rate has remained above the national average due to the entrepreneurial culture of the state's business community and the efforts of state governments across party lines. "Social development indicators have not been able to keep pace with economic development in this state of over 60 million people," UNICEF had observed about Gujarat back in 2013 (source). Maitreesh Ghatak of London School of Economics writes about Gujarat's development model: "When it comes to social indicators, the shine of the Gujarat model appears to fade." (source). While it is argued that a state with high growth rate over a long period will eventually improve upon its social indicators as benefits percolate down to every sector of development, it has not been the case with Gujarat. The state's social indicators lag behind its economic figures, indicating that the gains of growth have not reached a large segment of residents. According to the 2011 Census, poverty rate in Gujarat is 16.63 per 1 million people. Rajasthan, Uttarakhand and even restive Jammu & Kashmir have lower poverty rate than this second-most industrialised state in the country with the fourth-highest gross domestic product. The NSDP per capita has more than doubled between 2013–2022 in Gujarat (CMIE, 2022). Experts argue that the state has consistently maintained a higher economic growth rate than the rest of India since the mid-1990s, particularly in the first eight years of the new millennium (Hirway, 2014; Bhirud 2015; Dhaval S., 2019). Gujarat's annual GDP growth in previous two decades averaged almost 10% (The Economist, 2015) which is faster than

India as a whole (Table 1) and highlights its significant contribution to India's economy (Morris, 2014). This success has positioned Gujarat as an attractive destination for both national and international investments, leading to increased attention from neo-capitalists and private sector investors (Panagariya, 2012).

Development theory encompasses numerous factors known to affect a region's economic growth potential such as geography, institutions, infrastructure and natural resource endowments. However, these "indicators of potential" are not thoroughly evaluated across Gujarat's performance. Moreover, when placed in the context of its strong 2000s' potential and sustained equitable development framework, the supposed "growth miracle" may appear less extraordinary.

Table 1: Growth Rates of GSDP Level-Gujarat *vs.* India (%)

	1980–89	*1990–99*	*2000–10*	*2011–21*
Gujarat	4.9	8.0	9.8	8.29
All India	5.0	5.9	7.7	5.41
Difference	–0.1	2.1	2.1	2.88

Source: Author's construct.

India, as a whole, has been the dominant economic power globally for more than three-fourths of known economic history (Maddison, 2007). According to the convergence theorem (Barro, 1991), some regions with richer resources would initially grow faster than others when an economy's growth rate accelerates. However, the growth rates would converge eventually when the law of declining marginal returns took hold. According to studies, despite positive macroeconomic trends, India's goal of "growth with equity" is still eluded, and policymakers continue to have serious concerns about the country's substantial regional growth disparities (Datt & Ravallion, 2002; Khare, 2019; Kundu & Varghese, 2010). Due to differential marginal productivity of capital this may lead to income inequality across regions(Bhattacharya & Sakthivel, 2005). With India having become the fifth largest economy in the world in 2019 and aspiring to be the third largest by 2025, in this section we analyse India's situation in terms of growth across states and income inequality. Studies reveal that India's objective of 'growth with equity' continues to elude it and remains a matter of grave concern for policy makers as regional disparities in growth remain high despite good macro economic trends (Datt & Ravallion, 2002;Khare, 2019; Kundu & Varghese, 2010). Given the performance of India as a whole and existence of inter-state growth inequalities, it would be important to examine long term growth trends of Gujarat vis-à-vis other major states and examine where does Gujarat stands.). In order to do so, long term growth rates (LTGR) of net state domestic product (NSDP) were calculated (base year 2004–05[4]) for the period starting from 1993–94 to 2017–18.

We split the whole (1993–94–2017–18) period into three sub-periods: period I (1993–94 to 2000–01), period II (2000–01 to 2011–12), and period III (2011–12 to 2017–18) in order to examine the sustainability of growth, or if growth could be sustained over the long run (Table 2).

Table 2: Net State Domestic Product (base year: 2004–05)

States	*1993–94 to 2017–18*	*2011–12 to 2017–18*	*1993–94 to 2011–12*	*1993–94 to 2000–01*	*2001–02 to 2011–12*	*2001–02 to 2005–06*	*2006–07 to 2011–12*
Andhra Pradesh	6.48	7.20	5.87	5.08	6.01	4.93	5.16
Assam	4.47	6.33	3.56	1.73	4.67	3.71	4.71
Bihar	6.49	6.84	6.00	4.89	7.39	2.97	8.30
Gujarat	7.97	7.64	7.66	4.57	9.18	9.01	7.86
Haryana	7.42	6.83	7.24	5.24	7.98	6.66	7.16
Himachal Pradesh	6.83	6.22	6.69	6.52	6.32	5.88	5.36
Karnataka	6.75	7.49	6.12	5.54	6.37	5.47	5.38
Kerala	6.30	5.71	6.18	4.38	7.03	6.63	6.01
Madhya Pradesh	5.97	7.34	5.15	3.44	5.74	2.72	6.76
Maharashtra	6.84	6.62	6.55	4.02	8.10	7.46	6.31
Odisha	5.27	4.87	5.14	2.79	6.31	6.08	4.44
Punjab	5.00	4.64	4.86	3.81	5.51	3.54	5.37
Rajasthan	6.69	5.25	6.86	5.67	6.68	3.84	7.10
Tamil Nadu	6.82	5.56	6.93	5.43	8.22	6.45	7.09
Uttar Pradesh	5.21	5.71	4.74	3.45	5.51	3.85	5.57
West Bengal	6.07	5.50	5.95	5.81	5.38	4.43	4.85
All India	5.65	6.61	6.60	5.40	7.00	5.70	6.42
Mean	6.29	6.23	5.97	4.52	6.65	5.23	6.09
SD	0.92	0.95	1.06	1.26	1.24	1.77	1.17
CV	14.67	15.22	17.84	27.79	18.65	33.91	19.21

Source: Computed CAGRs for NSDP at factor cost, RBI Database from National Accounts Statistics (NAS), Central Statistics Office, (CSO), Ministry of Statistics and Programme Implementation, Government of India.

[4] The revised base year 2011–12 is widely contested by policy makers and academicians as the inflated growth estimates are hard to reconcile with other economic correlates (Nagraj, 2018).

Based on the LTGRs, the states can be classified into the following:

Table 3: Categorisation of States based on LTGR NSDP

Category	*States*
Sustained High GRs	Gujarat, Haryana, Maharashtra
Sustained Moderate GRs	Andhra Pradesh, Karnataka and Kerala
Sustained Low GRs	West Bengal, Punjab, Uttar Pradesh and Odisha
Un-sustained High/Low GRs	High to Low: Rajasthan, Himachal Pradesh and Tamil Nadu Low to High: Bihar, Assam and Madhya Pradesh

As discussed earlier, Gujarat underperforms on other social and educational indicator that raises queries on the kind of model the state follows. The state's social indicators lag behind its economic figures, indicating that the gains of growth have not reached a large segment of residents.

ECONOMIC GROWTH AND SOCIAL PROGRESS

Although excelling in economic performance, Gujarat compares poorly with other states in terms of social development indicators such as nutrition, healthcare, gender equality and so on. According to the 2011 Census, poverty rate in Gujarat is 16.63 per 1 million people.

Rajasthan, Uttarakhand and even restive Jammu & Kashmir have lower poverty rate than this second-most industrialised state in the country with the fourth-highest gross domestic product. (Weil, 2013) Further, sex ratio in Gujarat is 919 i.e. for each 1000 male, which is below national average of 940 as per latest census Table 4. Notably, across most social indicators, there was no considerable improvement in the last few years. For instance, the population of females (aged six and above) who attended school was 72% in 2015–16 and increased to 72.9% in 2019–20. The share of wasted children (low weight-for-height) improved marginally from 26.4% to 25.1%, while the share of underweight (low weight-for-age) children recorded a small rise from 39.3% to 39.7%. On both these indicators the State ranked

29 out of 30 states. What is striking is that the state's relative performance worsened in 2019–20 compared to 2005–06 on most social indicators. In the share of the female population who ever attended school, the State ranked 15 of 28 States in 2005–06; in 2019–20, it ranked 19 of 30. In the share of wasted children, the State's rank worsened from 16 out of 28 States to 29 out of 30 States.

Table 4: State's Performance in Select Indicators (2019–20)

Indicator	Value	Gujarat's rank	Top major States	Change from 2015-16
% women who ever attended school	72.9	19 of 30	Kerala: 95.5; Himachal: 81; T.N.: 80.4	-2
Women age 20-24 married before 18 years of age (%)	21.8	20 of 30	Himachal: 5.4; Kerala: 6.3 Punjab: 8.7	0
Infant mortality rate (per 1,000 live births)	31.2	19 of 30	Kerala: 4.4; T.N.: 18.6 West Bengal: 22	-1
Stunted children (low height-for-age) (%)	39	26 of 30	Kerala: 23.4; Punjab: 24.5 Tamil Nadu: 25	-2
Wasted children (low weight-for-height) (%)	25.1	29 of 30	Punjab: 10.6; Haryana: 11.5; Uttarakhand: 13.2	0
Underweight children (weight-for-age) (%)	39.7	29 of 30	Punjab: 16.9; Kerala: 19.7 Uttarakhand: 21	-3
Households with any member having a health insurance (%)	39	14 of 30	Rajasthan: 87.8; Chhattisgarh: 71.4; Andhra: 70.2	1
Population that use an improved sanitation facility (%)	74	18 of 30	Kerala: 98.7; Punjab: 86.6 Haryana: 85	-6

Source: Nihalani & Radhakrishnan, 2022.

Hence, the Gujarat model is widely acclaimed for its remarkable economic growth and performs poorly on social indicators. The assertion regarding the recent economic growth of Gujarat has faced growing challenges (Bagchi *et al.* 2005; Dholakia, 2009), prompting a re-examination of its purported success. This singular emphasis on Gujarat's economic growth and the rhetoric surrounding it may overshadow the achievements of other significant states such as Tamil Nadu, Karnataka, Kerala, Maharashtra and shift the focus from Gujarat's mediocre performance in the social indicators.

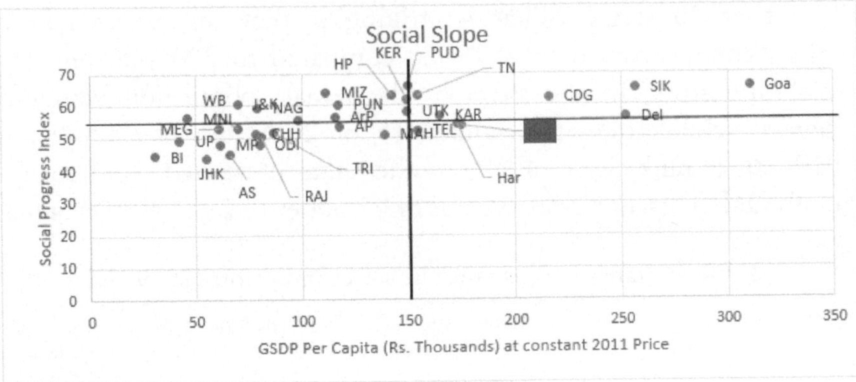

Figure 4: Social Slope Showing Social Progress Index's Scores for Indian States and UTs for the year 2021

Source: Author's construct using PIB and MOSPI data.

From the Figure 4 it can be seen that Gujarat despite being in the top five states in terms of per capita income falters when it comes to social progress index[5] and it lies in the second quadrant of high economic growth and low social progress. States like Kerala, Tamil Nadu, Himanchal Pradesh, West Bengal perform relatively well in social progress in comparison to Gujarat despite having per capita income less than it. Such a scenario makes Gujarat an anomaly to the theories of economic and social development that assert that as the economic

[5] Social Progress Index (SPI) for States and Districts made by the Institute for Competitiveness and Social Progress Imperative. The index assesses states and districts based on 12 components across three critical dimensions of social progress - Basic Human Needs, Foundations of Wellbeing, and Opportunity. The index uses an extensive framework comprising 89 indicators at the state level and 49 at the district level.

Basic Human Needs assess the performance of states and districts in terms of Nutrition and Basic Medical Care, Water and Sanitation, Personal Safety and Shelter. Foundations of Wellbeing evaluates the progress made by the country across the components of Access to Basic Knowledge, Access to Information and Communication, Health and Wellness, and Environmental Quality. Opportunity focuses on Personal Rights, Personal Freedom and Choice, Inclusiveness, and Access to Advanced Education.

Note: Further, the use of social progress index instead of HDI in the social slope (Figure 3) is because SPI is based on relatively more holistic social indicators in comparison to HDI. https://pib.gov.in/PressReleaseIframePage.aspx?PRID =1885039

growth accelerates, the social development follows. Further, Gujarat falls in medium category states in terms of Human Development Index (HDI) with HDI of 0.638 (2021). The three components of HDI are economic growth, life expectancy and education. As already discussed Gujarat, though performing well in economic terms, falters on the human capita aspect of development, which comprises health and education. Thus, despite having the highest SGDP per capita among larger states, Gujarat has failed to translate this advantage into human development and ranks 21st.

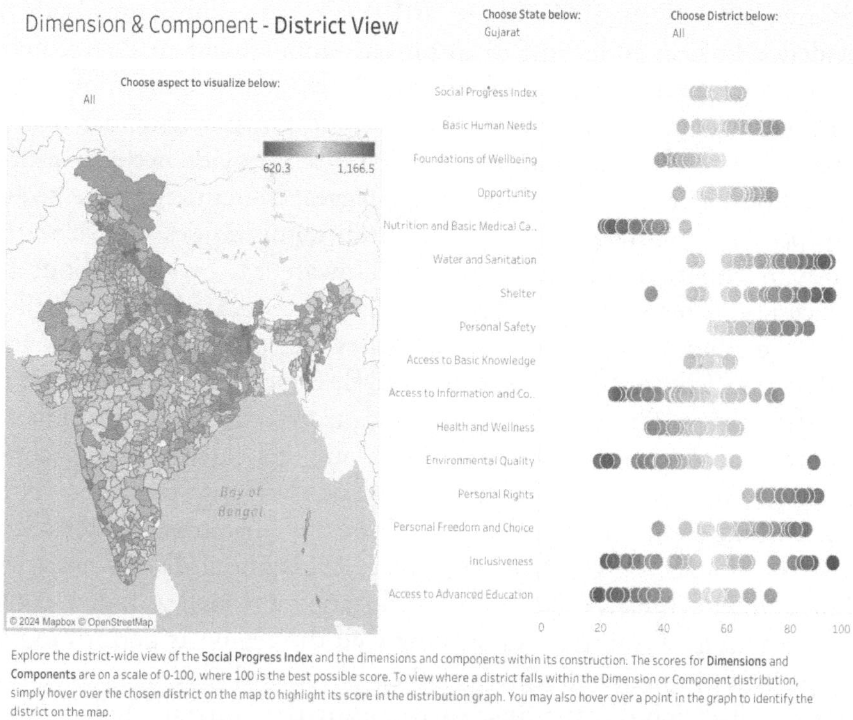

Figure 5: Range of the Districts Performance on Social Progress Index and its Components in Gujarat

Source: https://competitiveness.in/social-progress-index-states-and-districts-of-india

Figure 5, further highlights the range of the districts' performance of Gujarat on various social indicators. It is evident that Gujarat performs specifically poor on foundations of wellbeing, Nutrition and

Basic Medical facilities, Access to Information, Health and wellness, Environmental Quality, Inclusiveness and Access to advanced education. An economic model that has enjoyed adjectives like miraculous and has been extensively appreciated, if fails to deliver at the social level, then its effectiveness needs to be challenged. If the growth is not inclusive and not translate into the well-being and quality of life of the masses, the deeper scrutiny of the Gujarat Model and its mislinkage with social progress becomes significant.

From a development economics perspective, education is a vital instrument in promoting inclusive and sustainable development (Romer 1993; Tilak 2007, Khare, 2019). There is a substantial body of evidence linking education to improved employment quality, chiefly via the increased formalisation of jobs. As workers acquire more skills and knowledge, they become more productive and more viable candidates for formal sector jobs, which often provide better working conditions, greater security, and higher wages. Concurrently, the health prospects of individuals, families, and communities are elevated through enhanced health and hygiene awareness brought about by education. The informed decisions that an educated person makes about his/her health not only increases personal welfare but also reduces healthcare costs at a societal level. In addition, the increase in gender parity, facilitated by increased access to education, aids in societal advancement. When women are educated, they become better equipped to participate in decision-making processes, both within households and communities, thereby fostering greater social progress. Hence, in the case of Gujarat, leveraging indices such as the Employment Quality Index and Educational Quality Index could provide insightful inferences on how well the region is performing in its pursuit of quality education and employment. Understanding this nexus will enrich the discourse surrounding the Gujarat Model.

GROWTH, EDUCATION AND EMPLOYMENT STATUS—THE VIRTUOUS CYCLE

Notably, the growth model of Gujarat and its performance on select social and educational indicators present a curious case of study. Since, the state recorded the highest long run economic growth but didn't fair well on other important social indicators, it becomes an interesting case to analyse its performance and status on educational and employment dimension through an inter-state comparison.

Part A: Economic Growth and Employment Quality

Many research studies have shown that there exists a disconnect between India's recent growth and employment quantity and quality (MK SDG Paper). In fact, growth in the Indian states have had a very feeble but positive relationship with unemployment (MK SDG Paper). The cross-mapping of economic growth, human development and employment status reveals that not all the states deem to be experiencing virtuous circle of high growth and large gains in human development which are also the developed states of the country on various other parameters. Moreover, a majority of those that fall in the category of vicious circle carry a legacy of being lowly developed. Most of the states fall in the category of experiencing lopsided Economic Growth -Human Development circle and face the risk of falling into vicious cycle, if not taken care off, which is vulnerable category (MKSA IPE Paper).

There have been rising concerns about jobless growth in India as a majority of the states failed at achieving better employment outcomes despite high economic growth (MKSA IPE). In order to ascertain if Gujarat's model is also based on jobless growth and poor employment outcomes, we adopt the quadrant analysis replicated from MKSA SDG. The 14 major Indian states can be divided based on their GSDP per capita (2021–22) to correspondingly trace their performance on employment quantity and quality. The work force participation rate for the 15–59 age group serves as an indicator of employment quantity, illustrating the proportion of the working-age population that is engaged in economic activity. A higher WFPR suggests that a larger share of the potential labor force is being utilized. Quality of employment can be represented by the ratio of regular wage/salaried employees, which reflects stable, possibly more productive employment compared to informal or irregular work. Economic growth is typically measured by Gross State Domestic Product per capita, which reflects the average economic output per person.

We see that Gujarat falls in the very high economic growth quadrant along with Tamil Nadu, Maharashtra and Karnataka. A closer look at the employment indicators viz workforce participation rate (quantity of employment) and percentage of regular/wage salaried workers (quality of employment) reveals that Gujarat miraculously performs great on all three fronts. In Figures 6 & 7, it's seen that Gujarat falls in the virtuous cycle of high economic growth, high employment quality and quantity. The states have a WPR of 60.9 with 31.6% of regular/wage salaried employees.

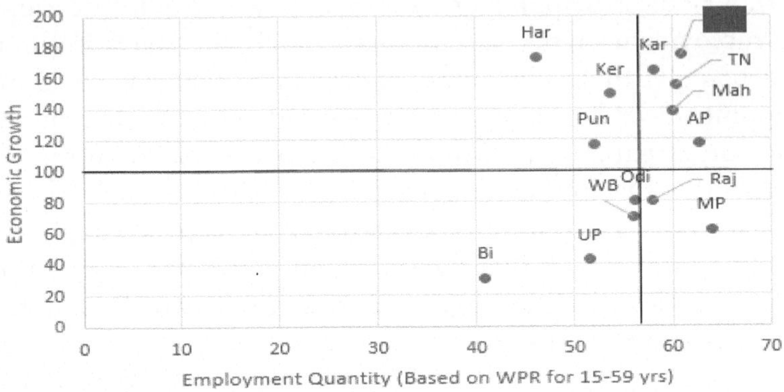

Figure 6: Quadrant Analysis: Employment Quantity and Economic Growth

Note: EG-economic growth as indicated by GSDP per capita, EM-QT – employment quantity as indicated by workforce participation rate of working-age.

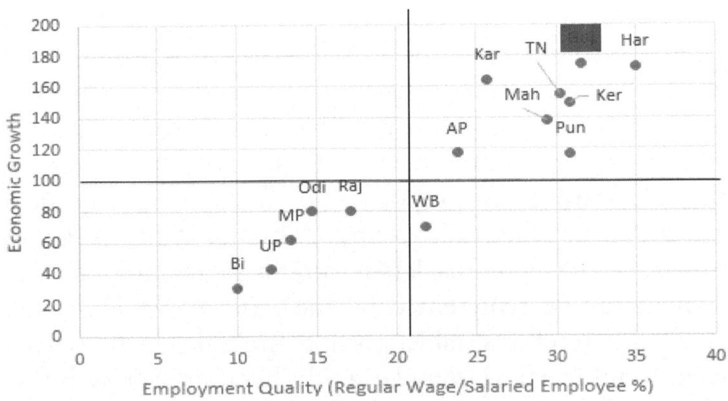

Figure 7: Quadrant Analysis: Employment Quality and Economic Growth

Note: EG-economic growth as indicated GSDP per capita, EM-QL – employment quality as indicated by percentage of regular/wage salaried.

The relationship between high employment quantity and quality (ratio of regular wage/salaried employees) to high economic growth is symbiotic. High employment quantity and quality can lead to increased consumer spending, more substantial savings and investment rates, and enhanced governmental revenue through taxation, all of which contribute to a robust GSDP per capita. Conversely, high economic growth often creates more jobs and leads to better wages and working conditions, as businesses thrive and demand for labour increases, which can then improve the WFPR and the ratio of regular wage/salaried employees. Dholakia (2009) has argued that the state has experienced significant economic growth with contributions from various sectors. Gujarat has capitalized on its strategic geographic location for industrial and export-led growth, enhancing its GSDP per capita. This industrial proliferation is likely to augment employment quantity and quality, as more factories and businesses require labour.

Part B: Educational Quality, Economic Growth and Social Progress

Educational quality is measured by creating and averaging two indices, namely Education Expenditure Adequacy Index (Appendix) and the Educational Effectiveness Index (Appendix), to assess the performance of Gujarat vis-a-vis other major states. The purpose is to see if the public spending on education and effectiveness of the education system of Gujarat is in alignment with its economic prosperity and social progress or not.

Education qualifies as quasi-public and merit good. Market is eloquently present but government intervenes with the paternalistic motivation to strengthen the sector and maintain equity. To calculate Education Expenditure Adequacy Index (EEAI) we have obtained the expenditure per student in elementary, secondary and higher education sector for each of the states. The rationale behind computing expenditure adequacy is to see how the states have relatively performed in carrying out their primary role of financing the access of the education across the levels. While analysing the results of the EEAI, it is important to consider the needs, economic potential and the cost constraints of the states and these variables can differ considerably between the states.

Effectiveness refers to the extent to which the output of the service provided meet the objective sets. Thus, here the focus is shifted from inputs to output. Output based grants would create an incentive regime that would promote a result based accountability culture. Output-based grants such as imposing conditions on achievement scores on standardised tests and reduction in dropouts' rates would help achieve accountability for results. The output indicators taken here are States' performance in National Achievement Survey (NAS) for the class III, V and VIII, transition rates from secondary to higher secondary and Gross Enrolment Ratio (GER) in higher education (overall, Schedule Cast (SC) and Schedule Tribes (ST)). The motive was to take one indicator each from elementary, secondary and higher education and to take such indicators that represent, learning outcomes and equity in access to education.

Results of adequacy index (Table 10) demonstrate that the top six rankers amongst the non-special states have an index greater than 100. This shows that their performance is better than the average. These states are Andhra Pradesh, Goa, Maharashtra, Kerala, Karnataka and Haryana. The other twelve states have EEAI below average including that of Gujarat. A comparison of the performance of the states under this head along with their performance on the effectiveness parameters will give us a holistic picture about whether the states doing well in adequacy i.e. spending better also are good at delivering output. Results of the effectiveness index show that seven states have the above average score i.e. above 100. These are Karnataka, Andhra Pradesh, Tamil Nadu, Goa, Rajasthan, Uttar Pradesh and Kerala. Thus, Maharashtra and Haryana, which were above average performers in the adequacy index, fare badly on effectiveness index. Whereas, Tamil Nadu, Uttar Pradesh and Rajasthan were in the list of above average spenders in the EEIA but are good performers in the effectiveness index. Odisha, Bihar, Chhattisgarh, Haryana, MP and Gujarat are the bottom scorers on the EI. This observation serves to underline the point that merely high expenditure do not translate into better outputs and outcomes. Thus, a special focus on output is

Table 5: Performance of Indian States on Educational Expenditure Adequacy, Educational Effectiveness and Educational Quality Index

Major States of India			
Index	*High Performers*	*Average Performers*	*Low Performers*
Education Expenditure Adequacy Index (EEAI)	Andhra Pradesh (259.33) Goa (216.50) Maharashtra (129.20) Kerala (105.85) Karnataka (104.74) Haryana (103.23)	Chhattisgarh (99.29) Gujarat (92.40) Tamil Nadu (81.44) Odisha (79.37) Uttar Pradesh (73.78) Madhya Pradesh (73.41)	Rajasthan (68.28) Jharkhand (66.28) Punjab (66.04) West Bengal (62.53) Bihar (59.56) Telangana (58.69)
Education Expenditure Effectiveness Index (EEEI)	Karnataka (241.07) Andhra Pradesh (208.14) Tamil Nadu (196.02) Goa (130.79) Rajasthan (128.98) Uttar Pradesh (120.89)	Kerala (111.03) Punjab (92.32) Telangana (77.41) Jharkhand (68.19) West Bengal (67.36) Maharashtra (66.51)	Gujarat (61.67) Madhya Pradesh (47.97) Haryana (47.67) Chhattisgarh (47.58) Bihar (43.59) Odisha (42.72)
Education Quality Index (EdQI)	AndhraPradesh (233.74) Goa (173.64) Karnataka (172.90) Tamil Nadu (138.73) Kerala (108.44) Rajasthan (98.63)	Maharashtra (97.86) UttarPradesh (97.33) Punjab (79.18) Gujarat (77.03) Haryana (75.45) Chhattisgarh7 (3.43)	Telangana (68.05) Jharkhand (67.24) West Bengal (64.95) Odisha (61.05) MadhyaPradesh (60.69) Bihar (51.58)

Source: Author's Construct.

crucial when earmarking resources. Gujarat performance even if average at education expenditure adequacy becomes poor when it comes to performance of outcome indicators. This flags the serious concern in the area of adequacy of expenditures and its utilisation in realising the education outcomes. Finally, we take the average of the adequacy and effectiveness index and derive the education quality index. Gujarat falls under the category of average performers.

Now putting the education quality and economic growth together in Figure 7, we observe some neat and interesting patterns. Most of the states which perform below average on education quality index also have relatively less GSDP per capita. For e.g. states like Bihar, UP, MP, Jharkhand, Chhattisgarh, West Bengal, Rajasthan and Odisha fall in the quadrant of low educational quality and low economic growth. Whereas, states like Kerala, Tamil Nadu, Karnataka, Andhra Pradesh and Goa fall in the quadrant of high educational quality and high economic growth. This highlights the positive relationship between the educational quality and economic growth. But, Gujarat, Haryana, Punjab, Maharashtra and Telangana fall in the category of low or average educational quality but high economic growth. And interestingly, there is no state with high educational quality but low economic growth. At the risk of oversimplification, we can generalise

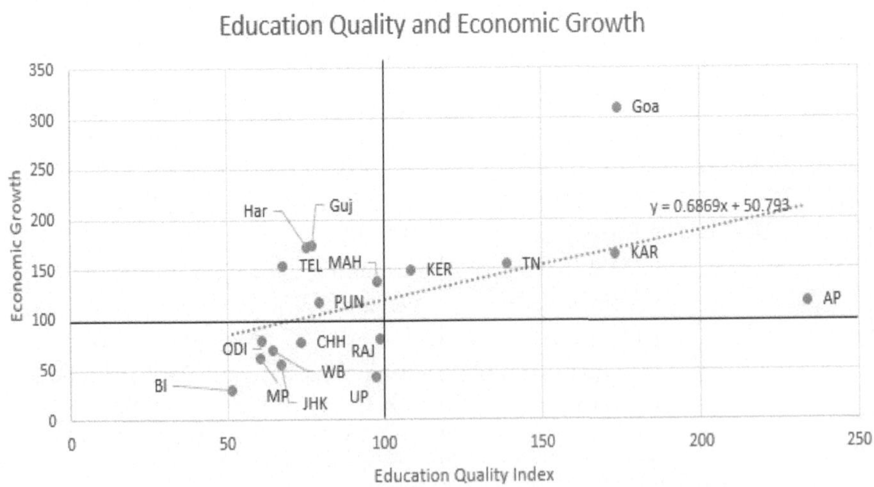

Figure 8: Quadrant Analysis of Major Indian States for Relative Educational Quality and Economic Growth

with the quadrant analysis in Figure 7 that high economic growth is possible with or without high educational quality but high educational quality almost always leads to economic development which is more sustainable and holistic.

From Figure 8, where we put educational quality and social progress on scatter plot, we observe that, the states with high educational quality and high social progress are almost those same states, which had high economic growth corresponding to the high educational quality in Figure 7. In addition, the states, which had low economic growth and low educational quality, fall in the first quadrant of low educational quality and low social growth in Figure 8 as well. However, most interestingly states like Gujarat, Haryana, Maharahstra and Telangana, which were in the third quadrant of low educational quality but high economic growth, fall in the first quadrant of low social progress and low educational quality in Figure 8. This shows that educational quality is vital to achieve social progress.

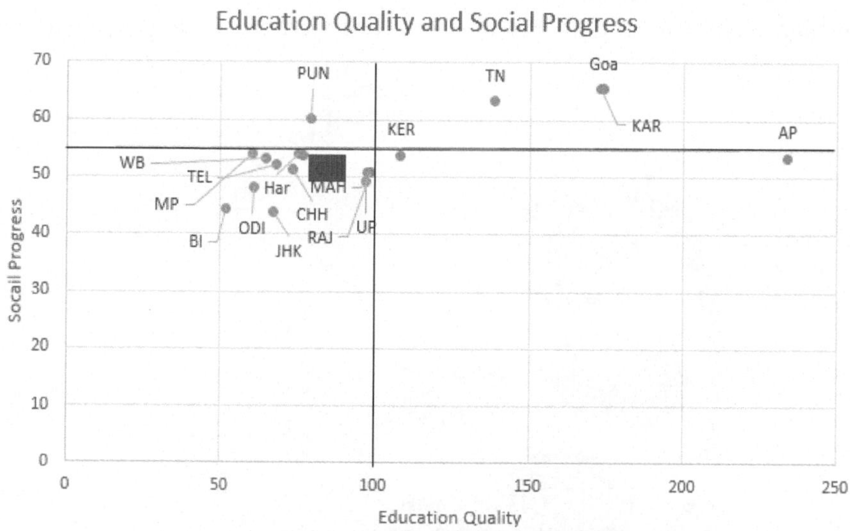

Figure 9: Quadrant Analysis of Major Indian States for Relative Educational Quality and Social Progress

Thus from the above exercise we conclude that on one hand Gujarat performs very well on employment quality and justifies the adjective "miraculous" which it has got for its growth model. But, on the other hand it performs below the national average in spending on education sector and is amongst the worst performers in the outcome indicators of the education sector measured by educational effectiveness index. This dismal performance of Gujarat is definitely not coordinated with its vision of economic growth and to an extent, explains the poor and mediocre performance of Gujarat on social progress index and HDI respectively.

CONCLUSION: GUJARAT WALKS HALF THE VIRTUOUS CYCLE

Drawing together the various threads of this paper, it is unequivocally evident that education is a linchpin for robust, sustainable, and inclusive economic development. Gujarat has achieved considerable success in terms of consistent high economic growth and high employment quality. However, Gujarat has only traversed half the path of the virtuous cycle of sustainable economic development (Figure 9) and half path is yet to be covered to enter into the sustainable spiral of high economic and social progress. The virtuous cycle proposes that

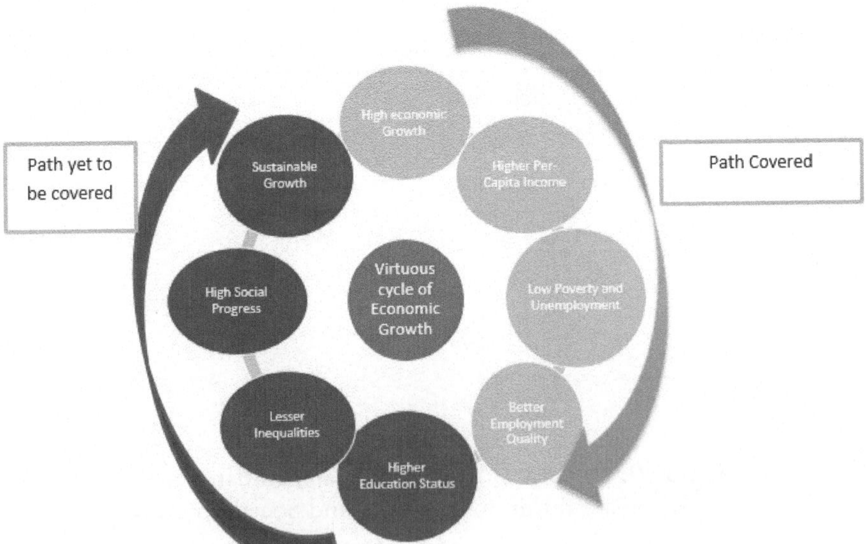

Figure 9: Gujarat's Journey on Virtuous Cycle of Sustainable Economic Growth

robust economic growth should be complemented by equally compelling human capital development, manifesting through quality education and healthcare.

Gujarat's impressive economic performance is laudable, but its modest and poor performance in education expenditure adequacy and effectiveness indices, respectively, indicate a missed opportunity to complete its virtuous growth trajectory. This explains well the dismal performance of Gujarat on social indicators. Hence, the state's lacklustre commitment to educational investment and ineffectiveness in utilizing existing educational resources inhibits the nurturing of a knowledge-based economy that thrives on innovation. To navigate through the remaining half of the virtuous cycle, the state must prioritize holistic educational reforms at all levels.

As a policy suggestion, implementing performance-based budgeting in the education sector could yield significant dividends. As Gujarat performs poor in educational adequacy and effectiveness index, this approach can improve the efficiency and effectiveness of spending, as resources are allocated based on demonstrable performance results rather than mere expenditure needs. By establishing clear performance targets, it allows for continuous learning and adaptation, which could optimize educational outcomes over time. In addition, in terms of education financing, reallocating around 6 percent of Gujarat's GSDP towards the education sector is suggested. These additional resources could be channeled towards enhancing the quality of education, expanding access especially for marginalized groups, improving school infrastructure, and augmenting teacher training and capacity. Furthermore, by strengthening the linkages between economic growth and the education sector, such a commitment could galvanize a virtuous cycle where more educated and skilled human resources contribute to higher productivity and sustained economic growth, with a portion of the growth dividends reinvested in further improving education and social progress. Hence, Gujarat's future development trajectory could be significantly enhanced by this strategic and forward-looking approach to education financing.

Further, the Gujarat Model hinges heavily on manufacturing and export-led growth. While these drivers undeniably fuel high economic growth rate, they somewhat neglect an equally important growth engine - innovation, a byproduct of robust higher education and research system. The pursuit of a revised Gujarat Model 2.0 could significantly benefit from channeling substantial investment towards higher education, research, and innovation. By infusing resources into these sectors, Gujarat could foster the development of a knowledge-based economy, wherein growth is fueled not merely by the production and export of goods but also by the creation and application of innovative ideas, processes, and technologies. In doing so, the state could also start developing a linkage with the social growth and education sector.

Gujarat Model 2.0, thus, should be one that embraces modern economic structures while still harnessing the region's manufacturing prowess. It should reflect a more balanced model of growth - one that is as focused on education and innovation as it is on traditional pillars of economic development. The new Gujarat model should demonstrate a seamless interplay between economic growth, education, research, innovation, and social development, making it more sustainable, inclusive, and resilient for the future.

REFERENCES

[1] Bagchi, A.K., Das, P. and Chattopadhyay, S.K. (2005). 'Growth and Structural Change in the Economy of Gujarat', *Economic and Political Weekly,* Vol. XL, No. 28, July.

[2] Banik, Arindam and Khatun, Rabia (2012). "Role of Knowledge in Supporting Growth across Indian States: A Co-Integration and Causality Approach", published by Modern Economy, Vol. 3, No. 3, 2012.

[4] Becker, Gray S. (1993). Human capital: A theoretical and empirical analysis with special reference to education, 3rd Edition. Chicago: University of Chicago Press.

[5] Bhirud, Vibha, Linkages between Economic Growth and Human Development: A Case Study of Gujarat (February 12, 2015). Bhirud, Vibha, Linkages between Economic Growth & Human Development: A Case Study of Gujarat (February 12, 2015) M.S. Gore Policy Evaluation Group., Available at SSRN: https://ssrn.com/abstract =2820248 or http://dx.doi.org/10.2139/ssrn.2820248

[6] Chadha, G.K. (2004). Human capital base of the Indian labour market: Identifying worry spots. *The Indian Journal of Labour Economics, 47*(1), 3–38.

[7] Dholakia, R. (2009). 'Regional Sources of Growth Acceleration in India', *IIMA Working Paper,* No. 2009-03-06.

[8] Dixit, A. (2014). 'A Balanced Critique of the Gujarat Growth Model', *Economic and Political Weekly,* Vol. XLIX, No. 39, pp. 30–33.

[9] Ghatak, M. and Roy, S. (2014). 'Did Gujarat's Growth Rate Accelerate under Modi?' Economic and Political Weekly, Vol. XLIX, No. 15, April, pp. 12–15.

[10] Hanushek, E.A. and Kimko, D.D. (2000). Schooling, labour force, quality and the growth of nations. *American Economic Review, 90*(5), 1184–1208.

[11] Hanushek, Eric A. and Ludger Woessmann (2007). "The Role of Education Quality for Economic Growth." Policy Research Working Paper No. 4122,World Bank, Washington, DC.

[12] Hirway, I., Shah, A. and Shah, G. (2014). *Growth or Development : Which Way is Gujarat Going?* New Delhi: Oxford University Press.

[13] Kannan, K.P. Growth without inclusion: the Gujarat 'model' for India's development exposed. *Ind. J. Labour Econ.* **58**, 653–676 (2015). https://doi.org/10.1007/s41027-016-0043-2

[14] Khare, M. (2019). Exploring the Relationship between Economic Growth, Employment and Education in Indian State in India's Social Sector and SDGs Problems and Prospects Edited by Rangachar Govinda, Poornima M. Routledge.

[15] Krueger, Alan and Lindhal, Mikael (2000). *Education for growth: Why and for whom?* Working paper 808. Princeton University, Department of Economics. Ministry of Human Resource Development, Government of India, Statistics of Higher and Technical Education 2009–10 (Provisional).

[16] Kingdon, Geeta and Soderbom, Mans (2007a). *Education, skills and labor market outcomes: Evidence from Ghana.* Background paper prepared for the World Bank study, *Linking Education Policy to Labor Market Outcomes.* Washington, DC: World Bank.

[17] Kingdon, Geeta and Soderbom, Mans (2007b). Education, skills and labor market outcomes: Evidence from Ghana. Background paper prepared for the World Bank study, Linking Education Policy to Labor Market Outcomes. Washington, DC, World Bank.

[18] Mathur, Ashok (1980). "Human Capital Spatial Disparities and Economic Development". *Manpower Journal,* 26 (3).

[19] Mayer-Foulkes, David (2007). "Human Development Traps and Economic Growth", in Guillem Meier; Gerald M. and Baldwin, Robert E, 1957. Economic Development: Theory, History and Policy. New York: John Willy & Sons.

[20] Mincer, J. (1974). Schooling, Experience and Earnings- New York: Columbia University Press.

[21] Morris, S. (2014). 'A Comparative Analysis of Gujarat's Economic Growth', in Hirway, I. Shah, A., and Shah, G. (eds.) *Growth or Development? Which way is Gujarat going?* New Delhi: Oxford University Press. pp. 20–81.

[22] Nurkse, Ragner (1953). Problems of Capital Formation in Underdeveloped Countries. New York; Oxford University Press.

[23] Panagariya, A. (2012). 'The Gujarat Miracle: There is no denying the major economic advances the state has made under Narendra Modi', *Times of India,* September 22nd. Accessed 11/3/15: http://timesof india.indiatimes.com/The-Gujarat-miracle-There-is-no-denying-the-major economic-advances-the-statehas-made-under-Narendra-Modi/

[24] Ranis, G. (2004). "Human Development and Economic Growth", Centre Discussion Paper No. 887, Economic Growth Centre, Yale University, USA.

[25] Ranis, G., Stewart, F. and Ramirez, A. (2000). "Economic Growth and Human Development", *World Development,* 28(2): 197–219.

[26] Schultz, T.W. (1963). The Economic Value of Education. New York: Columbia University Press.

[27] Soni, Dhaval and Jariwala, Vijay Sureshchandra, Social Expenditure and Economic Growth in Gujarat- Econometric Exploration (June 18, 2019). Available at SSRN: https://ssrn.com/abstract=3405962 or http://dx.doi.org/10.2139/ssrn.3405962

[28] The Economist (2015). 'The Gujarat model. How Modi-nomics was formed in one of India's most business friendly states', *The Economist Online.*

[29] Weil, D.N. (2004). *Economic Growth,* Boston: Addison Wesley.

APPENDIX

Calculating Education Quality Index

A. Education Expenditure Adequacy Index (EEAI)

Following are the steps involved in calculating the EEAI:

Step 1: We took the per capita expenditure for elementary, secondary and higher education sectors for selected State and average it over preceding and succeeding years (as per data availability) in order to avoid any sharp outliers. EEAI has been calculated for the period of 2019–2020.

Step 2: Each of the series was transformed by using the inverse of distance from the best performing State (indicated by c_{ij}, which was computed for each criteria indicator for each state). The rationale behind computing the inverse of this distance was that the closer a State was to the best-performing State (i.e., smaller the distance in the denominator) the higher would be the newly constructed series. Algebraically this could be expressed as:

$$c_{ij} = 1/(C^{*}_{ij} - C_{ij})$$

where,
i identifies the State; i =1…n

j identifies the two criteria indicators; j = 1, 2, 3 (*Note:* this refers to our three criteria: Elementary, Secondary and Higher Education.)

Cij* is the value of the indicator for the best performing State.

c_{ij} would then give the transformed series for the per capita expenditure across all the levels of education. Since the denominator of the equation above would be zero for the best performing State, it was given a notional number of inverse distance equal to that of the second-best state plus a bonus which was of the magnitude of the average inverse distance across States for that indicator.

Step 3: The aggregate performance indicator for each State i (P_{ij}) was obtained as an average of the three series.

$$P_{ij} = \frac{\sum_{j=1}^{3} c_{ij}}{3}$$

Step 4: The aggregate performance indicator was normalised with respect to the average for all States (denoted by eai_{ij}). Algebraically this would appear as:

$$eai_{ij} = \frac{P_{ij}}{\frac{\sum_{i=1}^{n} P_{ij}}{n}}$$

Step 5: The Expenditure Adequacy Index (EAIi) was obtained by setting the average of the normalised series to 100 (this is effectively scaling up by 100 as the average of the normalised series is unity) so that all the above-average States had an index greater than 100 and all the below average States had an index of less than 100.

$EAIi = eai_i * 100$

Table 5: Education Expenditure Adequacy Index and State Ranks

Major Indian States		
Rank	*States*	*EAI (2019–20)*
1	Andhra Pradesh	259.336
2	Goa	216.5049
3	Maharashtra	129.2081
4	Kerala	105.8513
5	Karnataka	104.7442
6	Haryana	103.2365
7	Chhattisgarh	99.29782
8	Gujarat	92.40062
9	Tamil Nadu	81.44189
10	Odisha	79.37341
11	Uttar Pradesh	73.7847

Major Indian States		
Rank	*States*	*EAI (2019–20)*
12	Madhya Pradesh	73.41363
13	Rajasthan	68.28409
14	Jharkhand	66.28638
15	Punjab	66.04602
16	West Bengal	62.53659
17	Bihar	59.56196
18	Telangana	58.69173
	Coefficient of Variation	0.5278

B . Effectiveness Index (EI)

Effectiveness refers to the extent to which the output of the service provided meets the objective sets. Thus, here the focus is shifted from inputs to output. The output indicators taken here are States' performance in National Achievement Survey (NAS) for the class III, V and VIII, transition rates from secondary to higher secondary and Gross Enrolment Ratio (GER) in higher education (overall, Schedule Cast (SC) and Schedule Tribes (ST)) (Table 6). The motive was to take one indicator each from elementary, secondary and higher education and to take such indicators that represent, learning outcomes and equity in access to education. The output indicators (like adequacy indicators) aim at providing the necessary condition for improving expenditure quality.

EI uses the specific output indicators of the states to analyse the performance of the states. It almost follows the same procedure as in the EAI except for one additional step. As two of the three criterion have more than one component, therefore component indicators need to be aggregated to obtain criterion indicators. These criterion indicators are further aggregated to obtain performance indicators and then the EI is calculated.

Table 6: Criteria and Components for Effectiveness Index

S. No.	*Criteria*	*Components*	*Data Source*
A	Elementary Education	Overall Achievement in class III, V and VIII	National Achievement Survey 2017
B	Secondary Education	Transition from secondary to higher	UDISE+ 2019–2020
C	Higher Education	GER (All Categories), GER SCs and STs	AISHE 2019–2020

Table 7: Education Expenditure Effectiveness Index and State Ranks

Non-Special Category States

Rank	*States*	*Effectiveness Index*
1	Karnataka	241.0746
2	Andhra Pradesh	208.1472
3	Tamil Nadu	196.0228
4	Goa	130.79
5	Rajasthan	128.9883
6	Uttar Pradesh	120.8913
7	Kerala	111.0356
8	Punjab	92.32017
9	Telangana	77.41478
10	Jharkhand	68.19948
11	West Bengal	67.36849
12	Maharashtra	66.51478
13	Gujarat	61.67499
14	Madhya Pradesh	47.97316
15	Haryana	47.67818
16	Chhattisgarh	47.58013
17	Bihar	43.59907
18	Odisha	42.7269
	Coefficient of Variation	0.5918

Now, the Education quality index is calculated taking the average of the adequacy and effectiveness index.

Rank	*State*	*Education Quality Index*
1	AP	233.7416
2	Goa	173.6475
3	KAR	172.9094
4	TN	138.7323
5	KER	108.4435
6	RAJ	98.6362
7	MAH	97.86144
8	UP	97.338
9	PUN	79.1831
10	Guj	77.03781
11	Har	75.45734
12	CHH	73.43898
13	TEL	68.05326
14	JHK	67.24293
15	WB	64.95254
16	ODI	61.05016
17	MP	60.6934
18	BI	51.58052

Seasonal Hostels: A Platform for Continuing Education in Dang

Naresh Chauhan[1] and Nasheman Bandookwala[2]

ABSTRACT: Economic hardship drives significant work-related migration from tribal areas in Gujarat, particularly impacting children. With limited childcare options, parents often take their children along, disrupting their education. These children either engage in unskilled labor or remain idle during the migration period, resulting in academic setbacks. The Sarva Shiksha Abhiyan's seasonal hostels provide a crucial intervention by ensuring educational continuity. These hostels, established in primary and upper-primary/secondary schools, allow children to remain in their communities while their families migrate. A study of 46 migrating families from three Dang district villages (Bhedun, Savarpada, and Govan), comprising 343 agricultural laborers and 124 casual laborers, demonstrates the effectiveness of seasonal hostels. They not only prevent educational disruption but also alleviate the financial burden on migrating families, which averages Rs. 6,000 to Rs. 7,000 per child for a 6–7-month migration period.

Keywords: *Seasonal Migration, Seasonal Hostels, UNICEF.*

PROLOGUE

Lack of employment opportunities in the rural surroundings of the districts of Dang has resulted in work related mass migration in or outside the state. Whilst intra- state migration is to, Surat, inter-state migration is to Maharashtra. The migrating families predominantly work as farm laborers in sugarcane and grape farms. These migrating laborers are mostly underpaid. Owing to their low income, it is difficult for them to shed extra penny and hence to have a facility-seasonal hostel, where their children can live is blessing in

[1] Assistant Professor, Department of Rural Economics, Gujarat Vidyapith, Ahmedabad, India.

[2] Assistant Professor, Department of Rural Economics, Gujarat Vidyapith, Ahmedabad, India.

disguise. The present study evaluates how seasonal hostels have lessened the financial burden of these families. The sample studied here is 46 migrating laborers, of whom 12 work as casual laborers and the remaining 34 as agriculture laborers.

GEOGRAPHICAL LOCATION OF SERVED VILLAGES IN THE DISTRICT OF THE DANG IN GUJARAT

OBJECTIVES

1. To evaluate the income of migrating laborers.
2. To evaluate expenses of migrating laborers.
3. To analyses the role of seasonal hostels.

THEORETICAL REVIEWS

'**Falling through cracks:** Children of seasonal migrants' is the sad chronicle of Sabuddin with his five children and Shivam a 10-year-old boy who wants to go back to school but is temporarily out of school due to his family's distress migration. The report discusses the problems faced by these children during their migration a and how a seasonal hostel has proved to be a blessing for them.

Raashid Shah, in his commentary "Seasonal Migration and Children's Education in India," discusses how children of migrants are left behind and intervention of state. He has emphasized that SamagraShiksha Abhiyan has evaluated the problems faced by children of migrants. The framework lays down provisions for seasonal hostels in source villages and schools at destination sites in addition to exploring the possibility of involving teaching volunteers. Furthermore, states like Gujarat and Maharashtra have also stepped in by creating seasonal boarding schools for migrant children, and engaging volunteers to provide after-school psychosocial support to leftbehind children. The report further emphasizes the problem of dialect at the site and the importance of appointing teachers that speak the mother tongue of migrant children. The Migrant Card initiative by the state of Gujarat has been incorporated in the study; it helps the state in monitoring interstate and intrastate migration and school dropouts. The recommendations in terms of school curriculum and bridge course are also included in the study, which makes it quite robust.

Understanding the community: The life in a seasonal hostel is interesting and robust study of seasonal hostels of migrant laborers in Odisha. The study covers the temporary as well as frequent groups of migrating laborers and their impact on the education of their children. Most importantly, it also examines life of children is seasonal hostels while their parents migrate to other states or different districts within of the same state.

Improving social protection probability for migrant-affected children by UNICEF is an interesting report examining the cause and impact of migration on children and evaluating various programs and policies for the social protection to the children of migrant laborers in Odisha. The report is a robust study of in and out migration of Odisha. The single and family migration in the state of Odisha is studied in the report and it is reported that single migration is for a longer period than family migration. Also, type of work and migration is dealt with in detail in the study.

Documentation of Seasonal Hostel in Kurnool district of Andhra Pradeshexamines and explains the concept and design of Seasonal hostels, along with feedback from children staying in them.

INCOME LEVELS OF MIGRATING LABORS

The survey was carried out for 46 migrating laborers; it is concluded that most of them live in fierce poverty. Out of 34 agricultural laborers 85.30% earn less than Rs. 7000 per month. While 50% of casual labourers earn less than Rs. 7000 per month (Table 1). This certainly indicates that the migrating laborers are poor and mostly live below the poverty line. Only 14.70% of agricultural labor earns more than Rs. 7000 to Rs. 10000 per month while 50% of casual labor earns more than Rs. 7000 to Rs. 10000 per month. During field work, it was observed that compared to other districts of Gujarat Dang has a high incidence of poverty.

Table 1: Income Levels of Migrating Laborers

Type of Work	*Upto Rs. 5000*	*From Rs. 5000 to Rs. 7000*	*From Rs. 7000 to Rs. 10000*	*Total*
Agriculture	13	16	5	34
Percentage	38.20%	47.10%	14.70%	100.00%
Casual Labor	1	5	6	12
Percentage	8.30%	41.70%	50.00%	100.00%
Total	**14**	**21**	**11**	**46**
	30.40%	**45.70%**	**23.90%**	**100.00%**

Source: Field work.

The wealth of the respondents is low. Owing to their low income and limited assets, these agricultural and causal laborers lead difficult lives. Of total respondents 56% of respondents reported wealth of maximum 2 lakhs whilst only 4.5% of the respondents reported wealth of 2.5 lakhs. This shows that selected sample of 46 respondents belongs to low level of income. Income earned during entire migration as reported by respondents is between Rs. 25000 to Rs. 75000. The various in income is due to females with young children working lesser hours and hence are paid less. The reported income is combined income earned by both the spouse in the entire seasons (6 to 7 months) Refer Table 2.

Table 2: Income Earned During Migration

Details	*Upto Rs. 25000*	*From Rs. 2500 1to Rs. 50000*	*From Rs. 50001 to Rs. 75000*	*Rs. 75001 and above*	*Total*
Agriculture Laborers	2	15	13	4	34
Percentage	5.90%	44.10%	38.20%	11.80%	100.00%
Casual laborers	0	3	6	3	12
Percentage	0.00%	25.00%	50.00%	25.00%	100.00%
Total	2	18	19	7	46
	4.30%	39.10%	41.30%	15.20%	100.00%

Source: Field work.

Work Hours of Migrating Labor

The migrating tribal laborers, whether in Maharashtra or other districts of Gujarat, work for predominantly 6 to 7 months. Field work data reveals that76% of respondents migrate to other districts of Gujarat and stay for 6 to 7 months, while 75% of laborers migrating to Maharashtra work for 4 months before returning to their native lands. The primary concern of the respondents was due to dearth of work in their own lands, forcing them to migrate. They expressed that if options of work are available or created locally, they would prefer to avoid migration. The issue needs to be addressed by the authorities.

Table 3: Details of Work Duration of Migrating Laborers

Details	*3 months or Less than that*	*4 months*	*5 mont hs*	*6 months*	*7 months*	*More than 8*	*Total*
Gujarat	0	2	2	15	11	4	34
Percentage	0.00%	5.90%	5.90%	44.10%	32.40%	11.80%	100.00%
Maharashtra	1	9	2	0	0	0	12
Percentage	8.30%	75.00%	16.70%	0.00%	0.00%	0.00%	100.00%
Total	1	11	4	15	11	4	46
	2.20%	23.90%	8.70%	32.60%	23.90%	8.70%	100.00%

Source: Field work.

Table 4: Number of Children in the Respondent Family

Details	*Number of Children 1*	*Number of Children 2*	*Number of Children 3*	*Number of Children 4*	*Number of Children 5*	*Number of Children 7/ More Than 7*	*Total*
Agriculture laborers	0	8	8	12	5	1	34
Percentage	0.00%	23.50%	23.50%	35.30%	14.70%	2.90%	100.00%
Casual laborers	1	2	5	1	2	1	12
Percentage	8.30%	16.70%	41.70%	8.30%	16.70%	8.30%	100.00%
Total	1	10	13	13	7	2	46
	2.20%	21.70%	28.30%	28.30%	15.20%	4.30%	100.00%

Source: Field work.

Table 4 indicates the number of children in families of respondents. Almost 73.7% of agricultural laborers have reported having 3 to 5 children while 66.70% of causal laborers have reported to have 3 to 5 children. In such scenario seasonal hostels provide an option for these children to stay in their own village and continue with their study as well as they are also provided with two square meal that suffice their living requisites. During the study it has been found that all the respondents leave their children studying in schools or colleges in seasonal hostel while they move for work to other state or districts.

Expenses on Children in Absence of Seasonal Hostel

The expenses on children rearing while they stay at home when parents are migrating comes to average Rs. 3000 to Rs. 5000 per child. It is evident that on an average the respondents have reported to have 3 to 4 children that comes to mean 3.5 children and hence expense will be approximately Rs. 14000 for the family.

The average income earned by migrating laborers is between Rs. 25000 to Rs. 50000 while average expenditure on children comes to Rs. 14000, which is approximately 28% of their total earnings. Hence seasonal hostels that provide stay as well as food to young ones of these laborers have saved 28% of their income.

Table 5: Expenses on Children While Parents are Migrating for Work

Details	*Upto Rs. 3000*	*Rs. 3000 to Rs. 4000*	*Rs. 4000 to Rs. 5000*	*Rs. 5000 to Rs. 6000*	*More than Rs. 7000*	*Total*
Agricultural labores	3	10	13	6	2	34
Percentage	8.80%	29.40%	38.20%	17.60%	5.90%	100.00%
Casual laborers	2	4	3	2	1	12
Percentage	16.70%	33.30%	25.00%	16.70%	8.30%	100.00%
Total	5	14	16	8	3	46
	10.90%	30.40%	34.80%	17.40%	6.50%	100.00%

Source: Field work.

Epilogue

The study carried out in the villages of Bhedun, Savarpada and Govan the Dang district has been an eye opener. The seasonal hostel facility provided by Sarva Shiksha Abhiyan to the children of migrating labor has proved to be a blessing for these poor laborers and their children. Firstly, children of these migrating laborers do not migrate with their parents and secondly and more importantly these children do not lose out son their education. The study has also tried to map the expenses of migrating laborers on children when they migrate. It has been concluded that the seasonal hostel facility has saved approximately 28% of income. Thus, in a way it is dual benefit for laborers. It is proposed that such facilities should be extended to more such villages where migration is rampant. The present study suggests that this initiative should be replicated in more areas where migration is rampant as it is home away from home for many children of migrating families. Owing to differences in caste and creed of migrating laborers and managing authorities (Gam Panchayat) many villages have reported that such applications have not been initiated and their children have remained deprived of such facilities.

REFERENCES

[1] https://samagrashiksha.ssagujarat.org/SuccessStories/Seasonal-hostel.pdf

[2] https://aif.org/understanding-the-community-life-at-a-seasonal-hostel/

[3] https://www.thehindu.com/news/cities/Vijayawada/Seasonal-hostels-for-children-of-migrants/article16365134.ece

[4] https://www.indiatoday.in/education-today/news/story/closure-of-seasonal-hostels-migrant-children-work-as-daily-wage-laborers-1832875-2021-07-26

[5] https://www.newindianexpress.com/states/andhra-pradesh/2020/nov/16/70-seasonal-hostels-for-kids-of-migrants-in-prakasam-2224094.html

[6] https://www.villagesquare.in/closure-of-seasonal-hostels-leaves-migrants-children-in-the-lurch/

[7] https://www.apteachers.in/2013/10/rc907-rvm-guidelines-to-run-seasonal.html

[8] https://timesofindia.indiatimes.com/education/news/surprise-checking-of-seasonal-hostels-meant-for-imparting-education-to-children-of-rural-labourers/articleshow

[9] https://repository.education.gov.in/wp-content/uploads/2017/07/seasonal-hostels-for-migrant-children-in-odisha.pdf

[10] https://www.indiaspend.com/development/falling-through-the-cracks-children-of-seasonal-migrants-858865

[11] https://sprf.in/wp-content/uploads/2021/07/SPRF-2021_Comm_Seasonal-Migration_Final.pdf

[12] https://cprindia.006Frg/wp-content/uploads/2022/02/Odisha-unicef.pdf

Impact of Public Health Programs on Maternal and Child Health in Gujarat

Mitulkumar Chaudhari[1] **and T. Shukkoor**[2]

ABSTRACT: Using NFHS-5 data, this study analyses the effectiveness of Gujarat's public health programs on maternal and child health outcomes. It examines the influence of these programs on key health indicators, including maternal mortality, care, anemia, institutional deliveries, and child health outcomes related to vaccination, nutrition, and pediatric services. While programs like Chiranjeevi Yojana, JSY, Mukhyamantri Matru Shakti Yojana, and Pradhan Mantri Matru Vandana Yojana have improved institutional deliveries and antenatal/postnatal care, significant challenges remain. High maternal mortality and widespread anemia in pregnant women persist, and despite programs like KPSY, Poshan Abhiyan, Matritva Sahyog Yojana, and ICDS, child malnutrition and anemia continue to be problematic. The study recommends ongoing monitoring and improved program implementation to address these persistent issues.

Keywords: *Public Health Programs, Maternal and Child Health, Gujarat, National Family Health Survey (NFHS-5), Malnutrition, Maternal Mortality Rates.*

---

[1] PhD Scholar of Sociology Discipline, Department of Humanities and Social Sciences Institute of Infrastructure, Technology, Research and Management (IITRAM), Ahmedabad, Gujarat, India. E-mail: mitchaudhary512@gmail.com

[2] Assistant Professor of Sociology, Department of Humanities and Social Sciences, Institute of Infrastructure, Technology, Research And Management (IITRAM), Ahmedabad, Gujarat, India. E-mail: shukkoort@iitram.ac.in

INTRODUCTION

Promoting the health of mothers and children and addressing nutritional issues is a critical objective for any country, especially in India, which has the highest global rates of maternal, newborn, and child mortality (Paul et al., 2011). To address these challenges, the Indian government and state authorities have launched several public health initiatives and schemes. One such initiative, the Maternal and Child Health (MCH) program, was introduced in the 1970s to prevent maternal and child deaths, particularly those that could be avoided through vaccination.

In 2013, the government implemented the Reproductive, Maternal, Newborn, Child, and Adolescent Health (RMNCH+A) framework to address major causes of mortality and illness among women and children, and to overcome obstacles that delay access to healthcare services. In line with the RMNCH+A framework, several programs such as Janani Shishu Suraksha Karyakaram (JSSK), Rashtriya Kishor Swasthya Karyakram (RKSK), Rashtriya Bal Swasthya Karyakram (RBSK), Universal Immunisation Programme, Chiranjeevi Yojana, Mission Indradhanush (MI), Janani Suraksha Yojana (JSY), Pradhan Mantri Surakshit Matritva Abhiyan (PMSMA), Navjaat Shishu Suraksha Karyakram (NSSK), and National Programme for Family Planning have been introduced by both central and state governments (source: https://pib.gov.in/pressreleaseshare.aspx?prid=1576128). As a result, there has been a steady decrease in fertility rates, maternal, infant, and child mortalities, and a reduction in the prevalence of severe nutritional deficiencies across the country. However, significant regional disparities in maternal healthcare coverage continue to exist across the country, influenced by cultural norms, socio-economic status, and awareness of the importance of maternal healthcare (Arokiasamy & Pradhan, 2013).

Several studies have examined the progress of maternal and child health development in Gujarat, focusing on state-initiated programs, challenges faced, and efforts to promote institutional delivery, vaccination, and address malnutrition and anemia among children (Soni *et al.*, 2023; Patel *et al.*, 2020; Rana *et al.*, 2019; Iyer *et al.*, 2017;

Sanneving *et al.*, 2013; Vora *et al.*, 2009; Mavalankar *et al.*, 2009; Bhat *et al.*, 2009). Soni *et al.* (2023) argue that despite the implementation of various public health programs and schemes, Gujarat has not fully leveraged the potential of these initiatives for maternal and child development, particularly in addressing malnutrition and anemia. In identifying barriers to reducing the maternal mortality ratio in Gujarat, Mavalankar *et al.* (2009) highlighted deficiencies in managerial expertise and a shortage of skilled human resources. Apart from studies by Soni *et al.* (2023) and Puranik and Shreya (2021), there is a limited number of studies specifically exploring maternal and child health development in Gujarat using data from the NFHS-5. While Soni *et al.* (2023) examined trends in nutritional outcomes, Puranik and Shreya (2021) focused on childhood anemia clusters across India, with Gujarat being a significant contributor to the prevalence of anemia. Most studies analyzing the impact of public health programs on maternal health in Gujarat have focused on the Chiranjeevi Yojana initiative and its effects on institutional delivery and neonatal care (Mohanan *et al.*, 2013; Iyer *et al.*, 2017; Ng *et al.*, 2013; Ganguly *et al.*, 2014; Vora *et al.*, 2015; Sidney *et al.*, 2016; Yasobant *et al.*, 2016; Yasobant *et al.*, 2017). Consequently, the existing literature underscores the need for further investigation to better understand the broader impact of public health programs on maternal and child health in Gujarat, particularly with reference to the most recent NFHS-5 report.

RESEARCH OBJECTIVES

1. To comprehend the public health programmes in Gujarat that are aimed at enhancing the health of mothers and children.
2. To evaluate the influence of public health initiatives on maternal health in Gujarat, with a focus on metrics such as maternal mortality rates, prenatal and postnatal care, anaemia during pregnancy, and institutional deliveries.
3. To assess the efficacy of public health initiatives aimed at child health development, including vaccination campaigns, nutrition programs, and paediatric health services, in improving child health outcomes.

The study utilized data from the National Family Health Survey (NFHS-5, 2019–20) for Gujarat. It examines key maternal and child health indicators as well as the coverage of healthcare programs.

Healthcare Programmes for Maternal and Child Health in Gujarat

The overall health status of a society is largely reflected in the condition of maternal and child health (MCH), which serves as an indicator of the efficacy of healthcare programs and interventions. The coverage of maternal healthcare services significantly influences maternal, neonatal, and infant mortality rates, as well as health complications during maternity (Navaneetham & Dharmalingam, 2000).

Gujarat has been proactive in implementing a range of healthcare initiatives aimed at enhancing the health of mothers and children. These initiatives, funded either solely by the state government or with support from the Central government, form a comprehensive strategy to foster a conducive environment for maternal and child health. A detailed understanding of these programs is crucial for formulating policies and interventions that can further enhance the overall health of the population in Gujarat. Key programs implemented in the state to bolster maternal and child health include:

1. **Chiranjeevi Yojana:** Promotes institutional deliveries and ensures safe childbirth through a Public-Private Partnership with private obstetricians.
2. **Poshan Abhiyan:** A holistic program that uses technology and community involvement to fight malnutrition in children, pregnant women, and lactating mothers.
3. **Mission Indradhanush:** A catch-up campaign under the Universal Immunization Program, aiming for complete immunization coverage for children and pregnant women.
4. **Janani Suraksha Yojana (JSY):** A centrally sponsored scheme aimed at reducing maternal and neonatal mortality by promoting institutional delivery among economically disadvantaged pregnant women.
5. **Janani Shishu Suraksha Karyakram (JSSK):** Offers financial support for maternal and child healthcare services, ensuring free

and cashless services for pregnant women, including delivery, newborn care, and postnatal care.

6. **Mukhyamantri Matru Shakti Yojana:** Initiated in 2022, it focuses on the health of pregnant and lactating women, providing nutritious food during the initial 1000 days.
7. **Mukhyamantri Poshan Sudha Yojana:** Strives to enhance nutritional and health status by providing nutritious food to pregnant and lactating mothers in tribal areas.
8. **Kasturba Poshan Sahay Yojana (KPSY):** A cash transfer scheme supporting Below Poverty Line (BPL) mothers during pregnancy, ensuring access to nutritious food and micronutrient supplements.
9. **Pradhan Mantri Matru Vandana Yojana:** Offers a cash incentive to pregnant women and lactating mothers, promoting maternal and child health.
10. **Integrated Child Development Services (ICDS):** Launched on October 2, 1975, as part of the National Policy for Children, aiming to comprehensively address the development needs of children.
11. **Kuposhan Mukt Gujarat Maha-Abhiyan:** In response to the rising rates of childhood wasting, the Government of Gujarat launched the Kuposhan Mukt Gujarat Maha-Abhiyan (KMGA) in 2015 as part of its Community-Based Management of Acute Malnutrition (CMAM) program.

Exploring Maternal and Child Health Development in Gujarat: Insights from NFHS-5

The NFHS, a comprehensive and regular survey conducted in India, explores multiple aspects of households, providing abundant information on Fertility, Infant and Child Mortality, Family Planning Practices, Maternal and Child Health, Reproductive Health, Nutrition, and Anaemia. Since 1992, NFHS has consistently served as a dependable source for nationwide maternal health indicators (Raj and Gupta, 2022). The most recent NFHS report (NFHS-5) for Gujarat highlights essential dimensions of maternal and child health within the state.

Maternal Health: Ensuring access to high-quality maternal healthcare is essential for diminishing maternal mortality rates and averting complications during pregnancy and childbirth. As per NFHS-5 data, in Gujarat, over 90% of mothers received antenatal care, and 94% of births took place in healthcare facilities.

Antenatal Care: Nearly four-fifths of mothers in Gujarat (77%) had at least four antenatal care visits. However, there is variation across districts. Navasari, Rajkot, Surat, Amreli, and Valsad districts reported good ANC coverage ranging from 94 to 93; while Banaskantha, Mahesana, Surendranagar, Kheda, Anand, Bharuch and Vadodara districts reported relatively poor ANC coverage ranging from 56 to 66.

Delivery Care: The majority, or 94%, of births in Gujarat occur in healthcare facilities, predominantly in government facilities, with the remaining 6% taking place at home. Institutional births are more common among women who have undergone antenatal checks, those with higher education levels, first-time mothers, and urban residents.

Postnatal Care: In Gujarat, 94% of mothers underwent a postnatal check following their latest childbirth, with 91% receiving the check within two days. Nevertheless, only 39% of home births underwent a health check in the initial two days post-delivery.

Maternal Mortality Rate: MMR is defined as the number of maternal deaths per 100,000 live births resulting from pregnancy or abortion.

The MMR in Gujarat decreased from 87 in Sample Registration System (SRS) 2015–17 to 57 in SRS 2018–2021. This is a significant improvement, and Gujarat is one of the eight states that have already achieved the Sustainable Development Goal of reducing MMR to less than 70 per lakh live births by 2030.

Anaemia: As per the NFHS-5 (2019-20) report, 62.6% of women aged 15-49 who are pregnant are found to be anaemic. This marks an increase from the rate of 51.3% reported in the NFHS-4 (2015-16) findings.

Child Health: The Child Health program combines interventions within the framework of the Reproductive, Maternal, Newborn, Child, and Adolescent Health (RMNCH+A) strategy of the National Health Mission (NHM). Its primary emphasis is on enhancing the health and nutrition status of children.

Vaccination of Children: The importance of vaccination as a cost-effective and safe method for primary prevention highlights its significance in the domain of maternal and child healthcare indicators. Full vaccination coverage for children aged 12–23 months has increased from 78.9% (NFHS 4) to 85% (NFHS 5). Noteworthy is that 95% of children have received the BCG vaccination.

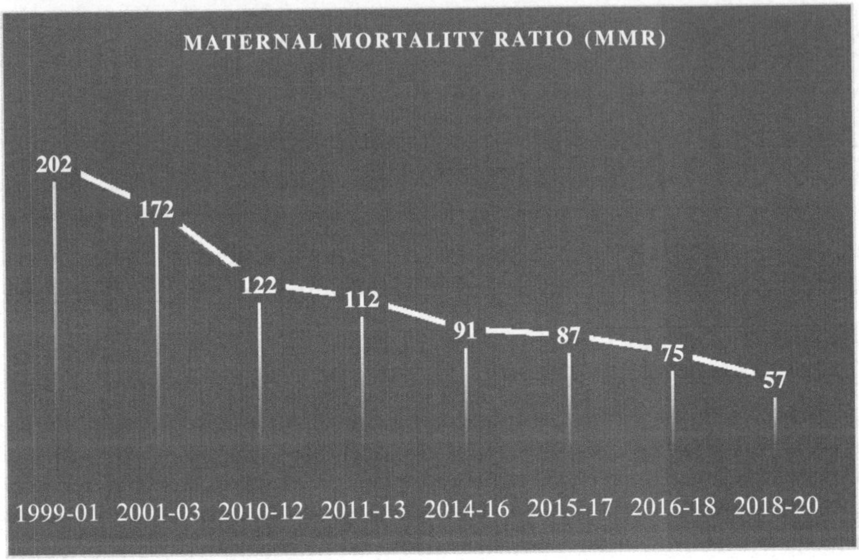

Source: Sample Registration System (SRS).

Infant Mortality: The infant mortality rate in the state fell from 34.2 deaths (before the age of one year) per 1,000 live births to 31.2 deaths between NFHS-4 and NFHS-5.

Under-five mortality Rate: It reduced from 43.5 deaths (before the age of five years) per 1,000 live births to 37.6 deaths per 1,000 live births.

Breastfeeding of Infants: The proportion of children under six months exclusively breastfed has risen from 55.8% (NFHS 4) to 65 % (NFHS-4). Children's Nutritional Status.

NFHS-5 discloses troubling statistics for children under the age of five in Gujarat, indicating that 39% are stunted (too short for their age), 25% are wasted (too thin for their height, and 11% are underweight. Even during the initial six months of life when breastfeeding is predominant, 27% of children experience stunting.

Anaemia: NFHS 5 reports says that an increase in childhood anaemia from 62.6% (NFHS 4) to 79.7% in children aged 6–59 months.

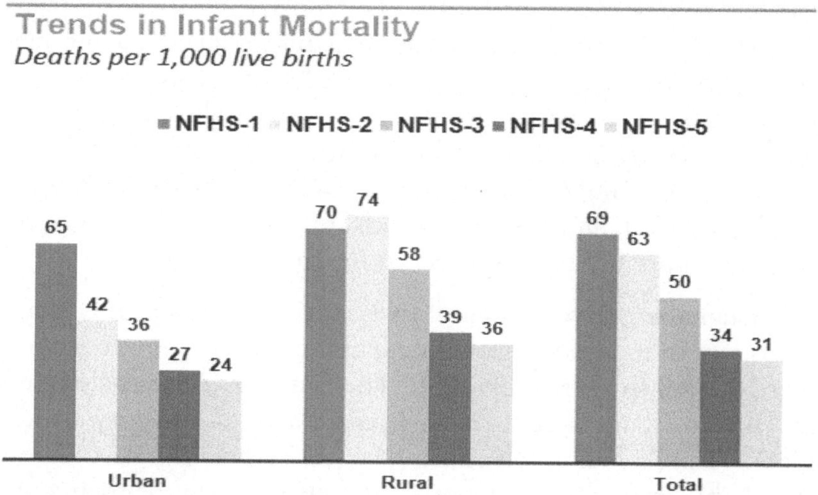

Source: NFHS 5.

Analysing Public Health Programs and Maternal-Child Health Progress in Gujarat

A health intervention involves activities or strategies aimed at assessing, improving, maintaining, promoting, or modifying health in individuals or populations. Health interventions, as defined by Clarke *et al.* (2019), have played a crucial role in India, particularly in enhancing maternal and child health.

The National Health Programme, initiated in India in 2013, has been instrumental in ensuring the quality of maternal healthcare, although there remains substantial room for improvement (Nair & Panda, 2011). The National Health Mission's (NHM) focus on Reproductive, Maternal, Newborn, Child, and Adolescent Health (RMNCH+A) underscores the significance of public health programs. Since 2005, India has witnessed a remarkable 77% reduction in maternal mortality, surpassing the global average reduction of 43% (Bhatia *et al.*, 2021). However, variations exist within the state and between different states in the country. According to Paul *et al.* (2011), potential reasons for these trends include social inequities, differences in healthcare systems both among and within states, and the consequences of urbanization and demographic transition.

Gujarat is among the eight Indian states that have already achieved the Sustainable Development Goals in reducing maternal mortality. According to the Ministry of Women and Child Development, the steps taken by the central government have facilitated remarkable progress in several states, including Kerala (19), Maharashtra (33), Telangana (43), Andhra Pradesh (45), Tamil Nadu (54), Jharkhand (56), Gujarat (57), and Karnataka with (69 with a significant decline in maternal mortality rate. It is shown in figure 1).

The Sustainable Development Goals (SDGs) set by the United Nations aim to reduce the global maternal mortality ratio to less than 70 per 100,000 live births by 2030. The fact that Gujarat, along with other Indian states like Kerala, Maharashtra, Telangana, Andhra Pradesh, Tamil Nadu, Jharkhand, and Karnataka, have already achieved this goal is a testament to the effectiveness of their public health initiatives.

It's important to continue these efforts and further strengthen healthcare infrastructure, enhance the quality of care, and ensure equitable access to health services to sustain and further improve these gains in maternal health. This will contribute significantly towards achieving the broader SDGs related to health and well-being.

Child Health: The Child Health program combines interventions within the framework of the Reproductive, Maternal, Newborn, Child, and Adolescent Health (RMNCH+A) strategy of the National Health Mission (NHM).

Its primary emphasis is on enhancing the health and nutrition condition of children.

Vaccination of Children: The importance of vaccination as a cost-effective and safe method for primary prevention highlights its significance in the domain of maternal and child healthcare indicators. Full vaccination coverage for children aged 12–23 months has increased from 78.9% (NFHS 4) to 85% (NFHS 5). Noteworthy is that 95% of children have received the BCG vaccination.

Breastfeeding of Infants: The proportion of children under six months exclusively breastfed has risen from 55.8% (NFHS 4) to 65 % (NFHS-4).

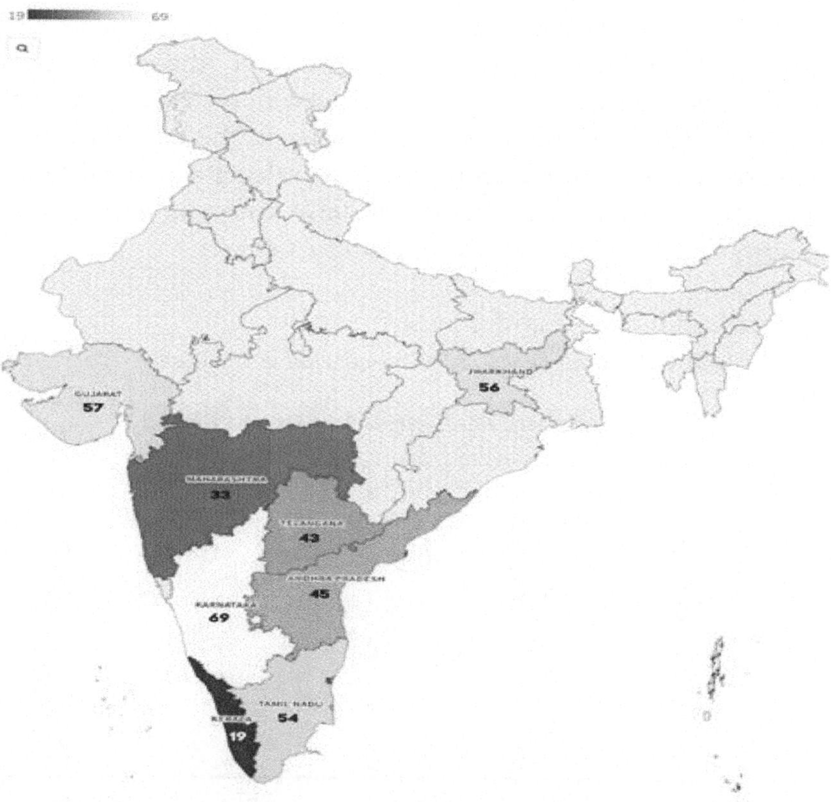

Source: Press Information Bureau, Government of India. https://pib.gov.in/FeaturesDeatils.aspx?Noteld=151238&Moduleld%20=%202

Children's Nutritional Status: NFHS-5 discloses troubling statistics for children under the age of five in Gujarat, indicating that 39% are stunted, 25% are wasted, and 11% are underweight. Even during the initial six months of life when breastfeeding is predominant, 27% of children experience stunting.

Anaemia: NFHS 5 reports suggest an increase in childhood anaemia from 62.6% (NFHS 4) to 79.7% in children aged 6–59 months.

As outlined in the Health Dossier 2021 for Gujarat by the National Health System Resource Centre, key indicators such as Antenatal care (ANC), institutional deliveries, C-sections, distribution of IFA tablets, follow-up of high- risk pregnancies, and provision of postnatal and newborn care have demonstrated substantial improvement since 2005, based on NFHS 4 & 5 data. However, the prevalence of anaemia in women aged 15–49 years has seen an increase from 56.5% (NFHS 4) to 69% (NFHS 5), with females in the reproductive age group experiencing more than twice the prevalence compared to men of a similar age group. (*Health Dossier 2021: Reflections on Key Health Indicators | National Health Systems Resource Centre.*)

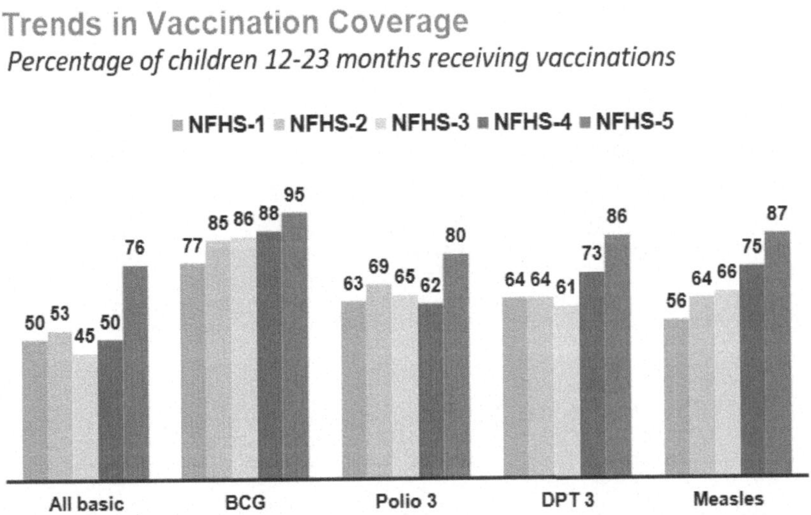

Source: NFHS 5.

Regarding the child health of the state, Gujarat has witnessed a noteworthy decline in Infant Mortality Rate (IMR) from 54 (2005) to 25 (2019). The improvement in these indicators can be attributed to various interventions at the state level, including infrastructure strengthening under the National Health Mission (NHM). NFHS 5 reports an increase in childhood anaemia from 62.6% (NFHS 4) to 79.7% in children aged 6–59 months.

NFHS-5 data indicates positive strides in child vaccination rates in Gujarat, reflecting increased coverage for various vaccines compared to NFHS-4. According to NFHS-5, more than three-quarters of children aged 12–23 months in Gujarat have received all basic vaccinations, with 96% being partially vaccinated. The improvement in child vaccination rates in Gujarat can be attributed to the nationwide efforts through Mission Indradhanush, showcasing the impact of enhanced vaccination strategies. A study by Bhatnagar *et al.* (2016) on child vaccination coverage in India since 2000 highlights improved routine vaccination services across all states of India. Parmar *et al.* (2020) conducted a study in the tribal Narmada district of Gujarat, revealing an elevated vaccination rate, particularly for DPT and BCG. Despite these gains, challenges persist, particularly in addressing anaemia and child nutrition. Programs like Poshan Abhiyan, Matritva Sahyog Yojana, and ICDS, as indicated by Chudasama *et al.* (2016), have not significantly improved the nutritional status of pregnant women or children in Gujarat, highlighting the need for targeted interventions and continuous monitoring.

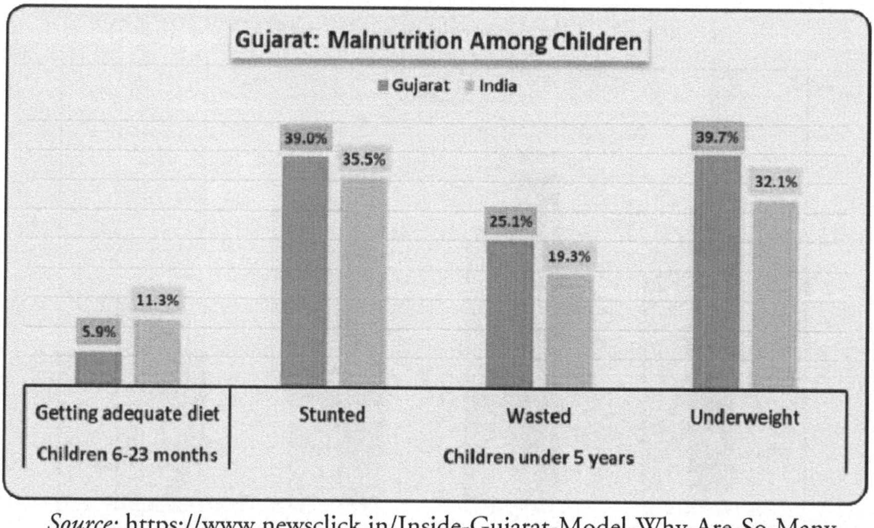

Source: https://www.newsclick.in/Inside-Gujarat-Model-Why-Are-So-Many-Children-Undernourished

The well-being of children under five is assessed through indicators such as stunting, wasting, underweight, and overweight. While overweight cases have increased, stunting, severe wasting, and underweight percentages have shown marginal shifts. In Gujarat, 39% of children under 5 are stunted, 25.15% are wasted, and 39.7% are underweight. Regions like Dahod, Tapi, and Panchmahal are severely affected, demanding targeted interventions despite the state government's acknowledgment of malnourished children and commitment to improvement. Gujarat ranks fourth in stunting and second worst in wasting among major states, experiencing sharper increases in malnutrition compared to tribal districts. NFHS-5 data reveals that over 9.7% of children under five years in Gujarat are underweight, with a significant increase in anaemia prevalence across demographic groups, particularly in urban districts like Ahmedabad, Surat, Vadodara, and Rajkot.

The National Family Health Survey (NFHS-5) 2019-21 reports an increase in childhood anaemia from 62.6% (NFHS 4) to 79.7% in children aged 6–59 months. It shows that despite numerous schemes and policies, Gujarat has yet to fully harness the potential of mandated policies to exhibit significant results in malnutrition and anaemia.

Maternal and Child Anaemia in Gujarat (NFHS 4 and 5)

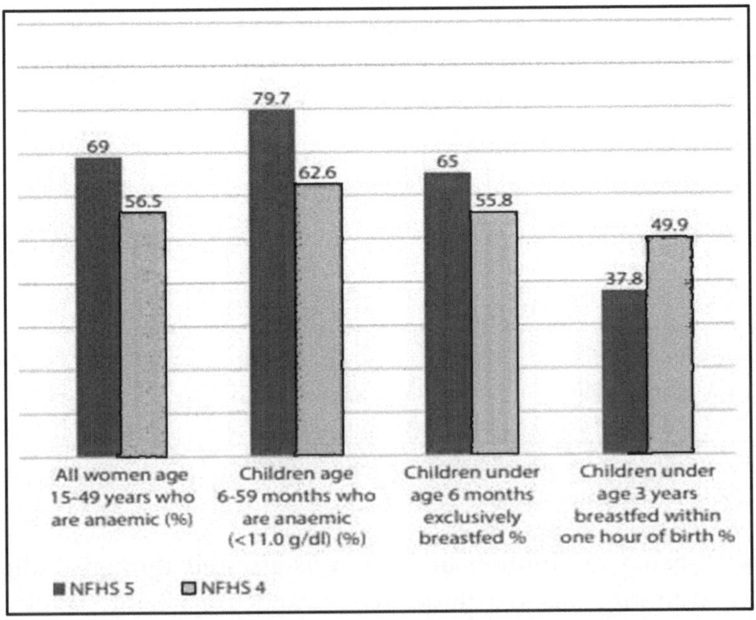

RESULTS AND DISCUSSION

Despite the implementation of various schemes and policies, Gujarat faces challenges in fully realizing the potential of health initiatives for maternal and child development. Malnutrition persists as a global public health issue, and Gujarat is among the states grappling with the complexities of addressing it. NFHS 5 reports an increase in childhood anaemia from 62.6% (NFHS 4) to 79.7% in children aged 6–59 months. A study by S.K. Singh *et al.* (2023) notes a notable reversal in the trend of anaemia prevalence among children under five in recent years. Pooja and Guddattu (2022) reveal in their study that approximately 33.56% of children in India are stunted, with high spatial disparity among districts. Another study based on NFHS-4 and 5 data by Soni *et al.* (2023) suggests that despite numerous schemes and policies, Gujarat has yet to fully harness the potential of mandated policies to exhibit significant results in malnutrition and anaemia. This study observes that every fourth child was thin for their age in Bihar, Gujarat, and Maharashtra. Spatial data analytics used by Puranik and Shreya (2012) identified clusters of childhood anaemia and its correlated factors across districts in India, revealing three significant local spatial clusters of anaemia, with Gujarat being a predominant cluster influencing anaemia prevalence.

In response to this pressing issue, the state government launched the Gujarat Health and Nutrition Mission, led by the Chief Secretary, with the ambitious goal of halving these indicators by 2029. The Action Plan outlines specific targets, including reducing Infant Mortality Rate (IMR) from 23 to 12 per 1,000 live births, Maternal Mortality Ratio (MMR) from 57 to 27 per 100,000 live births, stunting from 39% to 18%, wasting from 25% to 12%, and decreasing anaemia prevalence in women from 55% to 30%.

The nutritional status of children in Gujarat has seen minimal change since the National Family Health Survey (NFHS-4). The proportion of stunted children has remained steady at 39% over the four-year period between NFHS-4 and NFHS-5. The percentage of underweight children has only slightly increased from 39% to 40%, while the rate of wasted children has marginally declined from 26% to 25%. Despite these small shifts, the persistently high levels of undernutrition continues to pose a significant challenge in Gujarat. As part of the Community-Based Management of Acute Malnutrition (CMAM), the Government of Gujarat has rolled out several initiatives aimed at addressing malnutrition, including the Kuposhan Mukt Gujarat Maha Abhiyaan. This comprehensive campaign is designed to target all districts and municipal corporations within the state, with the goal of significantly reducing malnutrition rates and improving overall child health. Despite these well-intentioned efforts, the implementation of these schemes faces several challenges. Cultural practices in some communities may affect dietary habits and perceptions of nutrition, which can hinder the effectiveness of nutritional interventions (Patel *et al.*, 2020). Additionally, there is often limited awareness about the importance of proper nutrition and available resources, which further impedes progress. Economic constraints also play a crucial role, as low family incomes can restrict access to nutritious food and essential health services. These factors collectively create hurdles that complicate the successful execution of the Kuposhan Mukt Gujarat Maha Abhiyaan in certain districts. Addressing these challenges requires targeted strategies that account for local cultural contexts, enhance awareness through education and outreach, and provide support to families in need to overcome financial barriers to better nutrition.

Examining the implementation of maternal health policies in Gujarat, Sanneving *et al.* (2013) identified three prominent themes for poor maternal and child health: lack of continuity, complexity of coordination, and the absence of confidence leading to underutilization of the monitoring system. The decisions and actions were found to rely more on individual actors than sustainable structures. Mavalankar *et al.* (2009) pinpointed obstacles in reducing the maternal mortality ratio in Gujarat, including deficiencies in managerial expertise, scarcity of skilled human resources, unavailability of blood in rural regions, and infrastructure and supplies impediments. Manna *et al.* (2022) observe that the low socio-economic status of tribals reflected in their maternal health, especially in the low registration of pregnancies among tribals. Patel *et al.* (2020) emphasized the empowerment of mothers as a crucial factor initiating a step-by-step transformation in community behaviour. Navaneetham and Dharmalingam's (2000) research on the utilization of maternal health care services in South India highlighted the significant role of health workers and community participation in rural areas in delivering antenatal care. Bhatia *et al.* (2021) suggested that pro-poor policies in India, along with community-level involvement, have positively contributed to improving the maternal and child health initiative of the state. Gujarat should also explore the potential of community involvement in healthcare delivery as experienced in Kerala for the WHO-promoted community-based model of palliative care.

One area where Gujarat should focus is on public spending on healthcare, especially the development of maternal, neonatal, and childcare. Despite being an economic powerhouse, Gujarat faces social challenges, as evident in its ranking in the Human Development Index (HDI). While ranking sixth in Total Government Health Expenditure (TGHE), its total health expenditure (THE) is only 1.8% of the state's GDP, lagging financially constrained states. Our study suggests that Gujarat should focus on public spending on healthcare, especially the development of maternal, neonatal, and childcare.

Investments in female education are indispensable for decreased rates of infant and child mortality and morbidity. Studies by Govindasamy & Ramesh (1997) and Kruk *et al.* (2007) emphasize the significance of female literacy in influencing antenatal care utilization and the presence of skilled birth attendants. Additionally, there is a need to emphasize women's education to empower them to make better dietary choices for themselves and their children. Technology-enabled maternal and child health development is also a potential and cost-effective method. As suggested by S.K. Singh *et al.* (2023), the present study also recommends that the state should urgently implement a stringent technology-based monitoring mechanism for the food supplementation program to reduce childhood anaemia levels. One such scheme is TeCHO+, implemented by the Health and Family Welfare Department of Gujarat in 2018 to enhance comprehensive primary healthcare services. Modi *et al.* (2020) highlighted the potential of the TeCHO+ scheme to reduce the infant mortality rate in Gujarat, especially in tribal regions. Saha *et al.* (2023) compared key program indicators before and after the launch of TeCHO+ for maternal and child health in Gujarat, concluding that it is cost-effective and could be considered for replication. However, Rahman *et al.* (2022) point out that while mHealth interventions impacted maternal health outcomes.

One study conducted in Gujarat (George *et al.*, 2018) emphasizes the role of community could enhance service utilization in resource-limited settings, their overall effectiveness remains uncertain. A study conducted by Patel *et al.* (2020) further illuminated these challenges by exploring the perspectives of both healthcare providers and beneficiaries concerning the Kuposhan Mukt Gujarat Maha Abhiyaan (KMGA). The research delved into how different stakeholders perceive the effectiveness and impact of the initiative. It assessed the viewpoints of healthcare providers, who are directly involved in implementing the program, and compared them with the experiences and opinions of the beneficiaries who receive the services. This comprehensive analysis aimed to identify gaps and barriers in the program's execution, shedding light on the practical difficulties faced by both parties. The study's findings underscore the importance of understanding and addressing the various perceptions and challenges encountered in the field to improve the overall effectiveness of the KMGA initiative.

CONCLUSION

The insights derived from NFHS-5 underscore the critical state of maternal and child health in Gujarat, highlighting pressing concerns related to Infant Mortality Rate (IMR), child stunting, and anaemia among women of reproductive age. NFHS-5 reveals that a mere 5.9 percent of children aged 6 to 23 months in Gujarat receive an adequate diet. The prevalence of anaemia in children aged 6 to 59 months has surged by 17% across the state in a span of five years. Undernourished children are notably concentrated in the low socio-economic segments of rural areas and specific districts, including tribal dominated regions such as The Dangs, Narmada, Valsad, and Dahod. The study highlights that Gujarat has not made significant progress in maternal and child health, despite marginal improvements in indicators related to institutional delivery, antenatal/postnatal care, infant mortality rate and child vaccination. This suggests that the public health programs implemented in the state have not yielded substantial benefits or marked impact on the development of maternal and child health.

Both the NFHS5 report and the bulletin of the Sample Registration System (SRS) by the Registrar General of India underscore the need for sustained efforts to address persistent challenges and ensure the holistic well-being of mothers and 13 children in Gujarat. The concerning upward trend in anaemia prevalence across diverse demographics emphasizes the imperative for targeted interventions in the state.

REFERENCES

[1] Arokiasamy, P. and Pradhan, J. (2013). Maternal health care in India: Access and demand determinants. *Primary Health Care Research & Development, 14*(04), 373–393. https://doi.org/10.1017/s1463423612000552

[2] Bhat, R., Mavalankar, D., Singh, P.V. and Singh, N. (2009). Maternal healthcare financing: Gujarat's Chiranjeevi Scheme and its beneficiaries. *Journal of Health, Population and Nutrition, 27*(2). https://doi.org/10.3329/jhpn.v27i2.3367

[3] Bhatia, M., Dwivedi, L.K., Banerjee, K., Bansal, A., Ranjan, M. and Dixit, P. (2021). Pro-poor policies and improvements in maternal health outcomes in India. *BMC Pregnancy and Childbirth, 21*(1). https://doi.org/10.1186/s12884-021-03839-w

[4] Bhatnagar, P., Gupta, S.K., Kumar, R., Haldar, P., Sethi, R. and Bahl, S. (2016). Estimation of child vaccination coverage at state and national levels in India. *Bulletin of the World Health Organization, 94*(10), 728–734. https://doi.org/10.2471/blt.15.167593

[5] Chudasama, R.K., Patel, U.V., Kadri, A., Mitra, A., Thakkar, D. and Oza, J. (2016). Evaluation of integrated Child Development Services program in Gujarat, India for the years 2012 to 2015. *Indian Journal of Public Health, 60*(2), 124. https://doi.org/10.4103/0019-557x.184544

[6] Clarke, G.M., Conti, S., Wolters, A. and Steventon, A. (2019). Evaluating the impact of healthcare interventions using routine data. *The BMJ*, l2239. https://doi.org/10.1136/bmj.l2239

[7] George, A., Mohan, D., Gupta, J., LeFevre, A., Balakrishnan, S., Ved, R. and Khanna, R. (2018). Can community action improve equity for maternal health and how does it do so? Research findings from Gujarat, India. *International Journal for Equity in Health,* 17(1). https://doi.org/10.1186/s12939-018-0838-5

[8] Ghosh, A. and Ghosh, R. (2020). Maternal health care in India: A reflection of 10 years of National Health Mission on the Indian

maternal health scenario. *Sexual & Reproductive Healthcare, 25,* 100530. https://doi.org/10.1016/j.srhc.2020.100530

[9] Govindasamy, P. and Ramesh, B.M. (1997). Maternal education and the utilization of maternal and child health services in India. *International Institute for Population Sciences.* http://scholarspace.manoa.hawaii.edu/bitstream/10125/3472/1/NFHSsubjrpt005.pdf

[10] *Health Dossier 2021: Reflections on key health indicators | National Health Systems Resource Centre.* https://nhsrcindia.org/practice-areas/kmd/publications/health-dossier-2021

[11] Iyer, V., Sidney, K., Mehta, R., Mavalankar, D. and De Costa, A. (2017). Characteristics of private partners in Chiranjeevi Yojana, a public-private-partnership to promote institutional births in Gujarat, India – Lessons for universal health coverage. *PLOS ONE, 12*(10), e0185739. https://doi.org/10.1371/journal.pone.0185739

[12] Kruk, M.E., Galea, S., Prescott, M.R. and Freedman, L.P. (2007). Health care financing and utilization of maternal health services in developing countries. *Health Policy and Planning, 22*(5), 303–310. https://doi.org/10.1093/heapol/czm027

[13] Manna, S., Gupta, V., Sanchaya, S. and Garg, A. (2022). Inequities in maternal child health, education, and empowerment among tribal population in India. *Journal of Family Medicine and Primary Care, 11*(11), 7150. https://doi.org/10.4103/jfmpc.jfmpc_594_22

[14] Mavalankar, D., Vora, K.S., Ramani, K.V., Raman, P.S., Sharma, B. and Upadhyaya, M. (2009). Maternal health in Gujarat, India: A case study. *Journal of Health, Population and Nutrition, 27*(2). https://doi.org/10.3329/jhpn.v27i2.3366

[15] Modi, D., Saha, S., Vaghela, P., Dave, K., Anand, A., Desai, S. and Shah, P. (2020). Costing and Cost Effectiveness of a Mobile Health Intervention (IMTECHO) in improving infant mortality in tribal areas of Gujarat, India: Cluster randomized controlled trial. Jmir Mhealth and Uhealth, 8(10), e17066. https://doi.org/10.2196/17066

[16] Mohanan, M., Bauhoff, S., La Forgia, G., Babiarz, K.S., Singh, K. and Miller, G. (2013). Effect of Chiranjeevi Yojana on institutional deliveries and neonatal and maternal outcomes in Gujarat, India: a difference-in-differences analysis. *Bulletin of the World Health Organization, 92*(3), 187–194. https://doi.org/10.2471/blt.13.124644

[17] Nair, H. and Panda, R. (2011). Quality of maternal healthcare in India: Has the National Rural Health Mission made a difference? DOAJ (DOAJ: Directory of Open Access Journals). https://doaj.org/article/9fb3ea7b325e4691af3d52ff660b1195

[18] National Health Systems Resource Centre (2023). National Health Accounts Estimates for India (2019-20). New Delhi: Ministry of Health and Family Welfare, Government of India. https://nhsrcindia.org/sites/default/files/2023-04/National%20Health%20Accounts-2019-20.pdf

[19] Navaneetham, K. and Dharmalingam, A. (2000). Utilization of maternal health care services in South India. *RePEc: Research Papers in Economics*. https://econpapers.repec.org/RePEc:ind:cdswpp:307

[20] New Delhi: Ministry of Health and Family Welfare, Government of India. https://nhsrcindia.org/sites/default/files/2023-04/National%20Health%20Accounts-2019-20.pdf

[21] NFHS data reveals worrying levels of malnutrition among children in "Prosperous" Gujarat (2023). The Wire. https://thewire.in/rights/nfhs-data-reveals-worrying-levels-of-malnutrition-among-children-in-prosperous-gujarat

[22] Ng, M., Shanker-Raman, P., Mehta, R., De Costa, A. and Mavalankar, D. (2013). Initial results on the impact of Chiranjeevi Yojana: a public-private partnership programme for maternal health in Gujarat, India. *The Lancet, 381*, S98. https://doi.org/10.1016/s0140-6736(13)61352-5

[23] Parmar, R.J., Prajapati, N. and Shringarpure, K. (2020). Vaccination coverage of children in tribal Narmada district of Gujarat: a cross sectional study. *International Journal of Community Medicine and Public Health, 7*(2), 609. https://doi.org/10.18203/2394-6040.ijcmph20200436

[24] Parwez, S. (2016). A Comparative study of Gujarat and Kerala developmental Experiences. *International Journal of Rural Management, 12*(2), 104–124. https://doi.org/10.1177/0973005216660908

[25] Patel, A.S., Kumar, S. and Patel, J. (2020). A study on implementation of 'Kuposhan Mukt Gujarat Maha- Abhiyan' (KMGA) in Vadodara district, Gujarat. *Clinical Epidemiology and Global Health, 8*(4), 989–993. https://doi.org/10.1016/j.cegh.2020.03.009

[26] Pooja, B.S. and Guddattu, V. (2022). Understanding the Change in the Prevalence and Factors Influencing the Childhood Stunting Using District-Level Data from NFHS-4 and NFHS-5 in India. INQUIRY: The Journal of Health Care Organization, Provision, and Financing, 59, 004695802211271. https://doi.org/10.1177/00469580221127122

[27] Puranik, A. and Shreya, N. (2021). Anemia among children under 5 years in India: A District-Level spatial analysis using NFHS-5 data. *Asia Pacific Journal of Public Health, 34*(2–3), 206–212. https://doi.org/10.1177/10105395211058288

[28] Qadri, H.A. and Srivastav, S.K. (2015). Under-nutrition more in male children: a new study. *International Journal of Research in Medical Sciences*, 3363–3366. https://doi.org/10.18203/2320-6012.ijrms2015 1192

[29] Rahman, O., Yamaji, N., Nagamatsu, Y. and Ota, E. (2022). Effects of MHealth Interventions on Improving antenatal care visits and skilled delivery care in Low- and Middle-Income Countries: Systematic review and Meta-analysis. *Journal of Medical Internet Research*, 24(4), e34061. https://doi.org/10.2196/34061

[30] Raj, P. and Gupta, N. (2022). A review of the National Family Health Survey data in addressing India's maternal health situation. *Public Health Reviews, 43*. https://doi.org/10.3389/phrs.2022.1604825

[31] Rana, R., Vaze, G. and Christian, P. (2019). Determinants of Acute Malnutrition among Under Five Children in Aravalli District of Gujarat, India: A Community-Based Case-Control Study. *International Journal of Health Sciences and Research, 9*(6), 1–8. https://www.ijhsr.org/IJHSR_Vol.9_Issue.6_June2019/1.pdf

[32] Saha, S., Pandya, A., Raval, D. and Saxena, D. (2023). Cost-Effectiveness of MHealth Intervention (TECHO+) for improving maternal and child health indicators in Gujarat, India. PubMed, 47(4), 549–554. https://doi.org/10.4103/ijcm.ijcm_192_22

[33] Sanneving, L., Kulane, A., Iyer, A. and Åhgren, B. (2013). Health system capacity: maternal health policy implementation in the state of Gujarat, India. *Global Health Action, 6*(1), 19629. https://doi.org/10.3402/gha.v6i0.19629

[34] Sidney, K., Iyer, V., Vora, K.S., Mavalankar, D. and De Costa, A. (2016). Statewide program to promote institutional delivery in Gujarat, India: who participates and the degree of financial subsidy provided by the Chiranjeevi Yojana program. *Journal of Health, Population and Nutrition, 35*(1). https://doi.org/10.1186/s41043-016-0039-z

[35] *Significant decline in maternal mortality in India*. https://pib.gov.in/FeaturesDeatils.aspx?NoteId=151238&ModuleId%20=%202

[36] Singh, A. and Vellakkal, S. (2021). Impact of public health programs on maternal and child health services and health outcomes in India: A systematic review. *Social Science & Medicine, 274*, 113795. https://doi.org/10.1016/j.socscimed.2021.113795

[37] Singh, S.K., Lhungdim, H., Shekhar, C., Dwivedi, L.K., Pedgaonkar, S. and James, K.S. (2023). Key drivers of reversal of trend in childhood anaemia in India: evidence from Indian demographic and

health surveys, 2016–21. *BMC Public Health, 23*(1). https://doi.org/10.1186/s12889-023-16398-w

[38] Selvaraj, S., Karan, K.A., Srivastava, S., Bhan, N. and Mukhopadhyay, I. (2022). India health system review. New Delhi: World Health Organization, Regional Office.

[39] Soni, J., Sheikh, F., Saha, S., Wanjari, M.B. and Saxena, D. (2023). Nutritional Indicators for Gujarat, Its Determinants and Recommendations: A Comparative study of National Family Health Survey-4 and National Family Health Survey-5. *Cureus 15(5): e39175.*. https://doi.org/10.7759/cureus.39175

[40] *Vital stats.* PRS Legislative Research. https://prsindia.org/policy/vital-stats/national-family-health-survey-5

[41] Vora, K.S., Yasobant, S., Patel, A.R., Upadhyay, A. and Mavalankar, D. (2015). Has Chiranjeevi Yojana changed the geographic availability of free comprehensive emergency obstetric care services in Gujarat, India? *Global Health Action, 8*(1), 28977. https://doi.org/10.3402/gha.v8.28977

[42] Vora, K.S., Mavalankar, D., Ramani, K.V., Upadhyaya, M., Sharma, B., Iyengar, S.D., Gupta, V. and Iyengar, K. (2009). Maternal health situation in India: a case study. *Journal of Health, Population and Nutrition, 27*(2). https://doi.org/10.3329/jhpn.v27i2.3363

[44] Yasobant, S., Shewade, H.D., Vora, K.S., Annerstedt, K.S., Isaakidis, P., Dholakia, N. and Mavalankar, D. (2017). Effect of previous utilization and out-of-pocket expenditure on subsequent utilization of a state led public-private partnership scheme “Chiranjeevi Yojana” to promote facility births in Gujarat, India. *BMC Health Services Research, 17*(1). https://doi.org/10.1186/s12913-017-2256-6

[45] Yasobant, S., Vora, K.S., Shewade, H.D., Annerstedt, K.S., Isaakidis, P., Mavalankar, D., Dholakia, N. and De Costa, A. (2016). Utilization of the state led public private partnership program “Chiranjeevi Yojana” to promote facility births in Gujarat, India: a cross sectional community based study. *BMC Health Services Research, 16*(1). https://doi.org/10.1186/s12913-016-1510-7

[46] World Health Organization. Regional Office for South-East Asia (2010). Improving maternal and child health in Gujarat: initiatives for achieving MDGs 4 and 5. WHO Regional Office for South-East Asia. https://iris.who.int/handle/10665/205335

Inter-Taluka Health Infrastructure Disparities in Anand

Vijay S. Jariwala[1], Manish R. Patel[2] and Jignesh K. Barot[3]

ABSTRACT: This research examines inter-taluka disparities in health infrastructure within Anand, a relatively prosperous district of Gujarat, to identify gaps in healthcare access and promote health equity. Anand, despite being an economically strong district of Gujarat, is suffering from the problem of inter-taluka disparities in health infrastructure. The major objective of this research is to study the taluka-wise availability of health infrastructure in terms of hospitals, health centres, beds in medical institutions, doctors, nurses etc. in various talukas of Anand so that inequalities would be identified and remedies can be offered. Using the Coefficient of Variation, ratios, and deprivation/development indices, the analysis reveals significant variations, particularly in hospital bed availability, followed by hospitals and dispensaries. The ratios of health infrastructure indicators to population are generally low and imbalanced across most talukas. The deprivation and development indices identify Anand and Petlad as having relatively developed health infrastructure, Khambhat as moderately developed, and Anklav, Sojitra, Umreth, and Tarapur as underdeveloped and requiring urgent government intervention.

Keywords: *Health Infrastructure, Inequality, Development Index, Deprivation Index, Talukas, Anand.*

---

[1] Associate Professor, Department of Economics, Sardar Patel University, Vallabh Vidyanagar, Anand, Gujarat, India. E-mail: viju_19782004@yahoo.com

[2] Assistant Professor, Department of Economics, Veer Narmad South Gujarat University, Surat Gujarat, India.

[3] Associate Professor, Department of Economics, Sardar Patel University, Vallabh Vidyanagar, Anand, Gujarat, India.

INTRODUCTION

It hardly needs any justification that health infrastructure is an important factor for the development of human resources. In such era, health sector in Anand is facing various problems including inter-taluka disparities in the availability of health infrastructure in terms of hospitals, health centers, hospital beds in medical institutions, doctors, nurses etc. Health infrastructure refers to the resources needed to provide essential health services and have positive impact on the health of masses. Worldwide, health is considered as a right of every citizen and is defined as a state of complete physical, mental, social and spiritual well-being and not merely an absence of disease (Rao, 2004). Health outcomes like life expectancy, crude birth and death rates, infant mortality rate, eradication of diseases like malaria, leprosy, small pox, polio, tuberculosis and so forth are greatly influenced by the availability of health infrastructure (Subba Lakshmi and Sahoo, 2013). Therefore, it is the duty of the state to develop adequate health infrastructure in its territory. Accordingly, Anand – one of the progressive districts of Gujarat, has also developed substantial amount of health infrastructure since its inception as a separate district in 1997.

Health Infrastructure in Anand: An Overview

Anand is geographically a small district but it contributes to a good amount of share in state gross domestic product especially in Agriculture and allied sectors of the state. From the point of view of health infrastructure, Anand is also performing well. According to latest statistical abstract of Anand (2019–20), the number of medical institutions in Anand district has increased to 354 including 53 primary health centers (PHCs), 14 community health centers (CHCs), 251 sub-centers (SCs), 17 hospitals, and 62 dispensaries in 2019–20 from 56 (10 PHCs, 46 Dispensaries) in 2009–10. The total medical staff was only 251 out of which doctors and nurses were 45 and 206 respectively in 2009–10 but in 2019–20 this number has reached to 404 with 68 doctors and 318 nurses. There were only 3 medical institutions behind one lakh of population in 2009–10 but in 2019–20, their number has increased to 7.

The life expectancy of male and females increased to 65.50 and 70.00 years respectively in 2011. Birth rate and death rate (number of deaths per 1,000 people in a year) have improved and stood at 21.6 and 6.4 per thousand respectively in 2019 as against 33.34 and 9.21 respectively in 2009. Similarly, infant mortality rate (number of infants die before reaching the age of one year per one thousand lives in the same year) is also reduced to 42.0 per thousand in 2019.

Despite such progress the regional variations in health infrastructure are still a grave cause of concern for Anand district. Among eight talukas some are rich in health facilities while others are lagging behind. For example, in Tarapur taluka, health institutions are in very bad situation. There is lack of doctors in Government hospitals of most of the talukas of the Anand district. Moreover, many talukas are in serious condition with respect to the availability of health infrastructure.

In such circumstances, the attainment of the social goal of 'Health for all' (HFA) seems doubtful. Similarly, without balanced growth of health facilities in each region, the Sustainable Development Goals including reducing child mortality, improving maternal health and combating HIV/AIDS and other diseases cannot be achieved in any economy. Hence, the main purpose of this paper is to study the disparities among various talukas of Anand district with respect to health infrastructure which helps to identify disparities in access to healthcare resources. This information is crucial for promoting health equity and social justice within the district. And that will allow local Government and policymakers to get a clue to turn their eyes towards this problem.

The paper is organized as follows: Next section is dedicated on the review of concerned literature. After that in sections III and IV, objectives of the study and data & methodology are described respectively. Section V makes an analysis of inter-taluka disparities in health infrastructure in distinct ways. Finally, subsequent sections follow conclusion and policy implications.

REVIEW OF LITERATURE

The problem of regional disparities in health infrastructure has attracted the attention of economists, researchers, and policymakers in both developed as well as developing countries. In this regard, various studies have been conducted all over the world. However, to justify the need for the present study, the following studies have been reviewed. Goel and Ahlawat (1993) analyzed growth of health expenditure, existing infrastructure for health, medical staff and patients treated in hospitals and dispensaries in Haryana (India). It was emphasized to invest in health sector for creating health culture in the country. They concluded that better health and medical care services for the rural and poor people can be provided through proper health planning. Ghatak and Das (2012) found that health care system in the district of Birbhum of West Bengal is very far from the level of satisfaction, especially from the infrastructural point of view. Lack of this facility leads to inconsistency in the development of basic health care system as well as in overall development of the society. It was further seen that discrepancies existed both on spatial and temporal scales.

Gupta (2012) examined the degree of health inequalities across districts of urban Uttar Pradesh by applying the principal component analysis and found the existence of wide regional disparities regarding health of urban population. The study concluded that the Western region of the state was the leading region in urban health; though its performance is poor regarding illness, maternal and child health. Further, Eastern region performed poorly in terms of socio-economic development but other health indicators revea the success of this region. Panmei (2013) judged the spatial disparities of health care facilities in the state of Manipur. The study revealed that the better development of health care facilities mostly concentrated in the valley areas where, there is high accessibility level of better road connectivity and high socio-economic status. However, most of the hill districts are devoid of such facilities. Comparing valley and hill districts, the health care facilities are not the same as far as the quality and the order of services are concerned. Although considerable growth in health care facilities has been recorded but the uneven distribution and non-functioning of health centers in some districts resulted in disparities in the spatial distribution of healthcare facilities.

Sheet and Roy (2013) studied the regional disparities in health care infrastructure in nineteen blocks of Birbhum district (West Bengal).

They constructed the deprivation and development index for each block on the basis of eight indicators of health care infrastructure. It was concluded that the blocks of Sainthia, Bolpur -Santiniketan and Labpur are more developed with respect to the health care infrastructure and blocks including Nalhati-I, Suri-I, Mayureshwar-I and II are less developed. Hence the need of adequate planning was stressed to equally develop health care infrastructure. Motivating from the existing literature, the present study on inter-taluka disparities in health infrastructure for Anand district of Gujarat is undertaken.

OBJECTIVES OF THE STUDY

Growth with social justice and welfare has always remained at the highest priority in the plan strategy of Gujarat and therefore utmost preference has been given to social infrastructure including health and education. Yet, it cannot be denied that there is a wide gap in the availability of health infrastructure in various talukas of Anand which needs to be studied. A focused study on inter-taluka inequalities encourages community engagement. Local communities can engage in recognizing their health needs and play a role in designing and implementing interventions, which enhances their sense of empowerment and ownership. A detailed study can provide policymakers with data-driven insights to formulate targeted policies. This can aid in the allocation of resources and the development of strategies to address specific health challenges faced by different talukas within the district.

From this viewpoint, specifically the following objectives are worked upon.

1. To explore the inter-taluka variations in the availability of health infrastructure.
2. To make a taluka-wise comparison of health infrastructure on the basis of standards recommended by Government of India and World Health Organization (WHO).
3. To examine the disparities in the overall performance of each taluka in health infrastructure through deprivation and development indices.

METHODOLOGY

Selection of Data and Indicators for Health Infrastructure

The present study is exclusively based on secondary data which is collected from Statistical Abstract of Gujarat and Booklet on Anand district published by Government of Gujarat and by District Panchayat of Anand. To evaluate and assess the objectives of the study, seven indicators of health infrastructure are selected. The indicators relate to Allopathic medical institutions including, numbers of Hospitals[21], Primary Health Centers (PHCs)[2], Dispensaries[3], Community Health Centers (CHCs)[4], Hospital Beds, Doctors, and Nurses in these institutions are considered.

Research Method

Regarding research method, firstly, the existence of inter-taluka disparities related to above indicators is analyzed by the method of Coefficient of Variation (CV). Next, various ratios of the major indicators are computed to compare the health infrastructure of various talukas of Anand district on the basis of recommended standards.

---

[2] Hospitals imply government hospitals in any district where number of beds varies from 75 to 500 depending upon the size, terrain, and population of each district. Hospitals form an apex institute in the hierarchy of health care system and play an important role in providing the preventive, promotive and rehabilitative services to local community including training and research.

[2] Primary Health Centre (PHC) is a medical institute having one MBBS doctor. Also, 14 Para-medical and other supporting staff form a basic part of the health care system in PHCs. It may have 4–6 beds for patients and performs curative, preventive, promotive and Family Welfare services. A typical Primary Health Centre covers a population of 20,000 in hilly, tribal, or difficult areas and 30,000 populations in plain areas with 6 indoor/observation beds. It acts as a referral unit for 6 Sub-Centers and refer out cases to CHC (30 bedded hospital) and higher order public hospitals located at sub-district and district level.

[3] Dispensary is a medical institute where one physician and one pharmacist provide outdoor treatment.

[4] Community Health Centre (CHC) is a 30-bedded health institute with four specialists including a surgeon, a physician, a gynecologist, and a pediatrician supported by 21 Paramedical and other staff. It possesses one operation theatre, X-Ray machine, labour room and laboratory facilities providing specialist care in Medicines, Obstetrics and Gynecology, Surgery and Pediatrics.

Finally, the deprivation and development indices of health infrastructure for all individual talukas of Anand district are constructed in following steps:

Step I: Calculation of Deprivation and Development Indices: Firstly, level of deprivation of a specified region for selected indicator or variable is measured. In mathematical terms deprivation index (d) is obtained as shown in equation (1):

$$dij = \frac{Maxi - Xij}{Maxi - Mini} \qquad \ldots (1)$$

Where, dij is the deprivation index of ith variable (indicator of health infrastructure) for the jth region; Maxi and Mini denotes the maximum and minimum values of the ith variable in the series respectively; Xij is the actual value of ith variable for j^{th} region.

On the basis of equation (1), development index (D) of ith variable for j^{th} region is computed in terms of absence of deprivation and can be expressed in equation (2):

$$Dij = 1 - dij \qquad \ldots (2)$$

Step II: Average Deprivation Index and Average Development Index: In order to compute the average deprivation index (for j^{th} region), simple average of the deprivation index of all indicators (for j^{th} region) is taken as given in following equation (3):

$$dj = \sum_{i=1}^{n} dij \,/\, N \qquad \ldots (3)$$

Average development index (for j^{th} region) can be obtained if the average deprivation index (for j^{th} region) is known

$$Dj = 1 - dj \qquad \ldots (4)$$

Where, dj can be understood from equation (3). It is also possible to construct average development index by taking a simple average of the development index of all indicators (for j^{th} region)

$$Dj = \sum\nolimits^{n}{}_{i=1} Dij \,/\, N \qquad \ldots (5)$$

The values of deprivation and development indices range from zero to one. Besides, lower score in deprivation index or higher value in development index is desirable as it shows high level of development.

ANALYSIS AND INTERPRETATIONS

Investigation of Inter-taluka variations in the availability of Health Infrastructure in context of the first objective, inter-taluka disparities in the availability of health infrastructure are judged by estimating the co-efficient of variation (CV) for the seven indicators as shown in table 1.

Table 1: Taluka wise Availability of Health Infrastructure in Anand District during 2019–20

Taluka	*Hos-pitals*	*PHCs*	*Dis-pensaries*	*CHCs*	*Hospital Beds*	*Doctors*	*Nurses*
Anand	5	11	15	3	256	14	69
Umreth	1	6	7	1	66	6	27
Borsad	3	11	12	3	156	11	58
Anklav	1	3	3	1	48	4	25
Petlad	3	8	9	2	227	19	74
Sojitra	1	3	3	1	48	3	18
Khambhat	2	8	10	2	108	8	33
Tarapur	1	3	3	1	48	3	14
Total (Anand District)	17	53	62	14	957	68	318
Mean	4	12	14	3	213	15	71
SD	5	16	19	4	290	21	95
CV	136	134	135	134	136	136	135

Source: District Panchayat Office, Anand & Author's calculation.

It is clear from table 1 that Umreth, Anklav, Sojitra, and Tarapur talukas have only one hospital. However, Anand taluka has the highest number of hospitals that are five, followed by Borsad and Petlad talukas where number of hospitals are three each. These lowest and the highest values themselves are a confirmation of the variability in number of hospitals and the same is revealed by the value of CV which is 136 per cent for it. The number of PHCs is found to be comparatively less in Anklav, Sojitra and Tarapur talukas of the district. The CV is 134 per cent regarding this indicator. Further, Umreth, Anklav, Sojitra and Tarapur talukas have only one CHC and in this case, CV of 134 per cent highlights the differences in the districts.

Moreover, Anand taluka has the largest number of dispensaries whereas, the situation is worst for Anklav, Sojitra and Tarapur talukas as these talukas have only three dispensaries each and the CV is found to be 135 per cent showing wide disparities in availability of this facility. Additionally, the regional discrepancies are more in the case of availability of doctors (CV=136) than nurses (CV=135) where, Sojitra and Tarapur talukas are facing the shortage while Anand and Borsad talukas are rich in both of these resources. While considering the number of hospital beds in medical institutions, Anand taluka is prosperous and Tarapur, Anklav and Sojitra talukas are under-privileged. Here, the CV score of 136 per cent which is also very high compared to all other indicators. In this way, inter-taluka imbalances are observed for each indicator of health infrastructure for Anand district data for the year 2019–20. The high disparities have also been observed for all the talukas with respect to the availability of health infrastructural facilities like Doctors, Nurses, CHCs, PHCs and Hospitals.

Thus, irrespective of the case of low or high disparities, Anand is experiencing the inter-taluka discrepancies in the availability of health infrastructure. At one instance, such imbalances can be attributed to unequal population size in various talukas as it is general consensus that population is one of the indicators for the provision of infra-structural facilities by the Government. However, in order to have more remarkable conclusions, it becomes necessary to assess whether the talukas possess the recommended standards of health infrastructure as prescribed by Government of India and WHO.

Taluka-wise Comparison of Health Infrastructure based on Recommended Standards

The regional imbalances in health infrastructure in any economy can be judged on the basis of standards set by its government as well as WHO. Standards are a means of describing a level of quality that the health care organizations are expected to meet or aspire to achieve (IPHS, 2012). In India, Indian Public Health Standards (IPHS) are prescribed by Ministry of Health and Family Welfare, Government of India to attain and maintain an acceptable quality of health care infrastructure. In this regard, recommendations of IPHS are the provision of one Sub Centre (SC) for 5,000 people, one Primary Health Centre (PHC) for 30,000 people, one Community Health Centre (CHC) for a population of 1,20,000 in plains whereas in tribal, hilly and desert areas, there should be one SC for 3,000 people, one PHC and one CHC for 20,000 and 80,000 people respectively. However, it is also stressed by IPHS norms that each district should have at least one hospital. Moreover, the qualitative aspect of health infrastructure is also discussed by WHO in terms of standardized major ratios including doctor-to-nurse, doctor-to-population, hospital bed-to-population, nurse-to-population etc. According to WHO, the doctor-to-nurse ratio is said to be ideal when it is 1 Doctor: 3 Nurse (The International News; May 18, 2008). It is also prescribed by WHO that at least three hospital beds and one doctor must be available for the population of 1,000 (Jamwal, 2009; Kumar, 2013).

However, with reference to Nurse/Population ratio, WHO assumed the availability of one nurse for every 500 people to be best (Garari, 2014). Accordingly, in order to make taluka-wise comparison of health infrastructure on the basis of recommended standards, the ratios of some important indicators are calculated and presented in table 2.

Table 2 explains that doctor/nurse ratio is good and near to the ideal ratio (1:5) in most of the talukas except for Petlad taluka. With respect to the ratios of doctor to population and nurse to population, Tarapur (1 Doctor: 25333 People) and Petlad (1 Nurse: 3581.08 People) talukas respectively are good as compared to other talukas, still these are distant from the standard ratios (1 Doctor: 1000 People and 1 Nurse: 500 People). Whereas, Anand taluka with one doctor available for 43500 people and having one nurse for 8826 people is in worst situation. However, Hospital Bed/Population ratio is the best in Petlad i.e., 1 Bed: 1167 people which is near to WHO's recommendations (3 Beds for 1000 people). While, for Umreth taluka with one bed available for 2848 people is in poor condition.

In case of hospital to population ratio, Tarapur taluka is in good position with one hospital serving 76000 people whereas this ratio is worst in other talukas like Umreth, Borsad, Anklav, Khambhat and Anand in the district where one hospital is bearing the load of more

Table 2: Taluka Wise Major Ratios of Selected Indicators of Health Infrastructure in Anand District for the Year 2019–20

Taluka	*Doctor/ Nurse Ratio*	*Doctor/ Population Ratio*	*Nurse/ Population Ratio*	*Hospital/ Population Ratio*	*PHC/ Population Ratio*	*Dispensaries/ Population Ratio*	*CHC/ Population Ratio*	*Hospital Bed/ Population Ratio*
Anand	1:4.9	1:43500	1:8826.09	1:121800	1:55363.64	1:40600	1:203000	1:2378.91
Umreth	1:4.5	1:31333.33	1:6962.96	1:188000	1:31333.33	1:26857.14	1:188000	1:2848.48
Borsad	1:5.27	1:34545.45	1:6551.72	1:126666.67	1:34545.45	1:31666.67	1:126666.67	1:2435.90
Anklav	1:6.25	1:33750	1:5400	1:135000	1:45000	1:45000	1:135000	1:2812.50
Petlad	1:3.89	1:13947.37	1:3581.08	1:88333.33	1:33125	1:29444.44	1:132500	1:1167.40
Sojitra	1:6	1:32000	1:5333.33	1:96000	1:32000	1:32000	1:96000	1:2000
Khambhat	1:41	1:32625	1:7909.09	1:130500	1:32625	1:26100	1:130500	1:2416.67
Tarapur	1:4.67	1:25333.33	1:5428.57	1:76000	1:25333.33	1:25333.33	1:76000	1:1583.33
Total (Anand District)	1:4.67	1:30779.41	1:6581.76	1:123117.65	1:39490.57	1:33758.06	1:149500	1:2187.04

Source: Author's Calculation based on data in table 1 and Statistical Abstract of Anand District-2019–20.

Table 3: Taluka wise Deprivation Index of Health Infrastructure in Anand District for the year 2019–20

Taluka	*Deprivation Indices*							*Average Deprivation Index*
	Hospitals	*PHCs*	*Dispensaries*	*CHCs*	*Hospital Beds*	*Doctors*	*Nurses*	
Anand	0.00	0.00	0.00	0.00	0.00	0.31	0.08	0.06
Umreth	1.00	0.63	0.67	1.00	0.91	0.81	0.78	0.83
Borsad	0.50	0.00	0.25	0.00	0.48	0.50	0.27	0.29
Anklav	1.00	1.00	1.00	1.00	1.00	0.94	0.82	0.96
Petlad	0.50	0.38	0.50	0.50	0.14	0.00	0.00	0.29
Sojitra	1.00	1.00	1.00	1.00	1.00	1.00	0.93	0.99
Khambhat	0.75	0.38	0.42	0.50	0.71	0.69	0.68	0.59
Tarapur	1.00	1.00	1.00	1.00	1.00	1.00	1.00	1.00

Source: Author's calculations based on data in table 1.

Table 4: Taluka wise Development Index of Health Infrastructure in Anand District for the year 2019–20

Taluka	*Development Indices*							*Average Development Index*
	Hospitals	*PHCs*	*Dispensaries*	*CHCs*	*Hospital Beds*	*Doctors*	*Nurses*	
Anand	1	1	1	1	1	0.69	0.92	0.94
Umreth	0	0.37	0.33	0	0.09	0.19	0.22	0.17
Borsad	0.5	1	0.75	1	0.52	0.5	0.73	0.71
Anklav	0	0	0	0	0	0.06	0.18	0.04
Petlad	0.5	0.62	0.5	0.5	0.86	1	1	0.71
Sojitra	0	0	0	0	0	0	0.07	0.01
Khambhat	0.25	0.62	0.58	0.5	0.29	0.31	0.32	0.41
Tarapur	0	0	0	0	0	0	0	0

Source: Author's calculations based on data in table 3.

Table 5: Classification of Talukas as per the Development of Health Infrastructure

Taluka	*Development Level*	*Scores*	
		Average Deprivation Index	*Average Development Index*
Anand, Borsad, Petlad	High	< 0.400	> 0.600
Khambhat	Moderate	0.400–0.600	
Umreth, Anklav, Sojitra, Tarapur	Poor	> 0.600	<0.400

Source: Based on Calculations in table 3 and 4.

than one lakh people. With reference to the population served by PHC, Tarapur taluka is looking in better position in comparison with other talukas of the Anand district. In Tarapur, one PHC is available for 25333 people and this ratio is near to IPHS guidelines of 1 PHC for 30000 people. In this case, Anand and Anklav talukas are in poor circumstances. Further, Tarapur is at first position with respect to the ratio of dispensary to population where 25333 people depend on one dispensary. The most unfortunate situation is the case of Anklav where one dispensary is caring 45000 people. Moving towards to population pressure per CHC, Tarapur taluka has 1 CHC for every 76000 People which is a comfortable place as it has attained the ideal ratio of 130000 people per CHC. Besides, Sojitra taluka is also in good position where one CHC is serving 96000 people. But Anand and Umreth are such talukas where one CHC is providing service to more than 1.5 lakh people. On the whole, the above discussion reveals the existence of inter-taluka discrepancies in the health infrastructure for Anand district on the basis of prescribed standard. None of the taluka is found to achieve all the guidelines of IPHS as well as WHO standards. The situation of most of the taluka is disgraceful with respect to the health facilities. Thus, it becomes necessary to examine the taluka-wise development of overall health infrastructural facilities.

Examination of Inter-taluka disparities in the Development of Health Infrastructure in order to know the inequalities in overall performance of all talukas with reference to health infrastructure, their deprivation and development indices are prepared and highlighted in table 3 and 4 respectively. Further, table 5 presents the classification of the talukas according to the level of health infrastructural development. The scores of deprivation indices for hospitals, PHCs and CHCs, dispensaries, hospital beds and nurses, reveal that the Anand taluka is fully developed in all these five cases as the score of its deprivation and development indices are zero and one respectively. Borsad taluka is least impoverished or moderately developed with minimum values of its deprivation indices that are zero for PHCs and CHCs each and 0.27 for nurses. While the Tarapur taluka is completely deprived in the case of all the infrastructural indices as the scores of its deprivation index is one and development index is zero. Besides, Sojitra taluka is also facing full deficiency for hospitals, dispensaries, PHCs, CHCs, hospital beds and doctors as the deprivation indices are zero for this taluka. Anklav taluka is also having deprivation for to hospitals, dispensaries, PHCs, CHCs and hospital beds as indices for these indicators are zero for the taluka.

Khambhat taluka has moderate to high deprivation in various indicators of health infrastructural facilities. On the similar grounds, disparities are also seen for CHCs in which case Umreth, Anklav, Sojitra and Tarapur talukas are fully depressed but Anand and Borsad talukas possess zero score of deprivation index thereby it is said to be completely developed. However, from the point of view of the development of CHCs, Petlad and Khambhat talukas are having fifty percent development in this index of health infrastructure for Anand district for 2019–20 data.

With regard t the facility of hospital beds in medical institutions, Anand taluka is free from deprivation and can be considered as completely developed while Petlad and Borsad talukas are at second and third places respectively in the values of development index Anklav, Sojitra and Tarapur talukas are fully deprived with score 1 in deprivation index. In context of the number of doctors and nurses, Petlad taluka is wealthy (Deprivation Index = 0; Development Index = 1.0) Tarapur taluka is fully destitute (Deprivation Index = 1.0; Development Index = 0). The position of Anand and Borsad talukas are looking good with reference to availability of doctors and nurses respectively as the score of deprivation index is lower after Petlad.

On the whole, with regard to average deprivation and development indices, Anand taluka hits the best score (Deprivation Index = 0.06 and Development Index = 0.94). Alongside, Borsad and Petlad talukas with 0.29 score in deprivation index and 0.71 in development index each occupies second rank and can be placed under the first category of highly developed talukas along with Anand taluka (table 5). Next, it is evident that the values of deprivation and development indices are moderately high (between 0.400 – 0.600) for the Khambhat taluka. Therefore, with the hunches of mediocre development of health infrastructure, it is placed in the second category of moderately developed districts in table 5.

Contrary to the above, deprivation is said to be very high in the talukas having score above 0.600 in deprivation index or less than

0.400 in development index. Such talukas include Umreth, Anklav, Sojitra and Tarapur. These talukas are grouped in the third category showing poor development level of health infrastructure in Anand district as per table 5. Thus, the scores of deprivation and development indices vary among districts thereby highlighting the inter-district disparity in the development of health infrastructure in Anand district of Gujarat.

CONCLUSION

On the whole, it can be concluded from the present study that there is a substantial gap in the availability of health infrastructure in various talukas of Anand district of Gujarat. Firstly, the calculated values of Coefficient of Variation disclose the existence of inter-taluka imbalances which are on average with high values between 135–136 for all the talukas and for all the seven indicators of health infrastructure. Secondly, keeping in view the prescribed standards of health infrastructure, the inter-talukas comparisons for various indicators are made with computed ratios which highlights disparities among talukas regarding health infrastructural facilities. Among the ratios, doctor-nurse ratio in most of the talukas is near to recommended standards. However, hospital population ratio is also varying among talukas where Tarapur taluka is found to be comfortable while the hospitals in Anand, Umreth, Borsad, Anklav, Khambhat and Anand talukas are tolerating the heavy burden of population. But, what so ever be the population pressure, the talukas are fulfilling the norms of having at least one hospital in the taluka. Except the ratios of doctor to nurse and availability of hospital beds in medical institutions to population, rest of the other ratios in all talukas are not worth mentioning from the point of view of the standards prescribed by Government and WHO.

Finally, to examine the differences in the overall performance of each taluka with reference to health infrastructure, deprivation and development indices are constructed. The scores of these indices confirm the wide discrepancies among talukas in the development of health infrastructure. Also, on the basis of scores of these indices, the talukas are classified in to three categories. First category includes the

Anand, Borsad and Petlad talukas are having high level of health infrastructural development and are enjoying first, second and third rank respectively in this case. In second category Khambhat taluka with moderate level of development is placed. The third category comprises Anklav, Umreth, Sojitra and Tarapur talukas which are underprivileged with respect to the development of health infrastructure in Anand district. By identifying gaps and variations in health infrastructure, policymakers can optimize resource allocation. This ensures that resources are directed to areas with the greatest need, enhancing the overall efficiency of healthcare delivery. Health is a multi-faceted concept influenced by various socio-economic, cultural, and geographical factors. Analyzing inter-taluka differences provides a more holistic understanding of the complex dynamics shaping health outcomes within the district. The study contributes to the academic field by adding valuable insights into regional health disparities. It can serve as a reference for future research and contribute to the existing body of knowledge on public health and healthcare infrastructure. In summary, studying inter-taluka inequalities in health infrastructure in the district of Anand serves both practical and academic purposes. It provides a foundation for evidence-based policymaking, promotes social justice, and contributes to the overall improvement of public health outcomes within the region.

POLICY IMPLICATIONS

On the basis of the findings of the present study, it can be implicated that the Anand district needs balanced and unbiased development of health infrastructural facilities. For which there is emergence of constructing new hospitals, health centers, dispensaries and other institutions in the talukas facing shortage of these health infrastructural facilities. Along with this, there is logic and rationale for filling the vacant posts of doctors, nurses, and other medical staff to improve their availability for population in all talukas of Anand district. For the talukas experiencing lack of medical staff, Government may re-appoint retired medical personnel to overcome their shortage. The proper utilization of human as well as financial resources will be helpful to achieve the prescribed standards of health infrastructure in all areas. Tarapur, Sojitra, Umreth and Anklav talukas are proven as backward in health infrastructure, call for concrete plan of action from the Government of Gujarat. There should be separate programmes of health infrastructure development in each taluka according to their requirements. To support it, Government should increase budgetary allocations to health infrastructure in each district, every year. Moreover, the state needs to enhance the proportions of its gross state domestic product in health sector to attain efficiency, sufficiency, and equity in this sector. Besides, there is an urgent need to correct the financial leakages and corrupt practices. With the adoption of good governance, state should establish a statutory body to oversee the policy, programme and process of reducing inter-taluka disparities in health infrastructural facilities. Access to adequate health infrastructure directly influences public health outcomes. Analyzing inter-taluka differences allows for the identification of areas with potential health crises and enables the implementation of preventive measures to mitigate health risks.

REFERENCES

[1] Deswal, D. (2011). 'Haryana Faces Lack of Health Infrastructure, Doctors', *The Times of India* (November 11, 2011), Assessed on 24 November, 2020.

[2] Dhar, Aarti (2013). 'Now Health Sub-Centers to Provide Contraception Facilities' (11 July, 2013). Assessed on 06 December, 2020.

[3] Garari, K. (2014). 'Nurses Do Not Get Their Due', *Deccan Chronicle* (21 January, 2014). Assessed on 05 December, 2020.

[4] Garg, I. and Gupta, K. (2015). "A Study of Inter-District Disparities in Health Infrastructure in Haryana, India", *International Journal of Education and Management Studies*, 5(1):23–30.

[5] Ghatak, S. and, Das, P.P. (2012). 'Status of Rural Health Care and the Hidden Disparity: A Study of Birbhum District, West Bengal, India', *IOSR Journal of Humanities and Social Science*, 3(2): 13–18.

[6] Goel, M.M. and Ahlawat, S. (1993). 'Economics of Health in Haryana', A paper submitted in the 76th conference of Indian Economic Association at Ahmedabad.

[7] Goel, M.M. and Garg, I. (2011). 'Public Expenditure on Health and Economic Growth in Haryana: An Analysis', *Indian Journal of Applied Research*, 1(3):211–214.

[8] Goel, S. and Geetika (2014). 'Health Care System in Haryana: An Overview', *Edubeam Multidisciplinary-Online Research Journal*, 4(1):1–12.

[9] Government of Gujarat (2019). "Gujarat Economy", Department of Economic and Statistical Analysis, Gandhinagar, Gujarat.

[10] Gupta, A. (2012). 'Magnitude of Urban Health Disparity in Uttar Pradesh', *Asia Pacific Journal of Social Sciences*, 4(2):108–124.

[11] Indian Public Health Standards-IPHS (2012). "Guidelines for Sub Centers (SCs)" Issued by Directorate General of Health Services Ministry of Health & Family Welfare, Government of India, pp. 1–64. Assessed on 26 November, 2020.

[12] Jamwal, N. (2009). 'Not Enough Beds', *Down To Earth* (15 August, 2009). Assessed on 09 December, 2020.

[13] Kumar, A. (2013). 'Health Expenditure and Health Infrastructure in Class-I Towns of Uttar Pradesh, India', A Paper Presented in 3rd International Conference on Management, Economics and Social Sciences (ICMESS 2013) January 8–9, 2013 Kuala Lumpur (Malaysia). Assessed on 07 December, 2020.

[14] Kumar, U.A. (2013). 'India Has Just One Doctor for Every 1,700 People', *The New Indian Express* (22 September, 2013). Assessed on 05 December, 2020.

[15] Mahajan, N. (2014). 'Manpower Shortage Pushes Healthcare on Back Foot in Haryana' *The Pioneer* (18 July, 2014). Assessed on 28 November, 2020.

[16] Panmei, L.R. (2013). 'Spatial Disparities of Health Care Facilities in Manipur', *Indian Streams Research Journal*, 3(2).

[17] Park, K. (1994). *Preventive and Social Medicine*, Banarsi Das Publishers, Jabalpur.

[18] Rao, K.N. (2004). 'Trends in Health Status in Andhra Pradesh: An Empirical Analysis', *Indian Economic Journal*, 51(1).

[19] Sheet, S. and Roy, T. (2013). 'A Micro Level Analysis of Disparities in Health Care Infrastructure in Birbhum District, West Bengal, India', *IOSR Journal of Humanities and Social Sciences*, 7(3): 25–31.

[20] Subba Lakshmi, T. and Sahoo, D. (2013). 'Health Infrastructure and Health Indicators: The Case of Andhra Pradesh, India', *IOSR Journal of Humanities and Social Science*, 6(6):22–29.

[21] The International News (May 18, 2008). 'Doctor-Nurse Ratio Inadequate' Assessed on 09 December, 2020.

[22] The Tribune (May 30, 2014). 'Health Services on Ventilator at Narnaul General Hospital'. Assessed on 24 November, 2020.

Health Inequities in Gujarat: The Role of Infrastructure, Utilization, and Socioeconomic Factors

Rudra Narayan Mishra[1]

ABSTRACT: Gujarat is one of the leading states in the country in economic growth, infrastructure development and spread of urbanisation. On the other hand, the critiques often point out the state's position in crucial health outcomes not at par with its economic prosperity. Health outcomes are one of the major components in over all human development indicator and quality of life in any society. This study investigates the even distribution of health infrastructure throughout Gujarat, equitable access to these services across social groups, and the improvement of health outcomes while reducing regional disparities. While Gujarat has seen a significant increase in health facilities, often driven by the private sector, especially in tertiary care, the paper argues that grassroots-level health infrastructure requires greater state support. Although service utilization has improved, socioeconomic and regional disparities persist. Health outcomes, particularly nutritional condition, and anemia, require a more comprehensive and integrated approach. This paper studies primary health centres and anganwadis are crucial for improving health outcomes in rural and urban slums. Integrating health and nutrition services will optimize service utilization.

Keywords: *Health Infrastructure, Health Service Utilisation, Health Care, Health Outcomes, Health Service providers, Nutrition, Regional Disparities and Inequality.*

[1] Assistant Professor, Gujarat Institute of Development Research, Ahmedabad, India. E-mail: rudra@gidr.ac.in

INTRODUCTION

Gujarat is one the leading state in the country in economic development. The state in Indian west coast has the highest coastal line among all coastal state in India (1600 km). In terms of area the state is fifth largest in the country after Rajasthan, Madhya Pradesh, Maharashtra, and Uttar Pradesh. The geographical area is 196.024 square kilometres and population is little more than 60 million. It's the ninth most populous state as per census 2011. The size of the economy measured in Gross State Domestic Product (GSDP) at current prices, is estimated to be Rs. 22.61 lakh crore (US$ 275.78 billion in 2023–24, an increase of 15.5% over the previous year (State Economic Survey, 2023). In the Financial Year (FY) 2022–23, Gujarat contributed 8.6% to India's GDP. In terms of the contribution to GDP the state has fourth largest contributor to India's GDP in the above year after Maharashtra, Uttar Pradesh and Tamil Nadu. The state leads the export from India. It contributes nearly one-third to the country's turnover and export in pharma sector (35% and 28% respectively). It also contributed to one third of all exports from India between 2020–21 to 2022–23 (ToI 2023). The state is in third position behind Maharashtra and Tamil Nadu in both Projected GSDP (at Rs. 25.62 Lakh Crore for FY 2023–24) and Per Capita Net State Domestic Product (at Rs. 2.41 Lakh for FY 2022–23) among all states and union territories (ToI, 2023).

As per the report of the technical group on population projections for 2011–36, the state is likely to contribute 6.8% in the total projected population increase in India, sixth largest after Uttar Pradesh, Bihar, Madhya Pradesh, Maharashtra and Rajasthan (19.2%, 14.5%, 8.2%, 7.9%, and 7.25 respectively) (MoHFW, 2020, page 7). The projected sex ratio will be declining from 919 to 900 between 2011–36 (ibid, page 13), which perhaps indicates to rise in inflow of migrant population to the state in search of livelihood. During the same period the projected share of urban population to total population in the state is projected to be 53.6% (43.0% as per 2011 census), which will place the state in fifth most urbanised state after Delhi, Kerala, Tamil Nadu and Telengana (98.0%, 92.8%, 58.2%, and 55.0% respectively) (ibid, page 14). The term urban refers to towns (p laces with municipal corporation, municipal area committee, notified area committee or cantonment board); also, all places having 5000 or more inhabitants, a density of not less than 1000 persons per square mile or 400 per square kilometre, pronounced urban characteristics and at least three-fourths of the adult male population employed in pursuits other than agriculture.

By 2020, the state is projected to achieve Total Fertility Rate (TFR) of 2.1 which is considered as threshold for replacement level of fertility (ibid, 20). The projected life expectancy for males and females will be at 72.8 years and 77.3 years respectively which are more than projected life expectancy at birth at national level for males and females (71.2 years and 77.5 years respectively) (ibid, page 40). The projected values of net-migration rate (per 100) for males and females in Gujarat between 2031–35 will be 0.34 and 0.20 respectively, only Delhi and Haryana will be ahead of the state followed by Maharashtra.

While the dependency ratio for young 0–14 years is likely to decline from 29.0% to 19.9% due to decline in fertility, the per cent of old age population is likely to increase from 126 to 239 between 2011–36 (ibid, page 225). The increasing share of older population will alter the demand for health care needs in coming years. Both the incidences of Infant Mortality Rate and Under-5 Mortality Rate are projected to decline from 40 in 2011 to 23 in 2035 and 56 to 33 during the same period (ibid). Gujarat's population is relatively young compared to the national average, and a larger share of the population is of working age. However, the proportion of the elderly in the state is projected to double by 2036 and exceed the proportion at the national level. According to the 2011 Census of India, Scheduled tribes (ST) represent 14.8 per cent of Gujarat's population, and Scheduled Castes (SC) constitutes 6.7 per cent. We will look at the health service utilisation and health outcomes by these two marginal groups in following sections.

The state has reduced the poverty substantially from 33 per cent in 2005 to 17 per cent in 2012 (figure 1), which is attributed by the critiques to phenomenal economic growth in the state. the state government in a written reply stated there were a total of 31,56,541

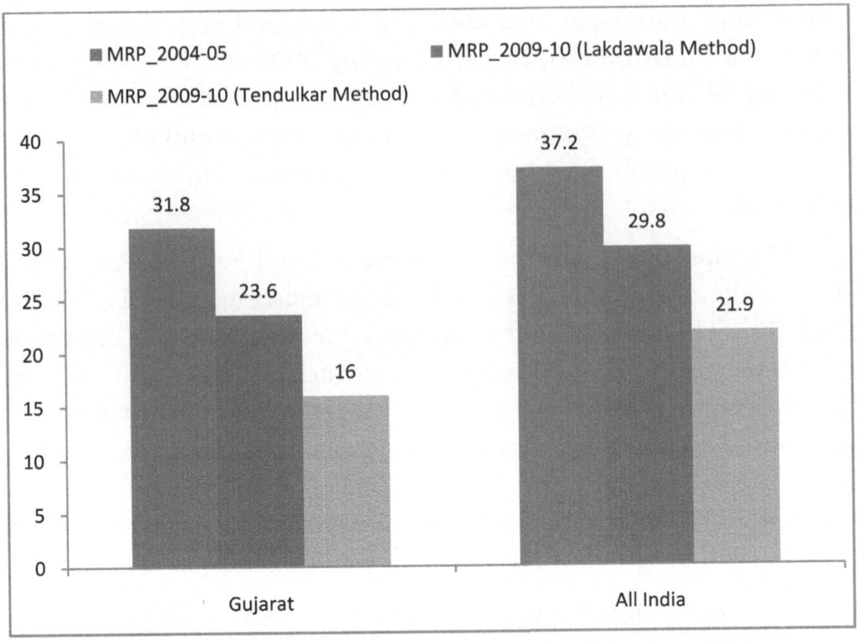

Figure 1: Percept below Poverty Line (BPL) as per NSSO Consumption Rounds (MRP): 2004–45 and 2009–10

Source: RBI Handbook of Statistics 2023.

BPL families in Gujarat and 2558 families got added to the BPL category list between September 2020 and August 2021. During this period, two families were also taken off the BPL list. However, the incidence of extreme poverty is still being reported as reported in media about the state government in a written reply in the assembly stated there were a total of 31,56,541 BPL families in Gujarat and 2558 families got added to the BPL category list between September 2020 and August 2021. During this period, two families were also taken off the BPL list (Indian Express, March 29, 2022).

Now if we look at Multi-Dimensional Poverty Index (MPI), Gujarat has shown improvement in all three parameters; head count ratio, intensity and MPI (Table 1) and these parameters are less than national figures. Other states in the table were included to look at the Gujarat vis-à-vis, the other two economically developed states ahead of the state; Maharashtra and Tamil Nadu. Both these two states show lesser poverty in all three parameters compared to Gujarat. Of course Kerala and Bihar are at top and bottom respectively among all states in India, and the latter is the lowest among all states in economic progress, therefore included in the comparison to locate Gujarat's achievement in poverty reduction.

Table 1: Population Estimates-Multi-Dimensional Poverty Index for Selected State and All India

Selected States/ All India	*NFHS-4 (2015-16)*			*NFHS-5 (2019-21)*		
	Headcount Ratio (Per cent)	*Intensity (Per cent)*	*MPI (NITI Ayog)*	*Headcount Ratio (Per cent)*	*Intensity (Per cent)*	*MPI (NITI Ayog)*
Gujarat	18.47	44.97	0.083	11.66	43.25	0.050
Kerala	0.70	38.99	0.003	0.55	36.92	0.002
Maharashtra	14.80	43.76	0.065	7.81	41.77	0.033
Tamil Nadu	4.76	39.97	0.019	2.20	38.70	0.009
Bihar	51.89	51.01	0.265	33.76	47.40	0.160
India	24.85	47.14	0.117	14.96	44.39	0.066

Source: RBI statistics, 2023.

Note: The estimates are based on India and States/UTs populations for the year 2021 by the Ministry of Health and Family Welfare (MoHFW), GoI.

According to the NITI Ayog (2023, page 37), 47,84,122 people in the state have escaped Multi-dimensional Poverty in 2021. However the same report suggests that 38.0% people in the state could be having some or the other form of under nutrition only Bihar and Jharkhand are above the state as per NFHS-5 figures (ibid, page 37). According to overall Human Development Ranking by NITI Ayog, Gujarat is among the medium-performing states in India with respect to human development, attaining eighth rank on the Human Development Index (HDI) among larger states in India. Of the three core dimensions of well-being in HDI, viz., education, health, and income, Gujarat's performance for the Health and Education Index is significantly lower than the comparator states like Kerala, Tamil Nadu and Maharashtra. As per the 2021 Multi-dimensional Poverty Index (MPI), this encompasses a broader set of indicators spanning over health, education and standard of living, Gujarat ranks 11th among larger Indian states. There is, however, significant variation in development across districts. Based on the state's MPI, the five worst-performing districts are: The Dang (0.278), Dahod (0.258), Panchmahals (0.190), Narmada (0.161), and Banaskantha (0.144).

EXPENDITURE ON PUBLIC HEALTH - GUJARAT

Often the state expenditure on health is considered as benchmark for health outcome of the state. Between 2012–13 and 2019–20, the expenditure has almost been doubled from Rs. 4675 crores to Rs. 10395.9 crores (figure 2). These are nominal figure which only indicates the broader trend in public health expenditure in the state.

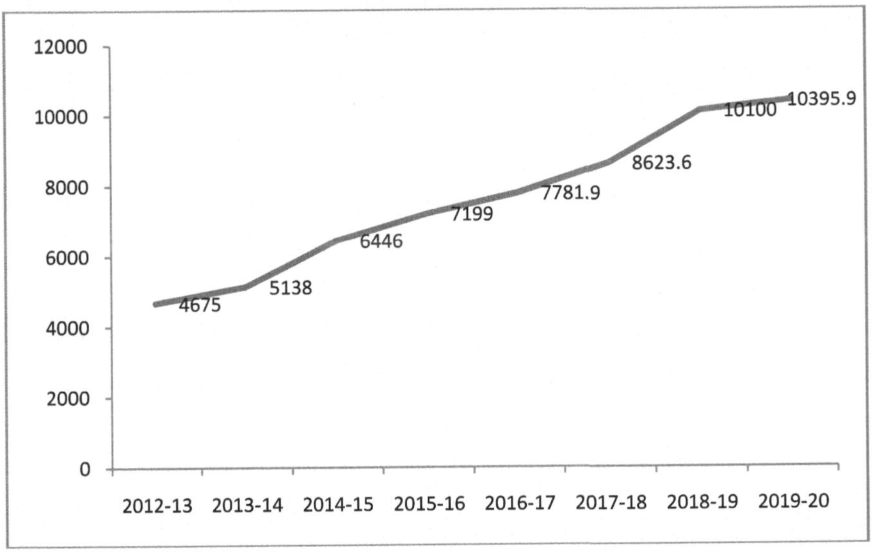

Figure 2: Expenditure on Health in Rs (Cr.) by the Government of Gujarat

Source: RBI Handbook of Statistics 2023.

However if we will look at the change in sector wise allocation by the state government for FY 2023–24 (current year) over revised estimate for previous FY (i.e. 2022–23), then on health sector we have only 5% increase in the allocation (figure 3). In fact the other important social sector expenditures like education and social welfare and nutrition have reported less increase than the health while rural development itself shows negative growth during the same period. Critiques often argue both education and health especially tertiary care and higher/technical education in the state have been opened for greater roles from private sector while state focusing on primary health care, especially in rural areas and primary and secondary education.

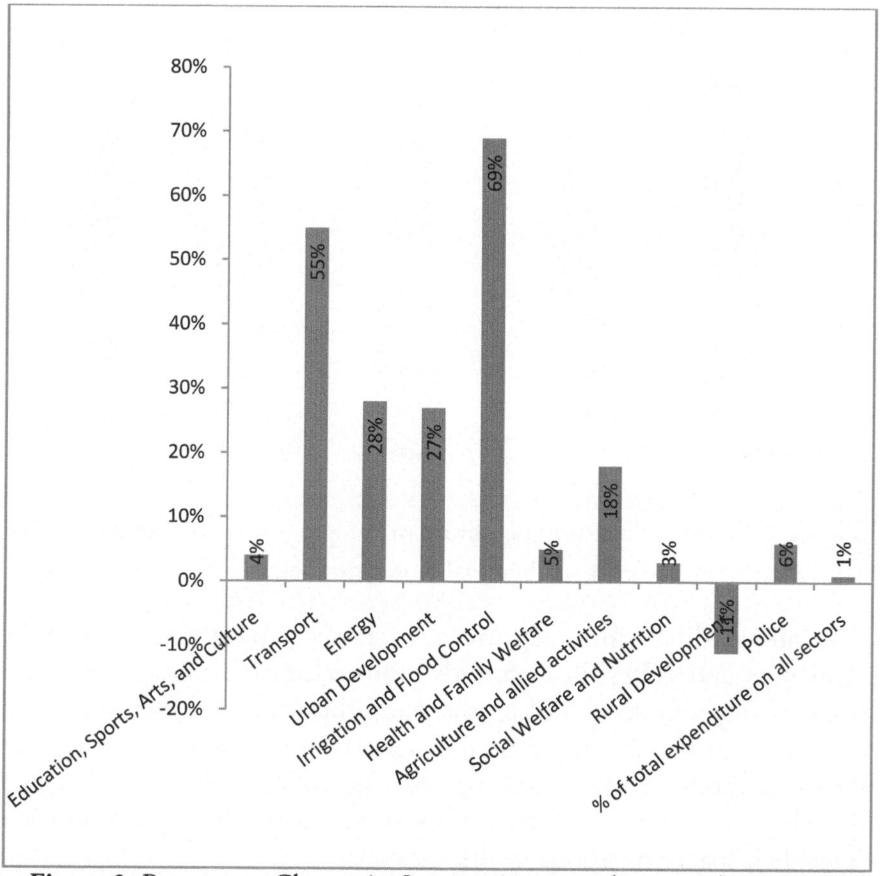

Figure 3: Percentage Change in Sector-wise expenditure under Gujarat Budget for FY 2023–24 from revised estimate for FY 2022–23

Source: https://prsindia.org/budgets/states/gujarat-budget-analysis-2023-24

If we look at the percentage share of the estimated health expenditure in total budget outlay of Gujarat for 2023–24, it is below average for all other states combined together (figure 4). This indicates that despite being the third largest regional economy the state allocation to health perhaps needs revisit in context of Gujarat. For year 2021–22 actuals one can see above 7% expenditure on health which was also a time when covid–19 pandemic was at its peak. The sudden surge in pandemic related loss of human lives and increasing number of infected persons needed additional expenditure to address the needs for health facilities and manpower to treat and save people.

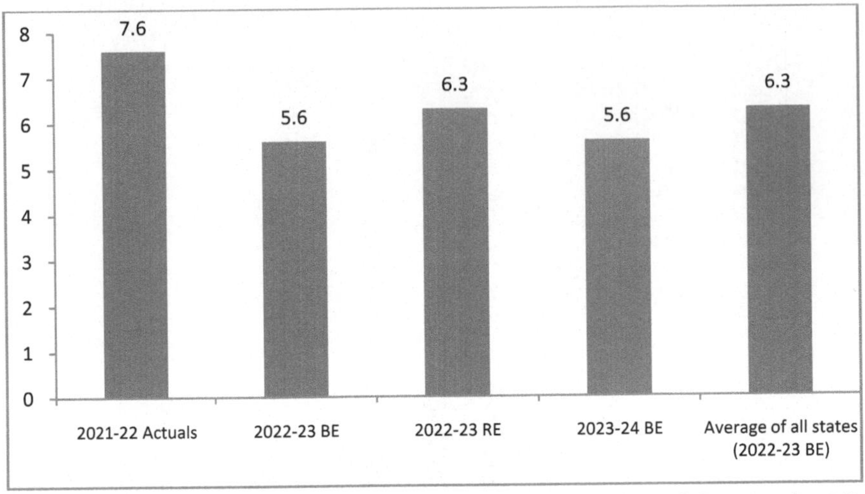

Figure 4: Share of Health Expenditure in Budget Outlay of Gujarat (in %)

Source: https://prsindia.org/budgets/states/gujarat-budget-analysis-2023-24

The above discussions capture the state's economy, demography challenges and state's fiscal towards health sector. The objective of this paper is very simple to look at the state's health infrastructure, health utilisation and health outcome through various numbers from various statistical reports and national surveys and collate them to understand the changing nature of state support to the health sector and it's possible impact on various health outcomes.

HEALTH INFRASTRUCTURE AVAILABILITY IN GUJARAT

Gujarat has almost the four times more number of government hospitals compared to most developed state in India, i.e. Maharashtra which is much larger in areas and population both compared to the state. In Gujarat most of the available health infrastructure funded by state is in rural areas, almost 4 out of 5 hospitals (Table 2). This trend is noticeable in selected states for which comparison has been made.

The reason for comparison of Gujarat with other four states have been elaborated in earlier section. For all the selected states the lion share of state funded government hospitals is in rural areas. When one looks at the figures for number of beds, Gujarat has the highest share of hospital beds in state supported hospitals among the selected states followed by Tamil Nadu and lowest in Maharashtra. From the available data its not possible to explain this pattern, but one possibility could be in rural areas the sanctioned capacity is lesser than urban areas. *Tamil Nadu shows most equitable distribution of hospital beds between rural and urban areas. While Bihar has the most inequitable distribution, as only 8.7% government hospitals in urban Bihar have 60.0% of hospital beds!! In case of Maharashtra even if one-third of total government hospitals are in urban areas but two-thirds of hospital beds in the urban area could be possibly explained in terms of hospitals in urban areas of the state could be much larger in capacity than their rural ones.* It then raises very important question; are there adequate hospital beds in rural areas given the number of hospitals!! But given the level of urban population in Gujarat, Maharashtra and Tamil Nadu, the three most economically developed states in India, which is almost half of the state's total population; the focus of these states on urban health needs require rethinking the strategy.

Table 2: Available Government Health Infrastructure in Gujarat

Selected States	*Number of Government Hospitals*			*Number of Beds*		
	Rural	*Urban*	*Total*	*Rural*	*Urban*	*Total*
Gujarat	81.3	18.7	2245	67.7	32.3	29402
Maharashtra	71.0	29.0	514	33.2	66.8	33028
Tamil Nadu	76.2	23.8	2445	50.2	49.8	52751
Kerala	83.7	16.3	1284	42.3	57.7	38097
Bihar	91.3	8.7	2132	40.0	60.0	29339

Source: RBI Handbook of Statistics 2023.

Note: Health Sub-centres not included. Government hospitals include central government, state government and local government bodies.

Now we will look into details about the health infrastructure in Gujarat. From the above table it is clear that Gujarat's effort in public health infrastructure is mostly towards rural areas. Now we will look at the status of rural health infrastructure including health sub centers, between years 2005–2022, which almost covers two decades. The Sub-Centre is the most peripheral and first contact point between the primary health care system and the community. Each Sub-Centre is required to be manned by at least one Auxiliary Nurse Midwife (ANM)/Female Health Worker and one Male Health Worker. Between two decades the number of health sub-centers (HSCs) has gone up by 25.5% in rural areas. If we look at the number of functioning sub-centers having own building only 13.5% increase is recorded. *If we look at the centers having their own building or not then the picture is not so promising; the proportion of functioning HSCs from their own building have gone down by 7.3% between 2005–22. In 2022 only two out of three HSCs found to be working from their own building in the rural Gujarat.*

Primary Health Centres (PHCs) is the first contact point between village community and the Medical Officer. The PHCs were envisaged to provide an integrated curative and preventive health care to the rural population with emphasis on preventive and promotive aspects of health care. The PHCs are established and maintained by the State Governments under the Minimum Needs Programme (MNP)/ Basic Minimum Services (BMS) Programme. As per minimum requirement, a PHC is to be manned by a Medical Officer supported by 14 paramedical and other staff (See Annexure-I for IPHS norms). Under NRHM, there is a provision for two additional Staff Nurses at PHCs on contract basis. It acts as a referral unit for 6 Sub Centres and has 4 – 6 beds for patients. Between 2005–22, there is 38% increase in number of PHCs in the state. There is also 96.5% rise in per cent of PHCs working from their own building. At present 88.4% of total 1474 PHCs in the state are functioning from their own building which is 26.5% higher from 2005.

Community Health Centers (CHCs) are being established and maintained by the State Government under MNP/BMS programme. A CHC is required to be manned by four Medical Specialists i.e. Surgeon, Physician, Gynaecologist and Paediatrician supported by 21 paramedical and other staff. It has 30 in-door beds with one OT,

X-ray, Labour Room and Laboratory facilities. It serves as a referral centre for 4 PHCs and also provides facilities for obstetric care and specialist consultations. There is 26.4% rise in number of CHCs in Gujarat between 2005–22. The percentage of CHCs working from own building has gone up by 40.9%. In 2022, 92.1% of CHCs were functioning from own building.

Out of 33 districts, Arvalli, Bharuch, Bhavnanagr, Dohad, Gandhinagar, Junagadh, Kachchh, Patan, Sabarkantha, Surat, Vadodara and Valsad have no district hospitals. Overall it can be concluded from the table 3 that HSCs somewhat need more attention in state planning to enable them to have their own building. Despite the increase in availability in the infrastructure the distance to the facility is still an issue in the state. According to one study more than 50 per cent of rural population in need of outpatient care travels to health facilities outside their locality (Dilip et al, 2019). Other states with similar issues are Tamil Nadu, Sikkim, Tripura, Rajasthan, Andhra Pradesh, Karnataka, Rajasthan, Bihar, Haryana, Madhya Pradesh, Jharkhand and Pondicherry (ibid).

Table 3: Status of Rural Health Infrastructure – Case of Gujarat

Sl. No.	*Name of the Infrastructure*	*2005*	*2022*	*Change in Number (4–3) (% change)*
1	*2*	*3*	*4*	*5*
Health Sub-Centers (HSCs)				
1.	Number of Sub Centers (HSCs)	7274	9132	1858 (25.5%)
2.	Number of HSCs functioning in own building	5554	6304	750 (13.5%)
3.	% of HSC functioning in its own building	76.3%	69.0%	–7.3%
Primary Health Centers (PHCs)				
4.	Number of PHCs	1070	1474	404 (38.0%)

Sl. No.	*Name of the Infrastructure*	*2005*	*2022*	*Change in Number (4–3) (% change)*
1	*2*	*3*	*4*	*5*
5.	Number of PHCs functioning in its own building	663	1303	637 (96.5%)
6.	% of PHCs functioning in its own building	(61.9%)	(88.39%)	26.5
Community Health Centers (CHCs)				
7.	Number of Community Health Centers (CHCs)	272	344	72 (26.4%)
8.	Number of CHCs functioning in its own building	225	317	92 (40.9)
9.	% of CHCs functioning in its own building	(82.7)	(92.1)	9.4

Source: Rural Health Statistics-India, 2022.

Along with the infrastructure the availability of medical staff is also very crucial to improve service utilisation from the state health facilities and health outcomes. There are increase in both sanctioned and in-position staffs between 2005–22, for various categories of staffs in rural health centers; HSCs, PHCs and CHCs. There are almost 50.0% increase in-position health workers/ANMs in HSCs and PHCs in the state between 2005–22. For doctors and pharmacists, lab-technicians and nursing staffs, the number for 'in-position', is almost doubled between 2005–22, in public health facilities in rural Gujarat. While for specialists (Surgeons, OB&GY, Physicians & Paediatricians) the 'in-position, staff has gone up by 38.0%, overall there is maximum short fall in this category. *In both periods less than 10% of the required specialists were available in rural health centers in Gujarat. Another exception being availability of radiographers in rural health facilities, who took X-Rays, whose number has declined from 113 to 72 between years 2005–22.* The radiographers job is crucial for diagnostics and absence of such crucial health worker may jeopardise the service delivery of the given health infrastructures, mostly at CHCs level, where one radiographer is mandated as per national guideline. The state has 10 doctors per one lakh population which is same as national level but very low compared to states like Maharashtra (12) and Tamil Nadu (14) and Kerala (18) (Venkateswarn, 2022).

Table 4: Availability of Health Specialists – Rural Gujarat (2005–22)

Sl. No.	*Name of the Posts in Rural PHCs*	*2005*	*2022*	*Change in Number (4–3) (% change)*
1	*2*	*3*	*4*	*5*
Health worker [female]/ANM at SCs & PHCs in rural areas (one worker per centre)				
1.	Required	8344	10606	27.1
2.	Sanctioned	7274	10889	49.7
3.	In Position	6508	9603	47.6
4.	Vacant	766	1286	67.9
5.	Shortfall	1836	1003	–45.4
6.	% of in-position to required posts	22.0	9.5	–12.5
Doctors at PHCs in rural areas (one doctor per centre)				
7.	Required	1070	1474	37.8
8.	Sanctioned	1070	1877	75.4
9.	In Position	848	1692	99.5
10.	Vacant	222	185	–16.7
11.	Shortfall	222	*	NA
12.	% of in-position to required posts	79.3	114.8	35.5
Total specialists in CHCs in rural areas [Surgeons, OB&GY, Physicians & Paediatricians]				
13.	Required	1088	1376	26.5
14.	Sanctioned	321	411	28.0
15.	In Position	92	127	38.0
16.	Vacant	229	284	24.0
17.	Shortfall	996	1249	25.4
18.	% of in-position to required posts	8.5	9.2	0.7

Sl. No.	*Name of the Posts in Rural PHCs*	*2005*	*2022*	*Change in Number (4–3) (% change)*
1	*2*	*3*	*4*	*5*
Radiographer in CHCs in rural areas				
13.	Required	272	344	26.5
14.	Sanctioned	271	113	–58.3
15.	In Position	113	72	–36.3
16.	Vacant	158	41	–74.1
17.	Shortfall	159	272	71.1
18.	% of in-position to required posts	41.5	20.9	–20.4
Pharmacist in CHCs in rural areas				
19.	Required	1342	1818	35.5
20.	Sanctioned	1413	1879	33.0
21.	In Position	807	1631	102.1
22.	Vacant	606	248	–59.1
23.	Shortfall	535	187	–65.0
24.	% of in-position to required posts	60.1	89.7	29.6
Laboratory technicians at PHCs & CHCs in rural areas (one per centre)				
25.	Required	1342	1818	35.5
26.	Sanctioned	1357	1861	37.1
27.	In Position	870	1682	93.3
28.	Vacant	487	179	–63.2
29.	Shortfall	472	136	–71.2
30.	% of in-position to required posts	64.8	92.5	27.7
Nursing Staffs at PHCs & CHCs in rural areas (one per centre)				
31.	Required	2974	3882	30.5
32.	Sanctioned	2769	4465	61.2
33.	In Position	1453	3901	168.5
34.	Vacant	1316	564	–57.1
35.	Shortfall	1521	*	NA
36.	% of in-position to required posts	48.9	100.5	51.6

Source: Computed by the author from Rural Health Statistics-India, 2022.

HEALTH SERVICE UTILISATION

Both Gujarat and India show that private healthcare providers and hospitals/clinics are the major sources of treatment for any illness. In urban Gujarat the service utilisation from any public services is only half of that the rural areas (figure 5). In fact private clinics are more preferred than private hospitals for ailments treated on medical advice. For the inpatient care in last 365 days from the survey the most preferred source seems to be the private service providers (figure 6). The perception of people about public health care system or service delivery might be linked to their preference for service from private service providers. But the dependence on private sector has also its associated cost for treatment. In Gujarat also the treatments in private hospitals are relatively cheaper than other two higher economically developed states as well as Kerala. Tamil Nadu shows the lowest average expense on treatment in government hospitals is followed by Gujarat (Table 5). One of the possible reasons for the low cost of treatment in Gujarat in private sector could be the nature of disease itself which may not require any major expenditure or there may be cheaper human resources available to work in health sector compared to other states. The use of public health centers was found to be higher among poor than non-poor across India (Dash and Mohanty, 2019). In India, about 61% of the poor were using public health centers compared to 40% of the non-poor. The proportion of poor utilizing public health centers for hospitalization is highest in states like Assam followed by Odisha, Delhi, West Bengal and Rajasthan while it is low in Gujarat, Haryana, and Telangana (ibid). *Gujarat is one of the states where low spending by state government on public health goes in hand with low private spending as well; reasons may be, the state is spending a small fraction but due to size of GDP it is huge which takes care of need for financing health care from the user, second may be due to high coverage of insurance in states like Gujarat (Manna et al, 2023) and third the private facilities are more accessible and dispersed reducing logistic cost for patients!!*

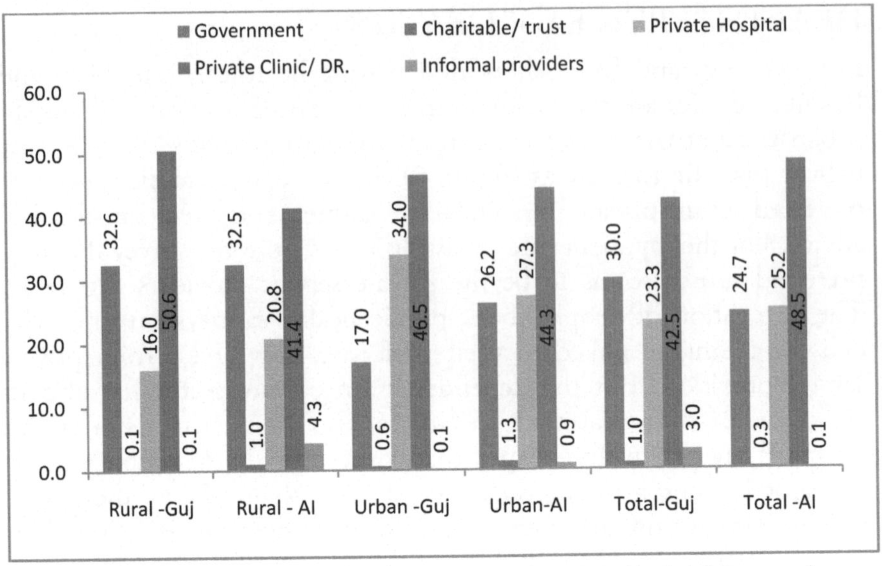

Figure 5: Percentage of Ailments Treated on Medical Advice, and Percentage Break-up of Such Ailments by (level of care received) Healthcare Service Provider (2017–18)

Source: NSS KI (75/25.0): Key Indicators of Social Consumption in India: Health.

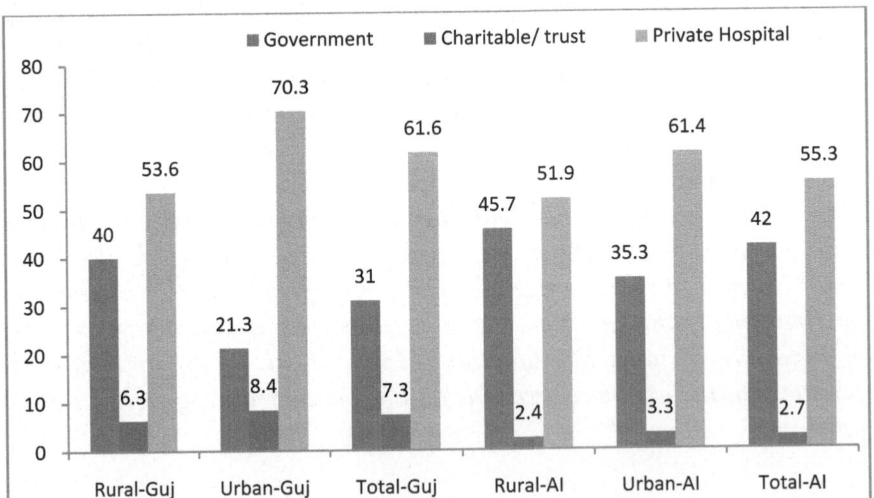

Figure 6: Percentage Break-Up of Hospitalisation (excluding childbirth) Cases by Type of Hospitals (2017–18)

Source: NSS KI (75/25.0): Key Indicators of Social Consumption in India: Health.

Table 5: Average Medical Expenditures per Hospital Stay (NSSO 75th Round, 2017–18)

		India	*Gujarat*	*Kerala*	*Tamil Nadu*	*Maharashtra*
Public hospital	R	4290	1151	4395	520	5606
	U	4837	3529	4589	433	7189
	T	4452	1936	4469	485	6177
Private Hospital	R	27347	25027	25949	28412	23821
	U	38822	29281	32746	41566	42540
	T	31845	27361	28775	35581	32566

Source: NSS KI (75/25.0): Key Indicators of Social Consumption in India: Health.

HEALTH/NUTRITION OUTCOMES

The prevalence of IMR in both rural and urban areas of Gujarat is lower than all India rate but higher than the other two economically developed states of Maharashtra and Tamil Nadu. Similar pattern is observed for U5MR as well. Within IMR, half of the deaths are neonatal deaths (deaths within 30 days from birth).

Table 6: Incidence of Mortality among Young in Gujarat and Selected States

	Infant Mortality Rate (IMR)			*% of Neo-Natal Deaths to IMR*			*U5 Mortality Rate (U5MR)*		
	R	*U*	*T*	*R*	*U*	*T*	*R*	*U*	*T*
Gujarat	27	17	23	51.5	48.1	50.5	28	17	24
Maharashtra	20	11	16	51.4	43.1	50.8	23	12	18
Tamil Nadu	15	10	13	56.6	46.1	50.0	16	11	13
All India	31	19	28	54.7	46.8	53.3	36	21	32

Source: SRS 2020.

Table 7: Nutrition of Children and Women in Gujarat

	Stunted Children	*Wasted Children*	*Underweight Children*	*Anemic Pregnant Women*	*Anemic Adolescent Girls*	*Anemic Women*	*Women BMI Below Normal*
India	35.5	32.1	32.1	52.2	59.1	57.0	18.7
Gujarat	39.0	25.1	39.7	62.6	69.0	65.0	25.2
District Median	37.8	26.0	41.0	62.9	70.8	66.4	24.4
Highest Prevalence	55.3 (Dahod)	40.9 (The Dangs)	53.1 (The Dangs)	82.6 (Aravali)	87.7 (Aravali)	78.9 (Chota Udepur)	43.4
Lowest Prevalence	18.2 (Jamnagar)	17.3 (Ahmedabad)	25.5 (Amreli)	43.1 (Kachchh)	47.0 (Amreli)	47.6 (Porbandar)	15.8
Districts higher than state average (number of districts)	Aravali, Banaskantha, Bharuch, Chota Udepur, Dahod, Gandhinagar, Gir-Somnath, Mahisagar, Narmada, Panchmahals, Patan, Tapi, Vadodara (13)	Anand, Aravali, Banaskantha, Bhavnagar, Botad, Chota Udepur, Dahod, Dwarika, Gandhinagar, Kheda, Mehsana, Mahisagar, Morbi, Navsari, Panchmahals, Sabarkantha, Surat, Surendrnagar, Tapi, The Dangs (20)	Anand, Aravali, Banaskantha, Bharuch, Chota Udepur, Dahod, Gandhinagar, Mahisagar, Narmada, Navasari, Panchmahals, Patan, Sabarkantha, Surendranagar, Tapi, The Dangs, Vadodara (17)	Aravali, Banaskantha, Bharuch, Chota Udepur, Dahod, Kheda, Mehsana, Morbi, Narmada, Panchmahals, Tapi, The Dangs, Vadodara, Valsad (14)	Aravali, Bharuch, Chota Udepur, Dahod, Gandhinagar, Kheda, Mehsana, Morbi, Narmada, Navasari, Rajkot, Sabarkantha, Surat, Panchmahals, Tapi, The Dangs, Vadodara, Valsad (18)	Anand, Aravali, Bharuch, Chota Udepur, Dahod, Gandhinagar, Kheda, Mehsana, Mahisagar, Narmada, Navasari, Panchmahals, Sabarkantha, Surat, The Dangs, Vadodara, Valsad	Anand, Aravali, Banaskantha, Bharuch, Chota Udepur, Dahod, Kachchh, Kheda, Mahisagar, Narmada, Panchmahals, Patan, Sabarkantha, Tapi, The Dangs

Source: National Family Health Surveys (NFHS-5) (2019-21).

The nutritional status of the state shows that the figures for the state are higher than national average for stunting, waiting, underweight among children, anaemia among women and adolescent girls and low BMI among women. Another aspect which is coming out from the data is that the phenomenon of under nutrition among pre-school children and women is no doubt high in tribal regions of the state but in non-tribal districts also the prevalence is higher than the state average for many of them.

REFERENCES

[1] Dash, A. and Mohanty, S.K. Do poor people in the poorer states pay more for healthcare in India? *BMC Public Health* **19**, 1020 (2019). https://doi.org/10.1186/s12889-019-7342-8

[2] *The Times of India (2023-06-07). Third year in row, Gujarat tops in exports.* https://timesofindia.indiatimes.com/city/rajkot/third-yr-in-row-guj-tops-in-exports/articleshow/100808013.cms

[3] *The Times of India (2023-12-02).* Richest State in India 2023- Top 10 Powerful, Most Developed, Highest GDP States. https://www.adda247.com/school/top-10-richest-states-in-india/

[4] *The Times of India (2020-02-03).* Healthcare in rural Gujarat second cheapest in India. https://timesofindia.indiatimes.com/city/ahmedabad/healthcare-in-rural-gujarat-second-cheapest-in-india/articleshow/73886041.cms

[5] Ministry of Health & Family Welfare, National Commission on Population (2020). Population Projections for India and States 2011 – 2036. https://main.mohfw.gov.in/sites/default/files/Population%20Projection%20Report%202011-2036%20-%20upload_compressed_0.pdf

[6] Dilip, T.R., Rajeev, Sadanandan and Sunil, Nandraj (2019). Importance of Proximity to Outpatient Care Facilities in Rural India. Social Science Spectrum, Vol. 5, No. 3, pp. 112-120. https://www.hstp.org.in/wp-content/uploads/2023/03/Importance-of-Proximity-to-Outpatient-Care-Facilities-in-Rural-India.pdf

[7] Indian Express 2022-03-29. Gujarat: Number of families below poverty line rose to 2,556 last year. https://indianexpress.com/article/cities/gandhinagar/number-of-families-below-poverty-line-rose-to-2556-last-yr-7841777/

[8] Ministry of Health and Family Welfare, Statistics Division (2022). Rural Health Statistics (RHS) 2021-22. file:///C:/Users/Rudra-Pc/Downloads/RHS%202021-22-1.pdf

[9] Manna, S., Singh, D., Ghosal, S. *et al.* Out-of-pocket expenditure and its correlates for institutional deliveries in private and public healthcare sectors in India: findings from NFHS 5. *BMC Public Health* **23**, 1474 (2023). https://doi.org/10.1186/s12889-023-16352

[10] Ministry of Home Affairs, Government of India, New Delhi (2020). Sample Registration System Statistical Report 2020. file:///C:/Users/Rudra-Pc/Downloads/SRS_STAT_2020.pdf

[11] Venkateswaran S. (2022). Health Status in India: Challenges and Opportunities (CSEP Working Paper 25). New Delhi: Centre for Social and Economic Progress.

SECTION 4

ENVIRONMENT

Environmental Costs of Industrialization in Gujarat

Rushiraj Upadhyay[1]

ABSTRACT: Gujarat has a long history of industrial activity, dating back to the Indus Valley Civilization. Its modern industrial development, particularly post-independence, has been fueled by factors like favorable geography, resource availability, accessible land policies, government support (including GIDC), technological advancements, and a receptive population. Often considered an industrial "growth engine," Gujarat's industrial development has brought numerous benefits, including commercial sector growth, increased exports, and employment opportunities. However, this rapid industrialization has also led to significant environmental damage. This paper examines both the advantages and disadvantages of Gujarat's industrial growth, including the factors driving it, major industries, and resulting issues such as environmental problems and the need for effective industrial policy. Finally, it proposes solutions to mitigate the environmental impact of industrial activity.

Keywords: *Industries, Industrial Growth and Development, GIDC, Industrial Policy, Environment Issues. Bioremediation, ETP.*

INTRODUCTION

One of the most crucial and influential states in terms of Industrial Growth and Development is Gujarat. Gujarat is also known as one of the most industrialized states of India. Leading industries in Gujarat are general and electrical engineering, textiles, vegetable oils, chemicals, soda ash, cement, ceramic, and the production of fertilizers. Moreover, the Pharmaceuticals and petrochemical industries are growing fast in Gujarat in the contemporary era. The report shows that 'Gujarat offers 30% of Petrochemicals,

---

1 *

50% Chemicals, and Pharmaceuticals business. Gujarat's six percent of total industrial production comes from the textile industry.[2] Furthermore, the role of Gujarat Industrial Development Corporation (GIDC) is crucial in Industrial Development. GIDC was established under the Gujarat Industrial Development Act, of 1962 to accelerate industrialization in the State. The purpose of GIDC is to identify and develop locations suited for industrial purposes. The role of GIDC is to provide core infrastructure for industrial development like water supply, roads and lights, power supply networks, and utilities like gas, telecom, and pipeline. Similarly, it provides supportive infrastructure like a skill upgradation center, commercial space, green spaces, public amenities etc. GIDC has developed 52 skill – upgradation centers to provide quality local manpower to the industries. GIDC handed over the Skill Upgradation Centers to respective training partners in consultation with the Center for Entrepreneurship Development. There are 225 GIDC estates comprising over 68,148 units across Gujarat. Out of which, 36% of estates are located in Saurashtra Kutch region, 27% are in central Gujarat, 25% are in Ahmedabad and north Gujarat and 12% estates are in south Gujarat. It has been noted that 35% of Gujarat State Domestic Products (in the year 2018–19) was accounted for by the manufacturing sector. According to the Gujarat Socio-Economical Review 2019–20, 11% of India's factories are in Gujarat and 16.8% of India's industrial output is from Gujarat.[3] Along with the government's efforts, many other determinants have stimulated Industrial Growth and Development in Gujarat. Industrialization is mainly seen in Urban areas due to the easy accessibility of basic facilities and infrastructure. Contemporarily, manufacturing sectors need skilled and technocrat employees that urban areas provide easily. Connectivity and transportation are important factors for industrial development. The export of manufactured goods is also an important factor in the growth of industries. Gujarat has enough basic facilities and infrastructure for industrial development. Geographically, Gujarat has a large coastline due to which the ports have been extensively developed and the

---

[2] https://gujaratindia.gov.in/business/major-indus.htm Access on 15th December 2023.

[3] https://gidc.gujarat.gov.in/Pages/Contents/GIDC_At_A_Glance_Key_Indicators Access on 15th December 2023.

manufactured goods can be exported on a large scale. These are some key factors behind the industrial development in Gujarat. On the other side, where the volume of industries is high, it has some limitations and hazards. There are high feasibilities of chemical and industrial hazards due to the heavy chemical industries. 'Gujarat, being a highly industrialized state is prone to chemical and industrial hazards which are well supported by the fact that 35% of the total Major Accident Hazard (MAH) units of the country are located mostly at Vapi, Hazira, Ankleshwar, Dahej etc'.[4] These are the affected places of industrial hazards in Gujarat. The focus of this paper is on the issues that emerged due to industrialization. It indicates that industrial hazards influence human life as well as entire living organisms. Cities with the largest number of industrial units are under the greatest risks. Industrial units dealing with different chemicals pose different hazards like chemical hazards, airborne hazards, and biological hazards are identified hazards that harm living organisms along with nature. In the race for industrial development, industrial hazards seem almost impossible to control, therefore, industrial policy regarding the industrial hazards damaging the environment should be observed and analyzed. Industrial development has caused major damage to the environment not only in Gujarat and India but also globally. Chemical, airborne, and biological hazards caused by industrialization *pose a threat to the health of people,* other living organisms, and the entire environment. The present paper has elaborately discussed some environmental consequences of industrial development in the state of Gujarat. Cement, Ceramic, Chemical, Fertilizers, and Textile industries in Gujarat are in major proportion. The hazards posed by these industries like cement, chemical, fertilizer and textile industries are also discussed here. Before that let us discuss the Major Industries in Gujarat State.

MAJOR INDUSTRIES IN GUJARAT

Gujarat is one of the fastest-growing states in India. The fastest-growing industries in Gujarat encompass a diverse range of sectors like chemical, textile, pharmaceutical, petrochemical, fertilizer, etc.

[4] www.gsdm.org access on 20th December 2023.

The main occupation of the people of Gujarat is agriculture and industrial production. A large proportion of Gujarat is associated with any business, which means these people have a business-oriented mindset. This region has been known since ancient times for a variety of productions. After independence, small-scale and large-scale industries have developed extensively in Gujarat. Various factors are responsible for industrial development like geographical conditions and natural resources, accessibility of basic amenities to establish it, and Industrial Policies. To promote industrial growth and production Government has introduced many schemes. Today, initiatives like the Vibrant Summit, Mudra Yojana, Start Up, etc. have played a pivotal role in the growth of small and medium-scale industries in Gujarat. Data noted that total number of 781615 MSMEs are registered under the Udyog Aadhar Memorandum in Gujarat till 2020.[5] Noted that 'Up to 30th September-2006, 312732 number of units are registered as SSI unit in Manufacturing sector having investment up to Rs. 1 crore in Plant & Machinery. From the year 2006 to September 2015, 376357 number of units are registered as an MSME in manufacturing as well as servicing activities under the MSMED Act-2006 having investments up to Rs. 10 crore in Plant & and Machineries and investment up to Rs. 5 crore in equipment of service sector.[6] Data show that the pharmaceutical industry in India is the world's third-largest in terms of volume and stands 14th rank in terms of value. It is growing at about 8 to 9 percent annually and is estimated to be worth 4.5 billion dollar. Different industries including pharmaceuticals, chemicals, paints, etc. are speedily growing in India which disposes of their effluents into the streams either directly or after partial treatment.[7] The number of industries has increased since the independence of Gujarat. Data show that 31040 industries were working in the year 2016 in various sectors which increased to 36726 by 2020 as registered under the Factories Act 1948. 'According to the Annual Survey of Industries 2018–19 results, Gujarat is first in the

---

[5] https://msmec.gujarat.gov.in/uploads/pdf/ANqKDPmQBetzCUNEisHgP3DoKvBo3Db6.pdf access on 20th December, 2023

[6] https://financedepartment.gujarat.gov.in/Documents/Bud-Eng_1096_2022-3-3_683.pdf Access on 20th December 2023.

[7] Patneedi Chanti Babu & Prasadu K. Durga. (2015) *Impact of Pharmaceutical waste on Human Life and Environment.* Rasayan 8(1), 67–70.

country in industrial production with a share of 17.4%, while it is second in NVA (Net Value Added) with 14.7%. With 20.47% fixed capital Gujarat is also first in the country's total fixed capital'.[8] Gujarat's major share of industrial products is from the petroleum, chemical, pharmaceuticals, and textile sectors. If we look at the share of major industry groups in Net Value Added (NVA) as per ASI (Annual Survey of Industry) 2018–19.

No	*Description of Industry*	*Percentage Share in Net Value Added*
1.	Mfg. of Chemical & Chemical Products	24.80
2.	Mfg. of Coke Refined Petroleum 16.39 Products	16.39
3.	Mfg. of Pharmaceuticals, Medicinal, Chemical & botanical	9.29
4.	Mfg. of Textiles	8.53

Source: Socio-Economic Review, 2021–22, Gujarat State.

These four leading industrial sectors in Gujarat have a notable contribution to the Economic growth of Gujarat. Looking at the economic growth and industrial development, 'Gujarat's State Domestic Products (GSDP) is estimated at Rs. 22.61 Lakh crore (US$ 275.78 billion) in FY23, an increase of 15.5% YoY. Gujarat has achieved the distinction of being one of the most industrially developed states. Accounting for 5% of the total Indian population, Gujarat contributes about a quarter to India's goods exports. In 2022–23, Gujarat contributed 8.6% to India's GDP' [9]. Data show that Gujarat is one of the most industrially developed states in India, with a 16.85% share of India's Industrial Output. Again it should be noted that Gujarat is the leading state in chemical, pharmaceutical, petrochemical, textile, cement & ceramic production in India. Let us discuss the various factors behind the Industrial growth and development in Gujarat.

---

[8] https://financedepartment.gujarat.gov.in/Documents/Bud-Eng_1096_2022-3-3_683.pdf Access on 20th December 2023.

[9] Report of India Brand Equity Foundation. June 2023. www.ibef.org

FACTORS AFFECTING INDUSTRIAL GROWTH AND DEVELOPMENT

Essentially, most of the industries are developed in urban areas and the urban periphery due to the ease accessibility of basic requirements for the Industrial establishment. Skilled human resources are the crucial requirements for Industrial development, that can be derived from the technical education campuses. Manufacturing industries need technical human resources, adequate infrastructural facilities, road and transport, communication channels, scope of trading etc., which are the major factors behind the Industrial development and Industrial Development in cities. The geographical advantage is one more crucial factor behind the Industrial Development in Gujarat. 1600 km. long coastline and the development of ports have played a crucial role behind industrial development in Gujarat. It is to be noted that Gujarat's industrial policy has played similarly a crucial role in industrial development. Both urbanization and industrialization are two sides of the same coin. Industrialization leads to urbanization and urbanization leads to industrialization. Both are socio-economic facts that can be seen.

One more cause behind industrial development is to emphasis on employment-based education. To prepare skilled human resources, Industrial Training Institutes (ITI) are established in Gujarat in large proportion. Gujarat is an industrialized state that needs skilled human resources, that fulfilled by the Industrial Training Institute. At present, there are 225 ITIs in the entire state. 103 ITIs are upgraded as a center for excellence for giving technical knowledge to the aspirants. Institutes have introduced a new syllabus for the requirements of various Industries such as Automobile, Chemical, Apparel, Mechanical, etc. 66 ITIs are upgraded under the public-private partnership which gives employment opportunities to their students.[10] Notable, to create and enhance skilled manpower, Skill University and Swarnim Start Up & Innovation University have been established. Strategically preparing skilled human resources is a crucial supporting factor for Industrial Development.

---

[10] Upadhyay R. (2014). *Gujarat: Decades of Development.* Ahmedabad. Rannade Publication.

Transportation facilities are also a key factor behind the Industrial Development. Gujarat's road network is approximately 74,000 km. The industrial development of Gujarat has been accelerated due to the 1483 km Delhi Mumbai Industrial Corridor. 'The state ranks first in cargo throughput amongst all Indian ports. The state has 42 ports which include 1 major port and 41 non-major ports which are geographically dispersed across south Gujarat, Saurashtra and Kutchch region'.[11] The state has 42 ports, including 1 major port and 41 non-major ports, which are geographically dispersed across South Gujarat, Saurashtra. Ease of accessibility and safe transportation are pushing industrial development in Gujarat.

Industrial development is a key factor for rapid economic growth. Major industries have been established—and developed in urban centers since Independence as mentioned above. Industries in different sectors are developed due to time-to-time upgradation in Industrial plans and policies introduced by the Government. A major determinant behind the large and small-scale industrial establishment is to provide an adequate atmosphere. Moreover, an open market for trading, business opportunities, policies for land on lease, capital subsidy, attractive investment policy, etc. are the crucial factors behind the Industrial development in Gujarat. Further, we will analyze some key factors of Industrial Policies in Gujarat.

ISSUES EMERGED DUE TO INDUSTRIALIZATION

Industrialization leads to many problems in the society. Over-industrialization can lead to economic growth in any state or nation but it also causes many problems, especially socio–economic and environmental damage. Industrialization is a major cause behind the urban migration. Rapid urban migration from villages has created issues regarding India's rural social and family structures. It has damaged the traditional family construction and created nuclear families. Rural-urban migration is rapidly seen in Gujarat. Villages are broken and youth are migrating to cities for employment. Industrialization and commercialization have created scope for employment and most importantly people are migrating for that. It

[11] www.gidb.org access on 21 December. 2023.

has also influenced the rural culture as well. On the other side, population density is increasing in cities and urban areas are expanding. The needs of the increasing population are rising. Industries to meet their needs have also expanded. Slums and related problems have emerged as well. Health and hygiene problems have arisen in congested areas. Environmental damage and environmental exploitation are increasing day to day. The fulfillment of human needs and the industrial development for that, both have damaged the traditional social system and the ecology.

Industrialization in Gujarat has harmed the environment and biodiversity as well. Air Pollution, Water Pollution, Soil contamination, Tree cutting, Deterioration of quality of life and life expectancy are the major issues that emerged due to industrialization. Along with that, exacerbated separation of labor and capital, child labor, discrimination against women, inequality in wages, deteriorated living conditions for workers, poor nutrition, temporarily developed slums and health, nutrition & hygiene related issues of slum dwellers etc. can be indicated as notable issues emerged during Industrialization era. Industrialization is a notable indicator to mention to economic development but parallelly it also damages the environment, emits pollutants, reduces soil fertility, pollutes rivers and groundwater, crops grown using chemicals influence the health of people, damage biodiversity and as mentioned above it damages the traditional social system. Cement industries in the costal of Gujarat pollute the land as well as impact plants around it. Pollution by cement dust impacts various plant species and crops.[12] Cement production produces the dust as a major source of Air pollution. It degrades environment quality, dust contaminates water which becomes harmful for human as well as animal health. Moreover, concrete made from cement damages the topsoil.

The environmental impact of Gujarat's industries, encompassing cement, textile, and chemical sectors, is a nuanced and intricate challenge. In the textile sector, high water usage and untreated wastewater discharge contribute to water scarcity and pollution, with

[12] Chaurasia S. Karawaria A. and Gupta A. (2013). *Effect of cement industry pollution on chlorophyll content of some crops at Kodinar, Gujarat, India.* International Journal of Ecology and Environmental Sciences. 3(4). 288-295

chemical use posing threats to water and soil quality. The chemical industry amplifies water stress, air pollution, and hazardous waste generation, affecting aquatic ecosystems and biodiversity. Shared elements among these industries include energy-intensive processes, dependence on non-renewable resources, and the crucial role of regulatory adherence and sustainable practices in alleviating environmental harm.

As per a report of the Gujarat State Chemical Disaster Management Plan, some of the chemical industries in Gujarat are considered to be more dangerous as they practice storage of large amounts of chemicals in the industrial unit. Among these, chlorine and ammonia are the most important chemicals in the picture which could be hazardous. Apart from these other chemicals are acrylonitrile, aniline, hydrogen fluoride, hydrogen sulfide, nitric oxide, phosgene, and oleum. The golden corridor of Gujarat i.e. Ankleshwar is believed to be generating many chemicals resulting in more pollutants being added to the environment. [13] Gujarat is also leading in the pharmaceutical industry now. While India's largest Pharma industries are established in Gujarat, proper disposal of the contaminated waste generated by these industries has become imperative. Pharmaceutical waste damages the environment and creates a risk for humans, aquatic, and wildlife. pharmaceutical industries are responsible for generating toxic effluent as a consequence of their operation. The wastewater generated from these industries possesses solids, biodegradable and non-degradable organic compounds, etc.[14] Pharmaceutical industries generate huge quantities of waste that creates an adverse impact on human health. The toxic elements are found in pharmaceutical effluents that contaminate the water and that water affects the health of the entire organism. Kapoor D noted the most common environmental hazards of pharmaceutical industries which are mentioned below.

- Ecotoxic damage is caused to the environment.
- Carcinogenic-contribute to the causation of cancer.

[13] Sharma S., Margi V. and Singh G. *et al.* (2017). *Dangers to the Environmental Health of Gujarat – A Forthcoming Industrial Hub of India.* International Journal of Trends and Research in Development. 4 (1). 602-604.

[14] Patneedi Chanti Babu and Prasadu K. Durga. (2015) *Impact of Pharmaceutical waste on Human Life and Environment.* Rasayan. 8 (1). 67–70.

- Persistent-remain dangerous for a long time.
- Bio-accumulative–accumulates as it makes its way up the food chain.
- Disastrous due to a catastrophe, mishap, calamity, or grave occurrence in any area.[15]

Thus, pharmaceutical companies are generating pollutants that are harmful to the health of entire organisms as well as hazardous to the environment.

Gujarat is known as a hub of Textile industries. Textile industries are largely established at various places like Ahmedabad, Surat, and Jetpur. Textile industries in Gujarat occupy a crucial position in the Indian economy in terms of industrial production. Textile industries are an important contributor to the industries that adversely affect the environment in Gujarat. Water, air, and solid waste pollution are more common due to these industries. A large quantity of water is needed for textile processing, dying, and printing. Along with the consumption and wasting of water, the disposal of polluted water also pollutes the land including rivers at large scale. These industries emit toxic gases into the air that include dust, oil mists, acid vapors, odours, and boiler exhausts. Textile manufacturing operations create large amounts of toxic and non-toxic solid waste. Fibers, yarn, and fabrics are solid wastes that are created directly from production lines. The cones, looms, and cardboard reels used to hold fibers and textiles during manufacturing add to a factory's solid waste pollution. Common toxic-solid waste pollutants include the storage drums and plastic containers used to hold hazardous chemicals and solvents. [16] The solid waste, air, and water pollution caused by the textile industry is alarming.

One more important industrial sector in Gujarat is chemical and petrochemical. Gujarat's Chemical and Petrochemical Industry comprises of about 500 large and medium-scale industrial unit, about

---

[15] Kapoor D. (2015). *Impact of Pharmaceutical Industries on Environment, Health & Safety.* Journal of Critical Reviews. 2 (4).

[16] Khurana Nisha S. (2018). *Major Environmental Problems Caused by the Textile Industries in Surat: A Study.* Inspira: Journal of Modern Management & Entrepreneurship. 8 (1). 307–313.

16000 of small-scale industrial units, and other factory units. Over 6500 chemical and petrochemical products are manufactured in the State[17]. Thus, the manufacturing of chemical and petrochemical products is large in Gujarat. These chemical-based industries are releasing air pollutants like Particulate matter, Ozone, and Eutrophication from high emissions of NOx and NH_3, CO, CFC, CO_2, Pb, etc.[18] These are the major harmful pollutants that adversely impact human health. We may say that these pollutants are dangerous for the environment. Chemical and petrochemical industries derive a major part of the industrial economy of the state. Thus, it becomes important for economic development as well. On the other side, it is a prerequisite to discuss and take steps against hazardous pollutants and try to reduce their emission.

Thus, if we look at the major industries in Gujarat, we can see that boilers, thermo packs, and diesel generators emit major pollutants. Pharma industries are emitting more amount of Iron, Textile industries are emitting major amounts of nitrogen and Sulphur oxide, Chemical industries emit large amounts of toxic metals and pollutants into the atmosphere, dyeing industries are emitting lead and many other manufacturing industries are responsible for the emission of pollutants like Sulphur dioxide (SO_2) and Nitrogen dioxide (NO_2), particulate matter, lead, arsenic (Ai), nickel (Ni), ammonia (NH_3), benzene (C_6H_6) etc. This section discusses the important industrial sectors of Gujarat and the environmental hazards they cause. Industrial development plays a crucial role in the economic development of any state but it is imperative to discuss its results. In this context, this section discusses the environmental violence caused by the textile industry, chemical industry, pharmaceutical industry, and cement industry. These industrial sectors in Gujarat are spreading environmental pollution but it does not mean that other industries have no role in spreading pollution.

---

[17] Pathak Maulik. (2019). *New Wave of Petrochemical expansion in Gujarat.* Time of India. https://timesofindia.indiatimes.com/city/ahmedabad/new-wave-of-petrochemicals-expansion-in-gujarat/articleshow/72628920.cms

[18] Jain N. Lakhani P and Gupta S. (2017) *Impact of Harmful Emissions near Chemical Based Industries in Gujarat on Human health and methods to scale down its impact.* International Journal of Engineering, Research and Technology. Conference Proceeding. 33-40

RESULTS & RECOMMENDATION

Industrial production has increased in modern times due to industrial development and technological advancement. As people's needs increase, production naturally increases. However, over-industrialization damages the environment and living organisms. Textile industries produce toxic effluent along with gaseous emissions that adversely impact human health and pollute land, air, and water. Hazardous pharmaceutical waste and chemical waste is also damaging the environment. Similarly, Cement and Chemical Industries are emitting more dangerous dust and chemicals into the air, land, and water, causing significant environmental damage. Modern industrial development is considered an important cause of global warming at the global level while industrial development has a huge contribution to environmental damage. Large amounts of carbon and other toxic gas emissions are increasing air pollution and toxic effluent released by the industries is a cause of land and water pollution. It creates an environmental disturbance that affects human health. 'Air pollution is a global public health emergency. Currently, 60,439,692 people in Gujarat are breathing toxic air that does not meet WHO's clean air guidelines. The district with the worst air pollution in Gujarat is Navasari. Where PM2.5 is forecast to be 72.2 $\mu g/m^3$. That's moderately polluted".[19] Gujarat's average air quality index is 94 which is poor. In cities like Ahmedabad, Ankaleshwar, Surat, and other major industrially developed cities AQI is very high which is harmful to the environment and entire living organisms. Gujarat needs a sound industrial policy to ensure environmental safety and protect biodiversity. However, industrial policy is focusing to achieve the objective of sustainable development. The policy also focused on industrial development without degrading the environment. It also emphasizes proper industrial waste treatment, environment assessment, promotion of eco-friendly products, and taking safety measures to avoid chemical hazards. However, there seems to be a need to focus more on sustainable development and environmental awareness.

In the contemporary environmental context, more attention has been focused on *Bioremediation*. Bioremediation is a technique or method

[19] https://www.airpollution.io/gujarat/ Access on 27th December 2023.

that employs the use of living organisms to clean up or neutralize contaminants, pollutants, and toxins from the environment. Similarly, for wastewater management '*Effluent Treatment Plants*' (ETP) has been designed. ETP is designed to clean up toxic materials and chemicals from Industrial wastewater. Today the concept of green building has evolved for sustainable development. This is the concept of sustainable structure or sustainable construction that is environmentally responsible. *Green buildings are designed to conserve and build energy, water, and material resources.* Thus, many other advanced plans should be innovated and implemented and steps should be taken scientifically to control environmental damage. Effective waste management, community engagement, and strict compliance with environmental regulations are underscored as vital components in addressing and reducing the environmental impact of these industries in Gujarat.

If economic growth is the only measure of development, then what kind of model we should adopt for a 'developed India' is worthy of consideration. The development of industries makes an important contribution to the economic development of India. Gujarat is a leading state in Industrial development. On the other hand, despite the existence of many laws and regulations, the emission of greenhouse gases continues on a large scale, causing damage to the environment, posing serious risks to human health, and becoming fatal for all living organisms. When discussing sustainable development, an industrial model should be adopted that proves the motto of SAVE EARTH, SAVE FUTURE, keeps sustainable development goals at the center and realizes the dream of a developed India.

ABBREVIATION

MSME	:	Micro Small and Medium Enterprise
ASI	:	Annual Survey of Industry.
NVA	:	Net Value Added
ITI	:	Industrial Training Institute
DMIC	:	Delhi Mumbai Industrial Corridor
SSIU	:	Swarnim Start Up & Innovation University
GPCB	:	Gujarat Pollution Control Board

ETP : Effluent Treatment Plant
CETP : Common Effluent Treatment Plant
PM : Particulate Matter
AQI : Air Quality Index

REFERENCES

[1] https://gujaratindia.gov.in/business/major-indus.htm Access on 15th December 2023.

[2] https://gidc.gujarat.gov.in/Pages/Contents/GIDC_At_A_Glance_Key_Indicators Access on 15th December 2023.

[3] www.gsdm.org access on 20th December 2023.

[4] https://msmec.gujarat.gov.in/uploads/pdf/ANqKDPmQBetzCUNEisHgP3DoKvBo3Db6.pdf access on 20th December, 2023

[5] https://financedepartment.gujarat.gov.in/Documents/Bud-Eng_1096_2022-3-3_683.pdf Access on 20th December 2023.

[6] Patneedi Chanti Babu & Prasadu K. Durga (2015) *Impact of Pharmaceutical waste on Human Life and Environment.* Rasayan. 8 (1). 67–70.

[7] https://financedepartment.gujarat.gov.in/Documents/Bud-Eng_1096_2022-3-3_683.pdf Access on 20th December 2023.

[8] Report of India Brand Equity Foundation. June 2023. www.ibef.org

[9] Upadhyay R. (2014). *Gujarat: Decades of Development.* Ahmedabad. Rannade Publication.

[10] www.gidb.org access on 21 December. 2023

[11] Chaurasia S. Karawaria A. & Gupta A. (2013). Effect of cement industry pollution on chlorophyll content of some crops at Kodinar, Gujarat, India. *International Journal of Ecology and Environmental Sciences.* 3(4). 288–295

[12] Sharma S. Margi V. Singh G. *et al.* (2017). Dangers to the Environmental Health of Gujarat – A Forthcoming Industrial Hub of India. International Journal of Trends and Research in Development. 4 (1). 602–604.

[13] Patneedi Chanti Babu & Prasadu K. Durga. (2015) Impact of Pharmaceutical waste on Human Life and Environment. Rasayan. 8 (1). 67–70.

[14] Kapoor D. (2015). Impact of Pharmaceutical Industries on Environment, Health & Safety. Journal of Critical Reviews. 2 (4).

[15] Khurana Nisha S. (2018). Major Environmental Problems Caused by the Textile Industries in Surat: A Study. Inspira: Journal of Modern Management & Entrepreneurship. 8 (1). 307–313.

[16] Pathak Maulik. (2019). New Wave of Petrochemical expansion in Gujarat. Time of India. https://timesofindia.indiatimes.com/city/ahmedabad/new-wave-of-petrochemicals-expansion-in-gujarat/articleshow/72628920.cms

[17] Jain N. Lakhani P & Gupta S. (2017) Impact of Harmful Emissions near Chemical Based Industries in Gujarat on Human health and methods to scale down its impact. International Journal of Engineering, Research and Technology. Conference Proceeding. 33-40

[18] https://www.airpollution.io/gujarat/ Access on 27th December 2023.

Weblinks

1. https://ic.gujarat.gov.in/?page_id=147
2. https://gujaratindia.gov.in/business/major-indus.htm
3. https://www.in.kpmg.com/pdf/Gujarat.pdf
4. https://financedepartment.gujarat.gov.in/Documents/Bud-Eng_1096_2022-3-3_683.pdf
5. https://msmec.gujarat.gov.in/statastics
6. https://www.india-briefing.com/news/major-industries-and-preferential-policies-for-foreign-investment-in-gujarat-29829.html/

Effectiveness of CETP in MSME Sector in Ahmedabad City: A Study

S. Muralidhar[1], C. Balaji[2] and S. Sandhya[3]

ABSTRACT: While industrialization has increased economic wealth, it has also increased pollution, led to urbanization, placed clear stress on the fundamental life support systems, and pushed environmental problems closer to the boundaries of tolerability. With booming industrial growth and a less proportionate land mass, environmental issues are now becoming a significant factor in industrial growth and development. A large amount of evidence constantly indicates that the transition of industries from traditional to eco-industrial networks, with green approaches, provides a viable solution to preserve the natural resources of the community. However, it requires an appropriate planning and an integrated framework aligned with the environment considerations, following a careful assessment of past and prevailing conditions. For this purpose, a study was conducted on the existing industrial pollution and environment in Gujarat.

Keywords: *MSMEs, Pollution, Pollutants, CETPs.*

INTRODUCTION

The environment is an integral part of our survival. Industrialization and the environment move in parallel. To excel in both the fields i.e. industrialization and environment, we should adopt clean technologies leading to sustainable development. A sustainable environment involves making eco-friendly decisions and taking

[1] Professor, Department of Commerce and Management Studies, Government First Grade College, Kolar, Karnataka, India.
E-mail: dr_muralidhar_s@yahoo.co.in

[2] Assistant Professor of Commerce, SDC Degree College, Bangarpet, Kolar, Karnataka, India.

[3] Principal, Koshys Institute of Management, Bangalore. Karnataka, India.
E-mail: sandhyatanuraj@gmail.com

relevant actions that conserve nature. In the present era, it is a vital issue, as everyone is realizing the impact of industrialization on the environment. Environmental protection is not just about reducing the waste we produce, but it is also concerned with developing technology and processes that will lead our business to become sustainable in the future and save our planet with eco-friendly technologies.

In recent decades, the concept of sustainable development and environmental protection has become a spotlight across the globe, and various international organizations and the government have taken several initiatives on national and international platforms to save the environment. All sectors of the economy, i.e., primary, secondary, and tertiary sectors will need to contribute to this collective objective of nation-building with sustainability.

Concerns about environmental degradation, quality of life and climate change are driving global consensus on the need to ensure environmentally sustainable economic growth. Supporting the greening of environmental footprint of individual small businesses may be small, their overall impact is significant. In the OECD area, but small and medium-sized enterprises account for approximately 99% of all businesses and two-thirds of employment. In India alone, SMEs are responsible for approximately 70% of industrial pollution. Improving the environmental performance of SMEs is essential for achieving greener economic growth.

While large enterprises have access to various resources, micro, small, and medium enterprises and businesses contribute to the major output and number of employment opportunities. One of the newest trends today is to start or transform a business into an environmentally friendly one, with many new opportunities every day, with new innovations, models and methods. As more and more people are moving toward green and organic products, making micro, small and medium-sized enterprises eco-conscious and eco-friendly not only helps to save the environment but also attracts consumer interest in the market. In recent years, an increasing number of people are becoming aware of their purchases, which affect the planet and its inhabitants, as well as consumers, and are increasingly choosing green and eco-friendly products and services. Sustainable upgradation booms businesses and tends to have significant growth potential because people are becoming aware of the need for sustainable development and nature-friendly goods.

Pollution problems manifest as deterioration of air quality, improper disposal of solid wastes and discharge of industrial effluents into water bodies. Industrial effluents are the source of some toxic pollutants and seriously pollute environment. In addition, they contribute significantly to the overall water pollution in the state and are considered more hazardous. Hence, this study focuses on industrial development in Gujarat and the challenges faced by MSMEs due to pollution.

LITERATURE REVIEW

Despite the existing literature on the impact of environmental issues on the success of MSMEs and the potential role of CETPs in environmental impact mitigation, there are still knowledge gaps that require further investigation.

Industries are unable to measure the financial, societal and conservational effects allied with their activities as highlighted by The National Institute of Standards and Technology (Hutchins *et al.*, 2013).

Sustainable technology, innovations in entrepreneurship and government policy, collaboration in technological development a positive impact on mitigating climate change. It gives an insight into green growth and sustainable living (Fernandes, C., 2021).

In a study titled "Assessment of Physio-Chemical Properties of Tannery Waste Water and its Impact on Fresh Water Quality", it is identified that most of the chemical parameters concentrated in the tannery waste water are above the BIS' prescribed standard limits. It is also found that the tannery waste water has an impact on people health and aquatic ecosystem (Shahida Praveen *et al.*, 2017)

In tannery effluents, the treated effluent was slightly brownish whereas untreated effluent was blackish. Consequently, the discharge of tannery effluents into the water bodies creates many pollution problems and affect the life of plant, animal and human (A. Sugasini and K. Rajagopal, 2015).

Research is required to evaluate the effectiveness and efficiency of CETPs in addressing the environmental challenges posed by MSMEs. Assessing the performance of different wastewater treatment techniques, including absorption methods, within CETPs can aid in identifying the optimal approaches for sustainable environmental management (Paolini *et al.*, 2018).

Investigating the role of government policies and support mechanisms in promoting the adoption of CETPs by MSMEs would be valuable. Analyzing the barriers and incentives for MSMEs to participate in CETPs can inform policymakers and facilitate the development of effective regulations and incentives (Hurst & Pugsley, 2011).

The performance of CETP in India has remained unsatisfactory because of disparate discharges, damage to treatment equipment, and clogging of pumping systems. The presence of organic impurities can affect the efficiency of CETP (Padalkar and Kumar, 2019).

Reusing non-potable water from wastewater treatment plant (STP) wastewater is an economical and water-saving preferred option and has become a common practice. Much research has been conducted on the reuse of gray water from domestic wastewater (Gruttner *et al.*, 1994).

METHODOLOGY

The data used in this study were taken from secondary sources. The data for pollution industries, pollution control facilities were collected from the Gujarat Pollution Control Board (GPCB), which is the apex agency at the state level for enforcement of environmental rules and regulations for the protection of the environment. It also regularly monitors the quality of water bodies and treated effluents from industries. To comment on the effectiveness of the performance of pollution control facilities, the data were compared with the standards set by the regulatory authority under the Environment Protection Act, 1986.

AN ANALYSIS: STATE CONTEXT

Table 1: Overview Statistics of the MSME Sector in Gujarat

MSME Sector Overview Statistics – Gujarat	*Units*
Total no. of MSMEs	3.5 Million (35 lacs)
Micro/Small/Medium	7.3/1.2/0.05 lacs
Share of Micro Units in MSMEs	85%
Employment in the MSME Sector	50.7 lakhs
Contribution to exports	20.82%
Total no. of ZED Certified entities	Fifty-two awarded ratings (Bronze 21, Silver 20, Gold 10 and Diamond 1)

Source: msme.gov.in

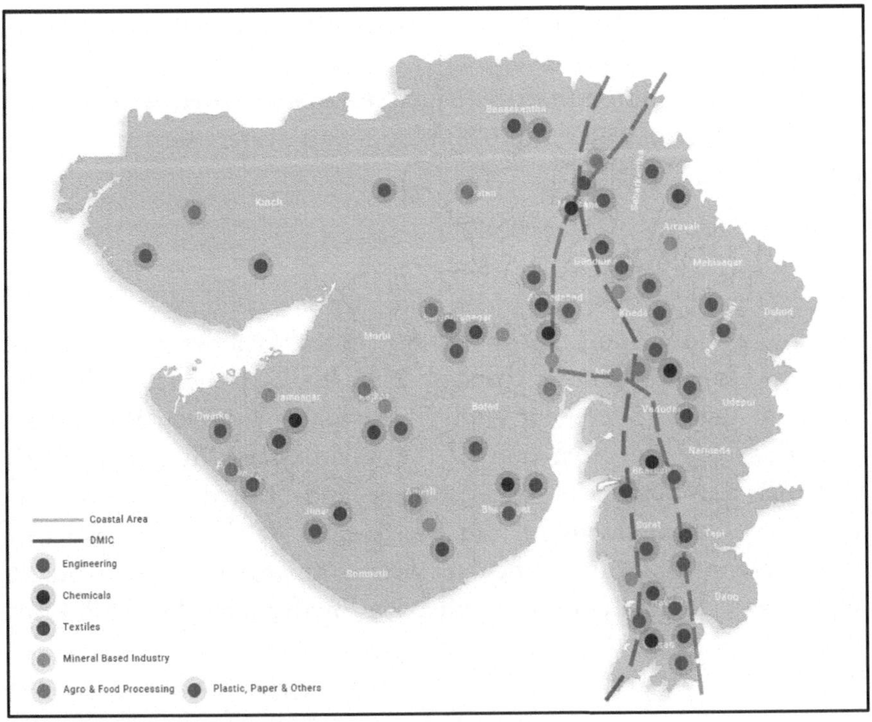

MSME Clusters in Gujarat (*Source:* https://indextb.com)

Comparative Distribution of MSMEs in the Top 10 States as a Percentage

Table 2: Statement Showing the Comparative Distribution of the Top 10 States

Sl. No.	*State/UT*	*5th Economic Census*		*NSS 73rd Round*	
		Number (in lakh)	*Share (%)*	*Number (in lakh)*	*Share (%)*
1.	Uttar Pradesh	89.99	14	44.03	12
2.	West Bengal	88.67	14	34.64	10
3.	Tamil Nadu	49.48	8	33.13	9
4.	Maharashtra	47.78	8	30.63	8
5.	Karnataka	38.34	6	20.19	6
6.	Bihar	34.46	5	14.70	4
7.	Andhra Pradesh	33.87	5	25.96	7
8.	Gujarat	33.16	5	21.78	6
9.	Rajasthan	26.87	4	16.64	5
10.	Madhya Pradesh	26.74	4	19.33	5

Source: https://msme.gov.in/sites/default/files/MSMEENGLISHANNUALREPORT2021-22.pdf

Details of Functional CETPs in Ahmedabad, Gujarat

Sl. No.	*Name of the CETP*	*Location*	*Installed Capacity (MLD)*
1.	The Green Environment Services Co. Op. Society Ltd.	Vatva, Ahmedabad	16
2.	M/s Naroda Enviro Project Ltd.	Naroda, Ahmedabad	14
3.	M/s Narol Dyestuff Enviro Society.	Narol, Ahmedabad	0.1
4.	M/s. Narol Textile Infrastructure & Enviro Management.	Ahmedabad	100
5.	M/s. Tata Motors Ltd Vendors Park	Sanand, Ahmedabad	1.5

Source: The table has been compiled from data collected from different sources. Retrieved from https://gpcb.gujarat.gov.in/Home/CETPResult (Feb 2023).

The CETPs mentioned in the above table have both physio-chemical and biological treatments to reduce the pollution load. There are five parameters on which the quality of water bodies is classified. They are:

(a) pH[1]
(b) COD[2]
(c) BOD[3]
(d) SS
(e) NH_3-N[4]
(f) Phenolic Compounds[5]

Since the treatment is performed with the help of bacteria, BOD becomes the most important parameter for evaluating the efficacy of CETP. In addition, some CETPs treat heterogeneous wastewater, and COD6, another important parameter, was also included in the analysis to investigate the effectiveness.

The Details of the Treatment for all CETPs have been Summarized and presented below:

Parameters	*Standards*	*The Green Environment Services Co. Op. Society Ltd.*	*M/s Naroda Enviro Project Ltd*	*M/s Narol Dyestuff Enviro Society.*	*M/s. Narol Textile Infrastructure & Enviro Management.*	*M/s. Tata Motors Ltd Vendors Park*
Wastewater treated in CETP (MLD)	–	23	5.2	0.045	90	0.12
pH in the treated effluent	Prescribed standard	6.5–8.5	6.5–8.5	6.5–8.5	6.5–8.5	6.5–8.5
	Observed values	7.4	6.92	7.17	8.09	7.51
COD in the	Prescribed	250	250	250	250	250

Parameters	*Standards*	*The Green Environment Services Co. Op. Society Ltd.*	*M/s Naroda Enviro Project Ltd*	*M/s Narol Dyestuff Enviro Society.*	*M/s. Narol Textile Infrastructure & Enviro Management.*	*M/s. Tata Motors Ltd Vendors Park*
treated effluent	standard					
	Observed values	138	264	277	93	42
BOD in the treated effluent	Prescribed standard	30	30	30	30	30
	Observed values	13	22	26	23	9
NH3-N in the treated effluent	Prescribed standard	50	50	50	50	50
	Observed values	17.86	21.78	18.26	13.66	11.42
Phenolic Compounds	Prescribed standard	1	1	1	1	1
	Observed values	0.96	1.41	1.33	0.31	BDL

Source: https://gpcb.gujarat.gov.in/Home/CETPResult (Feb. 2023).
Note: All the standards are in (mg/l) except for pH.

It is observed from the above analysis that pH and NH_3-N for the treated effluent from all CETPs meet the prescribed standards. For the most critical parameter, COD, two CETPs exceeded the prescribed standards of 250 mg/l for the treated effluents. This means that the effluents contain higher levels of oxidizable materials and the effects can be environmentally damaging to higher aquatic lifeforms.

As far as the performance of the pollution control system is concerned, it is unable to treat wastewater and does not meet acceptable standards.

A single policy for all issues cannot be used to deal with pollution contamination. Although the wastewater is different and the inlet standards prescribed in different CETPs are different, the same steps are taken to treat the pollution and the standards set for the treated wastewater are also the same. This is confusing because the reduction in pollution is directly proportional to the intake level and the emission control technology used.

This leads to the conclusion that the standard is arbitrarily imposed by regulatory authorities without considering the reduced efficiency of the system. Although CETP is regularly monitored by regulators, no action has been taken against violations of the prescribed standards. All CETP- treated wastewater is discharged into one or other water bodies causing pollution. Ineffective wastewater treatment by CETP and the presence of pollution far above acceptable levels are directly related to the poor quality of the water receiving industrial waste water.

Water Quality Index (WQI) of surface water at various sampling locations receiving industrial discharges:

Gujarat Regions	*WQI*	*WQI Range*	*Water Quality Indicators (Status) (CCME, 2005)*	
Fulzer River (Jamnagar)	55	44–61 (Poor to marginal water quality)	95–100	Excellent
SInhan River (Jamnagar)	56		80–94	Good
Asi River (Jamnagar)	59		60–79	Fair
Gangasagar Lake (Ahmedabad)	44		45–9	Poor (Marginal)
Ruper River (Patan)	61		0–44 Very Poor	
Banas River (Banas)	59			

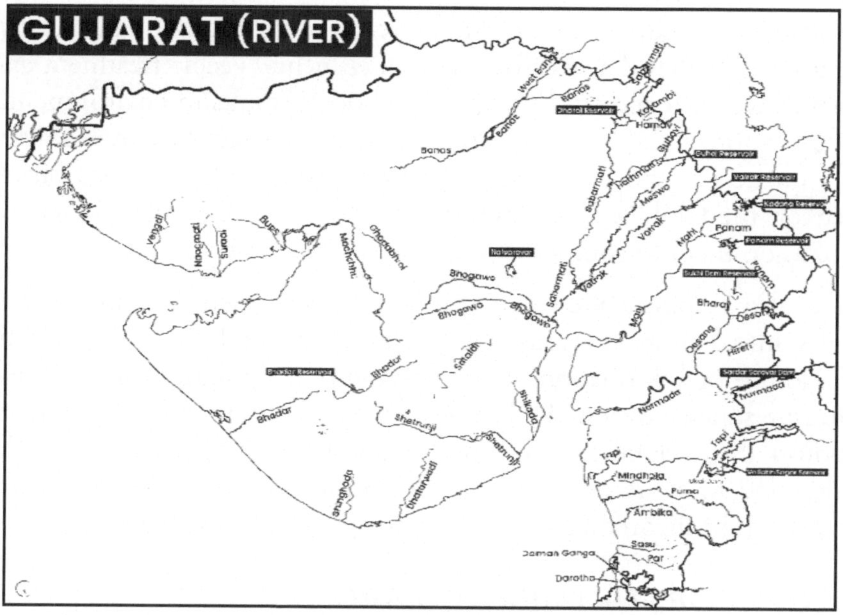

River Systems Flowing Through Gujarat

The quality of water bodies in Gujarat is analyzed in this section. It is realized that the presence of harmful viruses and protozoa in water bodies is responsible for causing illness. River bodies having a low WQI like Gangasagar Lake, Ruper River and Banas River have the presence of pollutants in water bodies above the acceptable levels and can have a negative impact on human health, livestock, agriculture, property, etc.

CONCLUSION

Gujarat may have to prepare itself for various challenges because of its location. A better understanding of future risks and responding accordingly requires a multidimensional approach that involves multiple agencies. There are no strict laws in place to regulate land use and prevent urban development. Unplanned or unscientific urban planning may lead to serious disasters and accidents in the future. Hence a detailed study needs to be conducted on risk zones to help stakeholders maki informed decisions. Hence, a detailed study needs to be conducted on risk zones to help stakeholders make informed decisions.

A state with unique characteristics in terms of the location of industries and water bodies that receive chemical effluents. Feeble treatment and ineffective enforcement by regulatory bodies results in environmental degradation. In addition, due to the constraints faced by the MSMEs i.e. financially and technologically, there are no other options but to rely on the CETPs. Therefore, it is important to enforce strict enactments on them to comply with the prescribed limits.

It is also recommended that the laws be amended to bring stricter rules into action. Various amendments like high penalties, public disclosure of information about pollution and polluters, and similar measures, are suggested. The challenges faced by the city due to industrial development and the resulting water pollution may be addressed to some extent if the conclusions of the discussion in this paper can be incorporated into the policies adopted by the city.

SCOPE FOR FURTHER RESEARCH

With the available secondary data, this study was done as an exploratory research. Going forward, an empirical study can be initiated for further analysis through the primary data to find effectives of CETPs in MSMEs and also to find the factors influencing the same. Since the present is restricted only to Ahmedabad City of Gujarat, the representation of all the states of the country can be considered for generalization of the findings.

REFERENCES

[1] National Institute of Urban Affairs (n.d.), "End to End Early Warning System for Ukai and Local Floods in Surat City" Available at: https://smartnet.niua.org/sites/default/files/resources/End%20to%20End%20EWS_Surat.pdf

[2] India Environment Portal (2006). *Environmental report. India Environment Portal.* Available at: http://www.indiaenvironmentportal.org.in/files/environmental.pdf

[3] OECD (Organization for Economic Cooperation and Development), 2006. Environmental compliance and enforcement in India: Rapid assessment."

Available at: http://www.indiaenvironmentportal.org.in/files/environmental.pdf

[4] Comptroller and Auditor General (2011). "Performance audit of water pollution in India" (New Delhi).

[5] Government of Gujarat (2015). "Annual Report-2014–15", Gandhi Nagar: Gujarat Pollution Control Board, Govt. of Gujarat.

[6] Singla, M. (2023). "MSMEs: The Growth Engine of India to Achieve Sustainable Development Goals and Self-Reliance. In Role of Micro, Small and Medium Enterprises in Achieving SDGs: Perspectives from Emerging Economies." Singapore: Springer Nature Singapore.

[7] Ministry of Micro, Small and Medium Enterprises (2022). "Annual report 2021–22", New Delhi: Ministry of Micro, Small and Medium Enterprises, Govt. of India.

[8] Canadian Council of Ministers of the Environment (CCME), WQI (2005). "Standard Methods for the examinations of water and wastewater", *American Public Health Association,* Washington, DC.

SECTION 5
FINANCIAL ASPECTS

An Analysis of Credit Management Practices and Their Influence on Profitability: Evidence from Listed Microfinance Institutions in India

Nilesh P. Movalia[1] **and Viralkumar M. Shilu**[2]

ABSTRACT: Microfinance institutions (MFIs) play a critical role in extending formal financial services to underserved populations, particularly those seeking small, short-term loans. In the current economic climate, ensuring the safeguard and sustainability of MFIs is paramount. This study investigates the credit management practices and the impact of non-performing assets (NPAs) on the profitability of listed MFIs in India. A descriptive analysis was conducted using secondary data, specifically annual reports, from seven listed MFIs spanning the fiscal years 2017–18 to 2022–23. Key financial indicators revealed an average credit growth rate of 20%, a capital adequacy ratio of 24%, and a significant decline in return on equity. The potential for Self-Help Groups to expand their membership and access to financial services was also noted. Regression analysis demonstrated a negative correlation between gross NPAs and provision coverage ratios with return on assets, consistent with existing literature (Ekinci & Poyraz, 2019). Conversely, other variables exhibited a positive relationship with profitability.

Keywords: *Credit Growth, Gross NPA Ratio, Return on Asset, Return on Equity, Provision Coverage Ratio, Write-offs, Self-help Groups and Microfinance Institutions.*

---

[1] Assistant Professor, School of Management, Shreyarth University-Ahmedabad, Gujarat, India. E-mail: nilesh.movalia@gmail.com

[2] Principal, Government Arts and Commerce College-Jafarabad, Gujarat, India. E-mail: prof.viralshilu@gmail.com

INTRODUCTION

Micro-finance institutions are the financial institutions or organizations which provide the primary financial services to the people. They offer savings accounts, insurance, small loans, funding for the education and primary needs of customer. These services are offered to the small income groups or low-income group people. It can also be called as the backbone of the rural economy.

As a developing economy, there is a significant portion of the population is living in rural area and associated with agricultural and allied activities. Rural economy is plays an important role in rural employment, gross domestic products and supply of food grains to the country. As a rural economy, it suffers from the many issues and problems like lack of infrastructure facilities, lack of formal financial system and mismatch of regional balanced development. Government emphasise on development of rural economy by providing support to improve the development of rural economy. Rural population is not aware about the basic financial products and services and Microfinance institutions.

There are various elements of the rural economy like Agriculture, small -scale industries, infrastructure etc. No question to think about the livelihood of the people without the support of the banking and financial services. Formal financial and banking system is unable to reach every-corner of the rural economy due to cost of operation and target customer. Hence small financial or informal financial institutions should step into the system and they can offer the suitable products and services to them for the upliftment of the rural economy.

Microfinance Institutions were established with the objective of financial inclusion to empower individuals and society in the rural areas which eventually leads to offering primary banking and financial services like, small size loans, saving accounts, Insurance, small business loans, loans to buy small things and family items. These services are basically offered to the individual with low income, lack of collateral or lack of any previous credit record and seasonal business etc.

Microfinance institutions are operating in an informal structure where customers are not aware about the regulatory framework and formal financial system. They always work based on trust. Sometime micro finance institutions are unable to get the interest and advances back from the customer because of one reason or anothe. Eventually it will affect the financial position and performance of the microfinance institutions. Therefore, this research has attempted to analise the credit management and its impact on profitability of Listed Micro-finance Institutions in India for a period of last six year i.e. financial year 2017–18 to 2022–23. Study has analised various financial indicators like credit growth, return on assets, return on equity, Gross NPA ratio, Provision Coverage Ratio and write offs and Capital Adequacy ratio.

PRESENT SCENARIO OF MICRO FINANCE IN INDIA:

There are more than 200 MFIs[2] operating in India across the different states of India as of March-2022. There are two different categories of extending microfinance services, which are as under:

1. The bank-led approach, Self-Help Groups-Bank Linkage Program (SHG-BLG),
2. The Micro Finance Institution (MFI)-led approach.

The program presently covers US$ 140 million families and US$ 11.9 million SHG groups, with a combined savings of US$ 472.4 billion, as of March 31, 2022.

Additionally noteworthy is the credit linkage thus far, with US$ 997.2 billion in loans given and US$ 3.4 million SHGs credit connected in FY 2021–22 (compared to US$ 2.9 million groups in 2020–21). As of March 31, 2022, there was a credit outstanding of US$ 1510.5 billion, representing US$ 6.74 million SHGs (or US$ 0.24 million on average). The numerous success stories in this magazine demonstrate that even while the average ticket size is not large, the impact can be life-changing.

The E-Shakti programme, under which financial and non-financial data of over US$ 1.2 million SHGs has been digitized to give comfort to banks for credit linkage of SHGs, is hoped to improve credit linkage.

The Malegam Committee provided three different margin caps for NBFC-MFIs: 10% for those with loan portfolios worth US$ 1 billion or more, 12% for other NBFC-MFIs, and 24% for individual loans.

A consistent margin cap of 12% was imposed for all NBFC-MFIs in the final rules published on December 2, 2011, along with a cap of 26% on individual loans. The set interest rate ceiling of 26% was lifted in 2012 due to the fluctuating costs of borrowing and to allow for operational flexibility, although with the restriction that the maximum difference between the minimum and maximum interest rate for individual loans cannot be more than 4%.

In India, microfinance is critical for achieving financial inclusion for the underprivileged in both rural and urban areas. When properly handled, lending to the impoverished can work wonders for the nation's growth and the reduction of poverty. Microcredit can significantly contribute to the reduction of poverty when government agencies and MFIs collaborate.

It is therefore expected that the industry has showed 40% annual growth rates until very recently. During this phase of fast expansion, there have been several crises and macroeconomic shocks, the most recent of which being the Covid-19 pandemic.

REVIEW OF LITERATURE

Tekalign Elias Era and Jaladi Ravi (2022) studied the effect of credit management and its impact on financial performance of MFIs in Hawassa. The study has analysed three micro finance institutions during the year 2008 to 2017. It was based on key financial indicators like Return on Investment, non-performing loan to total loan ratio, times interest earned ratio, average collection Period, by using a penal data to arrive at results. Finally, it was concluded that credit collection policy, interest rate and credit risk are significantly impacting the financial performance. Shanu Singh and Dr. Chandrama Singh (2017) examine the growth of NPAs in MFIs in India with reference to Bihar region. The purpose of the research was to know the major trend of NPAs and remedial methods. Research concluded that there was a decline in non-performing assets in micro finance institutions during the study period. **Ramazan Ekinci and Gulden Poyraz (2019)** have conducted study on how credit risk affects the Financial Performance of Deposit banks in Turkey. There were 26 commercial banks analised for period of 2005–2017 by using a secondary data. Various financial indicators like ROA, ROE, NPLs, etc. get the concrete result. Final results show that there was a relationship between credit risk and Profitability of deposit banks during the study. **Van Dan Dang (2019)** attempted to study the impact of growth in loan on performance of bank with reference to credit risk, bank solvency and profitability. Study was conducted on sample of Vietnamese commercial banks for a period of 2006 to 2017. It has concluded that the growth in loan affect the performance, solvency of banks. **Kwadwo Boateng (2020)** examined the credit risk and profitability of select saving and Loan companies with an aim to impact credit risk on profitability, non-performing loans, effectiveness of credit risk management. In study, end result showsadverse impact of credit management on profitability. **Smarika Jain and Dr Sangeetha R. (2021)** carried out research on how credit risk affect the financial performance of commercial banks. There were top thirteen commercial banks studied for a period of 10 years (2009– 2018) with an aim to know the effect of CAR and NPA on the ROE. Study concluded that there is significant impact of NPA on ROE and negative impact of CAR on ROE.

Research Gap

This study on credit management and impact of non-performing assets on profitability of listed microfinance institutions. It was observed that previous studies were focused towards the growth in non-performing assets and credit management during pre-2020 of microfinance institutions. Hence this study has identified the gap that there is an opportunity to undergo a study on 'how the non-performing assets impact the profitability of MFIs'? This has been studied by considering various independent variables like Capital Adequacy ratio, PCR, write offs, Credit Growth along with nonperforming assets ratio to know the true picture about the impact of non-performing assets on profitability of MFIs in India.

MAJOR OBJECTIVES

- To know the credit growth in Microfinance institutions.
- To know the non-performing assets among the Microfinance Institutions.
- To know the Capital Adequacy ratio of MFIs.
- To know the impact of NPAs on Profitability of Micro Finance Institutions.

METHODOLOGY

Research methodology is a process of identification of problem, collection of relevant data and analysis of data to reach out at meaningful conclusion. It also represents the in-depth investigation of the observation with a view to arrive at concrete conclusion. Research methodology has the aim to finalize the activities of research design and data collection procedure.

Research Design: Research design is a structure through which a study is conducted by the researcher. Here Descriptive research design has been adopted to conduct this study because it would help to make in-depth study of relationship between dependent variable on independent variable.

Data sources and Collection: Data was source from the Secondary source. It was collected from Annual reports of the MFIs, NSE, BSE, Screener websites.

Sample Size: There are 7 Micro finance Institutions (Listed on Stock Exchanges) were selected based on the market capitalization of more than 500 Crores for the study, which are

1. Arman Financial Services Ltd, 2. CreditAccess Grameen Ltd, 3. Fusion Micro Finance Ltd, 4. Muthoot Microfin Ltd, 5. Satin Creditcare Network Ltd, 6. Spandana Sphoorty Financial Ltd and 7. Ujjivan Financial Services Ltd.

Period of study: Financial Year: 2017–18 to 2022–23 (6 Years)

DESCRIPTIVE STATISTICS

Descriptive statistics show the measure of central tendency of the observation under the study which represent by the Mean, standard Deviation, Minimum, Maximum value. It will help to summaries the data in numerical term for the basic understanding and interpretation of the features and behaviour of data before the any inferences or estimation of the sample.

Table 1: Descriptive Statistics

Variable |	*Obs*	*Mean*	*Std. Dev.*	*Min*	*Max*
CAR |	42	25.75032	12.93967	.2358	50.74
Cgrowth |	42	38.15456	35.85039	–20.40459	158.6452
GNPA |	42	4.613831	5.119799	0	27.79856
NNPA |	42	2.756021	9.280465	0	60
PCR |	42	75.72737	116.9325	–106.6827	628.098
Writeoff |	42	19.43784	30.61572	0	142.1092
ROA |	42	1.931601	2.030724	–1.981707	6.308697
ROE |	42	9.907773	14.60364	–17.97235	76.42276

MEASURES

This research paper is focused in credit management and its impact on profitability of listed Microfinance institutions. There are seven microfinance Institutions that were studied for the period of financial year 2017–18 to 2022–23. There are two categories of variables have been identified first are independent variables which are Credit Growth, Gross non-performing assets, capital adequacy ratio, Provision Coverage Ratio, Write-offs ratio, and Dependent variable a measure of profit are Return on Assets, Return on Equity have been used to determine the impact of non-performing assets on profitability of Microfinance institutions. ANOVA was applied to know the significance difference in a financial indicator among the microfinance institutions and regression analysis was employed to know the impact of independent variables on profitability measures of Microfinance Institutions. Microsoft Excel and Stata software were used to compute the ANOVA and Regression respectively at 5% level of significance.

RESULTS AND DISCUSSION

This section of the research highlights the key aspects and results of the study.

Credit Growth

Credit Growth refers to the increase in the demand of the credit facilities in a country which included individual credit and industrial credit. This data represents the consumer spending and business interment and overall economic activity in a particular country or region.

H01: There is a no significance difference in credit growth among the MFIs.

Table 2: Credit Growth

ANOVA

Source of Variation	*SS*	*df*	*MS*	*F*	*P-Value*	*F Crit*
Between Groups	6333.32	6.00	1055.55	0.80	0.58	2.37
Within Groups	46361.96	35.00	1324.63			
Total	**52695.28**	**41.00**				

Table 2 shows that the *P-value* is 0.58 which is more than the 0.05 level of significance so null hypothesis is accepted. Hence there would not be a significance difference in credit growth among the microfinance institutions during the study period. It was declined when covid-19 spread in the year 2020 later on financial year 2021–22 it was back to normal growth path.

Capital Adequacy Ratio

The CAR (Capital Adequacy Ratio) is a key banking indicator to measure the financial strength and capital base of any financial institution to absorb the potential losses arising out of the unforeseen business. It is a key ratio which determines the lending and investment decision of a financial institutions.

H02: There is a no significance difference in Capital Adequacy Ratio among the MFIs.

Table 3: Capital Adequacy Ratio

ANOVA

Source of Variation	*SS*	*df*	*MS*	*F*	*P-Value*	*F Crit*
Between Groups	6013.74	6.00	1002.29	41.22	0.00	2.37
Within Groups	851.10	35.00	24.32			
Total	**6864.84**	**41.00**				

Table 3 shows that *P-value* is 0.00 which is less than the 0.05 level of significance. So null hypothesis failed to accept hence there would be a significant difference in capital adequacy ratio among the microfinance institutions during the study period (Jain & Sangeetha R., 2021).

Return on Assets

The Return on Assets shows an efficiency of a financial institutions to generate the income from its assets. It is computed by the net profit divided by the total assets of an MFI. Higher the ROA the better is the MFI and vice versa.

H03: There is a no significance difference in Return on assets among the MFIs.

Table 4: Return on Assets

ANOVA

Source of Variation	*SS*	*df*	*MS*	*F*	*P-Value*	*F Crit*
Between Groups	45.07	6.00	7.51	2.12	0.08	2.37
Within Groups	124.01	35.00	3.54			
Total	**169.08**	**41.00**				

Table 4 shows that the *P-value* is 0.08 which is more than the 0.05 level of significant so null hypothesis is accepted hence there is no significance difference in return on assets among the microfinance institutions during the study period.

Return on Equity (ROE)

The return on equity is a financial ratio to measure a return generated by the financial institution based on the shareholders' funds or on total Equity of MFI. It can be computed by the profit after tax divided by the total shareholders' funds. This measure is generally used by the shareholders to know the profitability on their interment and future growth prospects of an MFI.

H04: There is a no significance difference in Return on equity among the MFIs.

Table 5: Return on Equity

ANOVA

Source of Variation	*SS*	*df*	*MS*	*F*	*P-Value*	*F Crit*
Between Groups	1345.96	6.00	224.33	1.06	0.40	2.37
Within Groups	7397.96	35.00	211.37			
Total	**8743.92**	**41.00**				

Table 5 shows that the *P-value* is 0.40 which is more than the 0.05 a level of significance; so null hypothesis is accepted. Hence, there is no significant difference in return on equity among the microfinance institutions during the study period.

Gross Non-Performing Ratio (GNPA Ratio)

The Gross NPAs represent the bad loans and advances of the total loan book of a financial institution, which included substandard assets, doubtful assets and loss assets. As per the reserve bank of India instruct-tion financial institutions need to record the non-performing assets once an asset is unable to generate any return till 90 days. The criteria for identification on NPAs are different based on the priority sector and non-priority sector advances. Higher the GNPA ratio the higher the risk associated to the business of financial institutions and vice versa. So always financial institutions should have to keep quality assets.

H05: There is a no significance difference in Gross NPA Ratio among the MFIs.

Table 6: Gross NPA Ratio

ANOVA

Source of Variation	*SS*	*df*	*MS*	*F*	*P-Value*	*F Crit*
Between Groups	1278.28	6.00	213.05	2.02	0.09	2.37
Within Groups	3686.91	35.00	105.34			
Total	**4965.19**	**41.00**				

Table 6 shows that the *P-value* is 0.09 which is more than the 0.05 a level of significance; so null hypothesis is accepted. Hence there is no significant difference in Gross NPA Ratio among the microfinance institutions during the study period.

Provision Coverage Ratio (PCR)

The Provision coverage ratio is the financial indicator related to the non-performing assets which represents that the amount of money has been kept aside as a percentage of the non-performing assets. So in case of no recovery of the assets can be write off against the given provision and eventually it helps financial institutions to keep their balance sheet clean.

H06: There is a no significance difference in Provision coverage ratio among the MFIs.

Table 7: Provision Coverage Ratio

ANOVA

Source of Variation	*SS*	*df*	*MS*	*F*	*P-Value*	*F Crit*
Between Groups	230102.05	6.00	38350.34	2.05	0.08	2.37
Within Groups	655139.98	35.00	18718.29			
Total	**885242.03**	**41.00**				

Table 7 shows that the *P-value* is 0.08 which is more than 0.05 a level of significance; so null hypothesis is accepted. Hence there is no significant difference in Provision coverage ratio among the micro-finance institutions during the study period.

Impact of Non-performing Assets on Profitability of MFIs

Profitability of any organisation always always depends on the many other factors or variables and the same was tested by using the regression analysis in this study. There are five independent variables have been identified and studied in the study to arrive at meaningful result.

H07: There is a no significance impact of CAR, GNPA, Credit Growth, PCR and write offs on return on assets of MFIs.

Table 8: Regression Analysis Return on Assets

ROA	*Coef.*	*Std. Err.*	*t*	*P>|t|*	*[95% Conf.*	*Interval]*
CAR	.0060131	.0285627	0.21	0.834	–.0519147	.063941
Cgrowth	.0116864	.0094801	1.23	0.226	–.0075401	.030913
GNPA	–.0413987	.0680745	–0.61	0.547	–.1794602	.0966627
PCR	–.0036143	.0028141	–1.28	0.207	–.0093216	.002093
Write-off	.0073269	.0114646	0.64	0.527	–.0159244	.0305782
_cons	1.653161	.9208601	1.80	0.081	–.21443	3.520752

Table 8 of regression analysis of return on assets shows that the Gross NPA (Ekinci & Poyraz, 2019) and Provision coverage ratios are negatively related to the return on assets of the micro-finance intuitions during the study period however other variables like Capital adequacy ratio (Li & Zou, 2014), Credit growth are positively related to the return on assets. (Li & Zou, 2014)

$$ROA_{it} = \alpha_{it} + \beta_1 CAR_{it} + \beta_2 Cgrowth_{it} - \beta_3\, GNPA_{it} - \beta_4\, PCR_{it} + \beta_5 Writeoffs_{it} + \epsilon_{it}$$

H08: There is a no significance impact of CAR, GNPA, Credit Growth, PCR and write offs on return on Equity of MFIs.

Table 9: Regression Analysis Return on Equity

ROE	*Coef.*	*Std. Err.*	*t*	*P>|t|*	*[95% Conf.*	*Interval]*
CAR	.0007734	.1773585	0.00	0.997	–.3589263	.3604731
Cgrowth	.1687977	.0588661	2.87	0.007	.0494117	.2881836
GNPA	.8558179	.4227043	2.02	0.050	–.0014661	1.713102

ROE	*Coef.*	*Std. Err.*	*t*	*P>|t|*	*[95% Conf.*	*Interval]*
PCR	–.0194208	.0174741	–1.11	0.274	–.05486	.0160183
Writeoff	.007681	.0711887	0.11	0.915	–.1366964	.1520584
_cons	.8202475	5.718024	0.14	0.887	–10.77644	12.41694

Table 9 of regression analysis of return on equity shows that the Provision coverage ratio is negatively related to the return on equity of the micro-finance intuitions during the study period however other variables are positively related to the return on equity.

$$ROE_{it} = \alpha_{it} + \beta_1 CAR_{it} + \beta_2 Cgrowth_{it} + \beta_3\, GNPA_{it} - \beta_4\, PCR_{it} + \beta_5 Writeoffs_{it} + \epsilon_{it}$$

Where,

ROA: Return on assets,

ROE: Return on Equity

CAR: Capital Adequacy ratio

Cgrowth: Credit Growth

GNPA: Gross non-performing assets

PCR: Provision Coverage ratio

Analysis of Self-Help Groups

Table 10: Self Help Groups Under NRLM

Sr. No.	*State Name**	*SHGs Type*			*Sub Total*	*Total Members*
		New	*Revived*	*Pre-NRLM*		
1.	NRLP States	51,98,174	7,80,260	20,35,579	80,14,013	8,75,64,653
2.	North West States	2,73,301	15,442	1,922	2,90,665	25,23,335
3.	North East States	1,14,266	8,584	17,278	1,40,128	12,83,369
4.	Union Territories	8,137	2,535	990	11,662	1,36,331
Total		**55,93,878**	**8,06,821**	**20,55,769**	**84,56,468**	**9,15,07,688**

Source: https://nrlm.gov.in/shgOuterReports.do?methodName=showShgreport

Self-help group (SHGs) are the groups formed by the group of people of a society or community with an objective to address their common problems. SHGs works based on mutual support and under-standing which serve many issues based on the situation. It supports the livelihoods. In the year 2011, Government of India has started. The National Rural Livelihood Mission (NRLM) to support the rural poor and to enable them to increase their income and access to financial services. Here is the analysis of Self-Help Groups with reference to number of SHGs, total Members, SHGs as per social categories and SHGs with and without the bank accounts.

Above table 10 show that the number of Self-Help Groups are working under the NRLM in different parts of the country. It has been divided in to four different categories and all the categories includes different states. Looking at the highest number of SHGs, it is part of the NRLP states and it was significantly boost after NRLM (The National Rural Livelihood Mission).

Table 11: SHGs Group as per Social Category

Sr. No.	*State Name*	*SHGs Social Category*				
		SC SHG	*ST SHG*	*Minority SHG*	*Others SHG*	*Sub Total*
1.	NRLP States	16,47,620	10,09,789	6,66,578	46,90,026	80,14,013
2.	North West States	94,584	11,976	7,856	1,76,249	2,90,665
3.	North East States	10,033	97,201	6,322	26,572	1,40,128
4.	Union Territories	1,213	2,971	486	6,992	11,662
	Total	**17,53,450**	**11,21,937**	**6,81,242**	**48,99,839**	**84,56,468**

Source: https://nrlm.gov.in

Table 11 shows Self-Help Groups as per the social categories. More than the half of the total self-help groups comes under other categories, while around 20% belong to SC, 13% ST and 8% to minority SHGs.

Table 12: SHGs with and without Bank Account

Sr. No.	*State Name*	*Bank Account*		*Total SHGs*
		No Bank Account	*Have a Bank Account*	
1.	NRLP States	2,88,561	77,25,452	80,14,013
2.	North West States	982	2,89,683	2,90,665
3.	North East States	3,068	1,37,060	1,40,128
4.	Union Territories	14	11,648	11,662
	Total	**2,92,625**	**81,63,843**	**84,56,468**

Source: https://nrlm.gov.in

Table 12 represent that around 3.4% of the total SHGs do not have a bank account and among them, most belong to the NRLP States. Union territories are top iamong the fours in having a bank account as percentage of total SHGs they belong. Around 96.4% SHGs that belong to NRPL states, have a bank account and rest do not. There is scope for the further expansion (Singh & Singh, 2017) of the business by using a banking service.

FINDINGS

- **Credit Growth:** Looking at the test result, it shows no any difference in credit growth among the MFIs. When it look at the Average growth rate of the MFIs was around 20% which was quite good, while looking at individual companies, Arman Financial, Fusion Micro Finance, Spandana Sphoorty growth around 45% which is above the average of the peers. Rest of the companies has a scope to perform better.
- **Capital Adequacy Ratio:** There has been a variation in CAR ratios among the MFIs and it was decline during Covid-19 and now average of CAR of MFIs is above 24%. Arman Financial and Spandana Sphoorty have CAR of above 30% which is better than the peers. Credit access Gramin and Ujjivan financial services has a scope for the improvement in regard to the capital adequacy ratio.
- **GNPA:** Average GNPA ratio of MFIs is fall in the rage of 1.7% to 11%. Spandana Sphoorty, Satin Creditcare and Muthoot Microfin

having more GNPA ratios among the all the companies under study compare to the peer group.

- **PCR:** It shows that, there was no significant variation in PCR as per the ANOVA results among the MFIs. But looking at the last six years data, few among them have kept significant amount of provision during the last years. It inferences that there might be possibility of the default.
- **Write-offs:** ANOVA result shows that the there is a significance variation in write-offs of bad loans by the MFIs.
- **Return on Assets:** Overall MFIs generating 1.95 return on total assets which is not bad in a situation of COVID-19 phase. During the year 2020–21 their return sharply fell below the 50% of the return of the previous year. In the year 2022–23 they back to the normal return as pre-Covid level.
- **Return on Equity:** There was also no variations in ROE among the MIFs. Average returns of the MFI are near 9% which is below the pre-covid level which was 11%.
- SHGs have only 9.15 Crore members are associated in that so there is a need to have more members.
- Still 3.45% of SHGs need to connect to the banking system for better growth and opportunities.

SUGGESTIONS

- Credit Access Grameen and Ujjivan Financial Services should have to raise the additional capital to strengthen the financial position.
- Fusion Micro Finance, Satin Creditcare Network and Ujjivan Financial Services need to improve the quality of advances to minimize the bad loans.
- SHGs should expand the business in the unbankable area to increase the market share and improve the livelihood.

RECOMMENDATIONS AND EXPANSION

- It helps the MFIs, regulators and stakeholders to understand the present situation of selected MFIs.
- It helps researchers to conduct the study in the area of MFIs and their performance.

- This study can be extended to the unlisted companies operating the business in India.
- It has scope to undergo a comparative study with NBFC or banks.

CONCLUSION

Microfinance institutions have been working to meet the rising demand of the people of rural and semi-urban areas. This study examined that the average credit growth in the last six years was around 30% exception to the 2020–2021 due to the covid-19 pandemic. MFIs have an opportunity to expand the market share in rural India to meet the demand and improve the livelihood of the people. Credit has two sides. One is return and another is risk, so wherever any financial institutions are offering credit they will generate the return, but somewhere they also have to face a loan loss. Therefore, MFIs should have to develop a system to manage the non-performing assets in the proper way to minimize loan loss. Microfinance Institutions should keep enough capital to absorb institutions that arise due to default in payment of loans. Overall, the profitability performance was good of the microfinance institutions during the study irrespective of pandemic and competition.

REFERENCES

[1] Boateng, K. (2020). Credit Risk Management and Profitability in Select Savings and Loans Companies in Ghana. *International Journal of Advanced Research.*

[2] Chick Dieudone Ndab (2018). The Impact of Credit Management on the Financial Performance of Microfinance Institutions, Centria University of Applied Sciences.

[3] Dang, V.D. (2019). The effects of loan growth on bank performance: Evidence from Vietnam.

[4] Management Science Letters, 899–910.

[5] Deniz, Igan and Marcelo, Pinheiro (2011). Credit Growth and Bank Soundness, IMF Working Paper.

[6] Fan Li, Yijun Zou (2014). The Impact of Credit Risk Management on Profitability of Commercial Banks, Umeå School of Business and Economics.

[7] Gabriel, Di Bella (2011). The Impact of the Global Financial Crisis on Microfinance and Policy Implications, IMF Working Paper.

[8] Ramazan Ekinci, G.P. (2019). The Effect of Credit Risk on Financial Performance of Deposit Banks in Turkey. CPoromcpeudtiear C Socmiepnucete 0r 0S c(2ie0n1c9e, 979-987.

[9] Shanu Singh, D.C. (2017). Growth of Non-Performing Assets in Microfinance Institutions: Evidence from India. IOSR Journal of Business and Management, 19(6), 14–22. Retrieved from www.iosrjournals.org

[10] Smarika Jain, D.S. (2021). Impact of Credit Risk Management on Financial Performance of Commercial Banks. International Journal of Business and Management Invention, 10(7), 17–22.

[11] Tekalign Elias Era, J.R. (2022). The effect of Credit Management on Financial Performance of Microfinance Institutions in Hawassa, Ethiopia. Innovations, 108–120.

Websites

https://armanindia.com/quaterlyandannualreports.aspx
https://dbie.rbi.org.in
https://fusionmicrofinance.com/investor-relations/#annual-reports
https://growingscience.com/msl/introduction.html
https://muthootmicrofin.com/investors/annual-report
https://satincreditcare.com
https://www.bseindia.com/bseplus/AnnualReport
https://www.bseindia.com/bseplus/AnnualReport/539874/74257539874.pdf
https://www.creditaccessgrameen.in/investors/financials-and-investor-presentations/annual- reports
https://www.ibef.org/blogs/evolution-of-micro-finance-in-india
https://www.rbi.org.in/commonman
https://www.screener.in https://www.spandanasphoorty.com/investors?id=2
https://www.ujjivan.com/annual-reports
https://www.sa-dhan.net/wp-content/uploads/2023/05/MFI-Directory_Final_.pdf

ABBREVIATIONS

MFIs : Micro-Finance Institutions
PCR : Provision Coverage Ratio ROA: Return on Assets
ROE : Return On equity
CAR : Capital Adequacy Ratio

GNPAs : Gross Non-Performing Assets
NNPAs : Net Non-Performing Assets
NPAs : Non-Performing Assets
NRLP : The National Rural Livelihoods Project
RBI : Reserve Bank of India

State Name used in the analysis of self-help groups are given here:

A. NRLP States	*B. North West States*	*C. North East States*	*D. Union Territories*
1. Andhra Pradesh	1. Haryana	1. Arunachal Pradesh	1. Andaman and Nicobar
2. Assam	2. Himachal Pradesh	2. Manipur	2. Goa
3. Bihar	3. Jammu And Kashmir	3. Meghalaya	3. Ladakh
4. Chhattisgarh	4. Punjab	4. Mizoram	4. Lakshadweep
5. Gujarat	5. Uttarakhand	5. Nagaland	5. Puducherry
6. Jharkhand		6. Sikkim	6. The Dadra and Nagar Haveli and Daman and Diu
7. Karnataka		7. Tripura	
8. Kerala			
9. Madhya Pradesh			
10. Maharashtra			
11. Odisha			
12. Rajasthan			
13. Tamil Nadu			
14. Telangana			
15. Uttar Pradesh			
16. West Bengal			

SHGs and Savings in Gujarat: An Exploratory Study

Vrinda Dave[1], Maurvi Vasavada[2] and Suraj Shah[3]

ABSTRACT: Self-Help Groups (SHGs) in Gujarat have been actively promoting a culture of savings among their members. These groups encourage individuals, especially women, to save regularly, which helps in building financial resilience and creating a safety net for unexpected expenses. Savings within SHGs often serve multiple purposes: Emergency Funds where members contribute to a common fund that can be used during emergencies such as medical expenses or natural disasters. Investment Capital is where savings accumulated within SHGs can be used collectively to invest in income-generating activities such as small businesses or agricultural ventures and loan security, SHG savings often serve as collateral for accessing bank loans, as banks are more willing to lend to groups with a proven track record of saving and repayment. SHGs contribute to social cohesion and community resilience through collective action, ranging from health and sanitation initiatives to skill development programs. Supported by government policies and developmental interventions, SHGs have emerged as linchpins of Gujarat's development narrative, embodying the principles of self-reliance, solidarity, and inclusive growth.

Keywords: *Self Help Groups, Savings, Financial Resilience, Development, Collective Responsibility.*

---

[1] Research Scholar, Social of Social Sciences and Humanities, Ganpat University.

[2] Associate Professor, Ganpat University.

[3] Assistant Professor, Ganpat University.

INTRODUCTION

The concept of 'microfinance' was developed in India during the 1980s to address poverty and promote the empowerment of women. Although the microfinance sector in rural India has significant potential, it encounters obstacles to accessibility. Microfinance is a form of banking service that caters to individuals who face challenges in obtaining conventional banking services. It is aimed at the segment of the population that has little income and is unemployed. Microfinance institutions provide services such as loans, maintaining bank accounts, and offering micro-insurance products. In developing nations like India, conventional financial institutions fail to meet the needs of the impoverished rural population. Therefore, microfinance can play a crucial role in fostering the growth of small-scale enterprises by offering enhanced financial stability.

Microfinance and Self-Help Groups (SHGs) are interconnected entities that play crucial roles in providing financial services to underserved communities, particularly in regions like Gujarat. Microfinance involves the provision of small loans, savings, insurance, and other financial services to individuals who lack access to traditional banking services. SHGs, on the other hand, are community-based organizations where members pool their savings and resources to create a fund from which they can borrow for various purposes. Microfinance institutions (MFIs) work closely with SHGs to extend financial services to their members. MFIs provide loans and other financial products to SHGs, which then distribute these funds among their members based on their needs and repayment capacity. In Gujarat, Self-Help Groups (SHGs) have become a pivotal tool for economic empowerment and financial inclusion, especially in rural and marginalized communities. Microfinance institutions may provide loans directly to SHGs, which then disburse the funds among their members based on their credit needs and repayment capacity.

Self-help groups (SHGs) are community-based organizations formed by a small group of individuals, typically from similar socio-economic backgrounds, who come together to address common goals, particularly related to financial empowerment and social support. These groups, often comprising women in rural and marginalized communities, operate on the principles of mutual trust, cooperation, and collective responsibility. The primary objective of SHGs is to promote self-reliance and economic independence among their members. They achieve this by pooling their savings and resources to create a common fund, from which members can borrow for various purposes, such as starting or expanding small businesses, meeting household expenses, or addressing emergencies.

THE EVOLUTION OF MICROFINANCE IN INDIA

India sets a target of achieving a USD 5 trillion economy by 2025, and the microfinance sector will have a significant impact on improving the living standards of millions of poor families by empowering them to participate to the country's economic expansion. The future trajectory of the sector will be shaped by the capacity of participants to establish novel alliances, innovate new goods, provide fresh avenues for investment, and exploit technology to fulfil customer needs. Between February 2017 and June 2022, the field of microfinance in India has served as a financial assistance network for low-income households by providing credit opportunities to 60 million distinct borrowers through 118 million loan accounts. Throughout this period, the microfinance sector in the country experienced several changes in terms of inclusivity and growth, driven by a mission to generate money and expand services for its intended beneficiaries. In June 2022, the total gross loan portfolio (GLP) of the microfinance industry was INR 2,930 billion.

Microfinance activities in India are present in all 28 states and nine union territories in India. The eastern and Northeast regions have the largest share, accounting for 37% of the businesses. The south holds the second-largest portion at 27%, while the west holds a share of 15%. The figure below displays the distribution of loan portfolios among different institutions in India. In terms of distribution, as of June 2022, banks possess the largest portion of the market at 38%, while NBFC-MFIs hold a 35% share. SFBs, NBFCs, and other organisations collectively make about 27% of the total.

The Indian microfinance industry primarily functions through two operational modalities, and The Self Help Group Bank Linkage Programme (SHG-BLP) is one of them. It was created in the early

1990s, aimed to provide banking services to the vulnerable and unorganized sector. The NABARD initiated the plan in 1992 to establish a connection between the unorganized sector and the formal banking sector.

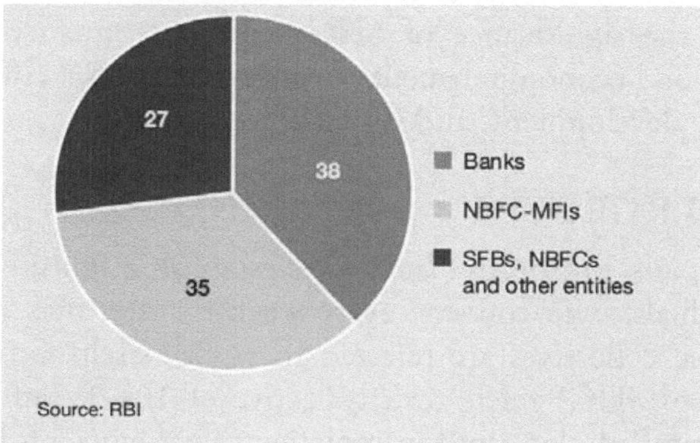

Figure 1: Distribution of Loan Portfolios among Different Institutions in India

As part of this initiative, banks were permitted to establish savings accounts for Self-Help Groups (SHGs). Self-Help Groups (SHGs) are often registered or unregistered organizations that consist of 10 to 20 members, primarily women, from economically disadvantaged backgrounds. They collect contributions from members and utilize the combined funds to provide loans to members in need. Under this scheme, banks offer loans to Self-Help Groups (SHGs) with a group guarantee. The amount of the loan can be multiple times the deposits made by the SHGs in the banks. Banks should take into account the comprehensive credit demands of self-help group (SHG) members, including (a) income-generating activities, (b) social necessities such as housing, education, marriage, etc., and (c) debt consolidation.

SHGs, often comprising women from rural and semi-urban areas, serve as catalysts for socio-economic transformation. By pooling their resources and accessing microfinance services, these groups enable members to engage in income-generating activities, such as small-scale agriculture, livestock rearing, and handicraft production. This not only enhances household incomes but also promotes women's empowerment and social inclusion. Additionally, SHGs in Gujarat serve as platforms for skill development, capacity building, and knowledge sharing, fostering entrepreneurship and innovation at the grassroots level. By fostering financial independence and entrepreneurship, these initiatives empower individuals to break the cycle of poverty and build a better future for themselves and their families. Therefore, the significance of SHGs and microfinance in Gujarat extends beyond economic benefits to encompass social empowerment, community development, and sustainable growth.

SELF HELP GROUPS

To secure loans, prospective borrowers establish a collective of at least five individuals, who convene every week for meetings to repay the loans. These collectives are referred to as Self Help Groups. A Self Help Group (SHG) refers to a collective of 10–20 individuals that serves as a unified platform for implementing a range of development initiatives. It is established and cultivated by a non-governmental organisation (NGO), a branch of a bank, or a self-help promoting organisation (SHPI). The purpose of financial intermediation is to facilitate access to affordable financial services while promoting self-management and development. A self-help group might be either registered or unregistered. Registration is mandatory for any group consisting of more than 20 members. Self-Help Groups (SHGs) have proved to be a successful tool and a very efficient means of delivering financial assistance to impoverished individuals in rural areas.

REVIEW OF LITERATURE

In their study, Maity and Sarania (2017) examined the efficacy of a Self-Help Group (SHG) programme in improving the employment rates, income levels, and poverty status of rural households. The research was conducted in the Bodoland region of Assam. The data was acquired by a primary survey conducted in two districts, including Bodoland, Baksa, and Udalguri districts. The poll was performed from May 2013 to October 2013. A combined total of 330 participants were chosen using the multistage purposive sampling technique, encompassing both the controlled and non-controlled groups. The study's findings revealed a substantial rise in the number of days of employment for the participants of the Self-Help Group

(SHG), rising from 108 to 119 days per year. The study employed the Foster, Greer, and Thorbecke (FGT) weighted poverty index to gauge the poverty levels of the participants. The Gini Coefficient and Atkinson measures demonstrate a significant reduction in inequality among the Self-Help Group (SHG) members compared to the non-SHG members, with a decrease of 0.07 and 0.05 percentage points respectively.

The research conducted by Manvar *et al.* (2019) demonstrated that the implementation of Self-Help Groups (SHGs) was an effective method to improve women's health by promoting greater understanding and awareness of health-related concerns, as well as providing financial stability in times of health crisis. The authors proposed engaging the entire community and raising awareness among men about gender equality by providing capacity-building trainings to women.

The quantitative data obtained by Modi (2019) for the research were evaluated using statistical techniques, specifically the t-test and multivariate analysis of variance (MANOVA). The results indicated that the training, as well as several demographic and group-related characteristics, had a noteworthy influence on multiple forms of empowerment, including social, personal, economic, and political empowerment.

Joshi (2002) noted that micro-credit programmes provide small loans to impoverished individuals for self-employment ventures that generate income, enabling them to support themselves and their families. Typically, micro-credit programmes provide a range of services and resources to their clients, along with credit for self-employment. These benefits typically encompass financial savings, educational training, professional networking, and support from peers. It is ironic that micro-enterprises and their contribution to the economy often remain unorganised. Impoverished women typically manage their own economic endeavours with great efficiency due to the intense need to survive. However, the lack of official backing for the economy makes it very challenging for impoverished women to enhance their economic circumstances on an individual and isolated basis.

The study conducted by Rathod and Devi (2019) concluded that the average economic empowerment index of Self-Help Group (SHG) members was significantly greater than that of non-SHG members. The study demonstrated a favourable influence of the Self-Help Groups (SHGs) on the economic and social standing of their members. The average socio-economic empowerment index for SHG members were significantly higher than that of non-members. This suggests that the group approach implemented through SHGs has proven to be a cost-effective method for addressing the social and economic needs of tribal women farmers in their living conditions.

Gujarat

Self-Help Groups (SHGs) play a significant role in empowering women and promoting socio-economic development in Gujarat, as they do in various parts of India. In Gujarat, SHGs are actively supported and promoted by various government agencies, NGOs, and microfinance institutions. The government provides financial assistance, training, and capacity-building programs to encourage the formation and sustainability of SHGs.

Gujarat, a state in western India, is divided into 33 districts. The SHGs are covered under NRLM. It is witnessed that Dahod records the highest SHG type with a total of 14695 SHGs and 140064 members in SHG. Porbandar records the least 2569 SHGs and 25639 members. Ahmedabad has 3430 new SHGs and 4527 revived SHGs. SHGs are prevalent in rural Gujarat and play a crucial role in empowering women economically. These groups provide a platform for women to come together, pool their resources, access credit facilities, and engage in various income-generating activities. SHGs also offer training and capacity-building programs to enhance women's entrepreneurial skills. Gujarat being a business state, SHGs have proved to be a successful initiative especially post-COVID-19. Mehsana has recorded a high demand for total members of 133801 with a total of 12813 SHGs. Gujarat has seen an increase in the number of SHGs in almost all districts.

Table 1: SHGs under NRLM (District Level)

S. No.	*District Name*	*SHGs Type*				*Total Members*
		New	*Revived*	*Pre-NRLM*	*Sub Total*	
1.	AHMADABAD	3430	4527	2341	10298	107070
2.	AMRELI	3968	3615	4105	11688	93896
3.	ANAND	4715	3902	3169	11786	118734
4.	ARAVALLI	2981	3214	2503	8698	85388
5.	BANAS KANTHA	7093	1127	2699	10919	107223
6.	BHARUCH	4060	1309	2494	7863	78991
7.	BHAVNAGAR	2050	1158	1615	4823	48255
8.	BOTAD	1198	458	2128	3784	32639
9.	CHHOTA UDAIPUR	6556	2124	1237	9917	105613
10.	DANG	1811	776	1669	4256	40894
11.	DEVBHUMI DWARKA	1079	115	2289	3483	30686
12.	DOHAD	7644	5186	1865	14695	140064
13.	GANDHINAGAR	1861	3390	747	5998	61982
14.	GIR SOMNATH	2498	1647	1526	5671	52232
15.	JAMNAGAR	3528	593	4789	8910	74269
16.	JUNAGADH	2459	2259	2208	6926	62212
17.	KACHCHH	2584	1758	2457	6799	58836
18.	KHEDA	4549	3222	3224	10995	111519
19.	MAHESANA	4535	4011	4267	12813	133801
20.	MAHISAGAR	3075	510	2394	5979	59067
21.	MORBI	1140	605	1262	3007	31430
22.	NARMADA	2824	1873	533	5230	54551
23.	NAVSARI	5841	2177	3235	11253	116374
24.	PANCH MAHALS	4268	2811	2571	9650	95262
25.	PATAN	5374	4058	1770	11202	114669
26.	PORBANDAR	844	622	1103	2569	25639
27.	RAJKOT	2818	2790	3295	8903	91520
28.	SABAR KANTHA	4672	2709	3542	10923	110091
29.	SURAT	3135	4186	3811	11132	112681
30.	SURENDRANAGAR	3695	1952	1704	7351	73146
31.	TAPI	5152	1749	3368	10269	106116
32.	VADODARA	5597	1704	2122	9423	91194
33.	VALSAD	5503	2181	3965	11649	116131
	Total	122537	74318	82007	278862	2742175

Source: nrlm.gov.in

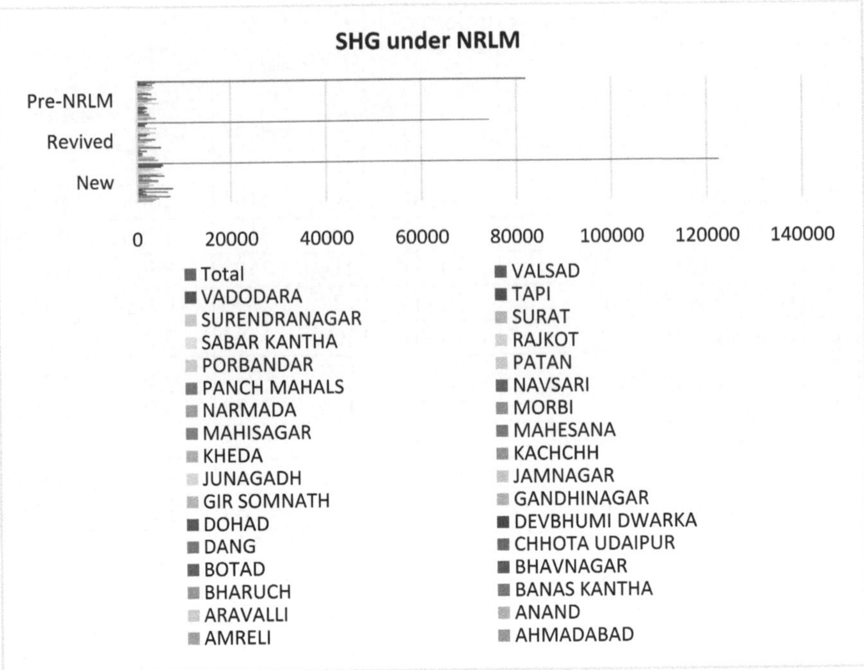

Gujarat SHG Overview

Self-help groups (SHGs) have emerged as powerful instruments for the promotion of the underprivileged classes, particularly in Gujarat. These groups empower marginalized individuals, including women, scheduled castes, scheduled tribes, and other economically disadvantaged groups, by providing them with a platform to collectively address their socio-economic challenges. In Gujarat, SHGs have been instrumental in promoting financial inclusion, social cohesion, and economic self-reliance among the underprivileged.

The table below indicates the present scenario of SHGs in Gujarat. In Gujarat, there are currently 278243 Self-Help Groups (SHGs) operating in all 33 districts of the state, with a total of 27,36,692 members. SHGs majorly promote women to have better livelihood. The social category SC SHG count in Gujarat is 25131, ST count is 82554, PWD is 3578 and Minority count is 6831. This indicates that Gujarat is focusing on its social growth in all ways and most importantly promoting the interests of the underprivileged.

Table 2: Gujarat SHG Overview

		Gujarat
Total District		33
Total SHGs		278243
Total Members		27,36,692
SHGs with less than 5 members		712
Social Category wise	SC SHG	25131
	ST	82554
	Minority	6831
	PWD	3578
	Others	163737

Source: nrlm.gov.in (May 2024).

One of the key ways in which SHGs promote the interests of the underprivileged is by facilitating access to financial services. Through collective savings and microfinance initiatives, SHGs enable members to access credit for entrepreneurial ventures, agricultural activities, and household needs. This access to finance empowers individuals to break the cycle of poverty, invest in education and healthcare, and improve their living standards. By harnessing the collective strength and potential of marginalized communities like PWD, Minority, ST, SC, and others, SHGs have become agents of change, driving inclusive growth and social justice in the state.

Table 3: Funds and Institutional Building Details

(Amount in lakhs)

Particulars	*Gujarat*	
	Numbers	*Amount*
Start-Up fund	16241	406.03
RF	209803	21734.04
CIF	56346	55587.45

Source: nrlm.gov.in

The effective allocation of funds and institutional building initiatives have played a crucial role in Gujarat's development trajectory. By fostering a conducive environment for investment, innovation, and skill development, these institutions have contributed to the state's emergence as an economic powerhouse and a model for sustainable development in India.

The effective allocation of funds and institutional building initiatives have played a crucial role in Gujarat's development trajectory. By fostering a conducive environment for investment, innovation, and skill development, these institutions have contributed to the state's emergence as an economic powerhouse and a model for sustainable development in India.

India has facilitated micro-enterprises by allocating dedicated funding under the category of 'Start-up funds'. According to the data by NRLM, 16241 SHGs were provided funds worth Rs. 406.03 lakhs to initiate their own business in Gujarat. They are anticipated to enact significant transformation at the regional level, consequently diminishing the rates of unemployment and poverty in rural areas of India. A Community Investment Fund (CIF) worth Rs. 55587.45 lakhs is also provided along with a Revolving Fund of Rs. 21734.04 lakhs to accelerate the internal loan procedure and facilitate the members' instant credit need.

Indicator-Wise Analysis of SHG-bank Linkage Programme in Gujarat

1. *Savings*

Table 4 represents the savings of the SHG with banks. The data shows that saving amount in Gujarat has only been rising with an increase in numbers of SHG as well indicates the cumulative number of SHGs saving by banks has jumped from 1105984.7 lakhs from 2014–15 to 5889267.56 in 202–23. The number of poor SHGs contributed to SHGs savings has increased from 7,697,469 in 2014–15 to 13403083 as of 2022–23. India has maximum accounts with commercial banks, as the banks have become a convenient source of finance and are reachable everywhere. On average, the savings amount was a total of commercial banks, regional rural banks and cooperative banks.

Table 4: Savings of SHGs with Banks Agency-wise position (2014–15 to 2022–23) (Amount in Lakh)

Year	*No. of SHGs*	*Savings Amount*
2014–15	7697469	1105984.07
2015–16	7903002	1369139.01
2016–17	8576875	1611422.64
2017–18	8744437	1959211.52
2018–19	10014243	2332448.15
2019–20	10243323	2615204.89
2020–21	11223400	3747761.37
2021–22	11893053	4724048.1
2022–23	13403083	5889267.56

Source: NABARD, Status of Microfinance, India.

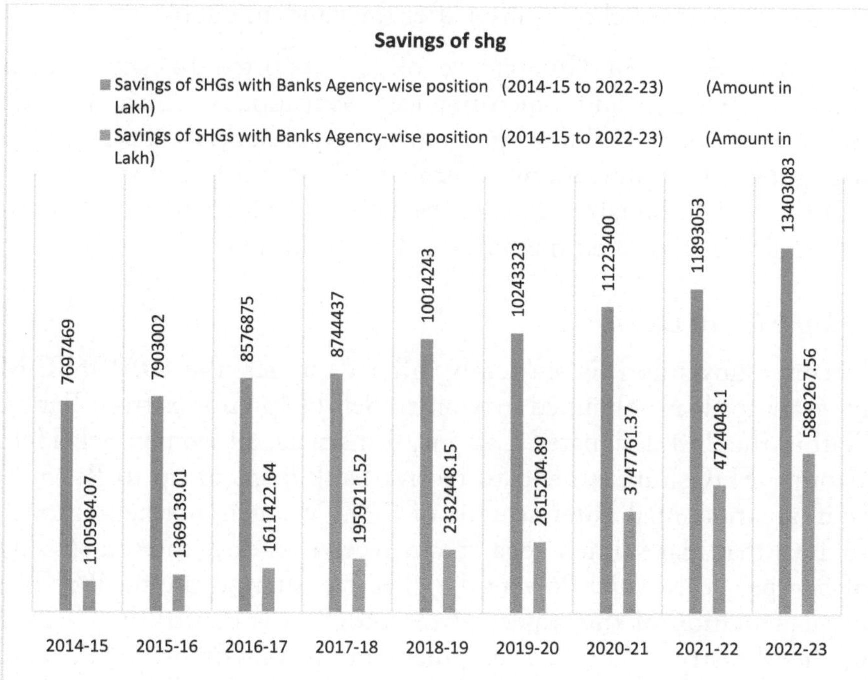

Self-Help Groups (SHGs) and savings culture go hand in hand in Gujarat, where these groups have become a cornerstone of economic empowerment and social cohesion, especially in rural areas. In Gujarat, SHGs have not only facilitated financial inclusion but have also instilled a culture of thrift and savings among members. These groups encourage members to contribute a certain amount regularly, which is then pooled to create a common fund. This collective savings mechanism not only promotes financial discipline but also serves as a safety net during emergencies and provides access to credit for entrepreneurial endeavors. The savings percentage in 2020–21 have been the maximum at 43.31 percent, indicating COVID-19 has impacted the household the most. The uncertainty caused by the pandemic has prompted many individuals and households to increase their savings as a precautionary measure. The pandemic has highlighted the importance of financial planning and resilience. Many people have become more aware of the need to manage their finances prudently, including budgeting, debt management, and savings strategies. This increased awareness may lead to long-term changes in savings behavior even after the pandemic subsides.

Moreover, SHGs in Gujarat are often supported by government agencies, NGOs, and microfinance institutions, which provide training, capacity-building programs, and financial assistance to strengthen their operations. Through these interventions, SHGs become self-sustainable entities capable of addressing the socio-economic needs of their members and communities.

2. *Bank Loans Disbursed*

Interest subvention is currently offered under the DAY-NRLM program for loans obtained by women Self Help Groups from Banks. Within the 250 designated Category-I districts, all women Self-Help Groups (SHGs) are entitled to receive bank loans of up to Rs. 3.00 lakh at an annual interest rate of 7%. Women self-help groups (SHGs) that make timely repayments receive an extra interest subsidy of 3% per year, which lowers the effective interest rate to 4%. The implementation of this aspect of the program is carried out directly by the Ministry of Rural Development and is fully funded by the core component of DAY-NRLM.

In Category-II areas of the country, women Self-Help Groups (SHGs) under DAY-NRLM who borrow loans up to Rs. 3.00 lakh from Banks are eligible for Interest Subvention. This means that the difference between the Bank's lending rate and 7% is subsidized, up to a maximum limit of 5.50% per annum. The implementation of this aspect of the program is carried out by the State Governments themselves and is financed through the allocation allocated to each State under DAY-NRLM, which includes the State's contribution according to established standards.

From table 2, it has been observed that Rs. 2758231.06 amount of loan has been disbursed in the year 2014–15. An upward trend has been observed, and in the year 2022–23 the total amount of loans disbursed increased to Rs. 14520023.3. This increase in trend denotes an increase in the borrower's financial capacity temporarily. The SHG women can plan their household expenses, entrepreneurial activities or any other income source activity.

Table 5: Progress under Microfinance - Bank Loans Disbursed to SHGs Agency-wise Position during 2014–15 to 2022–23
(Amount in Lakh)

Year	*No. of SHGs*	*Loans Disbursed*
2014-15	1626238	2758231.06
2015–16	1832323	3728690.09
2016–17	1898120	3878115.64
2017–18	2261132	4718587.61
2018–19	2698400	5831762.88
2019–20	3146002	7765934.84
2020–21	2887394	5807067.81
2021–22	3398267	9972922.5
2022–23	4295521	14520023.3

Source: NABARD, Status of Microfinance, India.

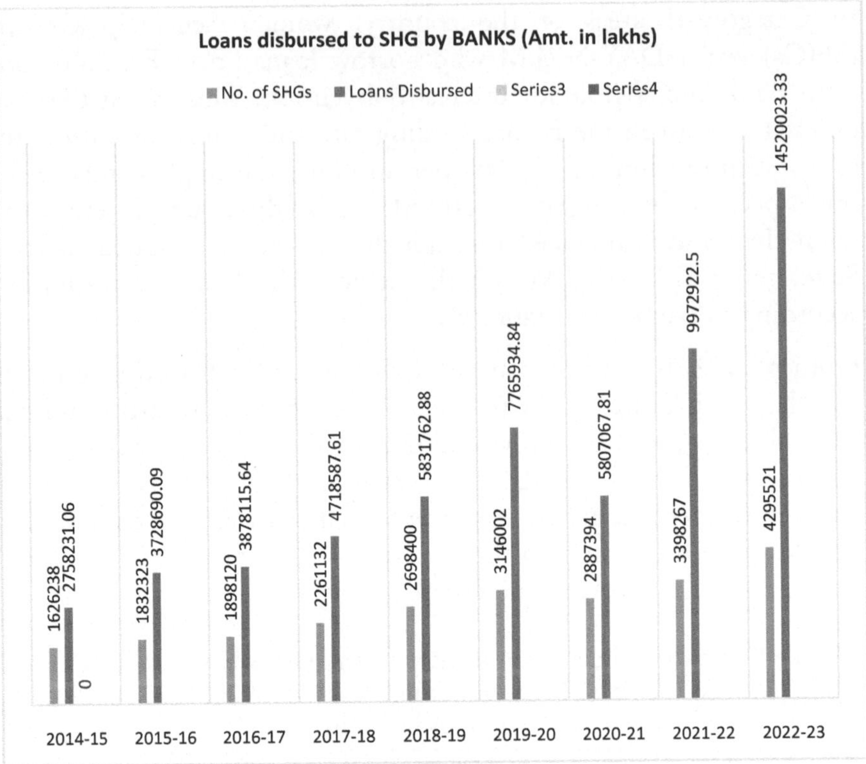

SHG groups empower individuals, particularly women, by providing them with opportunities for entrepreneurship and income generation.

Moreover, SHGs instill a sense of financial discipline and responsibility among their members, leading to improved financial literacy and management skills. Bank loan disbursement complements the efforts of SHGs by providing access to larger sums of capital for business expansion and investment in infrastructure. Banks play a crucial role in extending formal credit facilities, thereby integrating marginalized communities into the formal financial system. The timely and efficient disbursement of loans by both SHGs and banks not only stimulates economic activity but also contributes to poverty alleviation, social upliftment, and overall sustainable development. Thus, fostering an enabling environment for loan disbursement is pivotal in realizing the full potential of grassroots entrepreneurship and inclusive growth.

CONCLUSION

Self-help groups (SHGs) and microfinance are two interconnected concepts that have gained significant traction in the realm of economic development, especially in the context of empowering marginalized communities, particularly women, in developing countries like India. Savings accumulated within SHGs may serve as a source of collateral or co-contribution for loans obtained from MFIs or banks. SHGs and the savings culture they promote have emerged as powerful instruments for poverty reduction, women's empowerment, and community development in Gujarat. By fostering a spirit of self-reliance and collective action, these groups contribute significantly to the socio-economic progress of the state, particularly in its rural areas.

MFIs or banks may require SHGs to maintain a minimum level of savings or demonstrate a history of regular savings as a condition for accessing loans. The integration of savings with bank loan disbursement fosters a culture of financial discipline, encourages thrift among members, and enhances the creditworthiness of SHGs and their members. Additionally, savings within SHGs may be linked to formal banking channels, allowing members to access a broader range of financial services, such as savings accounts, insurance products, or other banking facilities offered by financial institutions. Overall, the synergy between SHGs, microfinance, savings, and bank loan disbursement create a powerful mechanism for financial inclusion, poverty alleviation, and community empowerment, particularly among marginalized populations in developing countries. SHGs often offer financial literacy training and capacity-building programs, enhancing the financial management skills of their members and promoting entrepreneurship. In Gujarat, this synergy between microfinance and SHGs has had a transformative impact, empowering marginalized communities, particularly women, and driving inclusive economic growth. Through access to credit and savings opportunities, SHG members have been able to start small businesses, invest in education and healthcare, and improve their overall standard of living. Thus, the combination of microfinance and SHGs represents a powerful tool for poverty alleviation, social empowerment, and sustainable development in Gujarat.

REFERENCES

[1] Aniket, K.G.-s. (n.d.).

[2] Ansari, S.A. (2011). SHG Bank Linkage Programme in India: An Overview. *International Refereed Journal of Arts, Science & Commerce.*

[3] Badajena, S.N. (n.d.). Self Help Group Bank linkage model and financial inclusion in India.

[4] Bali Swain, R. (2006). Microfinance and Women's empowerment: evidence from the self help group bank linkage programme in India.

[5] Chaitanya (2022, August). Importance of Microfinance in India.

[6] Chauhan, S. (2014). SHG-Bank Linkage Programme in Gujarat: An Exploratory Study.

[7] Chauhan, S. (January 2014). *SHG-Bank Linkage Programme in Gujarat: An Exploratory Study.* Bhopal.

[8] Garima Siwach (American Institutes for Research), S. (2020). *SHGs and Covid-19: Challenges, Engagement, and Opportunities for India's National Rural Livelihoods Mission* |. Women's Group Evidence (womensgroupevidence.org).

[9] Hose, T. (2017, April 5). What is Self- Help Group (SHG) -Bank Linkage Programme?

[10] Network, M.I. (2022–23). *Microfinance loan portfolio.*

[11] (2022, March). *Press Information Bureau (pib.gov.in).* Delji.

[12] Puhazhendi, V. adn (2002, November). SHG-Bank linkage programme for rural poor–An impact assessment. *In seminar on SHG bank linkage programme at New Delhi, micro Credit Innovations Department, NABARD,* Mumbai.

[13] PWC (2019). *vision-of-microfinance-in-india.*

[14] NABARD Annual reports 2015–23.

[15] RBI report 2023.

Fiscal Decentralization Efforts in Gujarat: A Critical Analysis

Himani Baxi[1] and Mandar Bhatt[2]

ABSTRACT: Fiscal decentralization is the process of empowering local government through the devolution of fiscal powers and responsibilities. The literature suggests a strong correlation between fiscal decentralization and development. In India, as per the 73rd and 74th Constitutional Amendment Act, the state are empowered to curate their own fiscal decentralization process. In this context the present study examines the efforts of fiscal decentralization and fiscal performance of local Government of Gujarat state. Provided the successful implementation of development model in the state, it is essential to examine how active the state has been in empowering its local government. However, the study finds that Gujarat has been one of the most passive states to implement fiscal decentralization and raised the concerns for the local development dynamics.

Keywords: *Fiscal Decentralization, Urban Local Bodies, Panchayati Raj Institution, State Finances, Finance Commission.*

INTRODUCTION

During the last few decades of the 20th century majority of federal nations worldwide have been undergoing the process of fiscal decentralization. During the same period some of the developing countries granted their local government additional constitutional authority. This includes Brazil in 1988, India in 1992 and South Africa in 1996. The process of transferring more fiscal authority to subnational or local government is known as fiscal decentralization. It

[1] Assistant Professor, Economics School of Liberal Studies, PDEU, Gandhinagar, India. E-mail: Joshi.himani@gmail.com

[2] Full time PhD scholar, Economics School of Liberal Studies, PDEU, Gandhinagar, India. E-mail: Mandarbhatt10@gmail.com

involves set of measures intended to boost fiscal autonomy of subnational government. It also consists of fiscal instruments and procedures that have the aim of helping in the delivery of public goods (Bird *et al.*, 1995). In India the third tier of government was given legal status through the 73rd and 74th Constitutional Amendments Act (CAA) 1992. Through this amendment the political and economic powers were transferred to third tier government which is Urban Local Bodies and Panchayati Raj Institutions. 73rd and 74th constitution amendment could be considered as a sort of culmination of the efforts. This is an important landmark because a two-tier federation has virtually become three tier federal polity. In India it is the state government who has complete autonomy and responsibility to implement process of fiscal decentralization. What is to be observed here is how Indian states have crafted fiscal decentralization within the state and how effectively an individual state is able to implement 73rd and 74th CAA 1992. In this context it is important to critically examine fiscal decentralization initiative and performance of Gujarat. For the state which is discussed and appreciated for its development model. Hence the objective of the study is to critically examine fiscal decentralization efforts in Gujarat. This paper is divided into primarily four sections. Section one provides details of the theoretical and empirical literature on fiscal decentralization, section two discusses fiscal decentralization framework in India section three examines the fiscal decentralization efforts and performance of Gujarat state and section four provides conclusion and recommendations.

REVIEW OF LITERATURE

There is a rich literature available that investigates the implementation and planning of fiscal decentralization as well as the interrelationship between fiscal decentralization and economic development of a region. The theories of fiscal decentralization are classified as; traditional theories or the first generation (1950 to 1980) and second-generation theories (1990 onwards). Tiebout (1956), Musgrave (1959), Olson (1967), Brennan and Buchanan (1980) are some of the prominent scholars who contributed to first generation theory, whereas economists such as Weingast (1995), Seabright (1996), Lockwood (2002), Besley, Coate (2003), Petchey, Levtchenkova (2002), Wagner (2007) contributed to second generation theory. The first generation fiscal federalism (FGFF) studies the performance of decentralized systems under the assumption of benevolent social planners. The second generation fiscal federalism (SGFF) theory builds on the first generation but assumes that public officials have goals induced by political institutions that often diverge from maximizing citizen welfare (Weingast, 2009). The FGFF theories assume that government is benevolent, and their policy aim is to maximize social welfare. However, it was also realized that the local government may also experience financial constraints and hence it will be a challenge to meet the expenditure requirements of local public goods. The theory has also extensively contributed in the functional classification of taxation powers and expenditure responsibilities. This functional distribution suggested by Musgrave and Oates is the pillar of fiscal decentralization theory. The logic behind this functional distribution is to allocate financial powers and responsibilities across national and sub-national governments in such way that there is possibility to obtain maximum gain from the allocated resources and thus economic efficiency can be achieved. Traditional theories perceive welfare gain and economic efficiency as a critical outcome of fiscal decentralization. It is argued that decentralized provision of local public goods maximizes social welfare when preferences differ across regions and spill-over effects are absent (Oates, 1993), (Tiebout, 1956) and (Musgrave, R.A., 1959). However, considering the financial constraints of the local government it is also proposed that delivery of public goods can be planned at local level but program design and financing will remain with the higher level (Bahl, 2008). Oates has in detailed discussed the rationale and pattern of distribution of functions and responsibilities between local and federal government. He argues that in the absence of monetary and exchange rate prerogatives and with highly open economies that cannot contain much of the expansionary impact of fiscal stimulus, local governments have very limited means for traditional macroeconomic policy and the local government will not be capable of handling economic stabilization policies (Oates, 1999). The local government is close to the community and has more information about their socio-economic conditions. This enables them to take care of the social services and allocations of resources in a local economy. The first-generation fiscal federalism theory has also extensively discussed division of taxation power between federal and local government known as 'tax assignment' problem. Taxation is one of the important sources for government. The issue of tax at the local government is certainly acknowledged in the fiscal decentralization and hence grants or transfers from federal government are considered as an important source of revenue. For the local government, the potential tax base is narrow and mostly in the informal sector, and their experience with tax administration is very limited (Bahl, 2008). Thus, revenue mobilization by small local governments is a special challenge.

As far as the literature on fiscal decentralization in India is concerned, the common issues raised by most of the studies was that the states have not been able to implement fiscal decentralization in its true spirit. Most of the Indian literature could only expand to the point of examining the pattern and implementation of fiscal decentralization process in Indian states. The studies examining relationship between fiscal decentralization and economic wellbeing of the local regions in India are almost absent, probably due to the unavailability of the data at the local government level. While the theoretical contribution in fiscal decentralization has accepted the significance of transferring fiscal powers and responsibilities to the local government however empirical literature particularly the studies on Indian fiscal decentralization are restricted to merely examining the pattern of decentralization rather than establishing any relationship between fiscal decentralization and economic wellbeing. The primary reason behind lack of empirical studies may be the unavailability of data at the local government. Many of the empirical studies about decentralization of Panchayati Raj have revealed that except few, most of the states in India have been passive in devolving powers and functions to Village Panchayats. As per the last report available on devolution index, out of the 29 functions to be devolved to rural local bodies (RLBs), only five states reported devolution of all 29 (Unnikrishnan, P.V. & Palanithurai, G., 2016). Many of the core functions, which traditionally belonged to local governments like, drinking water, rural roads, street lighting, sanitation, primary health etc. have not been transferred fully in some states and are being performed by the line departments of the State Government or the parallel para-statal (Alok V.N., 2016), (Rao *et al.*, 2011). Some states have also, instead of transferring the responsibilities to look after the domain or the sector, there is a transfer of responsibilities to implement particular schemes. Even those functions that have been delegated are 'without adequate administrative, financial and technical support' (Oommen *et al.*, 2017). This certainly indicates despite giving legal status to PRIs across almost all the states they are not fully empowered to execute and implement development programs on their own. As far as transfer of financial powers or taxation powers are concerned, most of the states showed a very passive attitude towards transferring taxation and revenue powers to PRIs. Given the fact that limited taxation powers are transferred to PRIs, out of them the Village Panchayats still have received higher taxation powers. The other two agencies of PRIs, District and Block panchayats have almost no taxing powers and little expenditure autonomy (Region, S.A., 2004). The district and blocks mainly function as an administrative body to implement the central and state programs. The sources of own revenue for District Panchayat in their total revenue basket is merely 2% – all India average (Accountability Initiative, 2019). There are numerous studies that have identified the resource gap for PRIs in India fiscal decentralization and have disused the issue of too much reliance on grants from higher level of government. The share of own sources of revenue for PRIs is very insignificant while the share of central and state grants has significant role to play (GoI, 2011), (Accountability Initiative, 2019; Aiyar & Kapur, 2019; NCAER, 2022; Oommen, 2022; Kapur, 2023). Although the taxes are levied and collected by PRIs, in most of the situations, it is the states who notify the PRIs of what rate to charge. The recent study of NCAER has also highlighted that barring Southern States, Village Panchayat in the rest of the regions do not appear to have any authority deciding the tax rate (NCAER, 2022).

While reviewing the various research studies related to the issue of fiscal decentralization with respect to Urban Local Bodies, there are two important aspects that have emerged. Studies by Oommen (2006), Simanti Bandyopadhyay (2014), Nallathiga Ramakrishna (2008), and the report compiled by YASHADA (2009) have observed that the efforts to promote fiscal decentralization through constitutional amendments have increased the fiscal responsibilities of ULBs but the capacity to generate required financial resources has not increased in accordance. Although one-third of the GDP comes from urban regions, the share of urban local bodies in the revenue and expenditure is highly insignificant about 0.5% when compared to that of Western countries. (Nallathiga Ramakrishna, 2008).

Studies done by Mohanty P.K., Misra B.M., Goyal R. and Jeromi P.D. (RBI, 2007) have found that with the limited resource capacity to augment financial resources, ULBs have been spending lower than that required for providing a minimum level of civic amenities. Rao and Bird (2010) have also shown a concern regarding ULBs finances and noted that not only adequate finance for the provision of services be found but it is critical to ensure that the money spent results in desired outputs and outcomes.

Based on the review of the brief literature it can be observe that the studies that analyzed the fiscal decentralization in contexts of local finances are less. Hence this study contributes to existing literature by critically examining the efforts of Fiscal decentralization at third tier government level in Gujarat.

FISCAL DECENTRALIZATION IN INDIA

The federal structure of India up to 1992 was of two tier having clear distinction between the fiscal power and responsibilities of central and state governments. The economic planning was highly centralized. Local bodies were only administrative units that were responsible for execution of the central plans and policies. It is after the 73rd and 74th Constitutional Amendments, the third tier of government that is Urban Local Body came into existence. The 73rd and 74th Constitutional Amendment Act, aims to address three issues (i) The constitution, composition and the structure of the panchayats and municipalities; (ii) Institutional arrangements for planning of economic and social development, and (iii) The functional and fiscal powers of the panchayats and municipalities. Referring to objective two and three, it implies that India is moving from a centralized planning to decentralize socio-economic development planning. The development agendas and planning have shifted from central level decision to more of the local government responsibilities. The very logic of decentralization is to empower local government to plan and execute their own development agendas as they would have greater insights into development issues and challenges at the regional level. This in fact is highly justified in a country like India which is more diversified in terms of cultural, economic and geographical parameters. The fiscal decentralization was designed in India in such way that it gave an autonomy to each individual state to transfer fiscal power and responsibilities to local government. The Eleventh Schedule of the Act (Article 243G) and Twelfth Schedule (Article-243 W) of the Constitution of India envisages that the State Government may, by law, endow the PRIs and ULBs respectively with such powers and authority as may be necessary to enable them to function an institution of self-government. Under the present structure of fiscal decentralization in India, it is at the discretion of state government to transfer power to raise revenue through taxes to the local governments and also to decide the revenue sharing of various state tax with local bodies. This has been a matter of concern.

The process of decentralization at the state level has raised issues related to lack of willingness to transfer fiscal power, absence of accountability and efficient financial management of local government. The PRIs and ULBs are left with limited power to raise their required financial resources despite the fact that the base of state taxes is local in its nature as most of the economic activities are conducted at a local level. State have been active in transferring the expenditure responsibilities but the same level of enthusiasm has not been seen in case of transferring the revenue generating powers or enabling the local bodies to create new sources of revenue. While legal status of governments has now been raised, they continue to exercise only such taxing and expenditure responsibilities as were devolved to them by their respective state governments.

ISSUES OF FISCAL DECENTRALIZATION IN GUJARAT

Gujarat is one of the top five economically advanced states in India. The development model is being highly appreciated with the state excelling in areas of GSDP growth rate (almost 15% average annual growth rate in last ten years), urbanization (42.58%, 2011 census), industrial growth etc. One may assume that the state with higher urbanization and higher growth rate probably would have empowered their local government and hence it would have helped achieve better development indicators. In this section we examine the fiscal performance of PRIs and ULBs and assess the fiscal decentralization efforts of the state. Broadly speaking there are two significant variables responsible for the fiscal performance of PRIs and ULBs can be classified as Exogenous and endogenous. The endogenous variables consist of the own efforts of PRIs and ULBs to strengthen their finances in terms of improving administrative mechanisms for tax collection, rationalizing expenditure, and implementation of the fiscal reforms. The exogenous variable includes the efforts to implement fiscal decentralization by the state government, transferring greater financial power to local government, adopting scientific approach for the devolution of financial resources to PRIs and ULBs, enhancing the capacity of PRIs and ULBs to build efficient financial systems, etc. Thus, it would be partial to study the fiscal performance of only local government to understand the issue of local finances in Gujarat. The study of exogenous variables is equally important. How decentralization affects access to, and quality of public services depends on the way it is designed and implemented. What local governments can achieve depends on the resources and responsibilities they are granted and on the power of national governments to override their decisions, (World Development Report, 2000). Hence along with fiscal performance of local government we also discuss the status of Gujarat State Finance Commissions – constitution and implementation.

The performance of PRIs and ULBs are assessed for the period from 2011–12 to 216–17. However, the audited data of PRIs expenditure is available only up to 2014–15. Due to the unavailability of audited data we are unable to extend the performance analysis to more recent years. The data are obtained from Comptroller and Auditor General Reports from various years.

While evaluating the fiscal situation of PRIs and ULBs in Gujarat, one of the major concerns is the data availability and data parity. Financial resources for PRI can be classified in three broad categories namely Grant-in-aid, own revenue, grant obtain from finance commission. While the expenditure can be classified into three categories General services, Social services and Economic services. However, the detailed classification of expenditure under these categories is not available and hence it is difficult to trace proper expenditure trends in Gujarat.

Table 1: Y-o-Y Growth Rate Receipts of PRI in Gujarat

Components	*2011–12*	*2012–13*	*2013–14*	*2014–15*	*2015–16*	*2016–17*
grants-in-aid	–	10.51	19.56	1.38	4.47	–13.4
Own Revenue	–	0.76	1.96	1.13	1.99	175.10
Finance Commission Grants	–	7.86	30.23	25.04	77.48	56.62
Total Receipts	–	**10.26**	**19.48**	**1.76**	**6.53**	**–7.40**

Source: C&AG report, GOG, 2018.

Table 2: Y-o-Y Growth Rate Expenditure of PRIS

Description	*2011–12*	*2012–13*	*2013–14*	*2014–15*
General services	–	54.19	41.08	48.43
Social services	–	28.17	18.74	–11.55
Economic services	–	7.86	41.83	14.46
Total	–	**25.71**	**–3.46**	**31.65**

Source: C&AG report, GOG, 2018.

Note: CAG data of PRIs expenditure is available only upto 2014–15.

The annual growth rate of revenue and expenditure of PRIs has been quite volatile (Table 1 and 2). For the year 2016–17 the total revenue had a negative growth of –7.40%. Similarly, the expenditure, particularly the social sector expenditure experience fluctuations. This certainly is worrisome as the finances of the government need predictability and consistency over time to be able to implement long-term development plans.

Chart 1: Composition of Revenue of PRIs

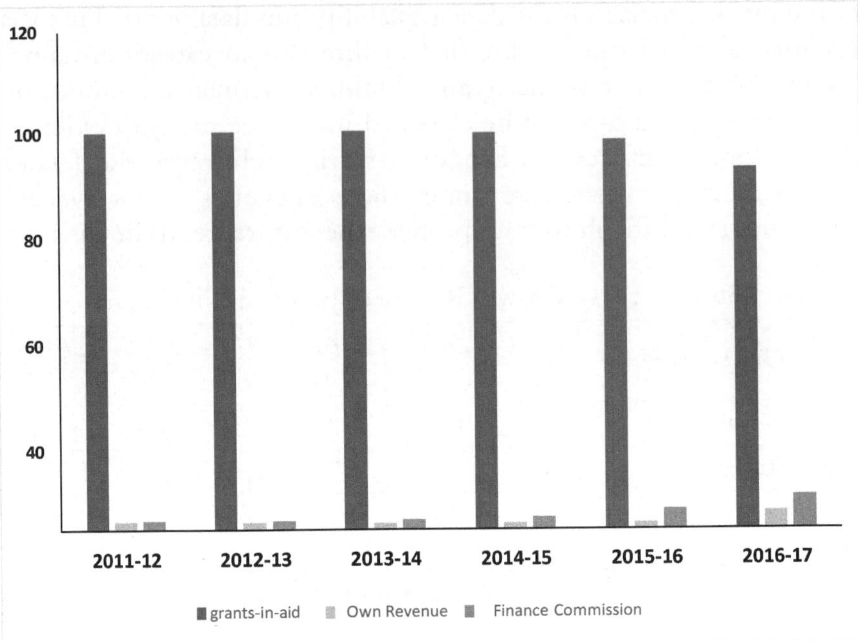

Source: C&AG report, GOG, 2018.

The condition of Panchayati Raj institutions is worse in terms of dependence on grants coming from the state government. Almost 90% (Chart 1) of the total revenue comes from grant-in-aid while own revenue which plays significant role in the independency of state

Table 3: CAGR of Receipts- and Expenditure of PRI

Receipt Components	*CAGR (2011–16)*	*Expenditure Components*	*CAGR (2011–2015)*
Grants-in-aid	3.08	General services	34.0
Own Revenue	18.67	Social services	7.72
Finance Commission Grants	28.8	Economic services	15.03
Total Receipts	4.57	Total	12.72

Source: C&AG report, GOG, 2018.

revenue has very small share of around 4%. Talking about finance commission grantd, it consist only 7% in total revenue. Despite being so much dependent on grant-in-aid the growth of those revenue coming from grant-in-aid had grown only about 3.08%.

Another observation from data is the differences in growth of expenditure and revenues of PRI. The receipts of PRI have increased by almost 4.57% (Table 3) during 2011–16 while the expenditure saw an increase of 12.72% from 2011–12 to 2014–15.

The similar issues can be observed while analyzing fiscal performance of ULBs. Financial resources of ULBs are obtained from two broad source, own sources, own receipts and grants and assistance from central govt/state govt. The own receipts consist of tax revenue, property tax and professional tax. The own non-tax revenue of ULBs comprises of fee for sanction of plans/mutations, water charges, etc. Table 4 and 5 provide annual growth rate of revenue and expenditure of ULBs.

Table 4: Y-o-Y Growth Rate Receipts of ULBs in Gujarat

Receipts	*2010–11*	*2011–12*	*2012–13*	*2013–14*	*2014–15*	*2015–16*	*2016–17*
Grants-in-aid	–	–37.74	49.76	15.58	–4.24	37.17	12.48
Own Revenue	–	18.05	15.80	–6.98	11.41	9.13	10.41
Finance Commission Grants	–	57.59	0.20	14.48	–7.33	202.85	79.23
Total Receipts	–	–14.60	30.15	4.65	2.42	27.02	14.49

Source: C&AG report, GOG, 2018.

Tables 4 and 5 provide annual growth rate of revenue and expenditure component of ULBs. It is evident that there has been very high fluctuation in the different components of revenue and expenditure over the years for the year 2011–12 there was a negative growth of –37.74% in grant-in-aid while in the immediate year it increased by 49.76%. In expenditure it can be observed that for year 2014–15 there was –0.28% growth in health care while in the year 2016–17 it increases by 287.62. This high level of fluctuations both in PRIs and

ULBs is indicating that budget exercise at the local level has not been done with required long term planning. This may certainly hamper the local development and local provision of public services.

Table 5: Y-o-Y Growth Rate of Expenditure of ULBs in Gujarat

	2010–11	*2011–12*	*2012–13*	*2013–14*	*2014–15*	*2015–16*	*2016–17*
Roads, Drains, Culverts	–	–14.49	195.79	24.88	– 12.27	5.29	76.96
Public Health and Sanitation	–	7.47	77.64	16.97	–0.28	15.97	287.62
Water Supply	–	7.47	77.64	16.97	–0.28	15.97	–21.49
Pay and Allowances	–	9.30	6.08	4.61	13.64	8.26	–3.79
Loan Repayment	–	76.58	129.84	–43.41	41.42	1.11	–59.78
Others	–	41.02	–14.71	248.92	46.20	9.56	–55.07
Total Expenditure	–	9.378	43.18	45.017	16.78	9.81	–3.25

Source: C&AG report, GOG, 2018.

The expenditure of ULBs of Gujarat is classified on the basis of purpose (Table 5). It includes expenditure on public utilities such as roads, water etc. It also includes expenditure on loan repayment and pay and allowance. As per Sections 87 to 92 of the Gujarat Municipality Act 1963 and Section 63 of the Gujarat Provincial Municipal Corporations Act, 1949, State Government devolved all the 18 functions envisaged in the Twelfth Schedule to the Nagarpalikas and Municipal Corporation to enable them to function as institutions of self- government (C&AG, GOG 2018).

Assessing the income of the ULBs almost 60% of the income is from grants-in-aid which comes from the state government, while the share of own revenue and finance commission grant is almost about 40% and 6% respectively (Chart 2). This can be grants for specific purpose or untied grants.

The composition of ULBs expenditure reveals for some years pay and allowances had a dominant share in ULBs expenditure while for the year 2013–14 to 2015–16 the share of expenditure in category of 'others' significantly increased see (Table 6). It was noted that the CAG also faced difficulty in terms on understanding and classifying the 'other' expenditure. No ULBs could provide the evidence for the other expenditure and also CAG could not obtain a similarity in the practices adopted by ULBs in classifying this other expenditure.

Chart 2: Composition of Revenue of ULBs

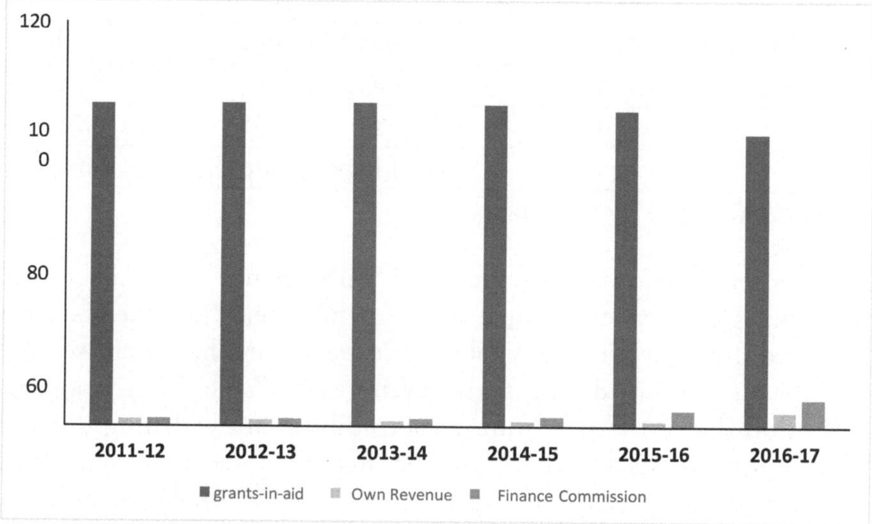

Source: C&AG report, GOG, 2018.

Table 6: Composition of Expenditure of ULBs

Expenditure Component	*2010–11*	*2011–12*	*2012–13*	*2013–14*	*2014–15*	*2015–16*	*2016–17*
Roads, Drains, Culverts	18.43	14.41	29.77	25.64	19.26	18.46	33.77
Public Health and Sanitation	4.54	4.46	5.53	4.46	3.81	4.02	16.12
Water Supply	15.37	13.02	16.52	10.03	8.05	9.13	7.41
Pay and Allowances	40.48	40.45	29.97	21.62	21.04	20.74	20.62
Loan Repayment	1.06	1.72	2.76	1.08	1.30	1.19	0.49
Others	20.12	25.94	15.45	37.17	46.54	46.42	21.55
Total	100.00	100.00	100.00	100.00	100.00	100.00	100.00

Source: C&AG report, GOG, 2018.

Table 7: Compounding Annual Growth Rate of Receipts & Expenditure

Receipt Components	*CAGR (2010–16)*	*Expenditure Components*	*CAGR (2010–16)*
Grants-in-aid	0.067	Roads, Drains, Culverts	25.83
Own Revenue	7.77	Public Health and Sanitation	38.05
Finance Commission Grants	36.21	Water Supply	4.39
Total Receipts	7.99	Pay and Allowances	5.19
		Loan Repayment	3.96
		Others	16.73
		Total Expenditure	15.60

Source: C&AG report, GOG, 2018.

Another observation about the fiscal performance of ULBs is the widening gap between income and expenditure. The receipts have increased by only 7.99% while the expenditure has increased by 15.60% per annum during these seven years (Table 7). It is a clear indication that the expenditure responsibilities are widening but the reliance on grants continues to be higher. One more alarming situation is the pattern of expenditure. Out of total expenditure, almost half of the expenditure is in the category of 'others' for five years from 2010 to 2015, for which there is no clarity.

From above given analysis it can be concluded that while the expenditures of local government are expanding the growth in revenue resources is remains at very low level. Both PRIs and ULBs reliance on their own sources of revenue are highly insignificant. Along with this the inefficiency in data collection and data availability as well as clarity in tracing the outflows is some concern that states need to look.

Gujarat State Finance Commission

As per Article 243I of the Indian constitution, each state was required to constitute state finance commission with one year from the constitutional amendment of 1992. The role of state finance commission as noted in their terms of reference is to review the finances of PRIs and ULBs, suggest ways to strengthen their financial position, to decide upon the transfer of proceeds of taxes, duties, user charges (levied by state) to local bodies and to fix the formula for distribution among PRIs and ULBs. This implies that it is the State Finance Commission which is primarily responsible for improving the fiscal performance of local government in the state. Fiscal decentralization process has unfortunately resulted into higher expenditure responsibilities of local government without being accompanied by fiscal power to raise their own sources of revenue. PRIs and ULBs till date are heavily dependent upon the revenue share and grants received from state government for their financial resources. These grants are either obtained under the state specific scheme or the transfer of tax revenue and grants as per the recommendations of the state finance commission. Hence, it is important to formulate appropriate mechanism for devolution of financial resources that would reduce the financial pressure of PRIs and ULBs. The devolution should maintain the right balance between the fiscal gap and the fiscal discipline of local governments. Also it is expected that the state finance commission contributes in terms of capacity building and strengthening the financial position of local level government. It should suggest the ways to transfer fiscal power to the ULBs along with suggestions to build more efficient system for collection of tax and non-tax revenue. Thus, the state finance commission plays a key role in improving the financial performance of local government. However, successive Central Finance Commissions have observed irregularity and delays in the constitution and functioning of state finance commissions in India. This in turn has indirectly contributed to the poor performance of local level government in India.

Along with other states of India, the approach of Gujarat government in formulation of state finance commission, implementation of the suggestions and recommendations of state finance commission has been very passive and disappointing. For the duration from 2021–22 to 2026– 27 the sixth state finance commissions should have been constituted across all the states. However, only nine states so far are able to constituted 6th SFC which include state like Assam, Bihar, Haryana, Himachal Pradesh, Kerala, Panjab, Rajasthan, Sikkim and Tamil Nadu (GoI, Ministry of Panchayati Raj, n.d.). Gujarat is far behind in the diligent implementation of the provision. The state has so far constituted only three finance commissions. Third State Finance Commission was constituted in 2011, initially the award period of which was 2010–11 to 2014–15, extended to 2016–17. The Commission submitted its report in May 2014. It was given extension to incorporate the recommendations upto 2019–20. Than the Commission submitted its supplementary report in March 2015. To appreciate, for the first time the State Finance Commission in Gujarat has devised a scientific formula for devolution of state's income to the local government (the details are yet not out, however this is the primary information received from the Finance Commission). However, the action taken report was tabled in the assembly on 31 March 2021, only at the time when the 15th Central Finance Commission made it mandatory. However, after almost nine months of the submission of the report, the report is yet not been placed in the Assembly. In the earlier finance commission also this process was delayed to a great extent. The status of formation of state finance commissions and submission of the report and also the status of action taken (as on December 2023) is summarized in the table 8. The details are obtained from Gujarat State Finance Commission.

Table 8: Status of State Finance Commissions Gujarat

Finance Commission	*Year of Constitution*	*Date of Submission*	*Report Placed in Legislative Assembly*	*Total Recommendations*	*Recommendations Accepted*	*Recommendations Implemented*
First	1994	1997–1998	2001	52 PRIs	27 (52%)	9 (17%)
	1998 Reconstitution			64 ULBs	29 (45%)	17 (26%)
Second	2003	2006	2011	41 PRIs	20 (49%)	7 (17%)
				42 ULBs	12 (29%)	8 (19%)
Third*	2011	2015	Action taken report place on 31st March 2021	33 ULBs	22 (49%)	13 (17%)

Source: Action Taken Report (previous finance commissions) and activities till date. Gujarat Third State Finance Commission. *CAG state finance report, March 2022. Data for PRIs are not available.

Some of the important inferences can be drawn from the table above. Although the first finance commission was constituted in 1994, the report of that was placed in an Assembly only in 2001. There was a gap of almost ten years between the first and second commission's constitution and the reports being placed in the Assembly. In case of the third State finance commission, the award period had already begun and the report was not tabled almost upto 2021. Thus there is a complete disconnect between the time of constitution of State Finance Commission and the award period. The government is not able to maintain the schedule starting from the timely formation of finance commissions to acceptance and implementation of the recommendations for the award period. This has led to quite an inefficient system of implementation of the fiscal devolution.

The problem with State Finance Commission is not restricted to only formation and report submission. There is also an issue with recommendations acceptance and implementation. The figures of recommendations accepted and implemented, summarized in the table are highly disappointing. As a result of such practices the financial resources transferred to ULBs do not follow any systematic pattern, making them non-committed, non-predictable and thus not guaranteed. One of the essential parameters for improving financial health of any level of government is to have consistent and assured or predictable flow of financial resources. This is certainly missing in case of ULBs. Due to irregularity in the formation of State Finance Commissions and non-compliance in terms of acceptance and implantations of Commissions' recommendations, the finances of ULBs have worsened.

CONCLUSION

As the this study tries to critically evaluate the Fiscal decentralization efforts in Gujarat it observes that the state has not been active in empowering local governments. While all the expenditure responsibilities are transferred to local bodies, the significant taxation powers are yet with state governments. The state finance commission is almost inactive which has resulted in a random transfer of financial resources. It is also observed that due to negligence of its efforts to improve local finance, the fiscal performance data of ULBs and PRIs are also no updated. This scenario might create a threat for the development of Gujarat. With the emphasis on rural development and urbanization, and the district panchayat's need to meet the Sustainable Development Goals, it is essential to strengthen decentralized development planning. For the local government to take ownership of the development planning, they must possess required financial powers along with fiscal autonomy to spend money. Based on the data it can be conclude that unfortunately the manner in which fiscal decentralization efforts are carried out in Gujarat it is alarming. If the state fails to take financial autonomy of local government seriously the chances are that other states will be able to achieve better development outcome at the village or block or district level. It is now time for the state government to initiate and empower its local government.

REFERENCES

[1] Accountability Initiative (2019). *Analysis of Fund Flows to Rural Local Bodies.* Centre for Policy Research. https://accountabilityindia.in/publication/analysis-of-fund-flows-to-rural-local- bodies/

[2] Aiyar, Y. and Kapur, A. (2019). The centralization v/s decentralization tug of war and the emerging narrative of fiscal federalism for social policy in India. *Regional & Federal Studies, 29*(2), 187–217. https://doi.org/10.1080/13597566.2018.1511978

[3] Alok, V.N. (2016). A Report Card of State Finance Commission: Recommendations of State Finance Commissions *of all Generations and their Implementation Status in India* (34160/2016/789). *The Indian Institute of Public Administration*, New Delhi.

[4] Bandyopadhyay, Simanti (2014). Critical Issues in Municipal Finance: A Summary for India, *American International Journal of Social Science*, Vol. 3, No. 4, July 2014.

[5] Bahl, R.W. (2008). Pillars of Fiscal Decentralization. *CAF Working Paper, 2008/07, Caracas: CAF.*

[6] Bird, R.M., Ebel, R.D. and Wallich, C.I. (Eds). (1995). Decentralization of the Socialist State Washington D.C.: World Bank.

[7] Govt. of Gujarat (2012). Report on C&AG on Local Bodies, March 2012.

[8] Govt. of Gujarat (2013). Report on C&AG on Local Bodies, March 2013.

[9] Govt. of Gujarat (2015). Report on C&AG on Local Bodies, March 2015.

[10] Govt. of Gujarat (2018), Report on C&AG on Local Bodies, March 2018.

[11] Govt. of Gujarat, (2015), Socio Economic Review, 2014–15.

[12] Govt. of Gujarat (n.d.), 'Gujarat Third State Finance Commission, Income-Expenditure Statement of all Mahanagarpalikas of Gujarat' Retrieved from http://gstfc.gujarat.gov.in/downloads/mc_all_gujarat.pdf

[13] Govt. of Gujarat (2013), Statistics of Municipal Towns and Cities, Gujarat 2012–13, published by Directorate of Economics and Statistics, GoG, 2013.

[14] GoI (2011). Roadmap for the Panchayati Raj (2011–17): An All India Perspective. Government of India, Ministry of Panchayati Raj.

[15] GoI, Ministry of Panchayati Raj. (n.d.). *Thirsty First Report Standing Committee on Rual Development and Panchayati Raj (2022–23).* Retrieved January 20, 2024, from https://loksabhadocs.nic.in/lsscommittee/Rural%20Development%20and%20Panchayati%20Raj/17_Rural_Development_and_Panchayati_Raj_31.pdf

[16] Kapur, A. (2023). The mission creep problem in panchayat finances. *Seminar, 763.*

[17] Mohanty, P.K., Misra, B.M., Goyal, Rajan and Jeromi, P.D. (2007). Municipal Finance in India: An Assessment, Department of Economic Analysis and Policy, RBI, Study No 26, December 2007.

[18] Nallathiga, Ramakrishna (2008). 'Trends and Perspectives of Urban Public Finance in Select Countries and India', *ICFAI Journal of Urban Policy*, Vol. 3, No. 1, 2008, pp. 16–32.

[19] Musgrave, R.A. (1959). The Theory of Public Finance—A Study in Public Economy. New York: McGraw-Hill.

[20] NCAER (2022). Study to Assess the Availability of Resources for Creating the Assets and Initiatives Taken for Generating Various Own Sources of Revenue (20220502). *National Council of Applied Economic Research*, New Delhi.

[21] Oates, W.E. (1972). Fiscal Decentralism, New York: Harcourt Brace Jovanovich.

[22] Oates, W.E. (1993). Fiscal Decentralization and Economic Development. National Tax Journal. https://doi.org/10.1086/NTJ41789013

[23] Oates, W.E. (1999). An Essay on Fiscal Federalism. *Journal of Economic Literature,* 37(3), 1120–1149.

[24] Oommen, M.A. (2006). 'Fiscal Decentralization to the Sub-State Level Governments, Economic and Political Weekly, Vol. 41, No. 10, March 11–17, 2006, pp. 897–903.

[25] Oommen, M.A. (2022). Essays on Fiscal Decentralisation to Local Governments in India. Concept Publishing Company Pvt. Limited.

[26] Oommen, M.A., Wallace, S. and Muwonge, A. (2017). Towards Streamlining Panchayat Finance in India. Economic & Political Weekly, 38.

[27] Rao, M.G. and Bird Richard, M. (2010). Urban Governance and Finance in India, *National Institute of Public Finance and Policy*, New Delhi, Working Paper No. 2010–68, April 2010.

[28] Rao, M.G., Raghunandan, T.R., Gupta, M., Datta, P. and Jena, P.R. (2011). Fiscal Decentralization to Rural Local Governments in India: Selected Issues and Reform Options. National Institute of Public Finance and Policy.

[29] Region, S.A. (2004). India Fiscal Decentralization to Rural Governments (26654-IN). World Bank Tiebout, C.M. (1956). A Pure Theory of Local Expenditures. *The Journal of Political Economy,* 64(5), 416–424.

[30] Unnikrishnan, P.V. and Palanithurai, G. (2016). Devolution Report 2015–16—Where Local Democracy and Devolution in India is heading towards? Government of India, Ministry of Panchayati Raj, Mumbai: Tata Institute of Social Sciences.

[31] Weingast, B.R. (2009). Second generation fiscal federalism: The implications of fiscal incentives. *Journal of Urban Economics,* 65(3), 279–293. https://doi.org/10.1016/j.jue.2008.12.005 World Bank, (2001). Decentralization and Governance: Does decentralization improve Public Service Delivery?'

[32] YASHADA (2009)3. Best Practices in the Financial Management of Urban Local Bodies in India. *Submitted to Ministry of Housing and Urban Poverty Alleviation, GoI,* June 2009.

Social Capital for Sustainable Rural Development

Forum Dave[1]

ABSTRACT: This study investigates the potential of social capital to address the multifaceted challenges confronting rural India, home to 62% of the nation's population, as per the 2011 census. Despite their pivotal role in the agrarian economy, rural areas are plagued by infrastructural deficiencies, alarmingly low literacy rates of 67%, and a concerning rise in unemployment to 2.5%, as indicated by PLFS 2023–24 data. These issues, compounded by limited access to financial resources, necessitate innovative and alternative development approaches.

Drawing upon Bourdieu's theoretical framework, this research argues that social capital, manifested in robust community bonds and shared norms, is a critical catalyst for rural empowerment. Norms, which foster trust and cooperation, underpin collective action, exemplified by Self-Help Groups (SHGs). SHGs, built on principles of trust and reciprocity, demonstrate the practical application of social capital, effectively empowering marginalised women through financial inclusion and information dissemination. However, the study acknowledges the inherent risk of social capital reinforcing existing inequalities, particularly through the formation of homogenous and potentially exclusive SHGs.

Employing Gujarat as a focused case study, this research analyses primary data collected from aspirational districts, with a specific emphasis on SHG awareness and operational function. The case study aims to address the fundamental question of whether social capital-based interventions can effectively transform rural India. By bridging the gap between theoretical constructs and practical applications, this study seeks to provide valuable insights into the role of social capital in fostering sustainable rural development.

Keywords: *Sustainable Rural Development, Social Capital, Self Help Groups, Gujarat.*

---

[1] Assistant Professor, Sardar Patel Institute of Economic and Social Research, Ahmedabad, Gujarat, India.

INTRODUCTION

As Mahatma Gandhi famously stated, 'Bharat lives in its villages.' must use this core idea to examine how India is growing. The 2011 census, revealed that 62% of our population resides in rural areas, which leads to various challenges that persist in these regions. Indeed, these regions are integral to the agrarian economy, and indeed, to the very fabric of our socio-cultural identity, they exhibit a persistent and deeply concerning deficit in essential services and infrastructure. The lack of adequate educational institutions, healthcare facilities, and sanitation infrastructure directly translates into lower productivity, diminished earning potential, and a reduced capacity for innovation within rural communities. The lack of financial services adds fuel to it. The stark disparity in literacy rates—67% in rural areas compared to 84% in urban centres—indicates a lack of investment in education and skill development in these regions. This, in turn, perpetuates the vicious cycle of poverty, limiting the potential for economic diversification and hindering the emergence of a robust, diversified rural economy.

Furthermore, the labour market indicators, as revealed by the PLFS data for 2023–24, present a worrying picture. The marginal increase in rural unemployment to 2.5%, compared with a decline in urban unemployment, signals a widening gap in economic opportunities. This divergence is not merely a statistical difference; it represents a fundamental imbalance in our economic development strategy and policy. The lack of vigorous financial infrastructure in rural India—limited access to formal credit, financial services, and efficient market linkages—further exacerbates these challenges. This lack of access smothers entrepreneurial activity, limits the ability of rural producers to access markets, and impedes the efficient allocation of resources. This, in turn, constrains rural economic growth, perpetuates regional disparities, and ultimately undermines our nation's overall development potential.

In rural areas, where financial and physical resources are often limited, social capital becomes paramount. It's the strength of community bonds, built on trust and shared norms (Coleman), that fills the gaps. Strong relationships facilitate information sharing and collective action, crucial for problem-solving. Community trust enables cooperation and resource mobilization, vital for overcoming adversity. Informal safety nets, formed through social capital, offer resilience during hardship. Ultimately, this interconnectedness empowers rural communities, making social capital indispensable for sustainable development. This means focusing on the strength of connections, not just their number. At the community level, this translates to collaborative efforts in resource management, infrastructure development, and economic growth. Bourdieu's concept emphasizes that building these meaningful relationships, whether through formal or informal channels, creates a vital asset for both individual and community success.

Norms play a critical role in the framework of social capital (Coleman, 1988; Putnam, 2000). Norms are shared common rules, expectations, and values that guide interactions within a social network. Emphasizing reciprocity, trust, and cooperation (Axelrod, 1984; Fehr & Gächter, 2000; Hardin, 2002), these norms are fundamental for fostering trust and enabling collective action (Ostrom, 1990). For a network's well-being, all members are required to contribute, which is possible through adherence to norms (Olson, 1965; Yamagishi, 1986). Norms also encourage collaboration and discourage free-riding (Olson, 1965). Moreover, they enhance social cohesion by cultivating a shared sense of identity and belonging among members (Durkheim, 1984; Tajfel & Turner, 1979).

The functioning of SHGs provides a clear illustration of social capital's effectiveness. Self Help Groups consist of groups of ten to twelve members mostly female who form a group. They save and provide loans within the group Built on networks of interpersonal relationships, they foster close bonds among members from similar socio-economic backgrounds, extending their reach to wider community support systems. Operating on shared norms of trust, reciprocity, and mutual support, SHGs instil a sense of collective responsibility and accountability. Trust is the cornerstone of their function, enabling members to pool resources and access financial assistance, while reciprocity ensures mutual aid. By facilitating collective action, SHGs empower members to address common challenges, promoting social cohesion and empowering marginalized groups, especially women.

They serve as vital platforms for information sharing, enhancing social status and enabling members to collectively voice concerns. In essence, SHGs generate and amplify social capital through strong relationships, shared norms, trust, and collective action, demonstrating its practical application in empowering communities.

However, Bourdieu also recognized that social capital is embedded within social structures and can contribute to social inequalities. Access to valuable networks is often unevenly distributed. This is well reflected in SHGs, though SHGs thrive on shared values and common backgrounds, leading to strong, unified groups, particularly among women, this very foundation can lead to biased or exclusive formations (Granovetter, 1973; Lin, 2001). If not addressed, this can inadvertently widen the gap between those who are included and those who are excluded, undermining the broader goals of social equity (Tilly, 1998; Bebbington, 1999). This occurs because the bonding social capital that creates strong in-group ties can simultaneously create barriers for out-group members (Putnam, 2000). Therefore, while shared values and homogeneity are vital for initial cohesion (Narayan & Pritchett, 1999), it is crucial to implement mechanisms that promote bridging social capital and inclusivity to prevent the reinforcement of existing inequalities (Krishna & Uphoff, 1999; Woolcock, 1998).

What are the implications of these observations for the validity of Self-Help Groups as social capital, and for the overall relevance of social capital in the context of Indian rural development? This research paper tries to address these objectives by taking the case study of Gujarat.

This paper commences with an introduction that highlights the pivotal role of social capital in mitigating India's rural challenges and outlines a practical model for its application. Subsequently, a comprehensive literature review is presented to contextualize the study in the first section of the paper. The second section details the methodology employed to analyze primary data collected from a selected sample within the state of Gujarat. Finally, the third section presents the analysis of the data and provides policy recommendations derived from the findings.

RESEARCH METHODS

The sample for the district of Gujarat has been identified based on NITI Aayoga's classification of aspirational and non-aspirational districts. Thus, two aspirational districts of the Gujarat state have been identified namely Narmada and Dahod. Districts categorized by NITI Aayog based on socioeconomic indicators, reflecting varying development levels, are subject to a stratified random sampling method. This method, which stratifies samples by district, block, village, and household, provides a nuanced understanding of SHG operations across different socio-economic groups.

Qualitative methods, such as interviews and focus groups, can be employed to understand how norms shape social interactions within specific contexts. Ultimately, comprehending the role of norms is essential for developing effective interventions aimed at strengthening social capital within communities. Fundamentally, social capital arises from the differential impact of norms, values, and beliefs on trust, networks, and institutions. It manifests as a collective asset comprising shared norms, values, beliefs, trust, networks, social relations, and institutions that facilitate cooperation and collective action for mutual benefit.

SHGs: A Platform for Social Capital Development

Social capital, with its dual potential to empower and exclude, manifests as an intricate network of relationships and trust. While it fuels cooperation and economic growth, it also risks perpetuating inequalities and fostering exclusionary groups. Self-help groups (SHGs) offer a promising approach to leveraging the positive aspects of social capital, serving as platforms for trust-building and collective action, thereby translating social connections into economic gains. Given Gujarat's long history of urbanization, reflected in its established cities and trade traditions, it provides a valuable context for examining social capital's impact on rural transformation. This study, therefore, explores the role of SHGs in facilitating social capital within Gujarat's rural landscape.

Self-Help Groups (SHGs) are small groups consisting of 10–20 individuals. They belong to comparable socio-economic backgrounds, formed with the primary objective of addressing shared challenges and enhancing their members' economic and social well-being. These groups are saving and providing loans to their members, fostering mutual support, trust, and collective decision-making. Often, these groups engage in income-generating ventures, such as small businesses or crafts, to bolster their members' livelihoods. Training covers bookkeeping, bank management, group leadership, and skill development. Beyond financial activities, SHGs act as platforms for social mobilization, raising awareness about critical issues like health, education, and rights. They also serve as vital intermediaries between their members and formal financial institutions. By nurturing a sense of community and shared responsibility, SHGs strengthen social capital and can play a pivotal role in poverty reduction and rural development.

To have a sustainable and effective functioning, these group is required to follow a common norm/protocol called Panchsutra. Panch-Sutra is regular meetings, regular saving, regular inter-lending, timely repayment, and maintenance of records. This framework not only strengthens the group's internal cohesion but also empowers members to enhance their skills and achieve greater economic prosperity. It is important to note that while three of these principles (regular savings, internal lending, and timely repayments) have a direct economic focus, they are intricately linked to and dependent upon the two non-economic commitments: regular meetings and maintenance of record.

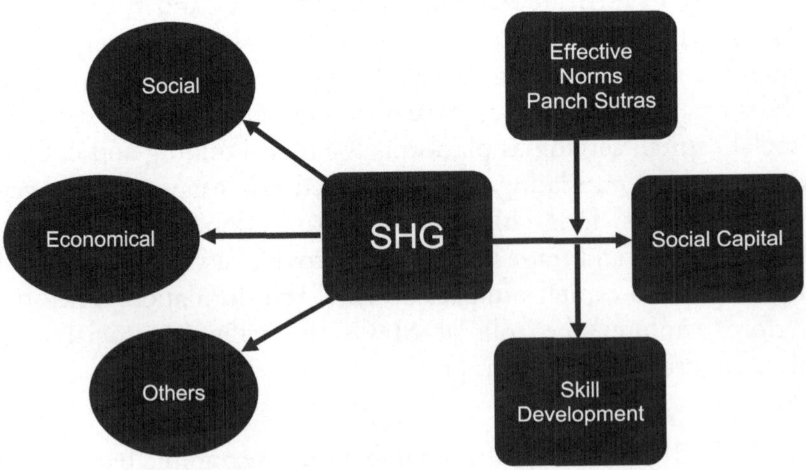

Characteristics of Selected Sample

Dahod and Narmada, Gujarat's aspirational districts, offer a crucial perspective on rural development, demanding targeted interventions to combat socio-economic disparities. Their demographics, characterized by predominantly rural populations (Dahod: 9.01% urban, Narmada: 10%) and substantial tribal communities (Dahod: 74.32%, Narmada: 81.55%), present unique development challenges. These challenges are further highlighted by educational disparities. According to the 2011 census, Dahod exhibits the lowest literacy rate among Gujarat's districts. Despite this, with a majority of its population belonging to Scheduled Tribes (ST) and Other Backward Classes (OBC), only 38% of the sampled population was found to be illiterate.

Table 1

Name of the District	*Total Population*	*Literacy Rate (In%)*	*Rural (In %)*	
			SC Population	*ST Population*
Dahod	1982758	58.82	1.63	78.62
Dang	225323	75.16	0.07	98.29
Mehsana	1581473	83.61	7.8	0.2
Narmada	555452	72.31	1.12	87.31

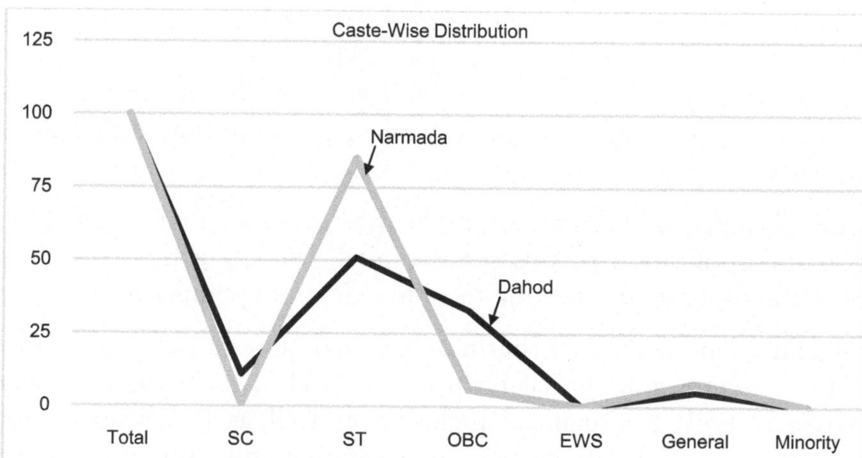

Graph 1: The Population in Caste

In contrast, Narmada's educational profile reveals that 38% of the sample attained education up to a lower primary level (6th–10th standard), with a slightly higher proportion achieving higher education (Narmada: 5%, Dahod: 3%). These educational patterns, as depicted in Graphs 1 and 2, underscore the need for tailored strategies.

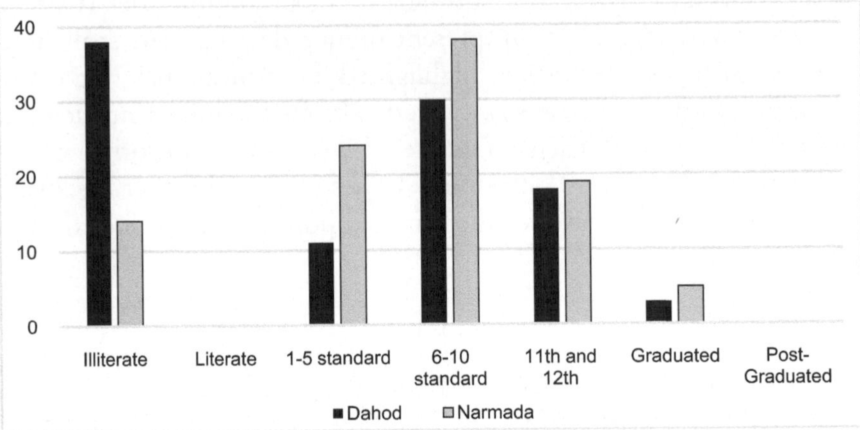

Graph 2: The Education Level

However, the inherent social capital within these tribal communities, characterized by strong kinship ties, traditional governance, and shared cultural practices, provides a foundation for development. This social capital, manifested in high social cohesion, mutual support, and collective resource management, is reflected in the functioning of Self-Help Groups (SHGs) while homogeneous communities with lower education levels can foster strong SHG networks, basic training is essential for members to fully utilize these networks.

The adherence of SHGs to norms like the Panchsutra demonstrates the practical application of this social capital, validating their role as a powerful tool for empowering these marginalized populations.

Gujarat's reputation as a business-oriented state is reflected in the high awareness among Self-Help Group (SHG) members regarding SHGs as tools for financial inclusion as well as Panchsutra. This indicates a pre-existing level of understanding and trust in collective financial mechanisms, a key component of social capital.

The age distribution, with over 80% of SHG members in the 25–60 age group across both aspirational (Dahod, Narmada). This working-age demographic represents a pool of active social capital, capable of driving community-level initiatives and economic empowerment.

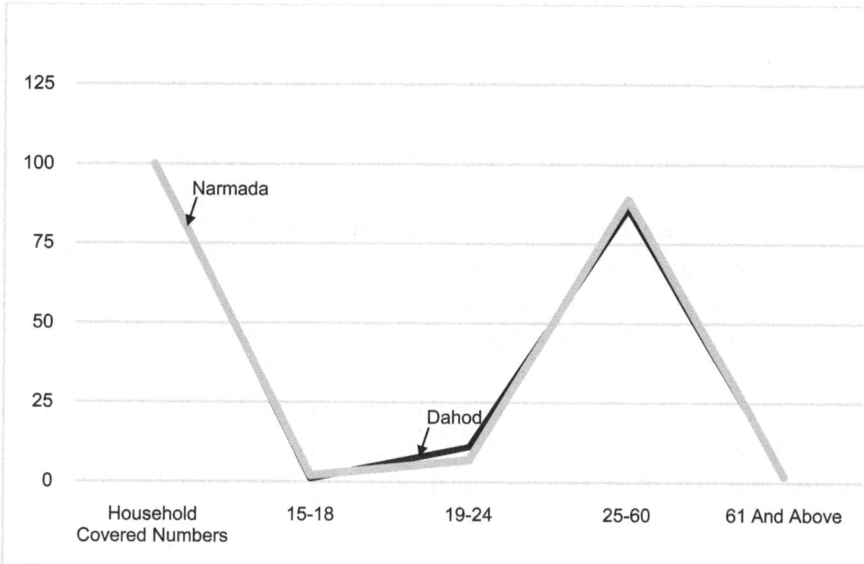

Graph 3: Age-Wise Distribution of SHGs

In the aspirational districts of Narmada and Dahod, the high percentage of working-age individuals (85–92%) suggests a strong potential for mobilizing this social capital for development. However, the high dependency ratios, particularly in Dahod (60.53%), highlight the need for targeted interventions. This dependency, comprising both elderly and children, necessitates a focus on intergenerational social capital, where working-age members leverage their networks and resources to support dependents. In the case of children, investing in education and health becomes crucial. These investments strengthen human capital, which in turn enhances social capital by creating a more skilled and healthy workforce. The recognition that health and education generate positive externalities underscores the importance of public goods provision, which can be facilitated through strong social networks and community participation. Therefore, the effective utilization of social capital, as demonstrated by the SHG model, is essential for addressing the specific challenges posed by the demographic profiles of aspirational districts in Gujarat.

Panch-Sutra and SHGs

The effectiveness of SHGs can transform rural regions if followed by norms such as PanchSutra. The observed variations in Panch-Sutra familiarity between Dahod (74%) and Narmada (54%) offer insights into the nuances of social capital within these aspirational districts. Dahod's higher awareness points towards potentially stronger internal cohesion and effective norm dissemination mechanisms. This could be attributed to a higher trial population and lower education. Due to a lack of education, they are largely dependent on each other for basic information. Conversely, Narmada's lower familiarity indicates a possible deficit in internal social capital drivers, suggesting that cultural, religious, or geographical factors may not readily facilitate the development of strong social bonds within its SHGs. This necessitates greater reliance on external interventions to bolster social capital.

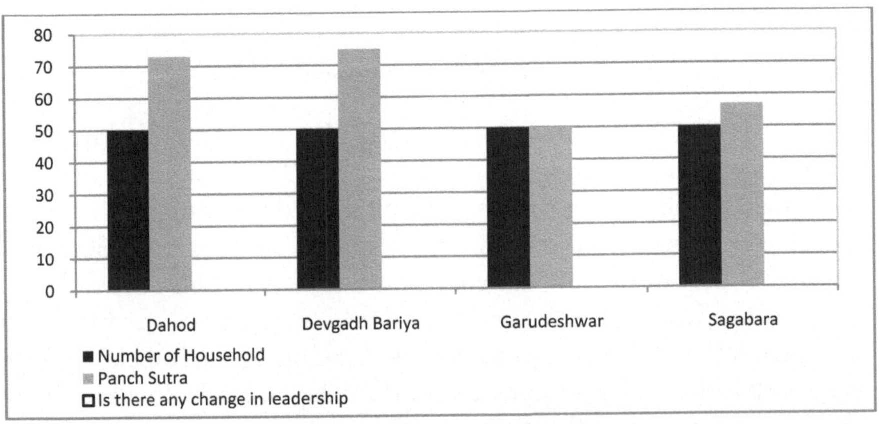

Graph 4: Awarness of Panch-Sutra

Despite these differences, SHG members' general familiarity with the Panch-Sutra across both districts signifies the presence of shared norms, a crucial element for SHG functionality. However, the prevalence of rote memorization, as reported by CRPs, highlights a significant gap in conceptual understanding. This reliance on external direction undermines the potential for autonomous functioning and suggests a need for deeper internalisation of the framework's principles.

Furthermore, the consistent absence of leadership changes, while indicative of stability, raises concerns about group inclusivity and the distribution of knowledge and capacity. This lack of turnover may suggest that leadership roles are not being rotated or that members lack the confidence or training to assume leadership positions. Consequently, the observed stability could mask underlying issues of limited participation and potential stagnation, hindering the long-term effectiveness of the SHGs and undermining the core principles of equitable social capital. Further, it indicates normal education does not always lead to financial literacy. It required special training for these members.

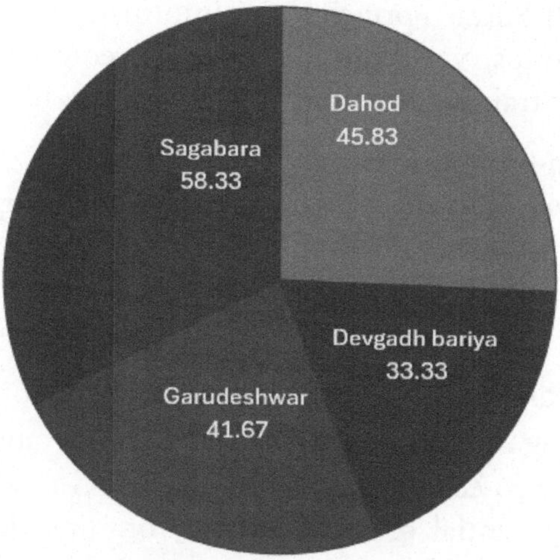

Graph 5: Meeting Attendance

The relationship between 'Panch Sutra' awareness and meeting attendance is unclear. While a block in Narmada showed higher attendance despite limited 'Panch Sutra knowledge, Dahod, with its more homogeneous population, did not follow this trend.

One member in Dahod Block expressed a lack of awareness regarding the value of regular meetings, asking, *'What is the importance of going into a meeting? I get the information that is being discussed.'*

This view likely arises from the group's social homogeneity.

CONCLUSION

This study examined the role of the Panch-Sutra framework in shaping social capital dynamics within rural SHGs While familiarity with the Panch-Sutra indicated shared norms, critical for SHG cohesion, a deep conceptual understanding was lacking. Rote memorization, rather than internalization, prevailed, hindering autonomous group function.

Intriguingly, Panch-Sutra awareness didn't consistently predict meeting attendance, revealing a complex social dynamic. Narmada showed higher attendance despite limited understanding, unlike Dahod's homogenous population. This highlighted that mere awareness doesn't guarantee participation. The study stresses a shift from memorization to comprehension, advocating for training that explains Panch-Sutra principles. Information flowed within homogenous groups, yet economic benefits required comprehensive financial literacy training for all members, not just leaders.

Focusing on non-economic aspects, the study affirms SHGs as effective social capital models in rural Bharat. Targeted training can transform this capital into a catalyst for rural upliftment. Social capital, embodying collective resources, offers a platform for sustainable development.

Ultimately, the effective implementation of Panch-Sutra hinges on both a deep conceptual understanding and its practical application. Empowering members through knowledge and skills enables SHGs to drive socio-economic change. The SHG model demonstrates the significant potential of social capital for rural development. To fully realize this potential, a nuanced understanding of the importance of norms in their practical application is necessary. Furthermore, integrating the non-economic factors explored here with economic considerations will likely unlock significant positive externalities, leading to transformative empowerment for women, their families, and the broader rural community.

This study is limited to only analyses of the non-economical sutra of norms called Panch-Sutra. This study underscores the need for nuanced SHG development and opens avenues for further research into the interplay of social and economic factors.

REFERENCES

[1] Axelrod, R. (1984). *The evolution of cooperation.* Basic Books.

[2] Bebbington, A. (1999). Capitals and capabilities: A framework for analyzing peasant viability, rural livelihoods and poverty. *World Development, 27*(12), 2021–2044.

[3] Coleman, J.S. (1988). Social capital in the creation of human capital. *American Journal of Sociology, 94*, S95–S120.

[4] Durkheim, É. (1984). *The division of labor in society.* Macmillan.

[5] Fehr, E. and Gächter, S. (2000). Cooperation and punishment in public goods experiments. *American Economic Review, 90*(4), 980–994.

[6] Granovetter, M. (1973). The strength of weak ties. *American Journal of Sociology, 78*(6), 1360–1380.

[7] Hardin, R. (2002). *Trust and trustworthiness.* Russell Sage Foundation.

[8] Krishna, A. and Uphoff, N. (1999). *Mapping and measuring social capital: A conceptual and empirical study of collective action for combating poverty in Rajasthan, India.* World Bank Publications.

[9] Lin, N. (2001). *Social capital: A theory of social structure and action.* Cambridge University Press.

[10] Narayan, D. and Pritchett, L. (1999). Cents and sociability: Household income and social capital in rural Tanzania. *Economic Development and Cultural Change, 47*(4), 871–897.

[11] Olson, M. (1965). *The logic of collective action: Public goods and the theory of groups.* Harvard University Press.

[12] Ostrom, E. (1990). *Governing the commons: The evolution of institutions for collective action.* Cambridge University Press.

[13] Putnam, R.D. (2000). *Bowling alone: The collapse and revival of American community.* Simon & Schuster.

[14] Tajfel, H. and Turner, J.C. (1979). An integrative theory of intergroup conflict. In W.G. Austin & S. Worchel (Eds.), *The social psychology of intergroup relations* (pp. 33–47). Brooks/Cole.

[15] Tilly, C. (1998). *Durable inequality.* University of California Press.

[16] Woolcock, M. (1998). Social capital and economic development: Toward a theoretical synthesis and policy framework. *Theory and Society, 27*(2), 151–208.

[17] Yamagishi, T. (1986). The structural goal/expectation theory of cooperation in dyadic exchanges. *Advances in Group Processes, 3*, 137–168.

APPENDIXES

Appendix I: % Distributed based on Caste

Caste-Wise Distribution	*Total Household Covered*	*SC*	*ST*	*OBC*	*EWS*	*General*	*Minority*
Dahod	100	11	51	33	0	5	0
Narmada	100	1	85	6	0	8	0

Appendix II: % Distribution based on Education

Education	*Illiterate*	*Literate*	*1–5 Standard*	*6–10 Standard*	*11th and 12th*	*Graduated*	*Post-Graduated*
Dahod	38	0	11	30	18	3	0
Narmada	14	0	24	38	19	5	0

Appendix III: % Distribution Age-Wise

Age-Wise	*Household Covered Numbers*	*15–18*	*19–24*	*25–60*	*61 and Above*
Dahod	100	1	11	86	2
Narmada	100	2	7	89	2

Appendix IV: % of Awarness and Leadership Change

Block Covered	*Total Household Covered*	*PanchSutra*	*Leadership Change*
Dahod	50	72.73	0
Devgadh bariya	50	75	0
Garudeshwar	50	50	0
Sagabara	50	57.14	0

Appendix V: Meeting

Block Covered	*Total Household Covered*	*%of Average Meeting Covered by SHG Members*
Dahod	50	45.83
Devgadh bariya	50	33.33
Garudeshwar	50	41.67
Sagabara	50	58.33

Section 6

Student's Corner

The Socio-Environmental Consequences of Industrialization in Hazira: A Case Study of the Fishing Community

Dipesh Jain[1]

ABSTRACT: The industrial growth of Hazira, a key transhipment port and developing suburb on Surat's western edge, Gujarat, presents a classic case of economic progress confronting environmental sustainability. This study thoroughly investigates the environmental problems arising from this rapid industrialization, with a particular focus on how pollution affects the fishing community, whose economic survival depends on a healthy ecosystem. The research utilizes a comprehensive analysis of secondary data from diverse sources, including news reports, academic articles, online resources, and scholarly journals, to provide a complete understanding of the challenges and their impact.

Keywords: *Industrial Development, Environmental Issues, Economic Growth, Rio Declaration, Fisherman Community.*

INTRODUCTION

The Rio declaration of united nation framework convention on climate change emphasized that human beings are at the centre of concerns for sustainable development and are entitled to a healthy and productive life in harmony with nature. This principle affirms that considerations of human well-being should guide policy making for sustainable development and that conservation of natural entities must be reckoned as part of such well-being. Unfortunately, these

[1] Assistant Professor of Economics, SDJ International College, Vesu, Surat-VNSGU, India.

points are not fully granted in the case of development induced environmental problems. Of course, during the past several decades, there has been an increasing concern over environmental problems throughout the world involving depletion of Ozone layer, acid rain, greenhouse effect, soil erosion, deforestation, water pollution, air pollution, etc.

With a total population of 71.6 million by May 2023, Gujarat ranks as the ninth most populous among India's 28 states, and it is the fifth largest state in terms of area encompassing 196,024 km2. Around 42.6% of Gujarat's population resides in urban areas, which is higher than the 31.2% urban population for India as a whole. Gujarat's position as a leading industrial state in India is demonstrated by the fact that it contributed 18% of India's total industrial output in 2023. It has also become a favored destination for Foreign Direct Investment (FDI) through the holding of biennial "Vibrant Gujarat Summits" that showcase the business-friendly policies of the state. However, as mentioned above, this narrative of industrial success needs to be qualified. First, Gujarat is also one of the leading states in terms of hazardous industrial waste production, generating about 28.76% of India's total industrial hazardous waste production. It also contains about 30.0% of all MAH units in the country. Second, social inequalities remain a key concern in the state both due to religious violence, as well as widening income inequalities. Industrialization has a long history in Gujarat and is famously associated with cotton textile production in Ahmedabad, the largest city in terms of population and state's main financial center. More recently, textiles have declined in importance and chemical industries have become a leading sector with the development of offshore oil and gas production contributing to the rising importance of petrochemicals. This shift has also changed the geography of industrial growth in the state. While the districts of Ahmedabad and Vadodara in central Gujarat and Surat and Bharuch in south Gujarat have been centers of industrial growth since the 1960s, this has now extended to include a coastal belt associated with petrochemical and port development, especially in south and west Gujarat. Industrial growth has also been spurred in new areas through the establishment of special economic zones (SEZs), and the growth of SEZ-related industries is especially prominent in the previously underdeveloped northwestern district of Kutch. The problem of hazardous waste production thus reflects both historical patterns and new geographies of industrialization, as Bharuch and Ahmedabad districts are the highest and second highest generators respectively of hazardous industrial waste in India, and Vadodara and Kutch districts are nationally ranked among the top Int. J. Environ. Res. Public Health 2019, 16, 42 3 of 13 ten districts producing hazardous industrial waste. These trends highlight the growing need to examine the distributive EJ implications of industrialization in Gujarat.

MODERNIZATION ACTIVITIES IN GUJARAT WITH SPECIAL REFERENCE TO HAJIRA

Following the economic reforms in 1991, India has adopted the structural adjustment package (SAP) designed by the International Monetary Fund and the World Bank to move towards a deregulated open economy to get integrated with the global economy as a solution to its basic problems of low growth and structural mass poverty. Development policies including industrial policy in India in the post-reform period have been formulated in accordance with this paradigm. After introduction of the new economic policy (NEP) in 1980s, more and more emphasis has been given to the industries, particularly the massive one. Gujarat can be said as one of the leading states throughout the country. Gujarat itself is experiencing phenomenal increase in investments both from mega- industrial sectors within the country and also from multi-national abroad. The coastal belt of Gujarat experienced rapid growth in terms of massive industrialization, infrastructure development and urbanization in post liberalization, privatization and globalization (LPG) era. The Government of Gujarat (GoG) plan out total 55 SEZs in Gujarat. It requires total area of approximately 27,125 hectares of land. GoG has initiated various incentives to boost the process of industrialization in the State. Total 12 special investment regions (SIR)s 8 are already declared under the SEZ Act.

INDUSTRIALIZATION IN HAJIRA

Hazira is one of the major ports of India and the most important element of Surat Metropolitan Region. The town is known as the industrial hub of India and is located on the bank of the Tapti River, eight kilometers away from the Arabian Sea. It is a centre for health tourism due to its natural springs, and a base for major industrial and shipping facilities like Essar, Kribhco, Shell, Larsen & Toubro, NTPC, ONGC, GAIL, GSEG power plant, Gujarat State Petroleum Corporation, UltraTech Cement and Hazira Manufacturing Division (HMD) of Reliance Industries.

The investment pattern shows that it has mainly concentrated in and around existing or potential port sites. Hajira, Dahej, Dholera, Jamnager, Mundra, etc. have emerged as the major industrial pockets in the costal belt of Gujarat. Hajira, witnessed phenomenal growth in terms of industrial activities, resulting in mammoth investment in very strategic areas. It is estimated that total capital investment of Rs. 350, 000 million will be made in Hajira Development Authority (HADA) 9 area (2003). This is expected to rise to over Rs. 500,000 million of investment in the near future-2025. Two SEZs are proposed in the HADA region. Hajira and Magdalla ports in the district provide logistic support to industrial operations in the state. Large scale industrialization has taken away major portion of land in and around Hajira village. The lands were taken by applying various techniques such as; acquisition, purchase, grabbing, encroachment, etc. for various purposes including erection of plants, construction of roads, railway, warehouses, townships, ancillary units and other logistic purposes. Socio-economic profile of HADA area suggests that majority of the affected population belongs to the socially, educationally backward caste (SEBC) s10 and is relatively of low educational background. They do not have much say in the state politics.

Table 1: Industries in the Hazira Port and Industrial Area

Sr. No.	*Industry Name*	*Sector/Type*
1.	Reliance industries Ltd	Petrochemical manufacture
2.	Essar Steel Ltd	Steel plant with power plants and jetty
3.	KRIBHCO Ltd	Fertilizer

Sr. No.	*Industry Name*	*Sector/Type*
4.	L&T	Forgings
5.	NTPC	Power
6.	ONGC	Petrochemicals
7.	HAEP	Atomic
8.	Niko Resources Ltd	Oil/Gas
9.	GSPC-Niko	Oil/Gas
10.	Hazira LNG Port by Shell	Port
11.	Magdalla Port	Port
12.	ABG shipyards Ltd	Ship Building
13.	GSEG Power Plant	Power

Table 2: Sources and Impacts of Pollution in the Tapi River

Sources of Pollution	*Pollutants*	*Some Impacts*
GIDC estates and CETP	High quantities of Silicate, phosphate and chloride	Categorized as grossly polluted low DO and BOD, High turbidity, High Alkalinity, phosphate, ammonia, potassium, release of hydrocarbons.
Hazira industrial Estate	Silicate	
Surat Municipal Waste	Presence of Cadmium, Magnesium and hard water	
Cleaning of oil tankers at port		High TDS, TSS and Turbidity, EC Suspended solids can clog fish gills, either killing them or reducing their growth rate. Reduced light penetration. Reduced ability of algae to produce food and oxygen.
Dredging and port construction		
Coastal erosion		

LITERATURE REVIEW

- Patel A. (2017). Industrial Development Induced Climate Change and its Impact on Various Segment of Rural Society: A Case of Hajira Village of South Gujarat, India. The aim of this study was to know the perception of people like agriculturists, animal husbandry, fishermen, etc. regarding impact of climate change. On the basis of respondents, it is clear that there is negative impact of environment degradation on people. The present study argues that in absence of proper policy and packages regarding the climate change, particularly of environmental problem, the 'quality of life' of the local people has deteriorated notably after following the development process through industrialization. It has impacted adversely on their socio-economic matters.
- Chakraborty, J. and Basu, P. (2019). Linking Industrial Hazards and Social Inequalities: Environmental Injustice in Gujarat, India. This paper examined the association between industrial development and significant economic and social inequalities. Researcher examined bivariate correlations between the density of each type of major accident hazards (MAH) unit (dependent variables) and each explanatory variable, at the subdistrict level. Bharuch in south Gujarat, and Ahmedabad and Vadodara in central Gujarat, these three districts collectively contain 254 of 402, or about 53% of all MAH units analyzed in this study. The density of all MAH units was significantly and positively correlated with population density, urban population proportion, and literacy rate, but negatively correlated with the proportion of home owning households. Bivariate correlation analysis did not indicate significant associations between MAH unit density and proportion of SCs or STs. When variables denoting socioeconomic status are considered, literacy rate suggested a positive association with several MAH unit density subcategories, after controlling for urbanization and other explanatory variables. The limitation of this study was that the quantity or quality of pollutants emitted by each MAH unit is not available and this prevents researcher from assessing human health risks posed by hazardous industries based on exposure and toxicity. This research only based on our

study is based on socio-demographic variables from the Census of India, which represent residential characteristics of subdistricts.

- Gandhi, P.J. & Agnihotri, P.G. (2022). Mapping the Socio-Economical and Environmental Impact of Weir Constructed on Tapti River and Industrial zone developed at Hazira of Surat. The main aim of the study is to find out the impact of weir and industrial belt development near the mouth of the river on earning capability or economic disruption of fisherman communities namely Machhi, Kahar and Kharwa and their common property rights, changes in the fisheries business practices, changes in the gender roles, migration of families and incidences of disease (i.e., dengue and malaria). There is negative impact of environment on fisherman communities. Many fisherman families shift their profession from fishing to rickshaw, textile, diamond job etc. Majority of the respondents (84.3%) has revealed that there was reduction in the fish catch as compared to past few years. This study recommended that NGOs and govt. education officers can increase the awareness through 'street drama' and 'puppet show' for importance of education in society through social engineering program. State government support in the form of subsidy is needed for the procurement of latest tools of fisheries.

Research Gap

Many researchers talk only general impact of environmental pollution on people but do not cover the specific communities like fisherman. Many researchers only talk about the communities of Surat but ignore the villages areas like Hazira where people highly affected due to environmental issues.

OBJECTIVES OF THE STUDY

- To study the industrialization in Hazira of Surat city.
- To assess the impact of industrial development on environmental degradation.
- To analyze the impact of environment degradation on fisherman community of Hazira area.

HYPOTHESIS

- There is negative relationship between industrial development and quality of environment.
- There is negative relationship between income of fisherman and quality of environment.

Data Collection

- Secondary data collected for the research and information from different newspapers, articles, relevant websites and portals, also based on various literature review of journals.

Impact of Environmental Degradation on Fisherman Community

According to the 1991 data of SMC around 2720 people were involved in fish catching and selling business. As per the information provided by fishermen community members during this survey, around 400 families are residing in the adjunct area of river bank. Majority of the family believes in joint family pattern with 3 to 4 earning persons in a family, in majority of the cases, both husband and wife are earning. The level of education is very low in community. Average members in the family are 12 to 15 persons. Hence, total population of around 8,500 people. During the survey, community members revealed that, even after the construction of Ukai and Kakrapar dams on river, they were getting sufficient water in river, which enabled them to maintain their hereditary profession of fish catching and selling but after the construction of weir near Singanpore village, the water flow is very minimal. Low flow of water has increased the salinity near their catching area. Also due to the polluted effluent discharged by Hazira based industries near the mouth of the river, the population of sea fish during the tide has been reduced to a great extent. Also, with the rising industrialization, their movement on coast has become restricted; these giant units became fiefdoms in themselves violating fishermen's traditional rights. They also revealed that, due to the exponential increment in population of the city (post 1995); the no. of 'Ganesha-statute' during Ganesh Chaturthi has increased to a great extent. The Hindu customs of statue submerge ('murti visarjan') in water is responsible for river depth reduction (due to the sedimentation of 'plaster-of-paris' used for statute making) and water quality problems. They also revealed that, in last five years, submergence of statute of other Hindu Gods and Goddesses has also been increased. Earlier when the population was low and sufficient water flows with velocity in river channel, a problem of sedimentation was not there but today is a reverse case. They also revealed that, during the summer season, one can cross the river by walking.

IMPACT ON FISH WORKERS

Village and history: As per the 2011 census, the Hazira village has a total population of 16,724 and 4,423 families, consisting of fish workers, traders and farmers. The village has 80 Adivasi fishing families who, historically, fished in the intertidal zone of the tapi river and the Arabian sea. The entire region is a rich intertidal zone with active mudflats. The Halpati community traditionally followed pagadiya fishing, and caste families such as Koli, Patel did fishing by boats. The fishing hamlet of Hazira village is only 2 km from the HPPL and AHPPL ports and is bound on the west by the open sea and on the east by the Tapi estuary. The hamlet used to have access to both fresh and marine waters where fishing took place.

Pollution/River flow: The traditional fish workers of Hazira have been pauperized by the development of the LNG terminals and ports, as the physical infrastructure of the port reclaimed land, blocked access to the sea and released oil sludge from cleaning tankers. According to fish workers of Hazira village, pollution in the estuarine region, traffic because of port activity and the cleaning of oil tankers in the sea are the main reasons for the disappearance of fish.

Fisheries and livelihood: There is negative impact on fish workers due to Adani project in Hazira. By 2009–10, the realization that the industry could destroy fish workers' livelihoods was dawning on the community and by 2016 the Hazira fish workers no longer followed their traditional occupation. The Hazira village has approximately 80 fish worker families who have lost their livelihoods. These are registered fish workers who have received no compensation or benefits from the fisheries department or the industries. Pagadiya fishing has stopped completely and only one boat goes out to sea, to a distance of 10 NM with approximately 7–8 people on boat. Each person has to pay Rs. 70 for a seat. The route to access fishing ground has been fenced off and villagers have to travel a few kilometers on foot, or by bike to reach the coast where their boat is moored. From catching big fish like swordfish, dolphins, jewfish, ghol, hilsa at the coast, the main catch now is low-value levta (mudskippers) that live in mud on nearby islands and are sold for Rs, 100 per kg. From making at least Rs. 10–12 lakhs per year, fish workers now barely manage Rs. One lakh.

Due to the above-mentioned reasons, the population of fish near the fish catching area has reduced to a great extent, which in turn results into low earnings per family and a loss of common property rights over natural resources. A questionnaire-based survey has been carried out to know the socio-economic and environmental impact of weir on Tapti River and its findings are summarized as follows: Reduction in productivity of downstream river fishery. Due to the development of weir, the river flow in the downstream of weir has been drastically reduced, which has reduced the fish population. Also due to the pollution in the delta region of river, the fish migration from Arabian Sea has been reduced. Due to this, even during the high tide level also, the fish population is very less. Direct discharge of Sewage water in the river at the Adajan and Pal area is also responsible for this reduction in population of fish.

Due to the pollution at mouth and low water flow from weir, lateral and longitudinal migration of fish towards the sea observed for breeding, i.e., a problem of ecology. The industries located at the Hazira are mainly hazardous process industries and discharging pollutant in the river, which has imbalance level of pH, low dissolved oxygen and higher COD. Due to these variation in the water quality in the delta region, the actual lateral and longitudinal migration of fish in river is absence and this has imbalance the cycle of ecology. This particular absence of the sea (guppy) fish in water river has increased the cases of Dengue and Malaria in the Surat city. Guppy fish has an ability to control the breeding of larvae of mosquitoes that cause dengue and malaria. Majority of the fishermen have changed their profession of low skill job, such as auto-rickshaw driver, peon in office, worker in textile mills etc. whereas some of the female members have started a job of home-servant. Instead of fish catching, some of the middle-income families have started a business of fish trading. They use to procure fish from Porbandar, Veraval, Daman & Mumbai, which has reduced the profit margin to a great extent.

LIMITATION OF THE STUDY

Due to limitation of time the study cover only Hazira area of Surat city. Research is fully based on secondary data. This study only talks about environmental impact of industrial development on the fishing community of Hazira, Surat.

BIBLIOGRAPHY

[1] Chakraborty, J. and Basu, P. (2019). Linking industrial hazards and social inequalities: Environmental injustice in Gujarat, India. *International Journal of Environmental Research and Public Health, 16*(1). https://doi.org/10.3390/ijerph16010042

[2] Gandhi, P.J. and Agnihotri, P.G. (2022). Mapping the Socio-Economical and Environmental Impact of Weir Constructed on Tapti River and Industrial zone developed at Hazira of Surat: A study focused on Fisherman community (Machhi Samaj) of city. In *International Journal of Innovative Research in Sciences and Engineering Studies (IJIRSES) www.ijirses.com*. www.ijirses.com

[3] Patel, A. (2017). Industrial Development Induced Climate Change and its Impact on Various Segment of Rural Society: A Case of Hajira Village of South Gujarat, India. *Journal of Governance & Public Policy (JGPP)*, 7(2), pp. 39–59.

Performance of the Agriculture Sector in Gujarat: Recent Experiences

Kalpana Kapadia[1]

ABSTRACT: The growth with inclusiveness can be achieved only when agriculture growth accelerates and is also widely shared amongst people and regions of the country. It is necessary to evaluate the performance of the sector periodically to find out the bottlenecks and adopt required strategies to facilitate the balanced growth of the sector in various states of the country. The present study evaluates the performance of agriculture in the state of Gujarat in recent years and also presents what could be the future options, given our objectives of accelerated growth, inclusiveness, and doubling farmers' income. This study is based on the secondary data collected from various published sources. Based on the findings, policy relevant suggestions have been made for improvement in the performance of the agriculture sector in the state. The study finds that share, Gujarat accounts for a 7.9 per cent share of the National GDP. Gujarat is the largest producer of Cotton, Groundnut, Condiments and Spices in India. However, there are many challenges to be addressed systematically to accelerate the agricultural growth in the state. Some of the major challenges for the agriculture sector in Gujarat include the expansion of irrigation provisions through developing microlevel water resources in rainfed areas of the state, ensuring efficient water management through micro-irrigation systems, reducing wide fluctuation in agricultural output, productivity, and prices, checking distress sales of agricultural output and rising cost of cultivation, making institutional credit available for a large section of marginal and small farmers so that agriculture in the state will be able to promote inclusiveness.

Keywords: *Agriculture, Performance Evaluation, Agricultural Growth and Challenges.*

---

[1] Research Associate, Agro-Economic Research Centre, Sardar Patel Univeristy, Vallabh Vidyanagar, Gujarat, India.

INTRODUCTION

Gujarat is one of the fastest growing states of India. Apart from this, it also has good support in the economic development of the country. The state has adopted a novel pattern of progress with the strategic development of key sectors such as energy, industry and agriculture. Agriculture and allied sector play a major role in the growth of State economy as activities of agriculture and allied sectors are the primary source of occupation for the majority of the rural people in the State. It has been estimated that more than two-third of total workers in the State are located in rural areas. Though the contribution of crop and livestock in the NSDP of the state has gradually declined from around 50 per cent during 1970s to around 12.4 per cent (at current prices) in 2021–22 (18.1 per cent at constant 2011–12 prices) (GoG, 2023), agriculture yet forms the spine of State development. More than half of the working population in Gujarat still depends on agricultural activities for their livelihood. About 49.6 per cent of total workers are cultivators and agricultural labourers as compared to 54.7 per cent at all India level (Census, 2011). Thus, agriculture in the state has been a major source of labour absorption. Moreover, agriculture provides indirect employment to the population in agro-based occupations. Thus, the prosperity and wellbeing of people in Gujarat is closely linked with agriculture and allied activities. The State is divided into eight sub agroclimatic zones based on the characteristics of their agriculture and climate. The state is endowed with abundant natural resources in terms of varied soil, climatic conditions and diversified cropping pattern suitable for agricultural activities.

Agriculture in Gujarat is characterized by natural disparities such as (i) drought prone areas and lowest annual rainfall amounting to only about 345 mm at the North West end of the states; and assured and highest annual rainfall amounting to about 2500 mm at the SouthEast end; (ii) well drained deep fertile soils of central Gujarat and shallow and undulating soils with poor fertility in hilly rocky areas in the east; (iii) moisture starved degraded areas and low lying waterlogged and saline areas; (iv) areas prone to frequent scarcity and areas prone to frequent cyclone or floods or locusts (GoG, 2012a).

Thus, the output of the agricultural sector in Gujarat has been largely dependent on the southwest monsoon. The state frequently experiences erratic behaviour of the southwest monsoon, which can partly be attributed to the geographic situation. The Gujarat government has aggressively pursued an innovative agriculture development programme by liberalizing markets, inviting private capital, reinventing agricultural extension, and improving roads and other infrastructure (Shah *et al.*, 2009; Kumar *et al.*, 2010). The massbased water harvesting and farm power reforms in dry Saurashtra and Kachchh, and North Gujarat have helped energize Gujarat's agriculture. These semiarid regions have outperformed the canalirrigated South and Central Gujarat. The net sown area of Gujarat is around 52 percent of the reported area of 188 lakh Ha. The cropping intensity is 141 percent and the gross cropped area is 138.15 lakh Ha. (NABARD, 2023) In this context, this study evaluates the overall performance of agriculture in the State of Gujarat in recent years and also presents what could be the future options, given objectives of accelerated growth, inclusiveness and doubling farmers' income. The present study is based on the secondary data collected from various published sources and the data were analyzed using suitable statistical tools.

POPULATION: RURAL, CULTIVATORS, AGRICULTURAL LABOUR

As per the Census 2011, total population of Gujarat was 6.04 crores, out of which rural and urban populations were 57.4 per cent (3.47 crores) and 42.6 per cent (2.57 crores) respectively. The decadal growth rate of the population in the state during 20012011 was 19.17 per cent as compared to 17.64 per cent at all India level. It can be seen from Table 1 that during the years census 1971 to 2011, In census 1971 were about 38 per cent of cultivators in the state which decreased census 2011 to 22 per cent. On the other hand, 52 per cent of total agricultural labourers were women. Thus, the dominance of women as agricultural labourers than cultivators can be noted.

Table 1: Distribution of Population and Workers in Gujarat

Particulars	*Census*				
	1971	*1981*	*1991*	*2001*	*2011*
Population (in lakh)	266.97	340.86	413.09	506.71	604.40
Rural population (in lakh)	192.01	234.84	270.63	317.41	346.95
Total workers (in lakh)	83.96	127.02	166.2	212.5	247.68
Main Worker (in lakh)	83.96	109.84	140.95	170.25	203.65
Marginal worker (in lakh)	NA	24.91	25.25	42.31	44.02
Cultivators (in %)	NA	38	33	27	22
Agri. Labourers (in %)	NA	23	23	24	28
Women share as agri. laboures (in %)				52	33

Sources: Socio-Economic Review various years, DES, Gov. of Gujarat.

STATE DOMESTIC PRODUCT AND PER CAPITA INCOME

In Gujarat, the share of agriculture has declined from 25.4 per cent to 18.1 per cent from 2011–12 to 2021–22, whereas the share of the manufacturing sector has increased to around 44 per cent in NSDP at constant (2011–12) prices in the year 2021–22 as compared to 36 per cent in 2011–12 (Table 2).

Table 2: Composition of Net State Domestic Product (NSDP) in Gujarat

Sr. No.	*Industry Group*	*NSDP by Industry Groups at Constant 201112) Prices (Rs. Crore)*		
		2011–12	*2015–16*	*2021–22 (Q)*
1.	Agriculture, forestry and logging, fishing and aquaculture, mining & quarrying	118950	141202	178857
		(25.4)	(21.0)	(18.1)
	of which, Crops and Livestock	93776	95232	120650
		(20.0)	(14.2)	(12.2)

Sr. No.	*Industry Group*	*NSDP by Industry Groups at Constant 201112) Prices (Rs. Crore)*		
		2011–12	*2015–16*	*2021–22 (Q)*
2.	Manufacturing, electricity, gas, water supply & other utility services & construction	168931	281762	429363
		(36.0)	(41.9)	(43.3)
3.	Tertiary Service	181244	249981	382402
		(38.6)	(37.1)	(38.6)
4.	Total Net State Value Added	469124	672945	990622
5.	Total Net State Domestic Product at Market Prices	532809	774775	1212454
6.	Percentage change over the previous year in NSDP		9.8	10.3
7.	Per Capita Net State Domestic Product	87481	120683	174539
8.	Percentage change over the previous year in per capita NSDP		8.4	8.9
9.	Agricultural Growth at a constant price (%)	()16.02	()5.10	5.91

Note: Figures in parenthesis are percentages of total NSVA.
Source: GoG (2022b).

DRIVERS OF STATE AGRICULTURAL GROWTH

Climate and Rainfall Pattern

Gujarat has more than two-third of its geographical area classified as dry but has slightly more rain than an arid region or climate (i.e. semiarid) and haslittle or no rain (i.e. arid land types). The state is divided into eight agroclimatic zones. As per climatic conditions and rainfall patterns state average rainfall varies from 350 mm to 1300 mm from 1971 to 2022 (Figure 1). The state frequently experiences unpredictable behaviour of the southwest monsoon, which may be partly attributed to the geographic situation.

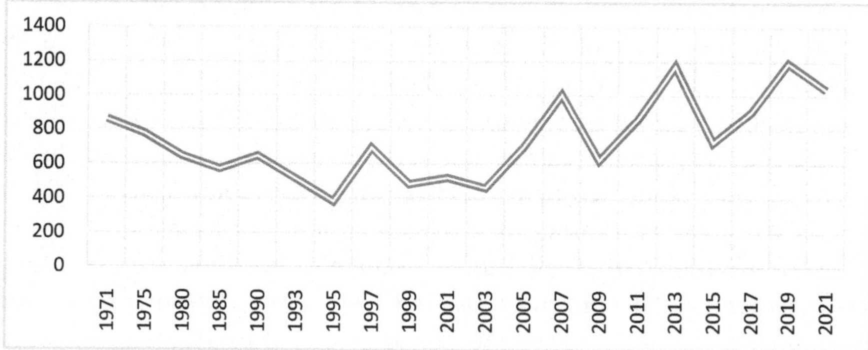

Figure 1: Yearwise Rainfall Pattern in Gujarat (1971–2022)
Source: GOG (2022b).

Agricultural Growth in Gujarat

The state's agricultural growth has been below average in most years. In the period between the years 2001–02 to 2021–22, the agricultural growth rate was 7.6% per annum (at 2011–12 constant prices) while the average economic growth rate was 9.2% per annum (Figure 2). However, agricultural growth has been stagnant in the last two decades.

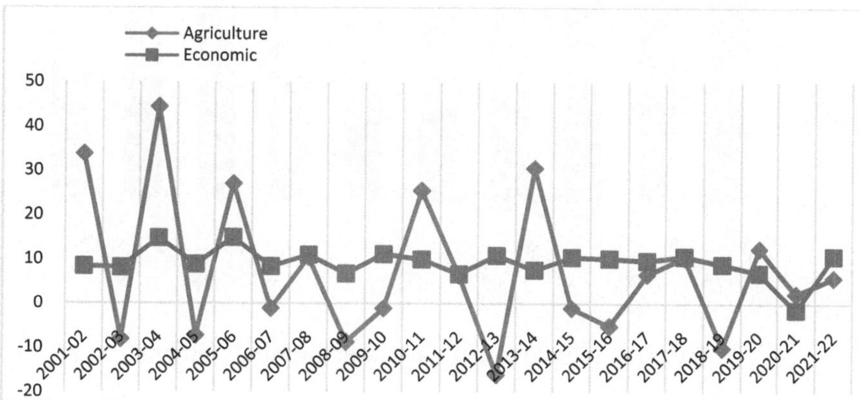

Figure 2: Growth Rate

Operational Land Holding Size

One of the important factors in determining the pace of the agricultural growth of any region of the state is the average size of operational holdings with the farmers. Due to the small size of the land, the majority of farmers do not use much machinery in agriculture, which is also a major reason for the decrease in production in agriculture. It can be (Figure 3) shown that in the year 1970–71 to 2015–16, the average size of operational holdings was 4.11 ha in 1970–71, which decreased to 2.33 ha in 2000–01 and now in 2015–16, it was 1.88 ha. Though the average operational land holdings in Gujarat are higher than all India's average of 1.08 ha, it is declining and becoming uneconomical to cultivate crops because of erratic rainfall and unremunerative rate for agricultural produce. In Gujarat, the highest size of operational holdings in 2015–16 was reported in Dang district (4.59 ha) and the lowest was in Anand district (0.95 ha) while across regions, Kutch region reported the highest size of operational holdings (3.07 ha) and while South Gujarat reported 1.57 ha operational size of holdings (GoG, 2016–17).

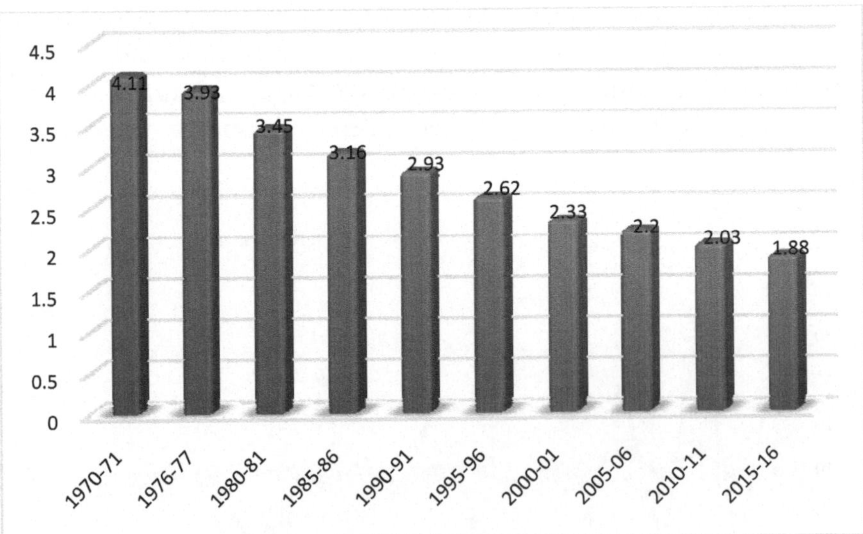

Figure 3: Aver. Size of Operationalholding: Gujarat

Source: GoG (201617).

Irrigation

Gujarat farmers have limited resources for irrigation. They have sources of irrigation that include canals, tube wells, open wells and tanks. Water is an important input for agricultural growth and it was possible only because of the Narmada dam which has turned many areas green with canal water for irrigation.

It may be noted from Figure 3 that percentage of gross irrigated area to gross cropped area has increased significantly from 26.5 percent in year 1980–81 to 61 percent in 2019–20, while irrigation intensity has increased from 117.9 percent to 160.9 percent during corresponding years (Figure 4). Major sources of irrigation are tube well account for 64.98 percent of net irrigated area followed by canal 22.46 percentage during 2019–20. Highest irrigation area coverage ratio of gross irrigated area to gross cropped area was Anand district 92.2 percent and the lowest was in Dang district. In total GIA in Gujarat, about 89 percent area was covered by North, Central and South regions while rest of 11 percent of irrigated area in two regions Surashtra and

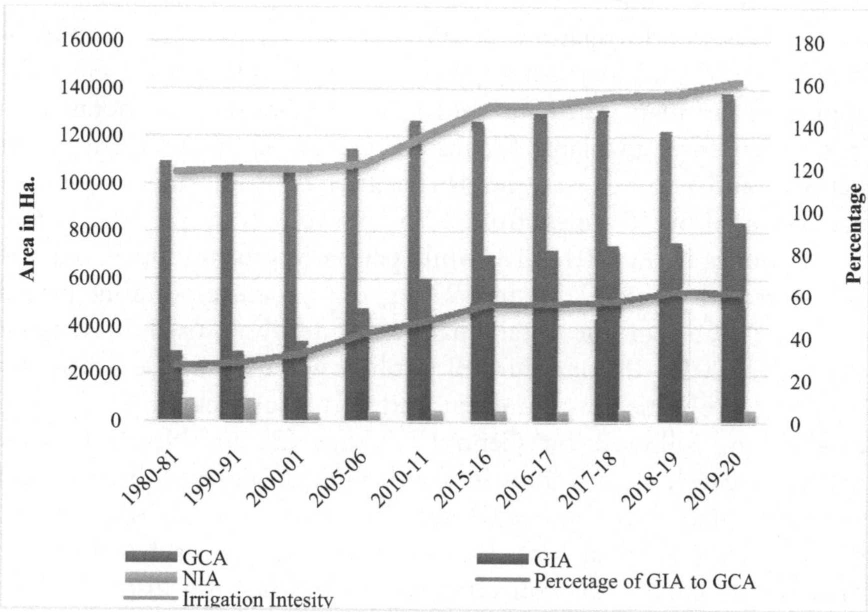

Figure 4: Growth in Area under Irrigation in Gujarat

Source: GoG (2020 various years).

Kutch (GoG, 2021–22). As mentioned earlier, Gujarat state has a limited source of irrigation facilities and therefore it is needed to save available water by using water judiciously through water saving technology such as drip and sprinkler methods of irrigation. The State Government has embarked upon "Jal Sanchay Abhiyan" (Drive for Storage of Water) in which the Micro Irrigation Scheme (MIS) is an integral part of the Programme. Gujarat Green Revolution Company Limited (GGRCL) has been implementing MIS in Gujarat. State has made remarkable progress in bringing area under micro irrigation. Since 2005–06 to March 2019, total 1.78 million ha land of 1.1 million farmers brought under MIS (Table 4.9). Saurashtra region accounts for highest share of 43 per cent in area as well as number of farmers covered under MIS in the State, followed by 32 per cent by North Gujarat, 14 per cent by Central Gujarat, around 7 per cent by South Gujarat and rest in Kuchch region. (GoG, 2021–22)

Fertiliser Consumption

After Green Revolution, farmers are adopting new technologies of seed, fertiliser and irrigation. Fertilizer is another important input for crop growth and increasing productivity. Fertiliser is a chemical application of plant nutrients (nitrogen, phosphorus, and potassium) in granular form to plants for instant use as per requirement. As at national and another state levels, fertiliser consumption in Gujarat has increased by 10 times, from 1.75 lakh tonnes in TE 1972–73 to 17.98 tonnes in TE 2017–18, while per ha of gross cropped area use has increased from 17 kg to 127 kg during corresponding period (Table 3). Out of the total quantity of fertiliser used in Gujarat during TE 2017–18, one-third of fertiliser was used in the Saurashtra region may be due to groundnut and cotton as well as paddy crop production, followed by Central Gujarat (29%), North Gujarat (25%). Sugarcane cultivation in South Gujarat along with fruits and vegetables may have increased fertiliser consumption while Dang district being a tribal area has reported less use of fertiliser and therefore declared to be converted as an Organic crop district by the State Government The coefficient of variation per ha use of fertiliser was the highest in Kutch region.

Table 3: Fertiliser Use in Gujarat

Particulars	*TE 1973*	*TE1983*	*TE 1993*	*TE 2003*	*TE 2013*	*TE 2018*
Fertilizer Use in tons						
Central Guj	59026	91205	209456	246673	505751	461660
South Gujarat	14883	44738	109612	131712	181757	170386
Saurashtra	79936	175050	231139	231526	589049	523892
North Gujarat	19805	65155	150434	178410	337883	400603
Kutch	1759	3938	15443	29214	56818	62869
Gujarat	175408	380104	716083	817535	1671258	1619410
Per ha use (kg)						
Central Guj	21.3	33.1	75.9	94.8	154.2	143
South Gujarat	19.4	59.4	129.2	148.4	203.7	204.8
Saurashtra	20.6	41.6	58	59.2	121.6	110.5
North Gujarat	8.4	26.8	60.9	67.9	115.3	125.4
Kutch	2.8	5.6	24.8	48	79.5	78.7
Gujarat	16.8	35	67	76.8	132	126.6
CV (%) per ha	*Period I*	*Period II*	*Period III*	*Period IV*	*Period V*	
Central Guj	22.38	30.43	17.46	21.31	56.92	
South Gujarat	33.58	33.87	16.61	28.37	59.41	
Saurashtra	38.51	32.17	20.92	29.68	59.52	
North Gujarat	52.02	26.69	21.63	21.3	60.65	
Kutch	106.59	168.82	36.08	24.02	83.28	
Gujarat	31.82	26.1	14.47	21.51	56.32	

Note: TE Triennium endings, CG – Central Gujarat, SG South Gujarat, SAU Saurastra, NG North Gujarat, KUT Kutch, GUJ Gujarat.

Source: GOG (2020b various years).

HYV and Seed Replacement Ratio

Seed is considered to be a catalyst of change in agriculture. The Green Revolution adopted in India during the late sixties and early seventies bear witness to this truth. And lately, during the decade of 2000s, Bt cotton seeds and hybrid maize seeds have shown spectacular results, particularly in Gujarat (GoI, 2012b). To complement good agricultural growth in the state, the availability of quality/certified seeds has been made available as required in various part of Gujarat. During the last four decades, the share of total area under HYV cereals in total area under cereals in the state has increased considerably, from 0.72 per cent in 1966–67 to 82.76 per cent in 2009–10. It is well discernible that the larger share of jowar crop (about 59.6 %) has not been with HYV seeds unlike other cereal crops (GoG, 2021). Though there has been substantial increase in area under HYV in the state, the interdistrict variations in area under HYVs of five major cereal crops have also been increased. Lately, during the decade of 2000 Bt cotton seeds and hybrid maize seeds have shown spectacular results, particularly in Gujarat. Though there is significantly surplus availability of quality/certified seeds in Gujarat, the Seed Replacement Rate (SRR) for majority of crops has been quite low. Even in the case of cotton and groundnut which are the pride of Gujarat, SRR has been as low as 25.5 per cent and 24.9 per cent respectively (GoG, 2021). Besides mustard and Bajra, the SRR needs further improvement in case of other crops.

Changing in Cropping Pattern

The changes in cropping pattern of Gujarat at four-point periods are presented in Table 5. It can be seen from the table that analysis of the cropping pattern in Gujarat brings out some unusual features. During 1970s and 1980s, Bajra (pearl millet) and Jowar (sorghum) were the main food crops and cotton and groundnut were the main nonfood crops. Some significant changes have taken place in crop pattern of Gujarat in the post-liberalization period. Area shares of Bajra which was 1331 per cent has declined to 3.1 per cent in 1990–91 to 2020–21. Though the area share of wheat has increased from 5.7 per cent to 9.3 per cent in 1990–91 to 2020–21, the share of food grains to GCA has declined by 44.7 per cent to 31.1 per cent during the period under study. The share of area under oilseed crops and cotton has remained around 23.5 percent and 15.4 per cent increased during year 2020–21, while spices, fruits and vegetables and flower crops have gained share in GCA in recent years. Overall, cropping pattern in the state after mid 1990s is responding to the impact of globalization. For some decades, farmers have also adopted a commercialization policy in farming, as the crops having greater market orientation are consolidating their share in the farm economy of Gujarat. Crops such as cotton, oilseeds, fruits, vegetables, spices and flowers, amenable to processing and value addition, are on the rise. These crops inherently provide higher returns per unit of land, resulting in higher incomes and employment generation in rural areas. Farmers need post-harvest facilities including foreign investments in processing, refrigerated

Table 5: Change in Cropping Pattern in Gujarat

Major Crops	*1990–91*		*2000–01*		*2010–11*		*2020–21*	
	Area (000' ha)	*% of GCA*	*Area (000' ha)*	*% of GCA*	*Area (000' ha)*	*% of GCA*	*Area (000' ha)*	*% of GCA*
Rice	623.0	(5.9)	583.5	(5.6)	808.0	(6.4)	906.6	(6.2)
Bajra	1394.3	(13.1)	989.2	(9.4)	873.0	(6.9)	460.3	(3.1)
Wheat	608.7	(5.7)	286.1	(2.7)	1589.0	(12.5)	1366.4	(9.3)
Maize	366.2	(3.4)	382.9	(3.6)	566.0	(4.5)	388.9	(2.6)
Total cereals	3799.8	(35.7)	2435.6	(23.2)	4014.4	(31.6)	3182.1	(21.6)
Tur	428.9	(4.0)	317.9	(3.0)	277.0	(2.2)	241.0	(1.6)
Total pulses	948.7	(8.9)	634.6	(6.0)	890.1	(7.0)	1397.5	(9.5)
Total food grains	4748.5	(44.7)	3070.2	(29.2)	4904.5	(38.6)	4579.6	(31.1)
Sesamum	237.0	(2.2)	356.9	(3.4)	251.1	(2.0)	258.9	(1.8)
Groundnut	1826.1	(17.2)	1744.8	(16.6)	1922.0	(15.1)	2162.9	(14.7)
R&M	348.6	(3.3)	186.6	(1.8)	222.7	(1.8)	214.7	(1.5)
Castor	384.9	(3.6)	458.6	(4.4)	490.6	(3.9)	652.9	(4.4)
Total oilseeds	2818.0	(26.5)	2746.9	(26.2)	3110.0	(24.5)	3438.5	(23.4)
Cotton	1041.6	(9.8)	1615.4	(15.4)	2623.0	(20.6)	2270.5	(15.4)
Tobacco	141.6	(1.3)	87.8	(0.8)	148.0	(1.2)	170.4	(1.2)
Horticultural crops	337.4	(3.2)	593.3	(5.7)	1404.0	(11.1)	1977.0	(13.4)
Fodder crops	1325.1	(12.5)	1371.1	(13.1)	1111.8	(8.8)	2000.4	(13.6)
Other crops	222.6	(2.1)	1012.6	(9.6)	598.8	(4.7)	285.8	(1.9)
GCA	10634.8	(100.0)	10497.4	(100.0)	12702.5	(100.0)	14722.2	(100.0)

Sources: Season and Crop Report various year, GoG.

transport and cold storage. Early 2000s period can be considered a watershed after which output has recorded a tremendous increase, making Gujarat the foremost state in India in terms of growth in the value of agricultural output. The strong performance of Gujarat agriculture is also reflected in terms of increased crop yields in groundnut, wheat and rice; whereas the yield levels have been more or less sustained in all the major crops.

Change Crop Output Growth in Gujarat

Paddy accounted for the major share in the total value of crop output 6.1 percent but declined from to 3.4 percent in 2020–21. Similarly, the value of wheat output reported a steady increase until 1999–2000 and declined thereafter. Same as Bajra and Jowar output reported decreased after 1990–91. Pulses (Tur crop) which registered a drop in their contribution to the total value of output from 4.7 per cent in 1990–91 to 0.9 percent in 2020–21. Meanwhile, Oilseed crop such as groundnut the value of output 11.7 percent in 1990–91 to increased 15.2 percent from 2020–21. But castor and mustard crop value output reported decreased from 1999–2000. The value of output of cotton increased to 20 per cent in 2020–21 from 10.8 per cent in 1990–91. Cotton is a profitable cash crop. It was found that productivity and profit from the cultivation of Bt Cotton is substantially higher than the conventional hybrid cotton varieties (Naik *et al.,* 2005). The share of condiments and spices in the total value of crop output also increased from 5 per cent in 1990–91 to 11.8 per cent in 2020–21. While Sugarcane, tobacco, chilli value of output decreased after 1999–2000. Value of output Fruits and vegetables were increased 10.9 percent in 1990–91 to 27.2 percent in 2020–21 and the reason the farmers get good value of output Overall, data analysis shows that agricultural production in the 1990s was broad. However, commercialization of agricultural production seems to have gained momentum in the early 1990s. There was a definite shift from foodgrains to non-foodgrains such as fruits and vegetables, oilseeds, fiber, and condiments and spices, whose share in both area and in value of output has been increasing during the study period. Further, the study reveals that diversification towards high value crops (HVCs) offers great scope to increase farmers' income.

These changes in the relative shares of crops in agricultural growth provide a clear indication of the growing importance of high-value crops in Indian agriculture (Table 6).

Table 6: Share of Major Crops in the Total Value of Crop Output (at 1999–00 constant price for 1990–91 to 2010–11 and at 2011–12 constant price for 2020–21)

Crops	*1990–91*	*1999–00*	*2010–11*	*2020–21*
Paddy	6.1	5.2	3.8	3.4
Wheat	8.4	5.1	6.7	4.3
Jowar	1.7	0.9	0.4	0.1
Bajra	5.1	4.9	1.9	1.2
Tur	4.7	1.9	1.5	0.9
Groundnut	11.7	9.2	14.1	15.2
Castor	11.7	7.8	4.5	7.3
Mustard	3.8	3.3	1.8	1.4
Cotton	10.8	11.9	25.9	20.0
Sugarcane	9.8	14.6	4.8	3.0
Tobacco	4.9	4.3	0.4	1.0
Chili	1.0	0.7	0.2	0.3
Potato	1.0	2.1	2.0	2.9
Fruits and Vegetables	10.9	23.1	23.3	27.2
Spices	5.0	3.3	7.0	11.8
Total	**100.0**	**100.0**	**100.0**	**100.0**

Sources: GoI 2023.

Marketing and Warehouse Facilities

As discussed in the above section, adequate returns on agricultural output is one of the driving forces for better agricultural growth. Better marketing channels and warehouse facilities are essential for ensuring adequate returns on the agricultural output of farmers. It may be seen from Table 7 that the total warehousing capacity under Gujarat State Civil Supply Corporation (GSCSC) has increased its

Table 7: Number of Storage Unit and Capacity of Warehouses in Gujarat

Performance of the Agriculture Sector in Gujarat: Recent ExperiencesPerformance of the Agriculture Sector in Gujarat: Recent Experiences	*Performance of the Agriculture Sector in Gujarat: Recent Experiences*			*Performance of the Agriculture Sector in Gujarat: Recent Experiences*		*Performance of the Agriculture Sector in Gujarat: Recent Experiences*	
	Performance of the Agriculture Sector in Gujarat: Recent Experiences	*Performance of the Agriculture Sector in Gujarat: Recent Experiences*		*Performance of the Agriculture Sector in Gujarat: Recent Experiences*	Capacity (In MTs)	Number of Storage Unit	Capacity (In LMTs)
		Govt. Owned	*Total (Incl. Hired)*				
1990–91	408	199418	252888	58	165787	26	2.78
2000–01	438	209339	226494	47	147579	28	3.97
2005–06	441	207370	214140	60	213148	30	7.02
2010–11	414	201920	215930	45	148156	28	7.68
2015–16	508	297950	308600	46	149766	29	7.12
2016–17	539	325700	336350	81	569199	31	6.24
2017–18	624	371650	406119	111	1887631	28	6.61
2018–19	638	399750	432469	103	504555	26	5.49
2019–20	684	496850	525172	167	782587	25	5.35
2020–21	677	525250	546248	110	456257	24	7.53

Source: Directorate of Economics and Statistics, Govt. of Gujarat, 2022.

capacity of storage from 2.1 lakh tonnes in 200506 to 5.4 lakh tonnes in 202021. It is astonishing to find that the level of utilization of the existing warehousing capacity has been very low. The Gujarat State Warehousing Corporation (GSWC) number of storage units has increased from 58 to 110 during 202021 "It may also be noted that, during the past five years, the Corporation has recorded losses in three of those years." This may be due to underutilization of the storage.

Post-Harvest Management and Value Addition

Agriculture has become demand-driven rather than supply driven. It is essential to produce and process agricultural commodities keeping in view the changing pattern of taste and preferences. Though the increase in agricultural production and productivity is the priority of the agriculture sector today, improved postharvest handling and processing is essential to ensure high quality products and further value addition. The value of agricultural output can be increased considerably by following improved methods of postharvest practices. Postharvest management plays an important role in production and marketing as a considerable quantity of valuable produce is lost every year due to improper postharvest management. Therefore, crisis in food availability is not only caused by natural disasters, but also by the absolute lack of postharvest management in India. The agricultural food industry contributes nearly 35 per cent to GDP in India which is the second largest producer of food next to China. India is the world's largest producer of milk, pulses and jute, and ranks as the second largest producer of rice, wheat, sugarcane, groundnut, vegetables, fruit and cotton. It is also one of the leading producers of spices, fish, poultry, livestock and plantation crops. Worth $ 2.1 trillion, India is the world's third largest economy after the US and China (FAO, 2021).

Gujarat stands fourth in the country in terms of per capita agricultural output. The horticulture sector is the supplier for large number of agro- based industries which has high avenues for generation of skill full employment and self employment opportunities both in rural and urban areas of the state. Better technology for post harvest management and market linkages are essential for increase in revenue from agro-products (Kalamkar *et al.,* 2015). The present scenario of existing and potential market linkages in the state reveals that there are no food parks in the state. Two food parks are planned at Hazira and Dahej. There are two AgriExport Zones (AEZs) in the state. One is for mango and vegetables and another for onions. The AEZ for mangos and vegetables is in central and southern Gujarat where about half of total mango production is produced. There are about 25 processing units and 100 cold storages in the region (GoG, 2018b). Exports from this region are primarily to Middle East and UK. The AEZ for onions has about 18 units out of which about 6 are HACCP certified. Onions in this zone are primarily exported in the dehydrated form to Europe and USA.

There are about 20 value addition centres (cold), 70 grading centres in the state. The processing units exist primarily for mango pulp, pickles, tomato ketchup, dehydration of onion and tutti –frutti. There are around total 16,400 food processing units in the state, out of which the total number of registered processing units is 56 with a capacity of 11.78 lakh quintals. Among these processing units, oilseeds processing, milk processing units, fruits and vegetable processing units and fish processing units are major ones. There are 185 cold storages in Gujarat having total capacity of 8.1 lakh metric tonnes, used primarily for potatoes and vegetables. The key issues with low level of processing in the state are poor post harvest infrastructure. It is estimated that Rs. 800 crores per annum are lost due to lack of post harvest infrastructure and processing (GoG, 2018). The post harvest loss for various fruits and vegetables is between 25 per cent and 30 per cent. Thus it is important to strengthen and expand the existing post harvest infrastructure and processing units.

CONCLUSIONS

Gujarat state registered an enormous increase in the rate of growth of agricultural output from just 0.90 per cent per annum during the period 198083 to 5.33 per cent per annum during the period 1990–93 to 2003–06. After the year 2005–06, the state has remarkable rehabilitation of agricultural growth. Due to significant and notable growth in crop output in Gujarat state during last two-decade period,

Gujarat occupies a relatively better position in terms of its contribution to the total production of different commodities in the country. Apart from this, some of the major challenges for agriculture sector in Gujarat include the expansion of irrigation provisions through developing microlevel water resources such as check dams, village tanks, farm ponds and recharging of wells under various water conservation programmes in rainfed areas of the state, ensuring efficient water management through micro-irrigation systems, reducing wide fluctuation in agricultural output, productivity and prices, checking distress sales of agricultural output and rising cost of cultivation, increasing agricultural exports and upscaling of farm validated modern technologies and agricultural innovations. There is a need for proper institutional mechanisms and organizational and management (O&M) reforms to overcome the felt constraints coming in the way of the farm prosperity in the state.

The improvement in water use efficiency is urgently required for irrigation expansion and reducing the excess pressure on groundwater in water-stressed areas of the state. More priority should be laid upon rainwater harvesting and effective water management through the promotion of micro-irrigation methods, while efforts should be made to bring more area under canal irrigation through the expansion of irrigation networks from neighbouring states. Gujarat is one of the leading states in the export of processed foods and high-value products. So the emphasis must be given to further development and expansion of agro-processing units and Agri Export Zones in the state. The farmers should be made aware of various improved cultivation practices required for high quality cash crops and about available incentives/schemes/programs by taking advantage of these schemes, farmers can increase their production and thereby increase their income. The addition of technology to traditional agriculture will be a game-changer for the state's agriculture. Enabling farmers to use GPS, GIS, drone technology, and remote sensing will help farmers to increase their productivity. The processors should be well-trained on various food safety measures and quality standards, adherence to sanitation and phytosanitation (SPS) standards and measures for minimizing export rejections. The scheme of the "Pradhan Mantri

Kisan Samman Nidhi" Yojana in the state assists the landholder farmer families as a part of increasing the income of the farmers.

REFERENCES

[1] FAO (2023). India at a Glance. Food and Agriculture Organization of the United States.

[2] GoG (1970 various years). Seasons and Crop Report. Directorate of Agriculture, Agricultural, Farmers Welfare and Cooperation Department, Government of Gujarat, Retrieved from https://dag.gujarat.gov.in/scrinfo.htm

[3] GoG (1970 various years). Socio-Economic Review. Directorate of Economics and Statistics. Gujarat State Budget Publication No. 34, Government of Gujarat, Gandhinagar, Retrieved from https://gujecostat.gujarat.gov.in/uploads/publicationsecmanagment

[4] GoG (2012a). State Agriculture Profile. Retrieved from http://agri.gujarat.gov.in/informations/state_agri_profile.htm), Government of Gujarat.

[5] GoG (2012b). Sector Profile: Food & AgriBusiness. Retrieved from http://www.vibrantgujarat.com/images/pdf/foodagrodetails.pdf Government of Gujarat.

[6] GoG (2018). District-wise Area, Production and Yield of Important Food & Nonfood Crops in Gujarat State. Directorate of Agriculture Gujarat State, Krishi Bhavan Sector10/A, Gandhinagar.

[7] GoG (2019). District-wise Area, Production and Yield of Important Food & Non Food Crops in Gujarat State (Year: 201516, 201617, 201718). Directorate of Agriculture, Government of Gujarat, Gandhinanagar.

[8] GoG (2020a). Socio-Economic Review 20192020, Directorate of Economics and Statistics. Gujarat State Budget Publication No. 34, Government of Gujarat, Gandhinagar.

[9] GoG (2020b). State Agriculture Plan and State Infrastructure Development Plan. Department of Agriculture, Farmers Welfare and Cooperation, Government of Gujarat, Gandhinagar (2020). https://rkvy.nic.in/

[10] GoG (2022). Statistical Overview of Gujarat State, Directorate of Economics and Statistics, Government of Gujarat, Gandhinagar

[11] GoG (2023). Performance of Development Indicators from 2001 to 2022, Directorate of Economics and Statistics, Government of Gujarat, Gandhinagar

[12] GoI (2011 various years). Provisional Population Totals, Office of the Registrar General and Census Commissioner, Government of India, New Delhi.

[13] GoI (2023). State-Wise and Item-Wise Value of Output from Agriculture, Forestry and Fishing year: 2011–12 to 2020–21 With Base Year: 2011–2012, National Statistical Office Ministry of Statistics and Programme Implementation Government of India.

[14] NABARD (2023). State Focus Paper – Gujarat State. National Bank for Agriculture and Rural Development, Gujarat Regional Office, Ahmedabad.

[15] Kumar, Dinesh M., A. Narayanamoorthy, O.P. Singh, M.V.K. Sivamohan, Manoj Sharma and Nitin Bassi (2010). Gujarat's Agricultural Growth Story: Exploding Some Myths, Occasional Paper No. 20410. *Institute for Resource Analysis and Policy,* Hyderabad.

[16] Kalamkar, S.M. Swain and Bhiya, S.R. (2015). Impact Evaluation of Rashtriya Krishi Vikas Yojana (RKVY) in Gujarat. Agro-Economic Research Centre, Sardar Patel University, Vallabh Vidyanagar.

[17] Shah, Tushar, Ashok Gulati, Hemant P., Ganga Shreedhar, R.C. Jain (2009). Secret of Gujarat's Agrarian Miracle after 2000, *Economic and Political Weekly*, 46(52), 4555.

Section 7
Commentary

Household Electrification in Gujarat and Rajasthan: A Saubhagya SWOT

Varinder Jain[1]

ABSTRACT: Rural electrification in India has historically been hampered by long distances and inadequate infrastructure, resulting in low per capita electricity consumption, a pattern mirrored in Gujarat and Rajasthan. Limited generation capacity utilization and utility inefficiencies further compounded the problem. To address these challenges, the Indian government launched the PM Saubhagya Yojana, aiming for 100% village and household electrification. This paper provides a comprehensive overview of the scheme's progress in India, with a specific focus on Gujarat and Rajasthan. The paper examines the state policy frameworks for rural electrification, the pre-Saubhagya household electrification status (up to October 2017), and the Saubhagya scheme itself. A SWOT analysis of the scheme, focusing on Gujarat and Rajasthan, is also presented, followed by concluding remarks.

Keywords: *RGGVY, Post-COVID-19, DDUGJY, SWOT.*

INTRODUCTION

Owing to long distances and fragile infrastructure, rural electrification in India has remained a challenge. With a large number of un-electrified households especially during the pre-Saubhagya period, per capita electricity consumption has remained at much lower levels. States of Gujarat and Rajasthan also followed a similar all-India pattern, with remote households facing considerable challenges in getting access to electricity. In fact, besides large population, limited generation capacity utilisation and power utility's commercial inefficiency remained a key factor affecting the operational dynamics, which significantly slowed the pace of rural electrification in India in general and in Gujarat and Rajasthan in particular.

[1] Assistant Professor, Institute of Development Studies, Jaipur, India.
E-mail: vjain2007@gmail.com

Recognising such lacunae, Government of India under able leadership of PM Narendra Modi announced PM Saubhagya Yojana which aimed at attaining 100 percent village and household electrification. This paper makes an attempt to provide a comprehensive picture about the progress made under Saubhagya Yojana in India in general and the states of Gujarat and Rajasthan in particular.

Including this introductory section, there are six sections. Next section provides an overview of state policy framework for rural electrification. Third section examines household electrification status till (October) 2017. Fourth section introduces Saubhagya scheme. Fifth section provides a SWOT analysis of Saubhagya Scheme with a specific focus on Gujarat and Rajasthan and the final section provides concluding remarks.

STATE POLICY FRAMEWORK FOR RURAL ELECTRIFICATION

Indian State has remained largely concerned about electrifying rural India. It has made significant interventions, from time to time, to attain this goal. Table 1 outlines some of the key interventions made by the State to promote rural electrification. It may be observed that the State has set up rural electric corporation in 1969 besides launching rural electrification program under Minimum Needs Programme in 1974. Kutir Jyoti programme was also introduced in 1988.

Table 1: Significant State Interventions to Promote Rural Electrification

Year	*Intervention*
1969	Setting up of Rural Electric Corporation
1974	Launching of rural electrification under Minimum Needs Programme which was introduced in first year of the 5th Five Year Plan (1974–78)
1988	Kutir Jyoti Programme
2001	Remote Village Electrification Programme launched by Ministry of New and Renewable Energy (MNRE)

2001	Rural Electrification Component was added to Pradhan Mantri Gramodaya Yojana
2003	Accelerated Rural Electrification Programme (AREP)
2004	Accelerated Electrification of One Lakh Villages and One Crore Households
2005	Introduction of Rajiv Gandhi Grameen Vidyutikaran Yojana (RGGVY)
2009	Decentralised Distributed Generation Scheme under RGGVY
2015	Deendayal Upadhyay Gram Jyoti Yojana (DDUGJY)
2017	Pradhan Mantri Sahaj Bijli Har Ghar Yojana (Saubhagya)

Source: Based on various web sources.

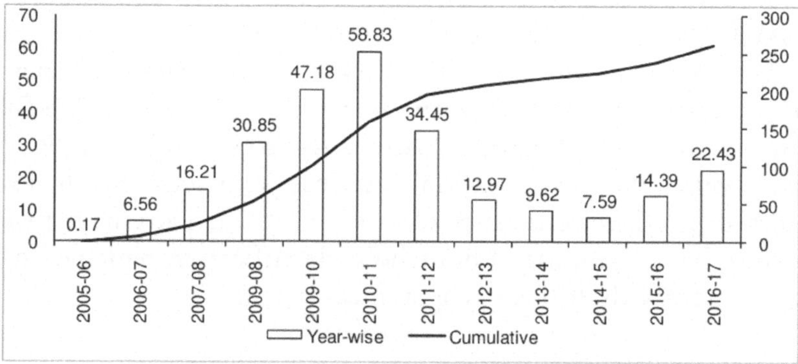

Figure 1: Year-wise Number (in Lakhs) of Electrified Rural BPL Households

Source: Based on GoI (2013) and Nair (2017)

MNRE introduced remote village electrification program in 2001. Similarly, rural electrification component was introduced under Pradhan Mantri Gramodaya Yojana in 2001. In 2003, accelerated rural electrification programme was introduced and in 2004, accelerated electrification of one lakh villages and one crore households was made. In 2005, Rajiv Gandhi Grameen Vidyutikaran Yojana (RGGVY) was introduced. In fact, this scheme has been a key intervention that aimed at electrifying all un-electrified villages/ habitations. Besides conventional modes of electrification, it also relied on non- conventional energy sources under Ministry of New and Renewable Energy's 'Remote Village Electrification Programme'. This scheme continued till the incumbent Modi government rechristened it as *Deen Dayal Upadhyay Gram Jyoti Yojana* on July 25, 2015. RGGVY remained in operation for 10 years. Figure 1 reports its year-wise and cumulative trend in electrification of rural BPL households. Its annual performance was at peak in 2010–11 beyond which it recorded slow performance. The pace of BPL household electrification got further momentum with DDUGJY in 2015–16.

HOUSEHOLD ELECTRIFICATION STATUS TILL OCTOBER, 2017

Till October 2017, there have been a few states which have recorded 100 percent household electrification (Figure 2). State of Gujarat has recorded 100 percent household electrification. Some other states have been Kerala, Punjab and Tamil Nadu who attained 100 percent mark in household electrification. There have been states like Bihar, Jammu & Kashmir, Madhya Pradesh, Rajasthan and Uttar Pradesh where household electrification rate has remained much lower. Almost all north-eastern states recorded a similar pattern. It may be observed that magnitude of household electrification remained much tense in states with difficult geographical terrains.

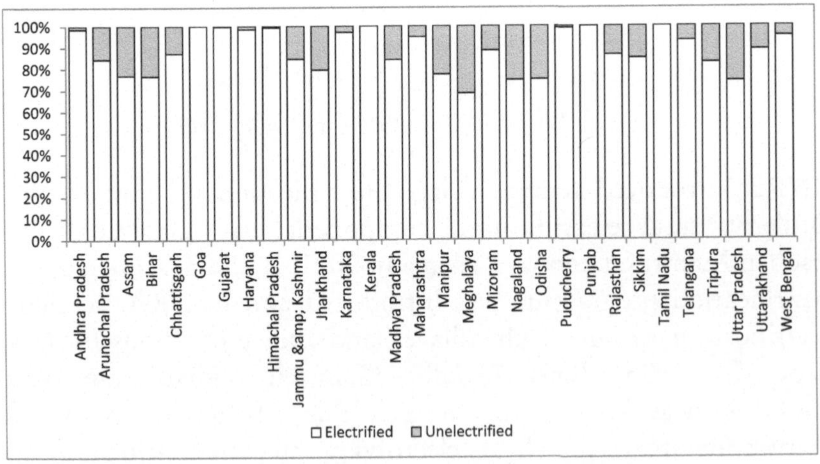

Figure 2: Household Electrification Status till October, 2017

Source: Based on https://saubhagya.gov.in

SAUBHAGYA SCHEME—A NOBLE INITIATIVE

In fact, it has been the unaffordability of BPL households to get new electricity connections on the one hand and the high capital cost for states to ensure 'last mile connectivity' that has hindered the access to electricity for such large proportion of households. Recognising such situation, the Hon'ble PM Narendra Modi announced a new scheme, *Pradhan Mantri Sahaj Bijli Har Ghar Yojana,* also called *'Saubhagya'* scheme with an estimated expenditure of Rs. 16,320 crore.[2]

Some of the salient features of the scheme are related to the provision of free metered connection to economically poor households. For other households, it takes a charge of Rs. 500 which is collected/ adjusted in electricity bills in 10 monthly installments and this collected after release of connection. To ease operational issues, it seeks to establish camps in villages or cluster of villages for spot registration.

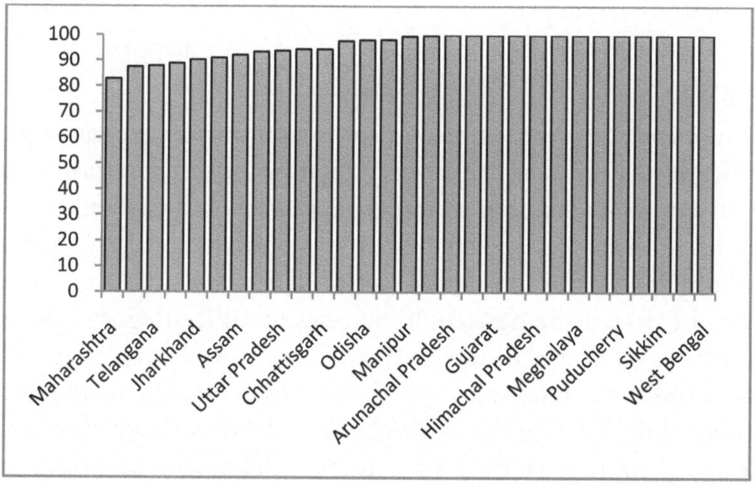

Figure 3: Progress Made in Household Electrification under Saubhagya Scheme

Source: Based on https://saubhagya.gov.in/

Figure 3 elucidates that a large number of states such Gujarat, Haryana, Punjab, Tamil Nadu, West Bengal, Bihar, Himachal Pradesh and a majority of north-eastern states have electrified 100 percent of their remaining households under the Saubhagya scheme.

In other states, attainment in household electrification remained somewhat limited and states like Maharashtra, Karnataka, Telangana, Andhra Pradesh, Jharkhand, Rajasthan, Assam, Uttarakhand and Uttar Pradesh could not attain the 100 percent mark in household electrification. In these states, progress in household electrification was made from February 1, 2019 onwards through various Saubhagya Rath campaigns, camps and control centres till March 31, 2019. Nonetheless, Chattisgarh has remained such state where 99.67 percent households are electrified and in all other states, 100 percent household electrification is attained under the Saubhagya Scheme.

A SWOT ANALYSIS OF SAUBHAGYA SCHEME IN CONTEXT OF GUJARAT AND RAJASTHAN

In such situation, a very useful analytical tool is of SWOT analysis which provides a balanced analysis of Successes, Weaknesses, Opportunities and Threats. Here, we conduct a SWOT analysis of 'Saubhagya' Scheme primarily in context of Gujarat and Rajasthan.

Strengths

The Saubhagya Scheme, given its aim to attain 100 percent household electrification, seems to be a very significant intervention. Its key strength lies in its concern to target, approach and electrify each left-out household and ensuring 'last-mile connectivity' in Gujarat and Rajasthan. It aims at providing connectivity without any monetary expense, i.e. free if the household belongs to BPL category.[3] As it aims for universal coverage, others may avail its benefit by paying Rs. 500 which would be recovered by DISCOMs in 10 instalments of electricity bills. It relies strongly on solar energy for off-grid connectivity and aims to power remote hamlets with solar power packs of 200–300 Watts having eight-hour battery backup along with five LED lamps, a DC fan and a DC power plug besides a five-year assurance of repair and maintenance service.

As its predecessors, it considers Rural Electrification Corporation as the national-level Nodal agency for scheme implementation and entrust other public institutions and Panchayats with the task of collecting application forms, distribute bills and collect payments.

Having robust financial support from the Centre, it provides a unique financing mechanism through Central support (60%), State support (10%) and bank/market loans (30%). Unlike its predecessors, its entire focus is not only on rural segment but it covers urban segment as well. The scheme also brings with it administrative ease. It ensures on-the-spot registration of applications and hassle-free receipt of connections.

Weaknesses

Given above strengths, there are some weaknesses as well. The scheme aims at providing electricity connection free of cost to BPL households but it does not guarantee free electricity. The households have to pay for it. In rural and remote areas where people remain the victims of faulty metering and other malpractices, the popularity of metered electricity supply is doubtful unless masses are adequately educated and made aware about its usage. There are apprehensions about DISCOMs inflating bills which add to reluctance in taking electricity connections. To contain bill recovery issues, option for pre-paid metering is under consideration with the government but how far it would be operationally feasible is yet to be seen.

Despite the fact that the scheme doesn't promise to measure the quantum or quality of power supply, it is considered as a step towards ensuring 24×7 power supply. In fact, the question of providing continuous and quality supply would depend on ability of DISCOMs. At present, most of DISCOMs are financially weak. Given the political pressures to provide free/subsidised electricity to agricultural or domestic consumers, they will continue to load-shedding and in such situation, 24×7 power supply to villages will remain a pipedream. Moreover, the cost of running scheme would come from the state and most of the states, given their fiscal health, would be reluctant in its effective implementation. In case the states agree to bear subsidy burden, the whole exercise of containing subsidy burden during recent years would turn out to be a futile exercise. Meeting additional subsidy burdens of this scheme would become difficult to meet due to state's fiscal targets.

One rationale behind this scheme, as proclaimed by government, is to raise employment opportunities. Surprisingly, it is not clear how the scheme would help when the households are provided single line connections. In order to enable productive usage of electricity, amendments in the Indian Electricity Act, 2003 would be required to allow commercial usage from domestic connections. Moreover, an effective usage would require access to three-phase connections but the scheme remains silent over this aspect.

DISCOMs in Gujarat and Rajasthan lack adequate staff to manage their daily operations, leading to a significant number of electric accidents and fatalities. If there is going to be an expansion of network, then there is more responsibility of the DISCOMs to avoid such unwanted incidents. But, the scheme does not say much on strengthening the staff strength, at least of those at ground level, of the DISCOMs.

Opportunities

The scheme brings with it various opportunities as well. It is largely seen as a landmark intervention that would help the poor in getting rid of candles and harmful kerosene used for lighting. Access to electricity would change household dynamics by lengthening duration of productive time in both Gujarat and Rajasthan. It would ease the life of women and children and thus, would contribute positively towards their better educational and health attainments. It would also lead to higher connectivity through radio, TV and mobiles, public safety and increased job opportunities. The scheme is going to yield economic dividends by pushing demand for power. Even a single unit daily consumption by the new four crore households would raise the daily electricity demand by forty million units which would help the DISCOMs, to some extent, in honouring 'Power Purchase Agreements'. Access to electricity would raise the demand for electric gadgets, LED bulbs and household appliances which would impact positively the manufacturing sector in both Gujarat and Rajasthan. It is noteworthy that since the announcement of the scheme, the share values of companies manufacturing electric meters, transformers, cables etc. are on the rise.

Besides improving per capita electricity consumption levels, the scheme would help both Gujarat and Rajasthan and thus India in meeting its global climate change commitments. Substitution of inferior fuels with electricity would reduce GHG emissions and thus, would help India in its move towards low carbon growth agenda. It is expected that due to economies of scale effect, UJALA[4] scheme will also get boost. This scheme popularises LED bulbs and other energy efficient appliances like fans through its non-subsidised financing model.

Threats

There are various threats as well. As the energy security framework has to work on the principle of equity, efficiency and sustainability, there are concerns over the last component under new scheme. Owing to imbalanced monsoon, poor agricultural performance and lopsided performance of rural employment guarantee scheme NREGA, there is limited purchasing power in rural areas of both Gujarat and Rajasthan but surprisingly, not much is done to deal with affordability issue. It is feared that new connection holders under the scheme would be the poorest of the poor who may be connected once but they may not retain connection for a sustainable period as they lack economic capacity to address recurring burden of electricity bills and thus, face the threat of default in bill payments. What is more required on the part of governments in both Gujarat and Rajasthan is to work on strengthening financial muscle of the rural poor so that they may start demanding electricity in a much more affordable manner which would also boost economic sustainability of the DISCOMs in both Gujarat and Rajasthan.

The tariff rates for these new connection holders, given the nature of consumer set, need to be relatively subsidised. In such case, the subsidy burden would be borne either by the States of Gujarat and Rajasthan or their DISCOMs as under *Ujwal DISCOM Assurance Yojana* (*UDAY*), the government has tried to bail out once the financial loses of DISCOMs. There is populism in power pricing (Jain, 2006) and even the UDAY has failed to address this problem. In such situation, providing electricity to these new customers in both Gujarat and Rajasthan at 'not-so-profitable' tariff rates would be the least priority of the DISCOMs in both the states which has diluted the whole purpose of this scheme.

Under RGGVY launched by UPA government in 2005, the Centre bore 90% of the cost with states only bearing 10%. At that time, the economy has been growing comfortably at 7.9 percent during 10th Five Year Plan (2002-07)[5] and it could mobilise resources. But, at present, in the post-COVID-19 scenario and the global slow-down amidst threats of tariff wars triggered by statements of U.S. President Donald Trump and the deportation of illegal migrants to India, the Indian economy in general and the economies of Gujarat and Rajasthan are experiencing somewhat slow economic progress - in such situation, mobilisation of required resources is a big concern. With limited Central funding, the resources available to power each household in both Gujarat and Rajasthan remain inadequate. Over the past several years since the inception of the scheme, it remains a concern why the government could not manage funds to finance this scheme in both Gujarat and Rajasthan. If so, then from where would the resources come when both Gujarat and Rajasthan are already under pressure to revive their struggling post-COVID-19 economies?

SUMMING-UP

In conclusion, one may say that a fair assessment of strengths, weaknesses, opportunities and threats leaves the impression that this scheme may go a long way towards achieving 100% household electrification target in both Gujarat and Rajasthan. However, the issues of getting rid of load shedding and power outages would remain in both the states and a lot of effort is required to ensure continuity and reliability. In fact, through this scheme, the governments in both Gujarat and Rajasthan envisage to transform their rural segments with the introduction of electric vehicles and other power- driven equipment. Such vision seems to be progressive as far as the development of power infrastructure in rural areas of both the states is concerned. Drawing insights from rich literature on energy-human development linkage, one may expect this scheme affecting significantly the quality of life especially for women and may play an instrumental role in strengthening educational and health outcomes, communications, public safety and job opportunities. Linking these outcomes with the progress made under UJALA Yojana, one may see pursuit of energy-efficient, low-carbon economy in both Gujarat and Rajasthan. Nonetheless, there are many-more milestones that both Gujarat and Rajasthan are yet to achieve to address their energy security challenges.

REFERENCES

[1] GoI (2013). *Implementation of Rajiv Gandhi Grameen Vidyutikaran Yojana*, 41st Report, Standing Committee on Energy, December 13.

[2] Jain, Varinder (2006). Political Economy of the Electricity Subsidy: Evidence from Punjab, *Economic and Political Weekly*, 41(38): 4072–4080.

[3] Nair, R. (2017). How Modi's Saubhagya Yojana Simply Repackaged an Already- Repackaged Scheme, *The Wire*, September 29.

Industrial Development and Environmental Issues—Scenario of Gujarat State

Bharat Jain[1]

ABSTRACT: This paper examines the progression of industrial development in India, emphasizing Gujarat's significant role, from pre-colonial handicraft dominance to post-independence planned industrialization through initiatives like GIDC, SEZs, and DMIC. While Gujarat's industrial growth has been substantial, it has also necessitated addressing environmental concerns through robust waste management systems and the proactive promotion of cleaner production practices via GCPC and policy incentives, demonstrating a commitment to balancing economic advancement with environmental sustainability, further solidified by integrating sustainable practices into engineering education.

Keywords: GIDC, Special Economic Zone, Special Investment Region.

INTRODUCTION

Industrial development is considered as one of the important indicators of socio-economic and human development. Before modern industry, India was a global hub for exquisite handicrafts. Renowned for its muslin, silks, and pottery, Indian artistry was highly sought after. However, the arrival of the English East India Company marked a shift. While some early attempts existed, modern industrial development in India gained momentum after 1854. This period saw the establishment of the first successful cotton textile mills in Mumbai and jute mills near Calcutta (now Kolkata), primarily driven by Indian entrepreneurship. India's industrial journey began in 1854

[1] Member Secretary Gujarat Cleaner Production Centre, Udhyog Bhavan, Gandhinagar, Gujarat, India. E-mail: gcpc11@yahoo.com; ms@gcpcgujarat.org.in; gcpc-env@nic.in

with the establishment of the first modern cotton textile factory in Mumbai. Thereafter, the first railway was introduced by Dalhousie who served as Governor General of India from 1848–1853. This pioneering effort was followed closely by the opening of a jute mill near Calcutta (now Kolkata) in 1855, marking the early steps towards a more industrialized India. Thereafter, first paper mill in India started at Ballygunj Circular Road in Kolkata, 1870. This marked a significant milestone in the country's industrial development. The growth and development of various industries such as chemical, iron and steel, sugar, cement and consumer goods, accelerated during the two World Wars. After Independence, the Government of India realized the importance of an appropriate industrial policy, which led to the Industrial Policy Resolution, 1948 focusing on socio-economic objectives like employment generation, increased productivity, reducing regional imbalance, promoting export oriented industries. According to this policy, the concept of mixed economy was introduced in which the state and the private enterprise were allowed to co-exist and co-prosper in the fields demarcated for them. This resolution divided the industries between public and private sectors. The real growth and development of the industrial sector in India started during the period of Five-Year Plans.

After the formation of Gujarat State on 1st May, 1960, the Gujarat Industrial Development Act, 1962 was published, under which the Gujarat Industrial Development Corporation (GIDC) was established to ensure smooth industrial development in the state. The main functions of GIDC include identifying and acquiring suitable land for industries, planning industrial estates and providing necessary infrastructure like roads, water supply, drainage, electricity, etc. With a staggering 224 industrial estates established, GIDC has played a significant role in shaping Gujarat's industrial landscape.

For the promotion of export oriented industries, Special Economic Zone (SEZ) Act was introduced in 2005. This act aimed to create special zones offering a range of benefits and incentives to attract export-oriented businesses. In SEZ the world class infrastructures are provided. At present in Gujarat there are total 20 functional SEZ established. Following the introduction of the SEZ Act in 2005, which focused on boosting exports, the Special Investment Region (SIR) Act came into play in 2009. This act aimed to take regional development a step further by fostering the creation of large-scale industrial hubs within specific areas.

The Delhi Mumbai Industrial Corridor (DMIC) is a massive infrastructure project stretching 1,500 kilometers. It runs alongside the Dedicated Freight Corridor, a high-speed freight rail line connecting Delhi and Mumbai. Traversing through the states of Delhi, Rajasthan, and Gujarat, DMIC aims to create a thriving industrial zone. In this corridor two prestigious SIR namely Dahej Petroleum Chemicals Investment Region (PCPIR) and Dholera Special Investment Zone (DSIR) are being developed.

Gujarat's Golden Corridor, a hub of industrial estates stretching from Ahmedabad to Mumbai, is dominated by the chemical industry. Despite existing environmental regulations like the Water Act (1974) and the EPA Act (1986), concerns about pollution from these industries were not adequately addressed. Despite existing environmental regulations such as the Water Act (1974) and the Environment (Protection) Act (1986), concerns about pollution from these industries were not adequately addressed. In response to these issues, the Honorable High Court of Gujarat took suo moto action (Special Civil Application No. 770). This bold move mandated the closure of certain industries in and around Ahmedabad until environmental issues were demonstrably resolved.

In response to the environmental concerns, Gujarat implemented a comprehensive strategy for industrial waste management. This approach emphasizes end-of-pipe solutions, focusing on treating waste after it's generated. Common Effluent Treatment Plants (CETPs): These strategically located plants have a combined treatment capacity of 817 MLD (Million Liters per Day), effectively treating industrial wastewater before release. Common Hazardous Solid Waste Secured Landfill Sites: Dedicated landfills provide a safe and secure disposal solution for hazardous solid waste generated by industries. Deep Sea Marine Pipelines: A sustainable approach for treated wastewater disposal involves pipelines that transport it far offshore for deep- sea release, minimizing coastal pollution. These combined efforts represent a significant step towards environmental protection.

Complementing the end-of-pipe solutions, Gujarat adopted a proactive strategy with the establishment of the Gujarat Cleaner Production Centre (GCPC) in 1999. Established under the guidance of UNIDO (the United Nations Industrial Development Organization), GCPC under the leadership of Dr. Bharat Jain, Member Secretary, GCPC champions the concept of cleaner production based on the 4R principles: Reduce, Reuse, Recycle, and Recover. This philosophy emphasizes minimizing waste generation at the source itself. GCPC promotes industrial symbiosis, where waste from one industry becomes a valuable resource for another. Resource Efficient and Cleaner Production (RECP) approach aligns perfectly with the circular economy, where resources are kept in use for as long as possible. A key advantage of Cleaner Production (CP) is its demonstrable return on investment. GCPC has documented numerous success stories showcasing how industries have implemented these practices and achieved cost savings through reduced waste.

The Gujarat Industrial Policy 2020 actively promotes Cleaner Production practices. To motivate industries, the policy offers financial assistance for implementation. Additionally, the state established the Gujarat State CP Award, a prestigious recognition program for outstanding achievements in cleaner production.

Furthermore, Gujarat has taken a significant step towards long-term sustainability by integrating Cleaner Production (CP) as a subject in the curriculum of Environmental Engineering programs at both graduate and postgraduate levels. This ensures that future generations of engineers are equipped with the knowledge and skills to design and implement cleaner production practices. The Resource Efficient and Cleaner Production (RECP) approach not only safeguards the environment but also paves the way for a more sustainable future.

REFERENCES

[1] https://www.gcpcgujarat.org.in
[2] https://gpcb.gujarat.gov.in
[3] https://kasez.gov.in/websites-of-sezs-in-gujarat
[4] https://ic.gujarat.gov.in

[5] https://www.unido.org
[6] https://cpcb.nic.in
[7] https://hdr.undp.org
[8] https://imd.gujarat.gov.in

Author Index